Motivation in War

This book fundamentally revises our notion of why soldiers of the eighteenth century enlisted, served and fought. In contrast to traditional views of the brutal conditions supposedly prevailing in old-regime armies, Ilya Berkovich reveals that soldiers did not regard military discipline as illegitimate or unnecessarily cruel, nor did they perceive themselves as submissive military automatons. Instead, he shows how these men embraced a unique corporate identity based on military professionalism, forceful masculinity and hostility towards civilians. These values fostered the notion of individual and collective soldierly honour, which helped to create the bonding effect that contributed towards greater combat cohesion. Utilising research on military psychology and combat theory and employing the letters, diaries and memoirs of around 250 private soldiers and non-commissioned officers from over a dozen different European armies, *Motivation in War* transforms our understanding of life of the common soldier in early-modern Europe.

Ilya Berkovich completed his PhD thesis at Peterhouse, Cambridge, and has since published items on crusader and eighteenth-century history. He has won the Polonsky Prize for Creativity and Originality in the Humanistic Disciplines from the Hebrew University of Jerusalem and the Moncado Prize for an Outstanding Article from the Society for Military History. Before starting his studies, Berkovich served three years as a conscript in the Israel Defence Forces.

Motivation in War

The Experience of Common Soldiers in Old-Regime Europe

Ilya Berkovich

Ludwig Maximilian University of Munich

CAMBRIDGE
UNIVERSITY PRESS

CAMBRIDGE
UNIVERSITY PRESS

University Printing House, Cambridge CB2 8BS, United Kingdom

One Liberty Plaza, 20th Floor, New York, NY 10006, USA

477 Williamstown Road, Port Melbourne, VIC 3207, Australia

314-321, 3rd Floor, Plot 3, Splendor Forum, Jasola District Centre, New Delhi - 110025, India

79 Anson Road, #06-04/06, Singapore 079906

Cambridge University Press is part of the University of Cambridge.

It furthers the University's mission by disseminating knowledge in the pursuit of education, learning and research at the highest international levels of excellence.

www.cambridge.org
Information on this title: www.cambridge.org/9781316618103
10.1017/9781316711835

First published 2017

A catalogue record for this publication is available from the British Library

Library of Congress Cataloging in Publication data
Names: Berkovich, Ilya, author.
Title: Motivation in war : the experience of common soldiers in
old-regime Europe / Ilya Berkovich, Ludwig Maximilian University of Munich.
Other titles: Experience of common soldiers in old-regime Europe
Description: Cambridge, New York : Cambridge University Press, [2017] |
Includes bibliographical references.
Identifiers: LCCN 2016046822 | ISBN 9781107167735
Subjects: LCSH: Military morale – Europe – History – 18th century. |
Soldiers – Europe – History – 18th century. | Sociology, Military – Europe –
History – 18th century. | History, Military – Europe – 18th century.
Classification: LCC U22.3 .B47 2017 | DDC 355.1/2309409033–dc23
LC record available at https://lccn.loc.gov/2016046822

ISBN 978-1-107-16773-5 Hardback
ISBN 978-1-316-61810-3 Paperback

To Christopher Duffy

I take the gallantry of private Soldiers to proceed from the same, if not from a nobler, Impulse than that of Gentlemen and Officers. They have the same Taste of being acceptable to their Friends, and go through the Difficulties of that Profession by the same irresistible Charm of Fellowship, and the Communication of Joys and Sorrows, which quickens the relish of Pleasure, and abates the Anguish of Pain. Add to this, that they have the same Regard to Fame, tho' they do not expect so great a Share as Men above them hope for; but I'll engage, Sergeant *Hall* would die Ten Thousand Deaths, rather than a Word should be broken at the *Red-Lettice*, or any Part of the *Butcher-Row*, in the prejudice of his Courage and Honesty

Richard Steele, Tatler 87, 29 October 1709

Wir müssen uns also zu Gott halten und ihn bitten, daß er unserm Könige und uns wolle gnädig sein, daß wir unsere Feinde mögen glücklich überwinden und den Sieg erhalten. Und ich hoffe, daß uns der liebe Gott bald den Frieden bescheren wird, daß wir anstatt der Briefe mündlich zusahmen sprechen können, welches ich von Hertzen wünsche, daß uns Gott Gnade verleihen wolle

[We must commend ourselves to God and implore him to be merciful to our King and us, and that we shall be able successfully to overcome our enemies and attain victory. And I hope that the Dear God will soon grant us peace, and that, instead of letters, we would be able to speak together again. I wish wholeheartedly that the Lord gives us this grace.]

Johann Hermann Dresel's last surviving letter to his father, 15 May 1759

Contents

Figures and Tables

Tables

Figures

Acknowledgements

This volume was conceived about fifteen years ago, when I was reading Christopher Duffy's history of Alexander Suvorov's Italian campaign. In the chapter surveying the armies of Habsburg Austria and Imperial Russia, Duffy brings as epigraph an excerpt from Tim Blanning's history of the French Revolutionary Wars, which reads:

The question of the motivation of Old Regime armies is almost wholly unresearched, partly because evidence is so spare and partly because it is tempting to assume that the soldiers signed up because of the bounty on offer, because they were pressed or because they were on the run and sought to desert at the earliest opportunity. In other words, the conventional picture corresponds to the Revolutionary rhetoric, which contrasted an army of citizen-soldiers with an army of mercenaries. Yet examination of the battles shows that the latter were capable of feats of heroism, both individual and collective, which cannot be explained simply in terms of iron discipline making the soldiers fear their officers more than the enemy.[1]

Five years later, as a master's student, I wrote to Professor Blanning, referred to the above quote and asked whether he thought it would make a good subject for a PhD thesis. One year later I began my studies in Cambridge.

The two years I spent working under Professor Blanning were truly inspiring. While never losing track of my immediate subject, Professor Blanning always prompted me to consider how my findings could relate to broader questions in early-modern European history. He also introduced me to Professor Duffy, whom I met at the end of my first term as a doctoral student. Professor Duffy's healthy scepticism regarding the availability of enough relevant primary sources has actually proven very heartening in its own way, as I entertained myself with the presumptuous belief of proving the great master wrong. I hope the material discussed over the subsequent pages demonstrates that old-regime soldiers did leave a substantial number of personal

---

[1] C. Duffy, *Eagles over the Alps*, 22; Blanning, *French Revolutionary Wars*, 119.

ix

recollections and more are to be found. Most importantly, without Professor Duffy and Professor Blanning the dissertation on which the current volume is based would never have been written and I would probably never have come to Cambridge in the first place. I am immensely grateful to them both, not only for helping me to become a better scholar, but also for changing my life.

Following Professor Blanning's retirement, I found myself under the aegis of Brendan Simms. To say that I am astonished by Professor Simms' encyclopaedic knowledge and incredible memory is to not express it strongly enough – I am stunned. The ability to recall all my arguments, including those which I myself have long forgotten, to know better than me what each of my footnotes says, the capacity to instantaneously recommend secondary literature on any conceivable subject; all this has left me in deepest wonder and greatly humbled. On a personal level, I must add that Professor Simms' kindness and patience with me were very generous.

I would like to mark for special thanks a number of colleagues who helped with particular aspects of the dissertation and its subsequent revision to publication. Simon Healy introduced me to some of the broader sociological concepts this study employs. Robert Selig shared with me his critical edition of the journal of Georg Daniel Flohr, although it is yet to appear to in print. William Tatum, whose forthcoming dissertation will certainly resolve once and for all many of the questions on eighteenth-century British military justice, forwarded me copies of rare material and shared with me parts of his own work. Lucia Staiano-Daniels provided a parallel perspective by sharing aspects of her ongoing PhD on common soldiers in seventeenth-century Saxony. Helen Roche helped me edit the book manuscript and provided additional constructive advice. A very special thanks goes to Debbie Bryce for her invaluable help in the Viennese archives.

Numerous friends, teachers and colleagues read, discussed, commented and otherwise supported me at various stages of research and writing. These include Tarak Barkawi, Steven Baule, the late Jacques Beauroy, Diana Beech, Ming Shun Chiang, Stephen Conway, Sir Christopher Clark, Andrew Cormack, Martyn Cowan, Marissa de Bruijn, Alan Forrest, Natali Gil, Yuval Noah Harari, Jasper Heinzen, Vicky Henshaw, Jennine Hurl-Eamon, Leighton James, Emrys Jones, Benjamin Zeev Kedar, Alisa Kunitz-Dick, Youenn Le Prat, Kevin Linch, Donald Londahl-Smidt, Matthew Lyle, Christopher Maine, Matthew McCormack, Hassan Metwally, David Parrott, Janine Rischke, Christian Schläpfer, Wolfgang Schmale, David Shiels, Adam Storring, Robert Tombs, Martin van Creveld and Joachim Whaley. I owe a special debt to Andrea Cobern, Dave and Debbie Faber,

Sebastian Pender, Tatsiana Senina, Frances Shih and Eva Steiner for their unconditional support at the moment when I most needed it.

I very much appreciate the help and assistance given to me by the staff of the Cambridge University Library, the Bodleian in Oxford, the British Library, the National Archives in Kew, the Templer Study Centre in the National Army Museum in London, the Austrian State Archives and the Austrian National Library in Vienna, the Military Archive at Vincennes and the National Library in Paris, the Institute for City History in Frankfurt, the André Malraux Multimedia Library in Strasbourg, the Patricia D. Klingenstein Library at the New York Historical Society, the Green Howards Museum in Richmond and the Luton and Bedfordshire Record Office. Some of the most enjoyable days doing research were spent in Wellington Barracks in London, where I worked in the regimental archives of the Grenadier and the Coldstream Guards.

I will always consider Peterhouse as my second home – no less! I have also benefited immensely from the generosity of the college, which awarded me the Graduate Research Studentship that enabled me to pursue my doctorate in the first place.

I am also grateful to the Hebrew University for awarding me the Golda Meir Postdoctoral Fellowship and then the Jacob and Lena Joels Memorial Foundation Fellowship. These helped to cover the period during which I revised my doctorate into a monograph.

I would also like to thank various employees of Cambridge University Press, especially the commissioning editor Michael Watson and members of the editorial team, Robert Judkins, Melissa Shivers and Lilian Dogiama. Together with Jeevitha Baskaran of Integra Software Services, they all helped bringing the manuscript to print.

With their usual generosity, my parents insisted that I forgo with the established custom of first-time authors and dedicate this volume to the man who got me interested in eighteenth-century history to begin with. However, my greatest love and thanks goes to them!

Abbreviations

AFS	*Armed Forces and Society* [Periodical]
BBS	Jürgen Kloosterhuis, *Bauern, Bürger und Soldaten: Quellen zur Sozialisation des Militärsystems im preußischen Westfalen 1713–1803, Vol. I Regesten,* (Münster: Selbstverlag des NW Staatsarchivs, 1992) [Book]
BL	British Library, London [Archive]
GG	Grosser Generalstab (ed.), *Briefe preußischer Soldaten aus den Feldzügen 1756 und 1757 und über die Schlachten bei Lobositz und Prag,* Beiträge und Forschungen zur Geschichte des Preußischen Heeres 2, (Berlin: Mittler 1901) [Book]
Hessians	*Hessians: Journal of the Johannes Schwalm Historical Association* [Periodical]
JSAHR	*Journal of the Society for Army Historical Research* [Periodical]
Liebe	Georg Liebe, 'Preußische Soldatenbriefe aus dem Gebiet der Provinz Sachsen im 18. Jahrhundert', *Jahresbericht des Thüringisch-Sächsischen Vereins für Erforschung des vaterländischen Altertums und Erhaltung seiner Denkmale,* 92-3 (1911-2), 1–37. [Article]
Methodists	Thomas Jackson (ed.), *Lives of Early Methodist Preachers, Chiefly Written by Themselves,* 4th edn, 3 vols., (Stoke-on-Trent: Tentmaker, 1998) [Book]
NAM	National Army Museum, London [Archive]
ÖStA	Österreichisches Staatsarchiv, Vienna [Archive]
SHD	Service Historique de la Défense, Vincennes [Archive]
TNA	The National Archives, Kew, London [Archive]

Introduction

For a long time, the conventional view of common soldiers serving in the armies of old-regime Europe was coloured by Frederick the Great's notorious assertion that men should fear their officers more than the enemy. The rank and file were largely an unwilling lot, recruited among the dregs of society; too drunk, dumb or desperate to resist the recruiting sergeant, or simply kidnapped into what one of the most prolific military historians of the last century has termed an outright form of 'military slavery'. No good could come out of such base human material and, to ensure their obedience, the recruits were subjected to harsh discipline and incessant drill until they were transformed into submissive military automatons. Then they could be marched into battle, closely followed by a line of cane-wielding officers and NCOs who would strike and even kill any man who would not fight earnestly enough.[1]

Although, in recent decades, scholarship has taken a more positive view of eighteenth-century common soldiers, assessment of their motivation remains largely unfavourable. This is particularly the case when the armies of old-regime Europe are compared to the troops of revolutionary and Napoleonic France. According to the traditional interpretation, old-regime tactics were based on direct control by officers to prevent their reluctant subordinates from running away. Such a system not only prevented any personal initiative coming from the rank and file, but also constrained the flexibility of the army as a whole. It was totally different for the French, whose willing soldiery freed their commanders from the necessity to police the men to make them fight. Moreover, France possessed not only enthusiastic but more trustworthy troops who could be sent to forage, employed in forests and broken terrain or dispersed to fight in open order, all of which resulted in enhanced military capability and higher combat effectiveness. In other words, the victories of

---

[1] Frederick the Great, 'Instruction für die Commandeurs der Cavallerie-Regimenter', in *Œuvres*, vol. XXX, 302 and repeated again in 'Das militärische Testament von 1768' in *Werke*, vol. VI, 233; Keegan, *History*, 343.

Revolutionary France over the united forces of old-regime Europe is portrayed not only as a military but also as a moral triumph.[2]

It is not that this view has gone wholly unchallenged. No one has provided a more vivid and succinct criticism of the conventional understanding of motivation in the armies of old-regime Europe than T.C.W. Blanning. Addressing the issue as part of a broader discussion of the Revolutionary Wars, Blanning contends that the ideals usually attributed to the French troops, such as patriotism and ideology, are constants, and are therefore expected to produce continuous military superiority. However, the conflict was not one-sided, and the revolutionary armies sustained numerous reverses. More importantly, the rank and file in the old-regime armies 'were capable of feats of heroism, both individual and collective, which cannot be explained simply in terms of iron discipline'. Their low reputation is not only unsubstantiated by their combat record, but also smacks of revolutionary rhetoric. 'Two awful possibilities loom: either that ideological commitment had little to do with fighting effectiveness or that the values of old regime were just as powerful as the ideals of the Revolution'.[3]

Blanning's critique is part of a historiographical trend, prevailing since the bicentenary of 1789, which re-examines some of the more established interpretations of the French Revolution and the wars that followed. The image emerging from those studies is far more ambiguous than the clear icon of the enthusiastic citizen-soldier so favoured by revolutionary orators and numerous modern historians. The French army was as much a product of the strengths of the new military system as of some of its less flattering aspects. Its members included genuine volunteers spurred by patriotism and ideology, but also numerous reluctant recruits produced by mass levies and conscription laws. The French nation did command the sympathy of many men, but others thought more of the homes and communities they left behind. Some recruits marched to the front inspired by patriotism, but their columns were often shadowed by detachments of the *gendarmerie*, the revolutionary successor of the old-regime *maréchaussée* or military police. Even French scholarship, which otherwise maintains a highly favourable view of the revolutionary traditions, acknowledges that, following the short upheaval of radical practices, disciplinary and hierarchical structures were restored to the military. But even before the late 1790s when, to use the subtitle of the English

---

[2] '[G]enuine and willing soldiers ... outfought opponents who remained trapped in the habits of doltish obedience and stereotyped tactics from which the French had escaped', Keegan, *History*, 352–3; For a kinder but essentially similar appraisal, see: Howard, *War*, 79–81.

[3] Blanning, *French Revolutionary Wars*, 119.

translation of Jean-Paul Bertaud's important study, it was again poised to become an instrument of power, the army was increasingly manned by coercive measures which caused widespread resistance, draft-dodging and desertion. As for those remaining with the colours, it was demonstrated that the longer a man served, the less likely he was to invoke official ideals. Soldiers' letters studied by Alan Forrest reveal that such men preferred to reflect upon their service by mentioning professional pride, prospects of promotion or drawing strength from the presence of their close comrades.[4]

Compared to this fuller and more nuanced treatment of the motivation of revolutionary and Napoleonic troops, views of old-regime soldiers remain surprisingly one-sided. Although intensive research into the social origins of their recruits has consistently dispelled the myth that the rank and file of eighteenth-century armies consisted of criminals and social misfits, their men are seldom credited with comparable idealism to that supposedly prevailing among the revolutionary soldiery. For instance, it is commonly agreed that eighteenth-century troops had little personal concern for the cause for which they were fighting. Although rarely expressed in the same condescending language, such views essentially repeat Frederick's low opinion on his own soldiers; but was that also the way these men saw themselves?

The last fifty years has witnessed a growing body of work devoted to what have long been socially marginalised groups, such as women, peasants, the urban poor and delinquents. A major conclusion emerging from those studies is that the lower orders in medieval and early-modern Europe were not an array of helpless brutalised individuals. Despite harsh, often cruel living conditions, their members had a sense of worth and a system of morals which often ran contrary to the officially sanctioned culture. Despite the lack of political and social rights, the lower classes could and often did resist the authorities in myriad ways, ranging from carefully orchestrated displays of defiance to open rebellion.[5] These findings often echo Michel Foucault's theories of power. Rather than being based entirely on coercion administered from above, Foucault suggests a more reciprocal model of power relations, where domination is rarely total and all participants engage in cycles of confrontation and cooperation which continuously reshape the existing system. The

---

[4] Forrest, *Conscripts and Deserters*; Forrest, *Napoleon's Men*; Bertaud, *Army of the French Revolution*; For a particularly revisionist account, see: Griffith, *Art of War of Revolutionary France*.

[5] For instance: Bercé, *Histoire des Croquants*; Davis, *Society and Culture in Early-Modern France*; Sabean, *Power in the Blood*; Härter, 'Soziale Disziplinierung durch Strafe?'; Shoemaker, *The London Mob*.

acceptance of authority is usually based on the consent of the subject, rather than upon coercion.[6] A despised group on the periphery of eighteenth-century societies, common soldiers should have been an optimal subject for cultural study in the current academic climate, which is otherwise so favourably disposed towards the rediscovery of the lost voices of common men and women. Nor should the apparent scarcity of personal narratives have been an obstacle. This did not prevent scholars from looking at similar groups by supplementing direct testimonies with administrative material, and employing innovative methodologies from other scholarly fields. In fact, many such studies have resulted in the rediscovery of long-forgotten autobiographical writings and similarly informative ego-documents by peasants, artisans and women.[7] Why should the same not prove true of old-regime common soldiers as well?

Irrespective of whether personal narratives by eighteenth-century common soldiers are indeed particularly rare, even well-known existing evidence has not been used in full. When one reads his political testament of 1768, Frederick the Great cannot easily be suspected of having much sympathy for his men. For instance, the need to ensure obedience by fear is underscored because the king does not believe that common soldiers could be prompted by ambition. The very same paragraph, however, begins by recommending the endorsement of a regimental *esprit de corps*.[8] Whatever his professed views on discipline, even Frederick acknowledged that there were other ways to encourage the troops. On campaign, the king usually maintained good-humoured interactions with his men, even adopting a certain degree of approachability. After the Seven Years War, while overtaken by a mindset that some of his biographers referred to as 'misanthropic', Fredrick was still willing to take issue with anyone who doubted the courage of his soldiers.[9]

Nevertheless, a single phrase appearing in two memorials – one intended for senior officers and the other for the king's innermost circle – long took precedence over any other single piece of evidence coming from the eighteenth century. This is not to say that modern scholarship ignored the existence of positive impulses among the old-regime soldiery, but these were rarely discussed at length, usually appearing in the marginalia of what are mainly social histories of armies or operational military

---

[6] Foucault, 'The Subject and Power'.

[7] For instance: Amelang, *Flight of Icarus*; K.J. Lorenzen-Schmidt and B. Poulsen (eds.), *Writing Peasants*; Ozment, *Bürgermeister's Daughter*.

[8] Frederick the Great, 'Das militärische Testament von 1768' in *Werke*, vol. VI, 233; the rephrasing of Frederick's ideas is based on Jay Luvaas' translation in *Frederick the Great on the Art of War*, 78.

[9] C. Duffy, *Frederick the Great: A Military Life*, 335; C. Duffy, *Army of Frederick the Great*, 67.

histories of their campaigns. Failure to examine the narratives composed by the men themselves in depth left little alternative to the ready availability of military regulations, which underscored the need for unrelenting subordination, or articles of war, which largely consisted of a catalogue of punishments for various disciplinary infractions. Although a number of superb recent German studies challenged the brutality of old-regime discipline and underscored the possible role of positive motivation in combat, their conclusions did not penetrate mainstream scholarship. The prevailing view, shared by both military historians and eighteenth-century specialists, still remains that old-regime soldiers were motivated primarily by coercion. It is the aim of this volume to offer a corrective to this view and present a broader examination of the motivation of the rank and file serving in the armies of old-regime Europe.

Within the framework of this study, motivation is defined as a set of attitudes and conditions which caused soldiers to perform their duty in peace and war.[10] These are examined by utilising surviving autobiographical accounts of the soldiers themselves, including letters, journals and, most importantly, memoirs. Direct statements as to why their authors served or fought is only one type of useful evidence which these sources can provide. Descriptions of daily conditions denoting the existence of military socialisation, references to camaraderie between peers and the leadership skills of their superiors are all relevant when one considers how and why these men were likely to act. Particular notice is taken of wartime activities, opinions about the aims of the conflict, attitudes towards the enemy and behaviour in combat. This study, however, is not limited to the subjective experiences of individual soldiers, but also to the external factors which were likely to make some incentives more effective than others. For instance, it is hard to deny that fear of punishment can be a great motivator. Therefore, before discussing the potential role of idealistic factors, we will examine the role and influence of discipline and, more specifically, to what extent it could be enforced successfully. On this point, soldierly narratives can be supplemented by administrative records. This material, some of which will be analysed statistically, will help determine whether discipline was indeed the mainstay of the old-regime motivational system, as the prevailing scholarly view generally maintains.

In addition to one-sided comparisons between old-regime and revolutionary armies and the innovative work on socially-peripheral groups in

---

[10] This definition is in line with the definition in the *Oxford English Dictionary* as 'the [. . .] stimulus for action towards a desired goal, esp. as resulting from psychological or social factors', see: q.v. "motivation" 1b.

early-modern Europe, another source of formative influence on the current study is John A. Lynn's *Bayonets of the Republic*. Investigating the tactics, morale and combat effectiveness in the *Armée du Nord*, the largest army fielded by France in the War of the First Coalition, this is a groundbreaking work that sets the standard for all future historical studies of military motivation. Lynn argues that, instead of overwhelming their opponents with hordes of undisciplined but highly enthusiastic citizen-soldiers, the French victories were a product of a new military professionalism and rigorous training. The revolutionaries outfought their opponents not *in spite* of disciplinary weakness, as argued by previous generations of scholars, but because of a new disciplinary system based on willing consent, whose introduction was made possible by the patriotism of the French soldiery and its association with the new order. And yet, despite shattering this long-prevailing view on the motivation of French troops, this study repeats many traditional assumptions about old-regime armies, often reflecting how the virtues of the revolutionary soldiers mirrored the drawbacks of their predecessors and opponents. According to Lynn, old-regime armies emphasised coercive discipline, which, together with their non-egalitarian ethos, precluded the creation of genuine attachment between officers and their soldiers, who also remained indifferent to the aims of the war.[11]

Although it takes issue with some of the assertions made in *Bayonets of the Republic*, the current volume owes much to its methodology. In this truly interdisciplinary study, Lynn combines more conventional sources, such as memoirs, regulations and archival records, with modern research on combat motivation. A highlight of Lynn's book is the theoretical model of combat effectiveness that shows how various factors contributed to the overall performance of the French troops. The current study follows Lynn's example. It considers primary sources in the light of modern findings on motivation, which, although employed to examine almost every conflict up to and including the French Revolutionary Wars, has seldom been applied to old-regime armies. Secondly, this study formulates a theoretical model that aims to establish the relationship between basic types of motivational incentives. Previous work on eighteenth-century armies has mentioned the existence of idealistic motives, but usually fails to comment on their relative importance compared to discipline or material factors. The current book seeks to bridge this gap.

Even if somewhat less stirring than the original French expression on which it is based, 'old regime' is a charged term, implying not only a radical break with the order antedating the Revolution, but also its

---

[11] Lynn, *Bayonets*, 24, 43, 62–3, 92–3, 101–2.

rejection.[12] Nevertheless, it is fitting to employ it in the current study. Firstly, it is an acknowledgement of the prevailing scholarly trend that underscores the alleged rift between the armies of eighteenth-century Europe and revolutionary France. Moreover, it is appropriate to use it in a work that examines not only the soldiers who participated in wars between old-regime states, but also considers the experience of those men who fought against revolutionary and early-Napoleonic France. Chronologically, this study fits neatly into the eighteenth century. It begins with the War of the Spanish Succession and ends in 1789 for old-regime France, and 1806 for the rest of Europe. The latter date is chosen to correspond with the crushing defeat of Prussia, whose army is considered as the embodiment of old-regime warfare. In that sense, the twin battles of Jena-Auerstedt mark the end of that era.[13]

Although this study does not share the view that the mere survival of a personal narrative by an old-regime common soldier renders it unrepresentative and, therefore, of little scholarly use, it is important to draw on as many such sources as possible. For the same reason, this study sets broad geographical limits, looking at western as well as central Europe. There is another important rationale beyond the relatively broad scope of the current study. This book shares the view that old-regime Europe was united by a single and relatively stable military culture, and that its armies shared basic similarities in their military experience and practice which outweighed their distinctive characteristics. From about 1700 until the outbreak of the French Revolutionary Wars, Europe saw little variety along national lines in fighting methods, weaponry and even in uniforms. Although some important tactical developments did take place, none proved strong enough to break the basic combat environment established on the battlefields of the War of the Spanish Succession. Introduction of effective light infantry in Austria, improved infantry drill in Prussia or the standardisation of the Austrian artillery under the Prince of Liechtenstein are good examples of military innovation in this period. These were practical improvements which added to the existing system rather than transforming it, and provided no lasting edge over other European opponents. Despite some variety in recruitment practices, the social composition of the old-regime armies was markedly similar. The soldiery originated from the lower orders of society; at its head, however, stood an almost exclusively noble and mostly cosmopolitan officer class. With regard to military administration, the century was

---

[12] Doyle, *Ancien Regime*.
[13] On the shocking influence of these battles their contemporaries, see for instance: Allmayer-Beck, 'Von Hubertusburg nach Jena'; Paret, *Cognitive Challenge*.

marked by continuous and largely successful attempts to bring broader aspects of military service under the aegis of direct state control at the expense of the proprietary rights of the officers.[14]

This important point provides the main justification for a study whose most significant primary sources originate from different countries over a substantial time period. Moreover, while every effort was made to locate and consult as many soldierly narratives as possible, the distribution of those sources proved unequal. The overall balance of published voices from the ranks tilts towards Britain. This discrepancy was addressed by research in major continental archives such as Vienna and Vincennes. However, it could not be remedied entirely. Moreover, a number of manuscripts located in American or small European archives could not be consulted.[15] Lack of linguistic capabilities precluded the study of Spanish or Scandinavian sources, although in the latter case a number of such writings were left by Swedish participants of the Great Northern War.[16] Yet, although this study cannot presume to be based on a completely balanced set of primary evidence, its conclusions are still useful. As long as they are drawn from autobiographical writings by common soldiers describing actual military service in old-regime Europe, findings for one army are likely to prove relevant for men in other forces who were undergoing similar service conditions and facing comparable challenges both in war and in peace.

The current study considers close to 250 such sources. It is possible to argue that this number is too insignificant for a period during which millions of men served. Moreover, it can be claimed that the mere fact that their authors were articulate or educated enough to express themselves in writing already marks them as extraordinary. Obviously, this is true, assuming that an ideal standard of completeness and representativeness is indeed achievable. Yet whatever the limitations of the current sample, it is definitely more representative and complete than anything attempted beforehand. The present study takes no greater liberty than

---

[14] The best overview of the military culture of old-regime Europe is C. Duffy, *Military Experience*; see also: Strachan, *European Armies*, 23–37; Conway, 'Eighteenth-Century British Army as a European Institution'; On the regularisation of Europe's armies, see: M.S. Anderson, *War and Society*, 56–63, 99–111; Corvisier, *Armies and Societies*, 64–72; McNeill, *Pursuit of Power*, 125–42; and for particular case studies: Redlich, *German Military Enterpriser*, vol. II; Hochedlinger, *Austria's Wars*, 303–26.

[15] For instance: 'Heinrich Georg Sigmund Q.', Deutsches Tagebucharchiv, Emmendingen, (1892 / II); 'Tagebuch eines Grenadiers im I. Bat. Des Hessen-Hanau Inf. Rgt. Erbprinz. Komp. Des Obristlieutenants Lenz', Staatsarchiv Marburg, Best 10e, Nr. 1/23.

[16] See the annotated bibliography attached to the English translation of Englund, *Battle of Poltava*.

that taken by James S. Amelang, whose examination of 300 years of experience of early-modern artisans is also based on about 250 personal narratives, or Barbara Donagan, whose excellent chapter on the rank and file in the English Civil War, which includes numerous interesting insights on their motivation, cites less than five writings by such soldiers themselves.[17] Moreover, while the quality and reliability of each and every one of the autobiographical writings employed in the following pages can be debated, it is hoped that, when combined, they can form a basis for informed generalisations. These narratives were produced by a diverse set of individuals with different experiences and perspectives. They include pressed men and volunteers, privates and NCOs, war veterans and men who served only in peacetime. Some authors served loyally until retirement, while others deserted. The perspectives held by the authors regarding their service are also different: some openly enjoyed it, others disdained it, and many state no clear opinion either way. Discarding their testimonies in the name of unattainable criteria would be a mistake.

Although it disagrees with some Lynn's notions regarding the nature of old-regime armies, this study looks up to *Bayonets of the Republic*, particularly to its model of combat effectiveness. It is very easy to make a long list of categories which pays attention to all kinds of factors, but is analytically sterile; it is as tempting to produce sweeping generalisations which make analysis easy at the expense of accuracy. Lynn's model strikes a delicate balance between these two extremes by subdividing combat effectiveness into distinct categories. These are first discussed separately, making it possible to consider their individual contributions towards the whole. The model offered in this study follows this example. Previous works commenting on the motivation of eighteenth-century soldiers often came to conclusions based on a selection of quotations from soldiers' writings. While demonstrating the existence of certain attitudes or the effectiveness of a particular motivational drive, such an approach cannot determine their overall significance. By considering motivation as a sum of separate categories, it is hoped to not only to establish the existence of distinct incentives, but also to evaluate their relative importance. Many of the ideas behind this model are not original. It owes much to Lynn's suggestion that we can consider military motivation as a set of three sequential stages. Another basic component of the current model is the theory of compliance, whose military aspects were formulated by Stephen Westbrook in a broader discussion of

---

[17] Amelang, *Flight of Icarus*; Donagan, *War in England*, 258–94; see also: Latzel, 'Vom Kriegserlebnis zur Kriegserfahrung', 6–10.

disintegration.[18] The claim for novelty of the current model is that it considers these two theories within a single matrix which defines the components of motivation. Although the subdivision of such a complex subject is artificial, it allows for the formation of distinct analytic categories which can be applied systematically, helping to counterbalance the anecdotal nature of narrative sources and their authors' choice of incident and choice of language.

This study advances the basic view that motivation is based on the availability of incentives. Those could be either positive or negative. In the former case, the incentive to pursue a particular course of action is based on reward; in the latter case, failure to pursue it leads to sanction. Neither the reward nor the sanction need to be material. For instance, both the desire to win approval from one's society and fear of shame could prove strong motives for action. Moreover, motivation can be based on external factors, as in the last example, but it is just as likely to be internal, that is, based on one's own values, irrespective of whether they correspond with those professed by the society at large. Essentially, motivation is not unlike the common dualist definition of honour, which distinguishes between internal and external measurements of worth. The former is based on intrinsic personal qualities – 'inner feelings of self worth and high-mindedness'. The latter owes its existence to the desire to acquire social capital for manifesting positive qualities in public, for instance: demonstrating 'valor for family and country [or] conformity to the community wishes'.[19]

Following Lynn, our model divides military motivation into three basic stages. Initial motivation covers the causes of why men enlist. Sustaining motivation considers reasons why soldiers endure the hardships of military life such as training, discipline, daily chores and, very commonly, boredom. Finally, combat motivation explains why soldiers fight.[20] Each stage has particular features which distinguish it from the other two. In the initial stage, the soldier comes closest to being an 'actor', that is, he is generally able to control the conditions he is under. In the later two stages, the soldier is a 'subject'; the challenges are external and his action will largely be limited to the choice of coping strategies. The combat stage, on the other hand, is made unique by the immediate presence of fear that needs to be surmounted. Moreover, throughout the first two stages, men usually have time to reflect upon their choice of actions, but in combat, decisions often have to be taken instantaneously.

---

[18] Lynn, *Bayonets*, 21–40; Westbrook, 'Potential for Military Disintegration'; Westbrook largely builds on ideas formulated in Etzioni, *Comparative History of Complex Organizations*.
[19] Quoted from Wyatt-Brown, *Southern Honor*, 4.   [20] Lynn, *Bayonets*, 35–6.

Despite that, it is the sustaining stage which is the most fascinating of the three. It is possible to ponder at length whether to enlist, but it all leads to one single action, and once the decision is made, the initial stage is gone, never to return. Combat would confront men with an intense challenge – clear and immediate danger to their lives – but actual fighting would rarely last more than a few hours, sometimes even minutes. This point is particularly relevant for old-regime warfare, when major field armies seldom engaged in more than two pitched battles per year.[21] Allowing for a grey area, such as low-intensity skirmishing between outposts or trench duty during sieges, periods of combat motivation can be likened to islets in a sea of sustaining motivation. In other words, the initial and combat stages are short and definite, while the sustaining stage is permanent and covers the bulk of one's military service.

While the three stages of motivation provide a diachronic element, as an individual cannot exist in more than one stage at any given moment, compliance theory provides a synchronic model. Its aim is to explain the choice and balance of external incentives which are applied to prompt an individual to pursue a desired course of action. This can be done using three basic types of power. Coercive power is the ability to inflict physical punishment on the disobedient. Remunerative power is based on the command of material resources, including rewarding the compliant, typically with pay. The first two leverages are thus easy to define: the former is based entirely on a negative incentive, and the latter on a positive incentive. Normative power is more complex, since it employs both incentives. The leverage is provided by the ability to award or withdraw desired status symbols. Unlike the two other leverages, normative incentives are immaterial. For this reason, this form of compliance can only be effective on individuals who have moral involvement within a larger collective whose values they share. For soldiers these could be immediate comrades, their units, or the general socio-political system in whose name the army operates. In the latter case, the involvement can be dynamic, but, according to Westbrook, it is usually latent. Ideological values would actively propel a minority to fight, but the majority of soldiers would invoke them as a consoling factor. Seeing one's socio-political system as basically worthwhile legitimises the demands made in its name.[22] Unlike the three stages of motivation, different types of compliance can operate simultaneously. For instance, promotion can carry both remunerative and normative elements: a rise in pay and the prestige accorded to

---

[21] For instance, during their seven years of service in the American War of Independence, even the most heavily engaged Hessian regiments spent only a few days in action; see: Atwood, *Hessians*, 234–5.
[22] This point owes much to the ideas developed by Charles Moskos, see Chapter 1, 26.

Table 0.1 *Model of military motivation*

				Continuity?		
				Singular	Recurrent	
				Stage of Motivation		
				Initial	Sustaining	Combat
Type of Incentive	Material	Compliance Type	Coercive	Conscription	Discipline	Fear
			Remunerative	Bounty	Pay	Greed
	Immaterial		Normative	Volunteering	Cohesion/ Ideology	Honour/ Faith

a higher position in the military hierarchy. On the other hand, an incentive factor belonging to one of the categories of compliance can play a role in each of the stages of motivation. For instance, patriotism, which is a normative factor, can spur a man to enlist, to serve and to fight. However, the precise incentive provided at every stage might have a different nuance, which can be either active or passive. For instance, a wish to fight the enemies of one's country might provide a reason to enlist. During the sustaining stage, belief in the just cause of a war against such enemies might reconcile the subject with the demands of military life. Lastly, in combat, hatred of the enemy can propel the subject into action. In previous studies, even when discussed as part of the same theoretical model, the three stages of motivation and the three leverages of compliance have always been considered separately. The current study merges them into a single model by crossing between them to create nine congruent sub-categories, as demonstrated in Table 0.1. Although it is possible to apply this model to any military organisation, we will discuss it in relation to old-regime armies only.

Eighteenth-century armies were supplemented by various forms of conscription. This included not only regulated and semi-regulated legal means such as cantonal recruitment and impressment, but also strong-arm methods, when individuals were abducted into the army. Ideally, however, armies were manned by voluntary enlistment, with the recruit receiving a cash bonus or bounty. Even though it was argued that old-regime Europe did witness instances of patriotic enlistment, such recruits were still entitled to a bounty. It is hard, therefore, to consider this category separately for old-regime Europe. In terms of sustaining motivation, discipline is traditionally perceived as the mainstay of the old-regime militaries. Pay is seen as another dominant incentive, in light of the deprivation supposedly prevailing in the social class from which the recruits came. There was also an element of informal earnings, as troops always welcomed opportunity to plunder. Although concepts of cohesion and ideology might appear anachronistic in an eighteenth-century context, elements of these did exist. For instance, the rationale traditionally attributed to *esprit de corps* is the creation of distinct regimental communities. Moreover, armies did call upon the ideals of their members. Sermons, celebrations and ceremonies were devised both to enhance the values of the military community, and also to underscore the legitimacy of its demands. Coercive incentives in combat were not limited to the presence of officers and NCOs who were placed along the line. As soon as battle was joined, the immediate presence of the enemy was likely to induce men to fight harder in hope of saving their own lives. Though quitting ranks for that purpose was strictly forbidden, looting was always a possibility, providing a potential remunerative incentive. As for normative motivation, honour, although traditionally considered as an officers' prerogative, could also apply to their subordinates. As demonstrated by Sascha Möbius' findings on fatalism in the Prussian army, the role of faith as a consoling factor could also prove very important.[23]

According to this model, the wartime motivation of an army as a whole is the sum of the nine above-mentioned categories, and, in peacetime, of the six categories of the initial and sustaining stages. However, since the stages of motivation are chronologically distinct, only three categories would be active in an individual soldier at any given moment, corresponding to the three types of compliance. The balance between them can be different, yet it is argued that their sum is a constant. The military organisation is based on compliance, with individual soldiers continuously being given orders that they can either obey or disobey. It is impossible to deny the existence of a grey area, as some men, either consciously or subconsciously, would not follow orders to the best of their ability. In combat, some soldiers would resort to external displays of fighting to satisfy one's superiors or pacify their fears, or skulk from the firing line

---

[23] See Chapter 1, 32.

without fleeing altogether. Others would be overtaken by passivity; neither fighting nor running. Nevertheless, when considered as a whole, the army either functions or it does not. When a critical mass of its individual members chooses to disobey, the organisation ceases to function. If that happened at the initial stage, there would not be enough recruits to man the army; in the sustaining stage, its soldiers would mutiny; in the combat stage, they would simply refuse to fight.

However, instances of such disintegration in old-regime armies are very rare. Despite continuous difficulties, no army raised too few recruits to cease operating. Eighteenth-century soldiers would sometimes mutiny, but those occasions were usually intended to redress particular grievances, and order would be restored quickly.[24] In combat, linear tactics did involve an element of disintegration because victory, in part, resulted from the psychological breakdown of the opposing infantry line. That said, old-regime troops showed surprising resilience. Armies could expect to lose up to a third of their men in the course of a single battle, while instances of individual units suffering casualty rates of over 50 per cent were also not unheard of. The fact that troops were successfully brought to fight in such circumstances speaks highly of their combat motivation, regardless of whether they were victorious or not. Moreover, defeated armies were able to regain their effectiveness very quickly. For instance, the Prussian army at Kunersdorf broke and run, sustaining an overall loss of 40 per cent. Within two days it was again a disciplined military force.[25] All this testifies to the overall success of the motivational system of old-regime armies, irrespective of the incentives on which it was based. The question should be, therefore, not whether old-regime troops were motivated, but the balance between the three levers of compliance at every one of the three stages of motivation. When the traditional views are reformulated according to the current model, coercive compliance was the most prominent lever, especially in the sustaining stage. Remunerative power, by contrast, was prominent in the initial stage, as most recruits chose to enlist for financial reasons. When it is considered at all, normative compliance is seen as the least important factor of the three.

---

[24] The only instance of an old-regime army coming close to disintegration in peacetime is the French army in 1789–90. But even in this case the disciplinary crisis was surmounted and the line army began its regeneration as an effective body even before the initial influx of volunteers; see: S.F. Scott, *Response*, chs. 2–3.

[25] For the conditions on the eighteenth-century battlefield, see: C. Duffy, *Military Experience*, 197–267. Instances of armies suffering losses of a third of its men and more include the Prussian army at Zorndorf, Hochkirch and Torgau. At the battle of Parma, a Swiss battalion in the Piedmontese service lost some 70 per cent of its men, but continued fighting. See: ibid., 245, 249–50, and also C. Duffy, *Army of Frederick*, 184–5, 195–6.

This model allows the current volume to take a more holistic approach to the subject. Coercive compliance is discussed in Part I (Chapters 1–3) which offers a counter-argument suggesting that discipline alone cannot account either for the service motivation of the great majority of eighteenth-century common soldiers or for the combat effectiveness of old-regime armies. Part II (Chapters 4–6) offers an alternative explanation which stresses the role of acceptance, as well as other forms of positive motivation among the rank and file.

Chapter 1 provides relevant background by discussing traditional views of old-regime common soldiers and their motivation. Although most historians no longer repeat older prejudices regarding the moral character of the eighteenth-century rank and file, the conventional understanding of its military experience still remains heavily influenced by established perceptions of the French Revolutionary Wars. Chapter 2 reconsiders desertion – the high level of which throughout the eighteenth century is commonly associated with the alleged brutality of old-regime armies and the overall unwillingness of their rank and file. However, comparative statistical analysis of samples drawn from Austrian, British and French archives demonstrates that only a minority of all deserters were actually arrested. Even among those who were apprehended, many deserters were still able to avoid punishment through bulk amnesties and pardon schemes. This suggests that desertion in this period had less to do with the harshness of service conditions than with the general incapability of the authorities in old-regime Europe to arrest and punish deserters. The standard view of military discipline is further questioned in Chapter 3. Instead of a stark choice between utter obedience and outright rebellion, power relations between soldiers and their officers were more nuanced. Just as early-modern peasants would wear down their lords by pushing the boundaries and making enforcement of obligations difficult and expensive,[26] the men of the line could protest against unpopular policies or partially defy the authority of their superiors without placing in question the military system itself – which most soldiers accepted and affirmed. Coercion alone was thus unable to enforce the continuous obedience of the rank and file, and their subordination was, at least in part, also a product of consent.

All this puts into question the centrality of the coercive factor in the running of old-regime armies, particularly in the sustaining stage. However, according to our model, for the motivational system to remain intact, a decrease in one element of compliance has to be compensated for. Chapter 4 looks at the role of remunerative compliance, particularly

---

[26] On this, see the classical account in Blickle's *Deutsche Untertanen*.

at the initial stage, where it is traditionally considered the strongest. Again, soldierly writings reveal a different reality from that described by modern historians. Although financial reasons are often mentioned, these were not the only important incentives to enlist. Military service held an appeal not only as a profession also but as an institution, which led some men to choose it over other forms of employment. In other words, there was a place for normative factors, even during the initial stage of military service. Chapter 5 continues the investigation of normative factors during the sustaining stage by showing that, once a man had enlisted, his successful socialisation into the military was largely dependent on his acknowledgement of established group standards. There are clear signs that the culture of honour not only penetrated deeply into the rank and file, but also formed part of a unique corporate identity, suggesting that soldiers developed a strong moral involvement with their immediate social surroundings. Chapter 6, which is devoted to wartime service, interweaves the theme of immediate military loyalties to comrades, units and the army with broader ideals. Soldiers' writings contain references to dynastic loyalty, national feelings and, at the time of the revolutionary wars, even ideology. Men were clearly not indifferent to these factors, making it likely that a demand to fight for them would have been seen as legitimate. It appears that a combination of normative factors that were internalised during the sustaining stage, together with the overall legitimacy of the hierarchical demands of officers, who typically led from the front rather than pushed from the rear, helped men to surmount their initial fear and enter battle.

1   Motivation

New Research and Contemporary Sources

One of the most important characteristics of old-regime wars was the relative indecisiveness of their campaigns. Although the century had its share of tactically decisive battles, such as like Blenheim and Roßbach, few were followed by comparable developments at the strategic level. High losses often meant that the victorious army was shaken as badly as its defeated opponent. Rapid exploitation of battlefield success was further hampered by cumbersome supply arrangements and numerous fortresses that could shield the defeated force in the unlikely case of swift pursuit. These fortresses were liable to hamper victors further. Although most sieges in that period ended successfully, a typical investment would last for weeks or even months. As fighting was rarely carried into the winter, a successful campaign would usually conclude with the capture of a number of border strongholds. The next six months would be spent on replenishing resources, training replacements and equipping magazines. The start of the next campaign season would likely see both sides evenly matched again. Significant military victory was not impossible, but it required maintaining a string of continuous successes over a number of years. This was achieved by Prussia in the two Silesian Wars and by Russia following their major gains against Turkey in the conflicts of 1768–74 and 1787–92, but such cases were the exception rather than the rule. For most old-regime belligerents, conflict turned into a long match of military and financial attrition, concluding with mutual exhaustion and diplomatic compromise.[1] However, the relatively limited political results of those conflicts were not mirrored on their actual

---

[1] C. Duffy, *Military Experience*, 10–2; Howard, *War*, 54–74; Strachan, *European Armies*, 9–16; Chandler, *Art of Warfare*, 12–23; Blanning, *French Revolutionary Wars*, 12–17; Bell, *First Total War*, 44–48; see also: McNeill, *Pursuit of Power*, 158–79; For an argument that the main reason for the 'limited' nature of old-regime warfare was that armies outstripped their supply arrangements, see: Van Creveld, *Supplying War*, 26–39; M.S. Anderson, *War and Society*, 82–90; Parker, *Military Revolution*, 38–44; Luh, *Ancien Régime Warfare*; For a criticism of the prevailing view of the 'indecisiveness' of old-regime warfare, see: Black, *European Warfare, 1660–1815*, 67–86; For a more nuanced overview of the period: P.H. Wilson, 'Warfare in the Old-Regime 1648–1789'.

battlefields, for old-regime combat experience was one of the most intensive in the history of warfare.

This was a result of the introduction of new weaponry in the late
seventeenth century, largely during the War of the League of Augsburg.
When it began, armies still fought in mixed formations armed with
matchlock muskets and pikes, but in the later years of the conflict, the
balance shifted in favour of infantrymen equipped with quicker-firing
flintlocks and socket bayonets. These allowed the musket to be turned
into a shock weapon without impairing its ability to fire.[2] As long as parts
of the infantry were equipped with blank arms only, a degree of active
fighting could be expected. The abolition of the pike meant that battles
were now decided predominantly by firepower or, perhaps, by the ability
to withstand it. While generally more reliable than its predecessor, the
flintlock was also apt to misfire, especially when loaded in battle conditions. Thus, in order to employ the new weapon with good results, the
effect of the first volley had to be maximised and '[i]n times of flat-
barrelled and front-charged guns this could only be achieved in one
way: massive use'.[3] To bring as many men to fire as possible, the depth
of the infantry line was decreased to four, three and, sometimes, even two
soldiers. While the front was thus extended, musketry had to remain
concentrated and the men were arrayed elbow to elbow, creating a thin
unwieldy formation unsuited for quick movement. A typical pace of
advance would rarely exceed seventy-five steps per minute, and pauses
were common to dress the formation and allow slower moving units to
catch up, in order that all muskets could be brought to bear when the
enemy was within range.[4]

But the fact that this slowly moving and closely packed formation made
an excellent target for enemy artillery tells only half the story. Smoothbore
muskets were inaccurate, and massed volleys ruled out the possibility of
aimed fire. A general discharge from 200 yards would hit no more than
a few men. At 100 yards the volley would have some effect, but when
delivered from half that distance, its results could prove murderous,
hitting as many as every third soldier in the enemy line. Thus effective
employment of infantry firepower required that firing had to be withheld
as long as possible. The troops marched towards the enemy without
pausing to shoot and ignoring whatever defensive fire came their way
until they were able to discharge the precious first volley that had been
calmly loaded before the battle. It made little difference whether the
shocked survivors fled immediately or the enemy required additional

---

[2] Chandler, *Art of Warfare*, 75–84; Luh, *Ancien Régime Warfare*, 156–60.
[3] Lynn, *Battle*, 144.   [4] Lynn, *Giant*, 482–3; C. Duffy, *Military Experience*, 200–4.

softening from more volleys or even a bayonet charge. The measured advance forward, while stoically enduring losses rather than actively inflicting them, became the prevailing characteristic of old-regime warfare from the War of the Spanish Succession onwards. Lynn fittingly called this 'the battle culture of forbearance', which required 'paying heavy cost in casualties as an essential downpayment on victory'.[5] The adoption of the flintlock also meant that the days of face-to-face combat were largely over. It could still occur in entrenchments, but instances of troops actually crossing their bayonets on the field were very rare. Not unlike the steady patient advance into the fire zone, the bayonet charge became a kind of psychological expedient. Its aim was not to transfix as many opponents as possible, but rather intimidate them into flight.[6] While still justified under the battle conditions of the time, the practice of induced passivity under fire was entirely counter-intuitive. Essentially, the old-regime battle tactics became a duel of mental endurance between the opposing troops. This alone should provide good reason for the study of old-regime soldiers' motivation.

Yet, despite the crucial importance of morale in linear combat, eighteenth-century military literature did not preoccupy itself with the inner motives of enlisted men. Only a few writers ventured any further than expressing the general expectation that soldiers were to act bravely. A typical military manual would include a few sub-sections on the duties of private sentinels and NCOs, but their content would be largely technical. Officers were generally advised to treat their men fairly and demonstrate interest in their well-being. The role of personal example was underscored by writers such as Humphrey Bland, who authored the most widely read military manual in Britain.[7] Nevertheless, these were mostly passing remarks. Even if the men were capable of acting from high motives, their lowly origins made them more likely to follow the vilest traits of human character. Such views were partially the product of the social chasm separating officers and men, but they also reflected a much broader social reality. The army essentially mirrored the practices of the patriarchal society of that time. Soldiers were seen as perpetually immature and mischievous children, and should be treated as such by their social superiors, who would chastise them whenever necessary, just as

---

[5] Lynn, *Battle*, 129; Strachan, *European Armies*, 16–7; C.J. Rogers, 'Tactics and the Face of Battle'; For a general discussion of infantry tactics: Chandler, *Art of Warfare*, 110–30; C. Duffy, *Military Experience*, 204–21; P.H. Wilson, 'Warfare', 88–94; For a view which underscores the evolutionary nature of the tactical changes in the late seventeenth and early eighteenth centuries, see: Nosworthy, *Anatomy of Victory*, particularly 9–10, 29–36.

[6] C. Duffy, *Military Experience*, 204–6; For more on bayonet charges, see Chapter 3, 101.

[7] Bland, *Treatise*, 144; Starkey, *War*, 53–4.

a caring and loving father would punish his son. For this reason, the foundation of the army rested on subordination and discipline, which was to be maintained constantly and, if need be, harshly.[8]

Nor were common soldiers likely to fare better at the hands of the more prominent civilian observers. The French *philosophes* considered them 'with a mixture of fear, disgust, and even pity'. In Britain, the memory of the Civil War placed the army under continuous suspicion. This reflected not only its association with despotic power, but also the army's role as the only available instrument of public order.[9] Less affluent members of society were likely to agree on that point, as troops were often employed to quell popular discontent. Moreover, the late introduction of barracks and their slow proliferation throughout the continent meant that, for much of the century, soldiers were often billeted on the civilian population, from whose resources they would frequently help themselves. Yet the dislike of soldiers had much deeper roots. Whatever the actual reasons, the choice to enlist was a brazenly individualistic act which questioned established traditional hierarchies of family and community. Moreover, the soldier looked and acted differently, worked with gunpowder (still often associated with the devil) and was subordinate to an alternative set of morals and laws.[10] Prevailing perceptions of the soldier as a rebel and an alien ring true in the semi-apologetic introduction to the memoirs of Sergeant William Kenward: 'I am the only man of the family [...], who ever had the Honour of serving His Majesty, (or to use the words of some and the opinion of many) that ever was fool enough to disgrace himself and Family, by becoming a Robber, Murderer and Runaway, to service his King and Country'.[11]

Common soldiers were sometimes seen more positively. One of the by-products of the prevailing sentimentalist fashion was a growing interest in the lower orders. In addition to farmers, prostitutes and midwives,

---

[8] Despite his positive view on the potential role of rewards and improvements, Stephen Payne Adye, the author of the standard British work on courts martial, considered the army to be composed from 'the refuse of society', see: *Treatise on Courts Martial*, 270; and also: C. Duffy, *Military Experience*, 82–4; Spring, *With Zeal and with Bayonets*, 107–10.

[9] Lynn, 'Treatment of Military Subjects in Diderot's *Encyclopédie*', 138; Brumwell, *Redcoats*, 55–7; On the army as an instrument of public order, see: M.S. Anderson, *War and Society*, 166–7; Ruff, *Violence in Early Modern Europe*, 66–71; Hayter, *Army and the Crowd*; P.H. Wilson, *From Reich to Revolution*, 302–3.

[10] Loriga, *Soldati*, 122–3; Snape, *Redcoat and Religion*, 15; In France, the view that soldiers associate with the occult due to their involvement with gunpowder prevailed well into the nineteenth century, see: Hopkin, 'La Remée', 140–1; Hopkin, 'Storytelling, Fairytales and Autobiography'; On similar attitudes in Germany, see: Ludwig, 'Der Zauber des Tötens'; On the hostility between peasants and soldiers in Russia, see: Keep, *Soldiers of the Tsar*, 190–2.

[11] Kenward, *Sussex Highlander*, 1.

common soldiers could now aspire to public sympathy and attention. In Britain, by the middle of the eighteenth century, there was money to be made from soldiers' memoirs. In addition to some genuine recollections, these included bogus publications as well as highly embellished biographies.[12] Across the channel, military theorists even toyed with the idea of a citizen-soldier. However, authors such as Maurice de Saxe and Antoine-Hypolite Guibert were more influenced by idealised perceptions of ancient Roman legionaries than by positive views of contemporary French soldiery.[13] At a time when most military thinkers were devising new tactical systems and the majority of military practitioners were occupied with the daily running of their units, it is unsurprising that some of the more insightful observations on enlisted men were made by those operating on the periphery of European military culture. These include the English essayist and retired captain Sir Richard Steele, whose thoughts provide the epigram for this study, the Prussian *Feldprediger* Carl Daniel Küster and the French surgeon-turned-materialist-philosopher Julien Offray de La Mettrie. Some of the shrewdest remarks on the motivation of common soldiers came from a most unmilitary character, Dr Samuel Johnson, who famously claimed that most men held soldiering in much higher esteem than they were actually ever willing to admit.[14]

Despite widespread recognition that motivation in the armies of Revolutionary and Napoleonic France was radically different to anything that preceded it, the bravery of the soldier continued to be taken more or less for granted. Despite Napoleon's high assessment of the role of morale in war, two of the greatest scholars who aimed to synthesise a general theory out of Napoleonic warfare gave little attention to the inner motivation of the rank and file.[15] There were some exceptions, however; these works were as interesting as they were unrepresentative in a field dominated by intellectual heavyweights such as Clausewitz and Jomini. One such example is the French officer Charles Ardant du Picq. Du Picq was

---

[12] Starkey, *War*, 25–6, 60–3; Harari, 'Military Memoirs', 297–9; Harari, *Ultimate Experience*, 184–6, 190–3; On the connections of sentimentalism and military culture, see: ibid., 135–59; and more generally on sentimentalist narratives: Denby, *Sentimental Narrative*. For examples of a real, a bogus and a disputed memoir from that time, see, respectively: Millner, *Compendious Journal*; Bates, *Life and Memoirs*; Davis, *Life and Adventure*.

[13] Hippler, *Citizens, Soldiers and National Armies*, 37–45; M.S. Anderson, *War and Society*, 199–201; Starkey, *War*, 51–2; Lynn, *Battle*, 185–6; Bell, *First Total War*, 78–82; At the same time, more and more civilian observers were willing to show sympathy to the common soldiers, see: S.F. Scott, *Response*, 42–3; Dejob, 'Soldat'.

[14] Küster, *Bruchstück seines Campagnelebens*; La Mettrie, *Machine Man*; S. Johnson, 'Bravery of the English Common Soldier'; see also the comments in Boswell's famous biography, *Life of Johnson*, 926–7.

[15] Clausewitz, *On War*, 184–9; Jomini, *Précis de l'Art de la Guerre*, 119–28.

aware of the moral support gained from the immediate presence of one's comrades and considered how this could be maintained when closely packed infantry formations were made obsolete by new advances in military technology. He also emphasised the role of fear, arguing, to use Keegan's vivid rephrasing, that 'men fight from fear: fear of the consequences first of not fighting (i.e. punishment), then of not fighting well enough (i.e. slaughter)'. Although du Picq's ideas anticipated some concepts which were later developed by twentieth-century researchers, his influence in his own lifetime was negligible.[16]

If the motivation of contemporary soldiers did not inspire much interest among active servicemen, it is unsurprising that the motivation of eighteenth-century soldiers was also largely ignored in the work of nineteenth-century scholars. The multi-volume histories of the Silesian and Seven Years War produced by the Prussian and Austrian general staffs say virtually nothing of the motivation of the men who fought in those monumental struggles. When the motivation of old-regime soldiers was mentioned, the comments it elicited were largely disparaging. French scholars, unsurprisingly, underscored the turning point of 1789 and the rise of the new citizen army, which replaced the degenerate military structure of the Bourbon monarchy. German writers were in a much more interesting position, as they had to reconcile their fascination with Frederick the Great with the apparently embarrassing conditions endured by the enlisted men who served under him. Some attempts in that direction were made in the publication of writings by Frederician soldiers. These were invoked to contradict the already much-quoted account of Ulrich Bräker, implying the superiority of the recollections of native Prussian recruits to the utterances of a pressed foreign mercenary.[17] Genuine interest in common soldiers and the forces influencing them began in earnest during the First World War. Initially, it was largely prompted by utilitarian concerns: treating a multitude of very unnerved men and patching their souls quickly enough to send them back into combat. Nonetheless, the growing trickle of studies in applied psychiatry soon swelled into a torrent of works of much broader scope on combat behaviour and its accompanying emotions. The systematic study of motivation, however, had to wait for another world conflict and, again, this was largely a by-product of practical interests – it emerged as part of a larger body of work on combat effectiveness. Although this concept had as much do with military hardware as with military spirit, American

---

[16] Ardant Du Picq, *Études sur le Combat*; Gat, *History of Military Thought*, 296–310; George, 'Primary Groups', 294–6; Kellett, *Combat Motivation*, 13–14; Keegan, *Face of Battle*, 71.
[17] See the introductions to Dominicus, *Tagebuch*, vii–viii; GG v–vi; Liebe, 1–2; For similar opinion by a son of a Frederician artillery NCO, see: Klöden, *Jugenderinnerungen*, 20–1.

analysts working in the immediate aftermath of the Second World War concentrated on the human side of the equation. Considering the carnage wrought by modern warfare, before one could even discuss why some units did better than others, one had to understand how soldiers were able to function in such an environment to begin with. Published within almost a year of each other, three works aiming to answer this question merit special mention, as their conclusions proved enduring, dominating the study of combat motivation ever since.

Hailed as a classic as soon as it was published, S.L.A. Marshall's *Men against Fire* presented combat motivation as inherently apolitical. Whichever ideological beliefs were held by the soldiers, these became irrelevant as soon as combat began. Rather than battling for abstract concepts such as nationalism or *esprit de corps*, men fought for their comrades. The reason for this is not only the moral support they received from their presence, but also a matter of reputation. Being considered a coward by one's immediate military circle is unbearable, and soldiers would put their life in jeopardy rather than have their courage questioned.[18] Marshall's views were further reinforced by sociologists Edward Shils and Morris Janowitz, who attempted to understand how, despite enormous hardship and growing losses, the Wehrmacht did not disintegrate and its men continued to fight against dire odds, even after it was clear that the war had been lost. Rather than ideological indoctrination, their study points to the resilience of a close-knit informal institution. The concept of the primary group, that is, a small group whose members know each other personally and whose cooperation plays a favourable and enticing role, was not new,[19] but Shils and Janowitz were the first to give it a military twist. Forged together by shared exertion and risk, and usually headed by a respected officer or NCO, a small, usually squad- or platoon-sized group commanded the loyalties of men. As long as this group and the relations between its members were maintained, the external pressures of the conflict mattered little.[20]

While the war was still ongoing, US Army researchers conducted a massive statistical survey of attitudes held by American troops. Based on interviews and questionnaires filled out by many thousands of soldiers, it was, as its editors rightly maintained, 'a body of data unique in the annals of warfare'. The analysis of combat motivation underscored the essential role of what it called the 'informal group', which fulfilled two important functions: 'it *set and enforced group standards* of behaviour, and it

---

[18] Marshall, *Men against Fire*, 44–63, 148–62.
[19] It was formulated by the American Sociologist Charles Hurton Cooley, who used it to explain education; see: 'Social Organization', 23–57.
[20] Shils and Janowitz, 'Cohesion and Disintegration', 269–72.

supported and sustained the individual in stresses he would otherwise not have been able to withstand'.[21] The norm expected from individual members was manly behaviour associated with courage, toughness and aggressiveness. A major bonding element within those groups was based on mutual trust. Each member was expected to 'do his share', that is, not to skulk during fighting, and, in exchange, be sure that he would nor be abandoned if wounded. This informal social contract did not provide an initial incentive to fight, but once battle started, it proved crucial in easing the stress of men.[22] This, together with the similarity of small-group dynamics described by Marshall, Shils and Janowitz, prompted much of the later literature to consider Stouffer as a mere corroboration of the two previous studies.[23]

What is usually forgotten, though, is that this study's actual conclusions are far more ambiguous, and that its authors continually advocate caution in interpreting their findings. For instance, they stress that the minor importance attributed by interviewees to formal discipline could equally point to the success of this and other coercive mechanisms to impress their values into the minds of the men. These values could be internalised so deeply that the requirements of the military organisation were considered legitimate not in spite but *because* of their institutional origin. Stouffer further shows that overt frowning upon idealistic impulses, commonly associated with the declining importance of patriotism, was often a direct reaction to the bravado of civilians and rear-echelon troops. While not overtly patriotic, American soldiers were deeply convinced of the justice of their cause. The study also points to the importance of religion, as well as fatalism and hedonism, as consoling factors for combat stress. The factor cited by the majority of the surveyed soldiers as the main reason which helped to reinforce their resolve in combat was what the questionnaires termed as 'a job to be done'. Essentially, this was the grim understanding that the surest way to return home alive was to win the war. Moreover, men had far more immediate concerns to attend to: food and sleep were often functions of battlefield success.[24]

Despite this relatively broad range of variables, the primary group became the dominant factor in the study of combat motivation. Military

---

[21] Stouffer et al., *American Soldier: Combat*, 130–1. Emphasis in the original.

[22] Stouffer et al., *American Soldier: Adjustment during Army Life*, 430–85; Stouffer et al., *American Soldier: Combat*, 111

[23] One recent example is a social history of the American Civil War, which cites one of Stouffer's surveys and then conclusively asserts that 'during World War II group loyalty was almost three times as important as ideology and fourteen times as important as leadership'. Compare this statement in Costa and Kahn, *Heroes & Cowards*, 118–9, with Stouffer's original charts in *American Soldier: Combat*, 107–12.

[24] Stouffer et al., *American Soldier: Combat*, 117–8, 150–1, 172–90.

sociologists pondered on the precise nature of this phenomenon. What was the actual size of the outfit the men would associate with? Was the relationship between its members based primarily on altruistic or self-serving motives? Was the character of the group determined by social or tactical considerations?[25] These questions were pursued not only for academic interest, but mainly because the belief that primary groups are the *sine qua non* for high combat effectiveness thus became important factor in military policy.[26] As the promotion of primary group cohesion became an aim in its own right, researchers tried to identify what factors were likely to enhance it. Studies from the 1950s and early 1960s cite the common background of group members, a trusted high command, good training, well-stocked magazines, functioning weapons, overall association with the aims of the war and even a strong identification with one's father as factors likely to promote primary group cohesion. However, as the concept of primary groups seemed to be engrossing all other variables of combat motivation, ambiguous evidence was also coming to light. It was unsurprising that studies found that cohesion was higher among troops who perceived their service conditions to be fair and considered their officers honest and considerate. At the same time, it was clear that harsh service conditions and an authoritarian style of leadership were just as likely to employ a strong bonding effect and foster groups which, 'though composed of dissidents, nonetheless promoted compliance by members with the organization's goal and demands'.[27]

More crucially, it became clear that, under certain conditions, strong group solidarity would actually *undermine* combat effectiveness. For instance, the policy introduced by the US Army in Korea that limited the duration of combat postings prompted groups to place great emphasis on the survival of their individual members. As returning home ceased to be a function of the war's progress, group loyalty now put an even greater stress on avoiding unnecessary risk. Social isolation threatened not only the coward who did not do his share but also the upbeat soldier apt to get everyone into trouble. Moreover, strong bonds between officers and men might induce the former to place the survival of their subordinates above the formal requirements of the military organisation. Officers could also be tempered from below. For instance, in Vietnam the combination of the vicious nature of the conflict, together with a single-year rotation policy,

---

[25] See the overview of scholarship in George, 'Primary Groups', 297–305; see also: Little, 'Buddy Relations'.

[26] For instance, a major question raised during the desegregation of the American army was the influence this move might have on the existing fabric of primary groups, see for example: Mandelbaum, *Soldier Groups and Negro Soldiers*, 89–126.

[27] George, 'Primary Groups', 308.

meant that soldiers would not hesitate to take matters into their own hands and get rid of over-enthusiastic superiors who were considered to disregard the lives of their subordinates.[28] Another important element put into question by the Vietnam War was the apparent insignificance of ideological factors. Writings by Charles Moskos emphasised the role of what he called 'latent ideology' in primary group cohesion which 'maintain[s] the soldier in his combat role only when he has an underlying commitment to the worth of the larger social system for which he is fighting'.[29] According to Moskos, while they could be very critical of the particular aims of the conflict, individual soldiers were convinced that their country was worth their effort. Thus, once faced by the need to fight, American troops retained their cohesion and combat effectiveness, while their socio-political commitment played a double role. Popular support for the war was unlikely to form a major incentive for combat. Lack of such support, however, convinced the combat troops that their sacrifice was unappreciated, making them even less willing to risk their lives. On the other hand, as long as the demands of military system were considered basically legitimate and direct superiors were not exposing the men to needless risk or unreasonable demands, basic compliance was ensured.[30]

Yet, despite those findings which demonstrated the ambiguous nature of primary group ties, belief in the crucial importance of interpersonal bonds as a prerequisite for military effectiveness has retained its prominence. Rather than being the single most important factor, studies from the 1980s and 1990s considered primary groups to be closely intertwined with variables such as ideology, leadership, discipline and *esprit de corps*.[31] Progressively, the whole issue of combat motivation came to be considered as part of a more fluid concept of group cohesion or a 'state where a group of relatively similar individuals holds together to accomplish its purpose, especially when the group is under stress'.[32] Although group cohesion has become the subject of a growing number of empirical studies and increasingly complex theoretical models, substantial similarities remain between it and primary groups, as theoretical as well as practical concepts. For instance, although the size of the group is less rigidly

[28] Little, 'Buddy Relations', 202–4; Moskos, *American Enlisted Man*, 141–4; see also: Lepre, *Fragging*.

[29] Moskos, *American Enlisted Man*, 147.

[30] Westbrook, 'Potential for Military Disintegration', 268–73; see also: Gabriel and Savage, *Crisis in Command*.

[31] Richardson, *Fighting Spirit*; Kellett, *Combat Motivation*; Dinter, *Hero or Coward*; Holmes, *Firing Line*; Manning, 'Morale'; For a study which underscores the role of ideology in motivation before combat, see: Chodoff, 'Ideology and Primary Groups'.

[32] Siebold, 'Military Group Cohesion', 187–8.

defined, research on cohesion deals almost exclusively with groups whose members know each other personally. As was the case previously with primary groups, the US Army official policy openly fosters cohesion, and studies conducted by its research psychologists often look at ways in which it could be enhanced.[33] The need to preserve cohesion is also invoked by those supporting the ban on homosexual soldiers serving openly in the military. It is on this last point that the prominence of cohesion has met a sustained challenge.

Since the early 1990s, a growing body of work by behavioural and social scientists rejects the relationship between group performance and social ties prevailing within that group. An influential paper by Robert MacCoun suggests the existence of two basic types of cohesion: social cohesion, that is the personal bonds and camaraderie between individual group members, and task cohesion, which he defines as 'the shared commitment among members to achieving a goal that requires the collective efforts of the group.' Social cohesion, according to MacCoun, rarely corresponds to actual performance. Task cohesion, on the other hand, shows consistent, if modest, correlation between the achievements of the group and the desired goals of the organisation in which the group operates. Thus, rather than being a function of social cohesion, group performance creates and reinforces bonds between individual group members.[34] Despite its growing prominence in some academic and political circles, MacCoun's theory did not find many followers within the military establishment. Possibly this has to do with the estrangement, prevailing since the Vietnam War, between American universities and the US Army.[35] A more obvious explanation lies in the practical implications of whichever view of cohesion wins the hearts and minds of civilian policymakers. At the moment, both supporters and opponents of social cohesion are entrenched in their positions and consider themselves to be defenders of established knowledge, each in their own professional sphere. For instance, a study commissioned in the wake of the Iraqi War by the Strategic Studies Institute of the US War College, aptly titled *Why They Fight?*, concludes that American troops fight primarily for each other. Although their main concern still rested firmly with their comrades, American troops, according to the study, were also prompted by ideological factors, such as the promotion of liberty and

[33] Manning, 'Morale', 457; Siebold, 'Military Group Cohesion', 185–6.
[34] MacCoun, 'What Is Known About Unit Cohesion and Military Performance', 291; Kier, 'Homosexuals in the U.S. Military'; Miller and Williams, 'Do Military Policies on Gender and Sexuality Undermine Combat Effectiveness?'; Herek and Belkin, 'Sexual Orientation and Military Service'.
[35] On that point, see the postscript in: Moskos, *American Enlisted Man*, 183–5.

democracy.[36] These findings came under withering attack by MacCoun and colleagues, who questioned the methodological apparatus of its authors and, particularly, their reliance on interviews and their failure to measure performance empirically. Wong and Kolditz reiterated that their aim was not to quantify performance but to understand what motivates men in combat. Moreover, they argued that interviews with genuine soldiers going in and out of combat provide more reliable evidence than studies conducted in a sterile and pristine academic environment.[37]

The discussion promoted by Wong's study demonstrates not only the conflicting views on combat motivation prevailing in contemporary research, but also the tendency of both sides of the debate to work by different methods and to address, essentially, different audiences within their respective establishments. But Wong's study is cited here for another reason. Its emphasis on camaraderie spiced with ideology, harking back to a combination of Marshall and Moskos, is also the view which currently prevails in the historical study of combat motivation. Geoffrey Elton argues that historians often tend to embrace views and methods from the social sciences just at the moment when social scientists discard these approaches in disgust.[38] Although this might also be the case here, the question of why men fight cannot be separated from the discourse prevailing outside specialised writings by social scientists and military psychologists. The view that soldiers fight for each other prevails not only in the popular imagination, being the subject of numerous films and books, but is also commonly invoked in contemporary military training.[39] Moreover, the appeal of this simplified understanding of primary groups is only increased when one considers the recent models formulated by both proponents and adversaries of the concept of task cohesion. These have become so complex[40] that it is hard to imagine how they could be applied meaningfully in a historical analysis. Thus, whatever the reason might be, the established view of combat motivation held by historians is the dominance of primary group cohesion. Its characteristics were discovered in almost every modern conflict, including the First

[36] Wong et al., *Why They Fight?*, 22–5.
[37] For the complete exchange, see the aptly entitled rubric 'disputatio sine fine', in: *AFS*, 32 (2005–6), 646–63.
[38] Elton, *Practice of History*, 25–6.
[39] Well-known films which underscore that soldiers fight for each other include Steven Spielberg (dir.) *Saving Private Ryan* (1998); Shekhar Kapur (dir.) *The Four Feathers*, (2002); and, of course, Phil Alden Robinson et al. (dirs.) *Band of Brothers*, (2001).
[40] See for instance one such model of morale in: Britt and Dickinson, 'Morale during Military Operations: A Positive Psychology Approach', 159–64.

World War, the American Civil War, the Napoleonic Wars and, of course, the French Revolutionary War.[41]

Yet, although it is still as powerful in military history as it was in military sociology from the 1950s and 1960s, the primary group paradigm did not remain unchallenged. In 1985, a groundbreaking study by Omer Bartov pointed to the potential importance of ideology, at least under extreme conditions. In his examination of three typical Wehrmacht divisions employed on the Eastern front, Bartov found that their casualty figures exceeded three or four times the nominal strength of these formations. Such a rapid turnover of men was detrimental to the formation of primary groups. According to Bartov, the units were kept together by a combination of brutal discipline and active ideological indoctrination. Although the latter was also prompted from above by Nazi propaganda, it was increasingly encouraged from below by the combat officers, who saw it as a useful tool for keeping their men together.[42] An alternative explanation of combat motivation in units suffering staggeringly high casualties was offered in Robert Rush's micro-study of the 22nd US Infantry Regiment during the battle of Hürtgen Forest. In a period of less than twenty days, this regiment lost 87 per cent of its initial strength, or some 54 per cent, if one includes the reinforcements continuously fed into the fray. As demonstrated by Rush, all existing primary groups could not have *physically* survived the initial few days of the battle. Moreover, the individual replacements were sent into combat immediately after arrival. Unable to form new social ties with surviving veterans, they fought on the side of men whom they never knew before. In such conditions, soldiers operated under what Rush terms situational motivation, which could be essentially summarised in a single word – survival. With no other alternative, cohesion was continuously formed and reformed around a dwindling cadre of surviving officers, NCOs and old soldiers, who were promoted once the former were killed.[43] Interestingly, these conclusions come close to those of the proponents of task cohesion, although

---

[41] Van Creveld, *Fighting Power*, 163–5; Hitoshi, 'Japanese Combat Morale', 347–8, 351; Watson, *Enduring the Great War*, 66–9; McPherson, *For Cause and Comrades*, 77–9; Muir, *Tactics and the Experience of Battle*; Coss, *All for a King's Shilling*, 191–210; Hughes, *Forging Napoleon's Grand Armée*, 209–13; Thoral, *From Valmy to Waterloo*, 102–7.

[42] Bartov, *The Eastern Front*. For similar arguments underscoring the role of ideology in the Wehrmacht based on soldiers' writings, see: Fritz, '"We are trying"'. Unsurprisingly, Russian historians of the Second World War also cite ideological factors, in particular hate of the enemy, as a major element in motivation of the Soviet troops. E.S. Seniavskaija even argues that this was the most dominant factor in the mentality of Russian and Soviet troops throughout the whole twentieth century, including the Afghan War; see her *Protivniki Rossij*; For another work which underscores the patriotism of the Soviet troops, see: Reese, *Why Stalin's Soldiers Fought*.

[43] Rush, *Hell in Hürtgen Forest*, 280–6, 332–5.

their citations give no indication that either side is aware of the other's work. Nevertheless, it is still reassuring that, although historians and social scientists studying combat motivation often tread different paths, some of their findings are actually much closer than one might initially expect.

However, even if the historical study of combat motivation does not use the latest material from the social sciences, the body of scholarly literature on motivation from the French Revolution onwards is substantial. In comparison, motivation in the armies of the old regime has received only scant attention. It is not that their soldiers have been wholly ignored, however. From the 1960s onwards, there have emerged a growing number of works on the social history of eighteenth-century armies, largely based on muster rolls, whose study was pioneered by André Corvisier. Corvisier's own monumental work, covering the history of the French army from the heyday of Louis XIV to the aftermath of the Seven Years War, shows that, rather than being the scum of the earth, a typical soldier usually came from a respectable, albeit poor background. Small as it was, the soldier's wage could be a serious incentive to enlist because it was paid regularly, making the soldiers somewhat better off than the urban poor or the peasant labourers from whom they were usually drawn. Those conclusions were then largely repeated by John Childs, Sylvia Frey, Glenn Steppler and Rodney Atwood, just to mention a few.[44]

As the social character of old-regime soldiers was steadily rehabilitated, scholars became more willing to consider positive aspects in their motivation after enlistment. Corvisier reflects that the status of the armies as distinct sub-groups in old-regime societies should have enhanced cohesion among their members. He is followed by Samuel Scott, who argues that the shared experience of harsh service conditions created bonds between individual soldiers. A similar factor was invoked in Frey's study of the British army in the American War of Independence, which also cites more affirmative incentives for cohesion such as regimental *esprit* and leadership. The role of officers is also mentioned in Christopher Clark's history of Prussia. The works of Christopher Duffy, the greatest living authority on old-regime warfare, combine many of those elements. He demonstrates that eighteenth-century armies had genuine volunteers and not just pressed men, and that the training of the recruits was often done

---

[44] Corvisier, *L'Armée française*, vol. I, 297–330, 471–506; Childs, *Armies and Warfare*, 64; Frey, *British Soldier in America*, 9–16, 21; Steppler, *Common Soldier*; Atwood, *Hessians*, 45, 211; Loriga, *Soldati*, 115–22; see also: S.F. Scott, *Response*, 16–9; Keep, *Soldiers of the Tsar*, 116–7, 143; P.H. Wilson, *German Armies*, 332–5.

with patience and gentleness, which compares favourably with the psy-chological bullying practised in modern boot camps. Duffy also argues that common soldiers had a sense of corporate identity and pride in their units. Finally, he points to the cohesive effect of regional recruitment and religion, as well as the role of cultural and political feuds in fuelling hostilities between particular armies.[45]

Yet despite these positive observations, the overall evaluation of the motivation of eighteenth-century common soldiers remains negative. Even among the above-mentioned studies, many underscore that religion, patriotism and even honour were not major motivational incentives.[46] The role of regimental attachment is often mentioned but rarely developed, failing to explain how such attitudes emerged and developed in a period when most regiments were dispersed in small packets over the countryside.[47] Lastly, and perhaps most importantly, the role of coercion in the running of old-regime armies is constantly underscored, far outweighing any positive feelings the men might have felt towards their service.

The Gordian knot presumably connecting harsh discipline and low positive motivation proved particularly influential in the analysis of primary sources. Possibly influenced by the *Sonderweg* interpretation of their country's history, German scholars tended to stress the grim-mest aspects of old-regime military service. Unlike the upbeat days when they were originally published, writings of native Prussian troops were now largely dismissed. Where their authors speak of their loyalty to King Frederick and to Prussia, their religious faith and their willing association with the aims of the war, modern German historians often saw signs of acquired fatalism inoculated by a barbaric system of military punishment. Even Klaus Latzel, who otherwise provides a highly empathetic analysis of a letter by a Prussian veteran of the Battle of Lobositz (1756), would not consent that this soldier could be motivated as positively as were the men who fought in the subsequent

---

[45] Corvisier, *Armies and Societies*, 171–94; S.F. Scott, *Response*, 34–5; Clark, *Iron Kingdom*, 206–9; C. Duffy, *Military Experience*, 7–10, 91–2, 129–136; C. Duffy, *Russia's Military Way*, 135; C. Duffy, *Instrument of War*, 86; Another work which brings much of the same arguments, but less elaborately, is Showalter, *Wars of Frederick the Great*, 11–2, 22–7, 101–4.

[46] On the last point, Armstrong Starkey remarks: 'There is little evidence that the rank and file embraced the culture of honor' and then proceeds to quote Roger Lamb and Joseph Sonnenfels, who actually state quite the opposite, see: *War*, 92–3. Scholars who consider the role of religion and patriotism in old-regime armies to be secondary or less include: Frey, *British Soldier in America*, 116; Brumwell, *Redcoats*, 117–8; Atwood, *Hessians*, 192; Keep, *Soldiers of the Tsar*, 204–8.

[47] Houlding, *Fit for Service*, 152.

wars against Napoleon.[48] This unwillingness to recognise the role of positive motivation among the old-regime rank and file also prevails in English-language scholarship, particularly among non-military historians and generalists.[49]

An exception is Sascha Möbius' recent excellent study on the Prussian army of the Seven Years War, which is also the first monograph devoted specifically to old-regime combat motivation.[50] Möbius begins his investigation by establishing that the practical aim of Prussian tactics was not to kill as many enemy soldiers as possible, but to break them psychologically, making victory a function of mental endurance. Möbius proceeds to analyse at length the feelings of the Prussian soldiers and their combat behaviour. While old-regime soldiers are usually studied through the eyes of their superiors, he underscores the value of surviving writings by the men themselves, particularly their letters. Möbius also emphasises the interaction between the soldiers and their officers, showing that the control exercised by the latter was far from absolute. Rather than simply compelling their men to fight, officers were more likely to encourage them through example. Soldiers were further propelled by a sense of honour and self-worth as professionals – a by-product of their highly demanding training. An additional factor contributing to their ability to endure the ordeal of combat was religious feeling, which promoted a strong sense of fatalism, coexisting with a firm inner belief that the soldier would survive unharmed.

Möbius' study is part of a broader trend among German scholars to reconsider the military history of their country. Although rejecting the prevalence of national attitudes in the eighteenth-century Saxon army,

---

[48] For a negative evaluation of eighteenth-century German troops, their motivation or battlefield capabilities, see: Redlich, *German Military Enterpriser*, vol. II, 185–230; Kunisch, *Der kleine Krieg*, 1–2; Kunisch, '"Puppenwerk" der stehenden Heere'; Bröckling, *Disziplin*; Sikora, *Disziplin und Desertion*, 45, 163–79; Latzel, '"Schlachtbank" oder "Feld der Ehre"?', 77–82.

[49] Examples of the dim view of old-regime soldiers and their experience are too numerous to cite here, but the following list of both historical and popular publications should suffice: Rothenberg, *Art of Warfare*, 13; Strachan, *European Armies*, 9; Bell, *First Total War*, 39, 238; Barnett, *Britain and Her Army*, 141–2; F. Anderson, *Crucible of War*, 286–7; Jennings, *Empire of Fortune*, 208–10, 242; Harari, *Ultimate Experience*, 160–5; In sociological studies of combat motivation, the eighteenth century is described as a period of brutal coercive discipline and a complete anathema to what more positively motivated modern armies would look like; see for instance: Westbrook, 'Potential for Military Disintegration', 249–50; Manning, 'Morale', 455.

[50] Möbius, *Mehr Angst*. Dorothée Malfoy-Noël's attempt to study the psychological aspects of combat during the War of the Spanish Succession published in the same year is brave but her primary sources are exclusively by officers. The attempt to fill the gap with modern French philosophical discourse on the body is unconvincing; see: *L'Épreuve de la Bataille*.

Stefan Kroll points to positive aspects of its service conditions and combat motivation. Preceding both of these is Jörg Muth's valuable but complc tely overlooked study of Frederician Potsdam. Muth's findings confirm many of Duffy's earlier suggestions that Prussian discipline was not as harsh as it is typically portrayed. Neither the military punishments employed in Prussia nor the desertion rates from its army were any worse than elsewhere in Europe. Moreover, members of the lower classes often saw military service as a chance to improve their daily lot. For a serf or minor artisan, becoming a soldier meant being placed under the aegis of royal service, which offered some safeguards vis-à-vis the junker land-owners, master craftsmen, community elders and even one's parents. Most importantly, Muth points to the contractual nature of old-regime military service. For their obedience, the men expected to be treated fairly and paid regularly; when this did not happen, they perceived the bond as having been invalidated. In other words, rather than being an instinctive reaction to brutal service conditions, desertion was the response to those instances when officers failed to meet their obligations.[51]

In addition to their more positive evaluation of the experience of old-regime common soldiers, the work of Möbius, Kroll, Muth, Duffy and Bleckwenn stresses the importance of writings by the soldiers themselves. In their studies, these scholars located not only new archival records but also rediscovered much neglected *published* material. Yet the view that common soldiers did not write remains extremely persistent, at least in the English-speaking world. Otherwise, it is hard to explain why out-standing recent studies still fail to make use of all the available printed sources. One such example is Matthew Spring's examination of the tactics of the British army in the American War of Independence, whose chapter on motivation is one of the first systematic examinations of *esprit de corps* in any old-regime army.[52] Judging by his citations, Spring was unable to take advantage of the work of Muth and Möbius, yet there is much more immediate material which he was, apparently, unaware of. The memoirs of Sergeants Roger Lamb and Thomas Sullivan are cited extensively, as are those of John Robert Shaw, who served as private in the 33rd Regiment. Spring, however, appeared to have missed the reminis-cences of Corporal George Fox, whose critical edition was published well over a decade before Spring commenced to work on his book.[53]

---

[51] Kroll, *Soldaten*; Muth, *Flucht*. Some similar points were made earlier by Hans Bleckwenn; see for instance: 'Bauernfreiheit durch Wehrpflicht'.

[52] Spring, *With Zeal and with Bayonets*, 103–37.

[53] Since the publication of Spring's volume, more first-hand accounts by British veterans of the American War of Independence have come to light thanks to the indefatigable efforts

Moreover, although modern theories on motivation were employed in studies on almost every major military force since the French Revolution, little comparable work was done for old-regime armies. One exception is Spring, who draws on a number of officers' accounts to demonstrate the existence of internalised group standards among the soldiery, indicating a social situation akin to primary group cohesion. Lynn, who serves as Spring's source on that point, is the only other scholar who suggests that factor could be relevant for old-regime armies. Lynn's study of the armies of Louis XIII and XIV identifies the *ordinaire*, or the soldiers' mess of some ten to eighteen members, as a potential equivalent of the primary group. Although Lynn underscores the inferential nature of this deduction, he considers such modern parallels to be generally reliable.[54] And yet, despite his readiness to apply such modern concepts to old-regime armies, Lynn falls victim to another trait which has long impaired the serious study of their motivation. The belief in the inherent superiority of the citizen-soldier over his regular counterpart often overshadows the similarities between revolutionary and old-regime armies. When such factors were noticed, their interpretation was always more favourable to the former. The example of the *ordinaire* is illustrative, here. Lynn acknowledges its possible contribution to the old-regime French armies; however, in his analysis of the combat motivation of the revolutionary forces, the same factor is attributed a crucial role.

The *ordinaire* in the revolutionary army numbered about a dozen soldiers who drew their provisions, cooked, ate and were quartered together, usually sharing the same tent or two. Moreover, whenever possible, its members also fought together, the *ordinaire* doubling as the corporal's squad, the most basic tactical unit of the French army. Lynn argues that the bonding effect of those common activities forged its members into a classic primary group.[55] However, as he himself demonstrates in *Giant of the Grand Siècle*, the *ordinaire* had existed in French armies at least since the first half of the seventeenth century. Moreover, like many other revolutionary regulations, those governing the mess were copied verbatim from the royal ordinance of 1778. Other eighteenth-century armies maintained a similar institution: the mess in Britain, the *Kameradschaft* or *Corporalschaft* in the German-speaking lands and the *Artel* in Russia. As we will see in Chapter 6, the mess is often mentioned in soldiers'

of Don N. Hagist. See his excellent *British Soldiers* and the Internet blog http://redcoat76 .blogspot.com.

[54] Spring, *With Zeal and with Bayonets*, 111; Lynn, *Giant*, 441.

[55] Lynn, *Bayonets*, 163–82; Lynn's argument is often repeated and some even consider the revolutionary *ordinaire* to be a great innovation; For instance, see the introduction to Karsten, *Motivating Soldiers*, ix; S.F. Scott, *From Yorktown to Valmy*, 198–9.

writings, denoting its role not only as a social institution but also as an enforcer of group standards. Therefore, assuming that the *ordinaire* was instrumental in instilling primary group cohesion in armies of Revolutionary France, why should it not play an equally significant role in the armies of old-regime Europe?

Lynn demonstrates that the French troops were then subjected to an intensive campaign of political education. Soldiers were provided with pamphlets and encouraged to participate in political meetings and ceremonies which underscored the just cause of the conflict. Old-regime armies, however, had comparable practices. The daily orders are just one such example. Rather than just notifying the assembled troops of regimental chores and other mundane matters, the orders often informed men of the ongoing events, usually accompanying them with a desirable interpretation. Eighteenth-century armies also had their own sets of ceremonies. Reviews, banner consecrations, church parades and public readings of the articles of war underscored different principles, yet served the same purpose: to reinforce the legitimacy of the system in whose name the men served and fought. Why is it taken for granted that showering soldiers with political newspapers motivated them more than a gill of rum handed out in honour of the king's birthday or a public address from their commander-in-chief? Considering the ideological aspect of the Revolutionary Wars, where is the proof that a feast around a liberty tree would necessarily invoke stronger emotions than attending a loyal demonstration, as was the case with many British regiments in the 1790s?

A point stressed by Lynn is the enthusiasm of the new French soldierly 'men who fought to fulfil their duties and to preserve their right as citizens' as compared to their old-regime predecessors 'who turned to military service because the society or economy offered them little alternative'.[56] Yet the emergence of the nation-in-arms rested squarely on conscription, whose introduction was the most obvious sign that revolutionary fervour had its limits. Moreover, as we will soon see, desertion in Revolutionary France was at least comparable, if not worse, than in most eighteenth-century armies. But even if we accept that a conscript army consists of more willing men than a fully professional force, the disparity between the revolutionary and old-regime armies is not as great as it first appears. The notion that military service is an obligation owed by the subject to his sovereign existed in Europe long before the French Revolution. Various forms of conscription were employed in all major eighteenth-century states, and the practice became more widespread towards the end of the century. Britain and pre-revolutionary France

---

[56] Lynn, *Bayonets*, 43.

used it more sparingly and resorted to it in wartime only, the former by impressment, the latter by drawing on its militia. Other states resorted to regional recruiting. One possibility was to request quotas of men from the provincial estates, as was done in the Habsburg Monarchy until the 1770s. Another option, which Austria eventually adopted, was the cantonal system. Pioneered by Prussia in the 1730s, every regiment was allocated a designated district from which it drew the manpower to meet its needs.[57] Undeniably, none of these methods was impartial, and the burden often fell on the weaker members of the society. Nevertheless, how do we know that those conscripted by a more egalitarian practice would necessarily make keener soldiers than those recruited selectively? Why should it be assumed that French conscripts were better motivated than the numerous Austrian, Prussian and Russian conscripts who faced them?

Lynn stresses that, following the revolutionary reforms, the social composition of the new French army became more representative of French society as a whole. The underlying assumption beyond this argument, though, is that socially heterogeneous armies fight better than socially homogenous ones. Although this particular question is discussed extensively in modern debates about social and task cohesion, this is not the place to answer it. Suffice it to say that even following the mass levy of 1794, the army still did not mirror French society. The proportion of peasants, for instance, was half of their share in the general populace. Likewise, soldiers from southern and western France were again underrepresented, just as they were under the old regime. Russia might well been unique, as the only major European power resorting exclusively to conscription, in drawing an annual levy from its enserfed peasantry. Yet, whatever one thinks of the morality of such a system, it produced an army which was a rather accurate reflection of its society, and definitely far more representative than the French one. While the situation in other old-regime armies varied substantially,[58] they shared another important

---

[57] Jany, *Geschichte der Preußischen Armee*, 679–700; Girard, *Service militaire*, part 2; Hochedlinger, *Austria's Wars*, 109–11; 291–5; P.H. Wilson, 'Social Militarization', 4–5, 10–8, 30–1; Keep, *Soldiers of the Tsar*, 144–61; Loriga, *Soldati*, 131–4. Other states which introduced the cantonal system include Schaumburg-Lippe, Hesse-Kassel and, for a short period, Württemberg, see: P.H. Wilson, *War, State and Society in Württemberg*, 80, 177–8, Ingrao, *Hessian Mercenary State*, 132–5.

[58] In old-regime France, for instance, the urban recruits and artisans were overrepresented, while the peasants, who made some 80 per cent of the population, provided only 15 per cent of the soldiers in 1789. The discrepancy could also be regional, as was the case with Ireland and Scotland which sometime provided between them close to half of the British rank and file. Similarly Bohemia and Moravia, which contained less than 15 per cent of the population of the Habsburg dominions, provided close 40 per cent of its rank

characteristic with revolutionary France. Whatever method was used to raise them, most soldiers in eighteenth-century Europe came from a single political and often a single national body.

Although almost every state actively sought foreign recruits to save its own subjects for more economically productive endeavours, there were never enough of them, especially in wartime. According to the samples studied by Duffy, only about one-fifth of the Austrian Army in the Seven Years War was recruited from outside the Habsburg dominions. As the conflict progressed, Prussia also had to draw more on its native-born cantonists. But even afterwards, when foreigners allegedly made up over half of the Prussian peacetime establishment, their actual numbers were much smaller. Any recruit drawn outside the regimental canton was designated as a 'foreigner' and, as estimated by Peter Wilson, many such men were actually Prussians who enlisted voluntarily. Most of the remaining foreigners came from the Holy Roman Empire, particularly neighbouring Mecklenburg and Saxony. Likewise, most foreign recruits into the Austrian army came from the Reich, Prussian Silesia and other German lands. The foreigners in Saxon service, whose numbers rarely rose above 10 per cent of the army, usually came from Prussia and nearby Thuringian principalities. Truly international recruiting was mostly the product of long-standing political and religious ties between states and particular communities. The Swiss in France, Spain and Piedmont; the Wild Geese in the Catholic monarchies; and the Scottish Brigade in the Netherlands cannot really be classified as mercenaries, but rather as allies or auxiliaries. But whatever definition is used, those contingents always remained a fraction of the troops raised locally. In the Seven Years War, France maintained over forty foreign regiments; however, they still comprised less than a fifth of its army.[59] In that sense, the majority of the soldiers who fought against revolutionary France were fighting in the service of their country, as the French did for theirs.

Lynn clearly demonstrates that the revolution increased the prestige accorded to the common soldier. From lowly members of the social periphery, they now became respected defenders of the fatherland. However, the stated worth of the individual French ranker should not

and file during the Seven Years War, see: S.F. Scott, *Response*, 9–11; Lynn, *Bayonets* 44–8; C. Duffy, *Instrument of War*, 52–8, 202.

[59] Hochedlinger, *Austria's Wars*, 292–3; C. Duffy, *Military Experience*, 32–4; C. Duffy, *Instrument of War*, 89–90, 202; Kroll, *Soldaten*, 156–62, P.H. Wilson, 'Politics of Military Recruitment', 539; Although British regiments were happy to recruit foreigners, particularly for service overseas, the majority of the army still came from the three kingdoms, see: Conway, 'Mobilization of Manpower', 380–1. For Irish Catholics serving on the continent, see: Murtagh, 'Irish Soldiers Abroad, 1600–1800'. For Germans serving in the British army, see: Wishon, *German Forces and the British Army*, ch. 5.

be taken at face value. One can debate whether the higher social status bestowed upon them by the republican authorities made the revolutionary soldiery more enthusiastic than their old-regime counterparts. What is certain, though, is that universal conscription guaranteed there were plenty of citizen-soldiers to be invested into the bloody business of war. Whether they were native-born recruits or foreigners, old-regime soldiers were valuable commodities: their enlistment was expensive, their training long and their replacement hard. For this reason, their commanders were often reluctant to commit their armies into battle. There were few such qualms on the French side, however. Fear of high losses ceased to be a deterrent for action, for as long as victory was delivered, its price would matter little.[60] Moreover, while old-regime troops were happy to plunder whenever an opportunity arose, many of their supplies were provided by a sophisticated system of convoys and depots. The French army largely discarded these, relying instead on a system of forced requisitions. This provided a powerful incentive to pursue the enemy into their own territory to make the war pay for itself. Old-regime soldiers might have been despised by their superiors, a point whose veracity we will address later; however, they were seldom treated as disposable assets. A cynic might even argue that becoming an object of haughty patriotic rhetoric is still a very sad recompense for men sent on almost indefinite service, to fight in what became continuous wars of aggressive political expansionism.

As we have seen, military motivation has been studied extensively by social scientists, military thinkers and analysts. Their conclusions, with a particular emphasis on primary group cohesion, were employed by historians studying armies from the French revolution onwards. The study of motivation in the armies of old-regime Europe is nowhere as methodical, which is an odd fact considering the demanding nature of linear tactics. Moreover, although they shared a number of important characteristics, their troops are seldom credited with the idealism commonly associated with revolutionary armies. Possibly, this subject was so little-studied because of the prevailing belief regarding the paucity of direct written testimonies by eighteenth-century common soldiers.[61] When personal narratives are cited, they are often approached, if not with downright distrust, then with a good degree of caution. The reliability of memoirs is often questioned on the grounds that they were written with the benefit of hindsight and that their authors had a reputation to defend or a patron to please. Published material is usually considered even more suspect, being likely to represent, so we are told, the attitudes of their

---

[60] Rothenberg, *Art of Warfare*, 61; Lynn, *Battle*, 189; Bell, *First Total War*, 150.
[61] For instance: Bell, *First Total War*, 121, 312.

authors at the time of writing or, even worse, a mere reflection of the prevailing public attitudes which the author was hoping to harness to sell his book. Considered far superior to memoirs are letters and private diaries. Being documents of a highly personal nature, their descriptions are generally taken to be a more genuine representation of their authors' thoughts and feelings at the time of writing.[62] Alas, from the little that was written, even less survives, making it extremely challenging to draw any informed conclusions about the mentality prevailing among the eighteenth-century soldiery. Undeniably, these are important arguments, particularly for the current study, which attempts to trace the inner world of old-regime common soldiers based on their extant writings. In order to justify such an endeavour, the quantity, availability and representativeness of those sources needs to be discussed.

Considering the social origins of most eighteenth-century soldiers, one might think that literate soldiers were uncommon. However, literacy among the lower classes in old-regime Europe was becoming less exceptional. It is estimated that up to 40 per cent of the labouring poor in Britain were literate. Between 1690 and 1790, the portion of French bridegrooms signing their parish records doubled to about half of the total male population. Interestingly, the corresponding figures in northern and eastern frontier regions, which provided most French recruits, were much higher, with some areas coming close to universal literacy. Literacy rates in the Holy Roman Empire fluctuated widely, yet it is telling that over 40 per cent of the day labourers in mid-century Coblenz were able to sign their names. In rural East Prussia, one of the poorest regions in Germany, comparable figures were reached only in 1800, although this was still a fourfold increase compared to only half-a-century before.[63] This has parallels with what is known about literacy in old-regime armies. Stephen Brumwell estimates that, during the Seven Years War, about a third of the British rank and file possessed rudimentary literacy. According to Jean-Pierre Bois, figures in late old-regime France were much higher. His samples of former royal veterans who volunteered in year II show that over 60 per cent of the men were fully

---

[62] C. Duffy argues that memoirists often saw their military service as part of the broader intellectual or religious journey resulting in the subjugation of their account to a higher meta-narrative, see: *Military Experience*, 134; On the opinion that letters are superior to memoirs and even diaries, see: Keegan, *Face of Battle*, 33; Forrest, *Napoleon's Men*, 23–4.

[63] Stone, 'Literacy and Education in England, 1640–1900', 109–12, 128–9; Schofield, 'Dimensions of Illiteracy in England, 1750–1850', 308–9; Furet and Ozouf, *Reading and Writing*, 25–7, 34–9, 48–9, 67–8; Woloch, *New Regime*, 174–5; Engelsing, *Analphabetentum und Lektüre*, 64; Gawthrop and Strauss, 'Protestantism and Literacy'; P.H. Wilson, *Reich to Revolution*, 62. For general overviews of literacy in early-modern Europe, see: Tóth, *Literacy and Written Culture*, 203–8; Houston, *Literacy*.

literate, while another 18 per cent possessed basic knowledge. Moreover, the use of recruiting posters with substantial textual content both by the British and the French armies further suggests that literate recruits were not necessarily exceptional.[64]

Moreover, whatever human material entered it, the army was one of the more conducive environments for learning in old-regime Europe. Promotion to NCO required basic knowledge of reading and writing, while growing bureaucratisation created a demand for literate soldiers who could help the officers with rolls and accounts. Although often justified on charitable grounds, provisions were often made for teaching soldiers' children in the hope that they would grow up into willing and educated NCOs. While garrison schools in Britain were usually random initiatives depending on the goodwill of individual officers, in some continental states, like Prussia and Austria, they became official state institutions. Even in Russia, the army was an agent for some sort of education. Samples of veterans cited by John Keep show that about 15 per cent were literate. Quite low by Western European standards, this was still a substantial fraction in an army conscripted from what remained, essentially, an illiterate society well into the nineteenth century.[65] Another major promoter of literacy was boredom. After mastering their drill, soldiers typically spent half of their time off duty. Many drank, some worked, but others studied. After enlisting, Sullivan found so much time to read and write that he decided to commence a journal. William Cobbett spent his free time in the recruiting depot reading books from a circulating library and practising writing. This caught the eye of his colonel, who encouraged Cobbett to study grammar. Moreover, armies often had enough educated men and foreigners who were happy to offer private tuition. Joining the Austrian army as a dissolute youth, Joseph von Sonnenfels picked up not only discipline and a sense of purpose, but also Italian and French from foreign comrades and Czech during manoeuvres in Bohemia.[66] Unlike Sonnenfels, who rose to become one of the figureheads of Austrian enlightenment, Friedrich Wilhelm Beeger had more humble prospects ahead of him, but his experience in the Prussian army

---

[64] Brumwell, *Redcoats*, 83; Bois, *Anciens soldats*, 278–82; Hagist, *British Soldiers*, 99. On recruiting posters, see Chapter 4, 133–9.

[65] Frey, *British Soldier in America*, 69–70; Hochedlinger. *Austria's Wars*, 314–5; Keep, *Soldiers of the Tsar*, 201–4; Brooks, *When Russia Learned to Read*, 3–4.

[66] Sullivan, *From Redcoat to Rebel*, 3–4; Cobbett, *Autobiography*, 25–6; Sonnenfels, *Über die Liebe des Vaterlandes*. For another soldier who used the diverse nature of the Habsburg army to acquire languages in tandem, see: Bersling, *Der böhmische Veteran*, 11; see also: Institut für Stadtgeschichte, Frankfurt am Main, S1/367 Johannes Reuber, 'Tagebuch', (4 August 1776); Stevenson, *Soldier*, 148; Haime 'Life', 213; Wright, 'Life', 318–9; Watson, 'Some Account', 107; Aytoun, *Redcoats*, 19.

sounds very similar. Essentially illiterate when he enlisted, Beeger learned to read from borrowed library books, even if it meant spending his last penny on them. After starting to earn during his off-duty hours, Beeger could afford to further his education, taking private lessons in writing, arithmetic and map-reading from a former student who served in his company.[67]

It can be argued that these individual examples provide only anecdotal evidence of a few exceptional cases. To quote Duffy's reference to Sonnenfels' future career: 'not many private soldiers could become Professor of Public Administration and Economics'. Yet they merge well with more general evidence for literacy rates among eighteenth-century soldiers. In 1704–5, the English army in Flanders was provided with 15,000 copies of the devotional *Soldier's Monitor*, whose distribution continued in later wars as well. In Protestant German states, soldiers were similarly provided with hymn-books. Some soldiers were actively corresponding with their families. Otherwise, it would be hard to explain the introduction of a subsidised postal service in the Prussian and the British armies.[68] Yet, sizable literacy rates do not guarantee the ready availability of written testimonies. The prevailing opinion is that, even if common soldiers did produce letters, diaries or journals, these must be long lost by now. Yet there is another major factor most scholars seem to remain unaware of. The scarcity of known testimonies by old-regime common soldiers stems not only from low survival rates, but also from established archival policies and prevailing scholarly interests, as the following example demonstrates.

Published at the approach of the second centenary of the American Revolution, an annotated bibliography of memoirs by members of Rochambeau's French expeditionary corps identifies over fifty sources by officers but not a single one by common soldiers. Today, three such

---

[67] Beeger, *Seltsame Schicksale*, 26, 30–1; For examples of literate soldiers offering tuition see: Bernos, 'Souvenirs de campagne', 677; Laukhard, *Leben und Schicksale*, 154; Todd, *Journal*, 10–2, Asteroth, 'Diary', (26–7 March, 1781), 443; Macdonald, *Autobiographical Journal*, 62–3; Sohr, *Meine Geschichte*, 115–6; New York Historical Society, RV Bremner, John, 'Diary and Memorandum Book', fol. 8; For officers sponsoring the study of their men, see: Greenleigh, *Veteran Soldier*, 35; Gee, 'Memoirs of an Eighteenth-Century Soldier's Child', 223; Hagist, *British Soldiers*, 103–5; Artillerymen were often taught mathematics and other professional skills relevant to their corps; see: Klöden, *Jugenderinnerungen*, 16.

[68] C. Duffy, *Instrument of War*, 225; Scouller, *Armies of Queen Anne*, 289; Steuernagel, 'Brief Description', 152; In German states this included also printed sermons; see for instance: Sohr, *Meine Geschichte*, 50–65; For more examples of religious literature handed to soldiers, see: Todd, *Journal*, 38; Snape, *Redcoat and Religion*, 25–6; One postal packet from a single regiment in Halifax in 1757 contained over fifty letters by common soldiers; see: Brumwell, *Redcoats*, 82.

sources are known. In the mid-1970s, Rudolf Karl Tröss rediscovered in the Municipal Library of Strasbourg the journal of Georg Daniel Flohr, private soldier of the Deux Ponts German Regiment. In the early 1990s, this four-hundred-page-long manuscript, with colour illustrations and maps drawn by the author himself, was brought to the attention of the English-speaking public by Robert Selig. Despite the ongoing efforts of Selig and the curators of the New Médiathèque André Malraux to which Flohr's diary was moved in 2009, a critical edition of this exceptional source is yet to appear.[69] Another journal by a common soldier from the French contingent is attributed to a grenadier from the Bourbonnais Regiment. Although acquired by the Library of Congress in 1907, scholars became aware of its existence only eighty years later. The cataloguing of this record under 'MCC 1907 Milton S. Latham Journal', provides a clue why it went unnoticed for so long. Despite its detailed description of sea battles by the French expeditionary corps on its way to America, this journal also awaits publication. Finally, in 2001–4 the reminiscences of a third ranker who participated in the expedition, André Amblard of the Soissonais Regiment, whose original manuscript is preserved in the departmental archives of Ardèche, was published in the *Review of the Society of Children and Friends of Villeneuve-de-Berg*.[70]

It is not impossible that Rochambeau's detachment, which numbered fewer than 6,000 men, contained all the literary-inclined common soldiers in an army of 150,000. It is far more feasible, however, that their writings were noticed because of the disproportionate attention devoted to this particular episode of the American War of Independence, which often overshadows what was, at least for France, a truly global conflict.[71] Moreover, this case demonstrates the challenges of locating such writings. Compared to the larger-state repositories where most scholars congregate, parish, regional and regimental archives are even more under-funded and understaffed. If available, electronic cataloguing of their holdings usually covers only new acquisitions. This explains the continuous dribble of original manuscripts whose existence

---

[69] Rice and Brown, *American Campaigns of Rochambeau's Army*, vol. I, 285; Robert A. Selig, 'German Soldier in America'; Personal communications by email with Dr. Selig 5 November 2010; Personal visit to the Médiathèque, Strasbourg, 10 November 2010, where the manuscript is preserved under Fonds Patrimoniaux MS 15.

[70] Amblard, 'Histoire des campagnes'; A transcript of Amblard's account is now available in the Military Archives at Vincennes under SHD GR 1 KT 800. A microfilmed copy of the manuscript, together with additional documents relating to Amblard's service, can be found under SHD GR 1 Kmi 78.

[71] Conway, *War of American Independence*, 133; see also: Dull, *French Navy and American Independence*.

only became known in recent years.[72] Yet, whatever was deposited beforehand still remains lying in small depositories all over Europe. This will continue until someone physically browses through all their holdings, takes note of the relevant manuscripts and reports their existence to the scholarly community.[73]

Identification of writings by common soldiers is also made challenging by the classification policy unique to every archive. Private letters and journals can be placed in diverse files, whose subject headings and research aids often contain no clue as to their actual holdings. Papers deposited by senior officers make a more obvious place to search. Indeed, their correspondence would typically contain an occasional letter from a subordinate, although these are apt to deal with administrative matters like reports and petitions.[74] Personal writings by common soldiers can also be gleaned from the administrative records held in more prominent state archives, as in the case of James Milligan, whose letter disclosing his desertion plans was attached to a court martial case. Petitions to monarchs or their ministers might be found in the relevant letter books,[75] but locating such items means browsing through vast amounts of irrelevant material. The same is true for another potential source for soldiers' writings. An examination of the 300 odd letters held in a single box of intercepted French correspondence from 1777 produced four letters by soldiers stationed in the French garrison in Saint-Domingue. Forming part of the High Court of Admiralty records in The National Archives, these letters are neither itemised nor catalogued; Kew preserves 110 such boxes from the American War of Independence alone.[76]

All this indicates not only that eighteenth-century common soldiers produced a significant amount of writing, but also that much more of it survives than is actually recognised. But while sole-surviving manuscript

---

[72] For example: 'Soldier's entire letter written by Private W. Hopkin', NAM 2008-06-4; Some of those recent discoveries were published, for instance, Pickert, *Lebens-Geschichte*.

[73] For more of the same attitude, see: Harari, 'Military Memoirs', 296.

[74] Henry Bouquet's papers contain numerous letters from his sergeants; see for instance BL add MS 21,646, fols. 25, 69, 227; See also letters such as that of Sergeant John Harvey to the Duke of Bedford (5 August 1746), Bedfordshire and Luton Archives and Record Service, R 769, 'Duke of Bedford's Regiment of Foot'.

[75] TNA WO 28/8 item 266, 'Copy of a Letter from a soldier 84th Reg'; WO 1/974 'The Humble Petition of Richard Brown'; see another such example in: Seriu, 'Déserteur et femme-soldat', 715. The military archive at Vincennes is exceptional by having a separate sub-series for papers of eighteenth-century common soldiers, but almost all are petitions for pensions, SHD GR YA 446–50.

[76] TNA HCA 30/281, 'Grand Don de Dieu'. In addition, this cartoon contains three more letters whose form and seals look much similar to those written by the soldiers, but there is nothing in their content to indicate the identity of their authors.

sources are understandably hard to locate, the same is also true of many published accounts. Contemporary editions prepared by the authors were often published by subscription and had a low circulation. Moreover, not every autobiographical narrative would be clearly distinguishable as such. In 1724, Donald McBane, a veteran of over thirty years of service, published a manual on swordsmanship; there is little to denote that his booklet also contains an incredibly lively autobiography of its author. Even David Chandler, a leading authority on Marlborough's army, and an editor of journals by common soldiers who participated in the War of the Spanish Succession, appears to be unaware of McBane's autobiography. It was finally identified as a personal narrative by Ian Morrison. His paper, rather than McBane's original manual, was used by Richard Holmes in *Redcoats*, the first general history to make mention of this source.[77] McBane's example demonstrates the extremely circuitous way by which soldierly writings can finally come to light. As mentioned by Brumwell in a recent critical edition of another overlooked eighteenth-century memoirist, it provides a 'reminder of just how much published primary source material awaits rediscovery and assessment'. Yet even a modern edition still does not guarantee that such sources are easily obtainable. The above-mentioned journal by Amblard appeared in the local history journal of a rural commune whose current population numbers less than 3,000 people. A similar example is provided by the diary of Private Valentin Asteroth, from the Murhard Library in Kassel. Thanks to the disproportionate interest in the American Revolution, it is one of the German repositories whose holdings were examined with particular attention, leading to the discovery of number of accounts by Hessian rankers. In 1966, its typescript version was prepared by the *Verein für Hessische Geschichte und Landeskunde*, yet even the German National Library in nearby Frankfurt holds no copy. Its English translation, prepared in 1990 by Bruce E. Burgoyne for the Johannes Schwalmm Historical Association, is long out of print.[78]

Thus, the potential to discover new manuscripts by common soldiers has to be tempered by the challenges of locating and consulting such sources. Although far from effortless, obtaining published sources is

---

[77] McBane, *The Expert Swords-Man's Companion*; see: Chandler's introductions to his editions of Deane, *Journal*, and J. Wilson, 'Journal'; Holmes, *Redcoat*, 142–3; Morrison, 'Survival Skills: An Enterprising Highlander'; It has now become a little easier to locate a copy of McBane after his manual was rediscovered by historical martial artists. This volume makes use of the reproduction published in 2001 by Mark Rector.

[78] Brumwell, in: Kirkwood, *Through so Many Dangers*, 27; Asteroth, *Tagebuch*; Asteroth, 'Diary'; Personal communication with Colonel Donald Londahl-Smidt, director of Military Research, Johannes Schwalm Historical Association, 11 April 2011. The new edition of Asteroth published in 1992 by Heinz Krause is almost as hard to come by.

much easier and, as we have seen, this material has still often been neglected. For these reasons, the present study has concentrated primarily upon locating published sources rather than searching for previously unknown manuscripts. Manuscripts by common soldiers were utilised whenever opportunities arose; however, the bulk of the evidence considered in the following pages comes from published accounts. This includes both letters and diaries, but the balance tilts heavily towards memoirs.

This, however, creates a number of methodological issues which need to be addressed. To quote Samuel Hynes, who discusses the basic types of military narratives, letters and diaries were intended to answer a need to record the events as they were happening. Consequently, they have the 'virtues of immediacy and directness'. Memoirs, on the other hand, are written retrospectively to answer the need to remember and, often, to justify. Either knowingly or unknowingly, their authors might further prefer prevailing public memories to their own lived experience.[79] To cite one such example, British veterans of the Peninsular War who published their memoirs after 1828 often drew on William Napier's standard history whenever their own memory failed them. Later accounts or histories might not only fill factual lacunae but also influence the authors to construct their experiences according to cultural expectations of remembrance. This aspect is well demonstrated by many of the later memoirs from the First World War, known for their motifs of 'disenchantment' and 'disillusionment'. Such themes became prevalent in publications appearing since the late 1920s, but writings composed while the conflict was still ongoing rarely mention anything of the sort.[80]

Nevertheless, many of the arguments raised against the trustworthiness of memoirs also apply to letters. Hynes does not mention that soldiers' narratives were produced to fulfil another need – the need to report. Letters were often intended to be read in public,[81] and their authors had to bear in mind the possible expectations of their audiences. Self-censorship is another important factor to be considered. Marie-Cécile Thoral, who studied personal narratives from the Napoleonic Wars, shows that some authors would tend to downplay their hardships in

---

[79] Hynes, *Soldiers' Tale*, xi-xiv; Hynes, 'Personal narratives and Commemoration'. More on the definition of memoirs, see: Harari, *Renaissance Military Memoirs*, 4–18; Harari, 'Military Memoirs', 298.

[80] Oman, *Wellington's Army*, 23–4, 29; C. Duffy, *Through German Eyes*, 15; see also: Harari, 'Military Memoirs', 302; Harari, 'Martial Illusions', 45–7.

[81] Forrest, *Napoleon's Men*, 40–1; For examples of letters clearly written for a wide audience, see: G. Robertson, 'Two Letters'; '*Feldwebel* G.S. Liebler to his wife and relatives' (12 October 1756), in GG, 33–5; 'Two letters by Musketeer Johann Christian Riemann to his family and friends' (16 June 1762 and undated, summer 1762), in Liebe, 30–5; NAM 1986-11-1, 'Letters of Sergeant Calder (American War) 1778–5' (19 June 1780).

order not to distress their correspondents. On the other hand, there was always the temptation to stress, if not exaggerate, the dangers experienced by the author in order to evoke awe, or underscore his toughness and achievements. Arguably, the need to consider such short-term goals could potentially influence the content of the letters much more than those of the memoirs, which were written with the benefit of hindsight, experience and reflection. Memoirs might arguably disclose less flattering details about the author or his service. A few instances when letters and memoirs by the same individual are available appear to support this point. Writing home after the storming of Seringapatam, Kenward states that, despite the tales about massive booty won by British troops, he had 'other business to employ himself'. In his memoirs composed after his discharge, Kenward admits plundering on other occasions. Likewise, the wartime letters of Saxon scholar Johann Gottfried Seume, who was pressed into the Hessian army and sent to America, describe the army positively and speak about his desire to be a courageous soldier. His memoirs, published some twenty years later, are one of the most damning indictments of the *Menschenhandel* or German soldiers' trade, whose victim Seume was.[82]

Moreover, the distinction between diaries and memoirs is not as clear as it is sometimes described. Good examples are Samuel Ancell's narrative of the Great Siege of Gibraltar or Corporal Robert Brown's journal of the British Flanders campaign in 1793–5. Both accounts include an added layer of digressions, opinions and interpretations; however, the bulk of both texts is a straightforward day-to-day account, too detailed to be remembered and too dry to be invented. It was likely to be copied directly from diaries which these authors kept while the events were ongoing.[83] But, just as published memoirs could contain unaltered material taken from contemporary notes, unpublished diaries could contain an additional layer inserted later. Surviving manuscript copies of the diaries of German auxiliaries Johann Conrad Döhla and Grenadier Johannes Reuber, who served in the American War of Independence, occasionally mention events which took place in Europe on the day they actually occurred – an obvious sign of later editing. Another such example is the journal of Corporal William Todd, who supplemented his notes from the Seven Years War with Guardsman John Tory's published account.

[82] Thoral, *From Valmy to Waterloo*, 6–9; Kenward, *Sussex Highlander*, 30–2, 51, 105–6. Also compare Seume, 'Mein Leben' in: *Werke*, vol. I, 62–6 with his letters in ibid., vol. IIb, 11–3, 26; For an example of subsequent editing out of unpleasant experiences, see: Hagist, 'Unpublished Writings of Roger Lamb', 281–2.

[83] Ancell, *Circumstantial Journal*; R. Brown, *Impartial Journal* who mentions his campaign notes in his introduction, iii–iv. Other authors who refer to the diaries or notes kept during the campaign and used in their later memoirs include: *Royal Dragoon*, 55; Beß, 'Aus dem Tagebuch', 200; BL Mss Eur B296/1 Hickson, 'My own Life', fol. 90.

In Todd's case, this appears to have changed little more than adding a few factual details which were of little relevance to Todd himself. Nevertheless, it can never be known for certain whether the experiences described in his and other journals were recorded at the time of the campaign. They might just as well have been embellished later.[84]

As for the claim that memoirs portray primarily constructed cultural experience, this applies equally well to any other type of personal writing and, in fact, any historical source. Lived experience can be influenced by cultural expectations just as remembered experience can. Moreover, perceptions of physical experiences can be shaped by the same factors.[85] Therefore, selectively dwelling on the constructed nature of a whole genre of sources is logically unfeasible. One can admit that all sources are equally constructed, but then this aspect becomes a constant and loses its value as a historical variable. Alternatively, one can consider every source individually on its own merits. This study follows the second option.[86] Moreover, the fact that sources were influenced by external considerations does not render them any less useful. Authors had the choice of what to write and which views to take. These choices are interesting and revealing, irrespective of the factual accuracy of their accounts. For instance, Richard Humphrys' journal includes official British casualty figures for the battle of the Plains of Abraham, a translation of Wolfe's declaration to the Canadians upon his landing before Quebec and the full articles of the surrender of Havana. The description of this last achievement concludes with a reference to the harmony prevailing between the army and the navy and by quoting Admiral Pocock's own words that 'both corps strived equally for their glory of their king and country's service'.[87] Throughout the memoir, Humphrys does not mention himself a single time. But even if we assume that he is just a passive consumer of official rhetoric, Humphrys' case

---

[84] See the introduction to Döhla's English translation, by Bruce Burgoyne, *Hessian Diary*, xii–xiii; see the introduction to Todd's *Journal*, xv–xvi; Atkinson 'Soldier's Diary of the Seven Years' War', 119 n. 1.

[85] Harari, 'Military Memoirs', 306; For examples of studies arguing about the constructed nature of physical experiences, see: Kleinman, *Illness Narratives*; Bracken, 'Hidden Agendas: Deconstructing Post Traumatic Stress Disorder'.

[86] For a recent defence of the use of memoirs as primary sources, see: Thoral, *From Valmy to Waterloo*, 10–12; For similarly positive consideration as part of a broader category of ego-documents, see: Peters, 'Zur Auskunftsfähigkeit von Selbstsichtzeugnissen schreibender Bauern'.

[87] BL add MS 45,662, Richard Humphrys, 'Journal', fols. 73–5, 125, 127–138. Wolfe's declaration appears unpaginated at the end of the manuscript. For more examples of accounts quoting from peace treaties and capitulation articles, see: J.R., 'Journal', 36; Archives Nationales, Paris, Mar/B4/288, Jacques Gruyer, 'Letter to his father', (17 January 1782).

provides valuable evidence of the efforts of the military authorities to encourage their men. Official statements and figures were often highly embellished, if not overtly false.[88] Yet it is telling that soldiers, like Humphrys, readily accepted these. Moreover, the willingness of soldier-authors to internalise elements of official discourse[89] is not unimportant when we consider why they chose to serve and fight.

The view adopted in this study, however, is that soldier-authors were active creators of their texts rather than passive conduits of official propaganda, as well as of more general cultural influences. Writers of the narratives considered in the following pages had no difficulty demonstrating their disdain, ranging from specific complaints about an unpopular superior to general themes such as the injustices of military service. In fact, the bluntness of some of the authors is striking. John Scot's poem on his regiment in the War of the Spanish Succession begins by reproaching his colonel for failing to honour a promise to discharge him. This officer is one of the persons to whom the poem is dedicated, so it is unlikely that he missed this point, together with other uncomplimentary references, including his alleged miserliness. A major motif which continuously reappears in the poem is ingratitude, as the soldiers get very little in exchange for their sacrifices, and often fall victim to irregularities. As for the supposed payment of subsistence money, Scot remarked 'when it is payed I cannot tell you, And I wot not who can tell me [sic]'.[90] Financial abuses by superiors were a common cause for complaint. The Waldeck Sergeant Carl Philip Steuernagel protests that the cost of

---

[88] In his memoirs John Johnson ridicules the overoptimistic letter full of false promises of forthcoming French support, sent by Governor Vaudreuil to the commanders of the Canadian militia only a short time before the final surrender of the colony. Johnson himself, however, was also influenced by official rhetoric, as his account quotes verbatim the whole the capitulation articles of Montreal: 'Memoirs of the Siege of Quebec', 134–5, 140–54.

[89] Just to mention a few examples: official casualty figures are quoted in Dominicus, *Tagebuch*, 35, 41; Scot, 'Remembrance', 553–5; Also compare the identical figures appearing in different letters in GG, 12, 21–3, 34. Sources with quotations from daily orders include: Sullivan, *From Redcoat to Rebel*; Steuernagel, 'Brief Description' 127–9; Sermons are quoted verbatim by Sohr, *Meine Geschichte*, 50–65. For letters written to resemble a battlefield bulletins, see: Grenadier Guards Regimental Archive, London A03/03, George Darby, 'Letters'.

[90] Scot also complained of a general who gave a French garrison too lenient surrender terms and unfairness that rear-echelon men received the same siege bounty as frontline troops, see: 'Remembrance', 328, 384–6, 423, 426, 476, the quotation is from page 458. His anonymous contemporary who served with the Royal Dragoons in the British contingent in Spain criticises officers for making bad tactical choices, despoiling soldiers of their pay and refusing to take interest in their well-being. In one particularly appalling case, they imprisoned a man who came to warn them of an upcoming enemy attack. According to the narrator, the officers should have been put in jail themselves; see: *Royal Dragoon*, 47, 55.

hymn-books received as gifts from the prince was deducted from the soldiers' pay. Kenward indulges in a sarcastic tirade about prize agents who helped themselves to ivory, gems and jewellery but who, after learning that 'some loose characters had got possession of a few gold chains and bangles', forbade all plunder for patriotic reasons. 'Shuddering of the idea of seeing their dear countrymen loaded with chains, an appearance so derogatory to the nature of a Briton'.[91] Such criticism was not limited to manuscripts intended to be read by a few individuals, but also to published memoirs. Writing about the debacle at Saint Cast, the author of a Seven Years War journal known only by his first name, Jonas, openly admonishes the British commanders for holding the life of their men in lesser value than captured livestock which was given priority for embarkation from the beachhead, despite news of the French approach. Duncan Cameron's account, published within a few months of the disastrous battle of Monongahela, complains that after their return to Will's Creek, the survivors were subjected to unjustly severe discipline. Describing the courts martial and the heavy floggings that followed, Cameron hints that the officers apparently learnt something from the savages.[92]

But, just as they could be disapproving of their superiors and the army in general, authors did not necessarily withhold unfavourable information about themselves or their experiences. The Prussian cantonist Dominicus admits running for his life at the battles of Paltzig and Kunersdorf.[93] Other less savoury aspects described by Dominicus include details on how the army was procuring its supplies. A typical dry entry from October 1756 reads: 'We found a house where bread is just taken out from the oven – it is immediately taken. The women there had many children and weeps, I returned her my share, the others did not'.[94]

---

[91] Steuernagel, 'Brief Description', 152; Kenward, *Sussex Highlander*, 31–2, 40, 58; For more financial complaints against superiors, see: Aytoun, *Redcoats*, 32–33, 35–6, 40; Centre of Kentish Studies, Maidstone, U1350 Z9A, James Miller, 'Memoirs of an Invalid', 77–8; Laukhard, *Leben und Schicksale*, 232, 249.

[92] Jonas, *Soldier's Journal*, 39–40; D. Cameron, *Life*, 14; Compare the latter account with 'Journal of Captain's Cholmley's Batman', 34–5. For tyrannical behaviour by some officers and NCOs, see: Aytoun, *Redcoats*, 9–11, 17–8; Beeger, *Seltsame Schicksale*, 24–5; Pickert, *Lebens-Geschichte*, 38; Laukhard, *Leben und Schicksale*, 148–9; Le Roy, *Souvenirs*, 45, 54, 58; Bersling, *Der böhmische Veteran*, 247–52.

[93] Dominicus, *Tagebuch*, 56, 60; More examples of soldiers fleeing combat include Scott, 'Remembrance', 325, 487, 494; McBane, 'Expert Swords-Man's Companion', 25–6; In his first battle against the American rebels, Stephen Jarvis' 'pantaloons received a wound, and I don't hesitate to say, that I should have been very well pleased to have seen a little blood also', 'American's Experience in the British Army', 200.

[94] Dominicus' generosity on that occasion was rewarded as he found a large sack of apples in the next house. The opinion of its owners remains unrecorded; see: *Tagebuch*, 7; For more admissions of looting, both nuanced and not, see: Bernos, 'Souvenirs de

Some narrators openly describe how they deserted. In addition to their own less flattering deeds, authors also describe hardships they underwent: hunger, exhaustion and sleep deprivation. In some of the narratives which were composed over a long period of time, one can distinguish war weariness and a genuine desire for peace.[95] Most descriptions of combat include highly disturbing details. Although some are brought to enhance the reputation of the narrator, most must surely be interpreted as genuine expressions of shock and anguish.[96]

Considered as a whole, the sources used in this study present a diverse picture. Some underscore the positive aspects of military service, reinforcing their descriptions by official language. Others appear to be doing everything to dispute it. As shown by Paul Fussel, who studied the First World War, memoirs, personal narratives were often written to challenge official representations of the war. This is definitely true of some veterans, like Prussian cuirassier guardsman Johann Christoph Pickert, who apologises sardonically for leaving all battle descriptions out of his account because he would be unable to compete with the knowledgeable men who read all the official bulletins while sitting in the safety of their homes.[97] Most sources do not appear to be taking an overt position, however. Instead, they include elements acknowledging and praising some official aspects and criticising others, both openly and subtly. A good example of the latter kind is the journal of Quartermaster Sergeant John Johnson of the 58th Regiment of Foot, describing the British conquest of Canada in 1759–60. It is a representative case of a soldier's memoir. It is based on notes Johnson made while serving in the campaign itself, while the narrative was written only in the early 1780s. The endeavour was made with the encouragement of 'some gentlemen from the regiment' – an obvious sign of patronage. Official language appears often in the memoir: the surrender articles of Canada are quoted verbatim, the conduct and sacrifice of the officers, particularly Wolfe, is praised, as is the 'intrepid spirit' of his successor General Murray. The same text, however, contains another

campagne', 757–8; Todd, *Journal*, 55, 147–8; 153; Döhla, 'Tagebuch', (22–3 March, 1780); Laukhard, *Leben und Schicksale*, 225, 235.
[95] For references to hardships, see the letters of La'rka Stepanov and Avakum Belkin in: Kozlov, 'Okopnie pisma', 201, 205; J. Miller, 'Memoirs of an Invalid', 65; 'Grenadier Adam Becker to his wife and family' (18 November 1756), in GG, 38; For results of exceptionally grievous hunger: Tory, *Journal*, 59; Zahn, 'Soldatenbrief', 76; For examples of war-weariness, and desire for peace see: Deane, *Journal*, xvii, 99, 122; Scott, 'Remembrance', Grotehenn, *Briefe*, 84, 120.
[96] For examples of particularly gory descriptions, see: J. Wilson, 'Journal', 78; R. Brown, *Impartial Journal*, 37–44; Grotehenn, *Briefe*, 57–8, 124; see also: 'Letter by Franz Reiß to this wife' (6 October 1756), in GG, 30.
[97] Pickert, *Lebens-Geschichte*, 5; on the iconoclastic stance of memoir writers in general: Harari, 'Military Memoirs', 298; see also: Fussell, *Great War and Modern Memory*.

layer which uses official language, if not to subvert, then at least to amend the account of the campaign. Johnson's narrative is essentially a hymn of praise to the British common soldiers. Heroic actions by individual NCOs are described equally to those of the commissioned officers. Other soldiery virtues that are praised are humility, when a gallant sergeant refuses a commission; humanity, when men share their last supplies with starving Canadian civilians; and sacrifice, when the sick leave the hospitals to join their comrades as the garrison is marching out of Quebec to fight the French army. The defeat in the subsequent battle of Sainte-Foy is presented as a moral victory of the soldiers who held out for so long against a much stronger enemy. What follows is a scathing criticism of General Murray, whose vainglory in accepting battle under unfavourable conditions not only almost lost Quebec, but also cost the lives of many of his brave subordinates.[98]

Authors such as Johnson demonstrate that soldier-authors were not only conscious of what they wrote, but were also willing to adopt complex perspectives. Furthermore, irrespective of whether their authors had a stated or subtle agenda, many narratives are useable simply because of the vast amount of detail they provide. Such details are likely to be reliable for they are often too specific or are of too minor importance for the author to justify their invention. For instance, conversion narratives by Methodist preachers might not be the most trustworthy sources regarding the religious sentiments of the typical ranker, but they contain much useful material on daily life in the army. Originally published in *The Muscovite*, one of the major literary vehicles propagating Emperor Nicholas I's doctrine of Official Nationality, the memoirs of Colonel Yakov Starkov might seem suspect when depicting the Poles and the French revolutionaries against whom Starkov fought as a junior NCO during the 1790s. On the other hand, there is no apparent reason why Starkov should have made up his description of the informal control mechanism employed by the men of the line to correct the behaviour of unpopular fellow soldiers.[99] Likewise, there is no reason to single out for

---

[98] J. Johnson, 'Memoirs of the Siege of Quebec'; For official language, see: 80, 102, 126, 131; For examples of gallantry by common soldiers and criticism of superiors, see: 98, 113, 116, 118–9, 120–3. Compare a description of the battle of Kloster Kampen whose author interlaces the story of the selfless sacrifice of Chevalier D'Assas with descriptions of similarly heroic acts by French commons soldiers: Lamy, *Précis historique sur le régiment d'Auvergne*, 45–8.

[99] For examples of surprisingly coherent political, religious and national views expressed by Starkov and his comrades, see: *Raskazi*, 4, 14, 107, 144, 168, 203, 242; For a description of peer pressure in the ranks, see: ibid., 23; More on *The Muscovite* and on Official Nationality in Czarist Russia more generally, see: Peace, 'Nineteenth-Century', 191–2; Riasanovsky, *Russian Identities*, 132–43.

criticism the accounts of intellectuals for whom military service was just a passing stage of their lives. Firstly, there was substantial movement of individuals in and out of the military profession. Soldiering was not just a stage in the lives of *Magister* Friedrich Christian Laukhard and Sonnenfels, but also of John Macdonald, who worked as a schoolmaster, butler and shopkeeper, the chimneysweep Franz Karl Cura and the Hessian *Feldscher*-turned-preacher Charles Lahatt. Moreover, greater education of an author could actually add to the overall usefulness of the source. Former student Seume was promoted sergeant and was relieved from duty to help his colonel with the regimental paperwork. However, why should this diminish from his description of his early days in the army, or his transportation to the New World?[100] In fact, Seume's education and interests made him a shrewd observer, and his account provides many valuable details of daily life in camp, as compared to narratives of less-educated soldiers, who often describe the ongoing campaigns rather than their own experiences.

A final methodological point is that none of these concerns regarding the reliability of soldierly narratives has precluded their use when they have been employed to reinforce the traditional view of old-regime armies. This can be demonstrated with the help of a well-known example – Ulrich Bräker – whose autobiography appears to possess all the attributes of the story of an archetypical old-regime soldier. A nineteen-year-old lad from a poor rural Swiss family, Bräker was tricked by Prussian agents into seeking employment as a valet. Guided into a nearby town, Bräker was hired by a generous gentleman who turned out to be a Prussian recruiting officer. Ordered to travel ahead of him to Berlin, Bräker was forcibly enlisted in his master's regiment. The new pay proved ludicrously small and Bräker was further distressed by the officers' habit of shouting and even beating their men. Not surprisingly, many deserted, but Bräker tells us that all were taken and severely punished. Fortunately, the Seven Years War soon began and Bräker deserted and returned home to Switzerland. Neither the fact that Bräker wrote his memoirs thirty years after his service nor that he was a self-made scholar precluded scholars from using this account to demonstrate the dire conditions of the Prussian rank and file. Bräker's account of his desertion is considered to be one of the few genuine testimonies of this kind available.

Taken at face value, Bräker's memoir has little sympathy for the Prussian service. Yet, when examined in detail, it testifies to the existence

---

[100] Macdonald, *Autobiographical Journal*; Cura, 'Tagebuch'; Lahatt, 'Autobiography', More in favour of sources by educated soldiers, see the introduction to Todd, *Journal*, xiv–xv.

of elements usually associated with positive motivational incentives. Despite his initial unwillingness, Bräker quickly formed comradely ties with individual members of his unit. In peacetime, the soldiers were billeted in small groups: while on campaign six men lived in a tent together with an NCO, 'making one table one household one bed'. When it came to combat, Bräker fought actively, quickly firing his sixty cartridges, despite the fact that the troops were advancing in open order outside the immediate sight of their officers. After deserting during a lull in the fighting and arriving in the Austrian camp, Bräker notes with displeasure how their soldiers concoct stories about defeating numerous Brandenburgers. Lastly, after returning home, Bräker not only did not dispose of his uniform, but tidied it up before going to church, as if he was about to head out to a Berlin parade.[101] Moreover, Bräker's other writings, particularly his voluminous diaries, suggest that his time in the army had a profound influence on him, leading him to adopt military terms and jargon. All this implies that Bräker was genuinely proud of his time in the army. This obviously did not make him wish to return to Prussia; nevertheless, it is fair to day that his experience there was not entirely one-sided. Despite the ready availability of his memoirs, which were republished numerous times, only in the last decade have scholars finally acknowledged that Bräker's portrayal of the Prussian army is more intricate than that of a mere coercive enterprise.[102] This illustrates that prevailing negative views on the motivation of old-regime common soldiers do not stem as much from lack of autobiographical writings or their unreliability, but rather from constrained interpretation of existing evidence. Although he did employ previously unused material, Möbius' novel conclusions are not so much the product of new evidence as the careful reconsideration of existing sources. The present work takes a similar approach. Although it did discover new material, its main focus is placed on scrutinising previously known testimonies.

Although personal narratives are a challenging source, they remain the most useful form of evidence for the purposes of the current study. The literacy of their authors does not necessarily diminish the representativeness of their military experience. Moreover, soldier-authors could adopt a critical stance or combine varied perspectives, both official and unofficial. Produced by a large group of diverse individuals, these writings offer a wealth of evidence. The random survival of autobiographical accounts by old-regime common soldiers adds further weight to their

---

[101] Bräker, 'Lebensgeschichte', 442–3, 449, 453, 462, 465–6, 470.
[102] See: Kloosterhuis' excellent, 'Donner, Blitz und Bräker'. This study builds in turn on some of the ideas in: Eckert, 'Ulrich Bräkers Soldatenzeit und die Preußische Werbung in Schaffhausen'.

overall trustworthiness. In fact, when critical editions of their writings are available, it is interesting how many of their statements can be confirmed. For these reasons, this volume embraces a positivist approach to soldierly narratives. Unless there are reasons to doubt the authenticity of a particular source, the statements of the authors are taken as they stand. Historians should remember that it is presumptuous to assume that they should always know better what were the actual thoughts, feelings and acts of the people whom they study.[103] Nevertheless, this study takes no greater liberty with its primary material than previous studies which have commented on the motivation of eighteenth-century soldiers. Many of these comments were based on a partial reading, while others had nothing but prevailing assumptions to support them. Negative views of the motivation of old-regime soldiers did not require particular scrutiny. This study seeks to provide a fuller picture of their experiences and the reasons why they enlisted, served and fought.

---

[103] On that point see: Harari, 'Scholars, Eyewitnesses, and Flesh-Witnesses of War'; Harari, 'Armchairs, Coffee, and Authority'.

2   Reconsidering Desertion in Old-Regime Europe

Unlike the motivation of the rank and file, desertion from the armies of old-regime Europe has been a relatively well-studied subject.[1] One of the lasting legacies of the decline of military entrepreneurship in the decades following the Thirty Years War was not only the emergence of regular standing armies, but also a substantial amount of formal paperwork.[2] As monarchs and their generals expected to know how many troops were available for service, manpower reports now had to be submitted on a regular basis, usually to the relevant ministry of war. Consequentially, muster rolls and monthly returns, or their continental equivalents such as the French *contrôles des troupes* or the Austrian *Musterliste*, form a substantial part of the holdings of the surviving military archives. Deserters would figure on these documents among those men who had left the unit, together with the men who were discharged, transferred or those who had died. Moreover, if the fugitive was captured, this fact was likely to leave a trace of a different kind. Guilty of one of the severest military crimes, the deserter could be brought before a court martial. While not a general rule across Europe, the regulations of some old-regime armies, including the British and the French, instructed that the proceedings of such trials had to be confirmed by a senior officer, reported to the ministry of war or, at the very least, have their verdicts recorded in some way. All this generated additional reports and correspondence and some of this material has survived as well.

However, the quantity and quality of the available source material is not the only reason why modern historians study desertion. The current scholarly consensus, as neatly put by Michael Sikora, is that 'the

---

[1] Recent monographs include: Sikora, *Disziplin und Desertion*; Muth, *Flucht*; There are also important chapters in: Kroll, *Soldaten*; Corvisier, *L'Armée Française*, vol. II, 693–880; Lynn, *Giant*, 398–414; Atwood, *Hessians*, 184–206; and particularly: Steppler, *Common Soldier*, ch. 6; For an interesting micro-study, see: Rea, 'Military Deserters from British West Florida'.

[2] For instance, the systematic accumulation of French military archives begins in 1688; see M.S. Anderson, *War and Society*, 100.

eighteenth century was the age of the deserter'. Corvisier, whose work on the French army has set the standard for all subsequent studies on the social history of old-regime enlisted men, estimates that between 1700 and 1763, one-fifth of all French soldiers deserted.[3] And, indeed, desertion in wartime could reach spectacular proportions. During the Great Northern War, the Russians lost as many as 20,000 deserters per year. The failed campaign in Bohemia in 1744 cost Frederick over 10,000 deserters, some 15 per cent of his entire force. In the Seven Years War, the Austrian army had over 60,000 deserters, while in 1759 it was estimated that the first two months of campaigning alone cost the French army over 2,000 deserters. The Hanoverian army, which is said to have one of the lowest desertion rates during that conflict, lost 14 per cent to that cause.[4]

Unsurprisingly, desertion is said to have had a noticeable effect on old-regime tactics. One of the arguments raised against the use of light infantry was the fear that its men would escape as soon as they had left the sight of their superiors. Foraging had to be limited, leaving armies at the mercy of a cumbersome supply system of magazines and convoys.[5] A camp would be just as alert to the internal threat of desertion as that of an approaching enemy force. A good example of the importance placed by eighteenth-century commanders on preventing desertion comes from Frederick the Great's instructions to his generals. This first and most influential of his military writings begins by outlining the preventive measures to be taken against desertion.[6] Contemporary disciplinary regulations left little doubt of the fate awaiting a captured fugitive. 'Death or such other punishment that by the said court shall be inflicted' stated the British articles of war, the court in question being a General Court Martial which tried capital cases. The Austrian articles threatened the equivalent *'leib-und lebens-Straf'* for those absent without leave, and

---

[3] Corvisier, *L'Armée Française*, vol. II, 736–7. These figures are often repeated whenever old-regime desertion rates are discussed; see for instance: Gooch, *Armies in Europe*, 11; Frey, *British Soldier in America*, 16; Iain Cameron mistakenly cites those figures as indicating 20 to 25 per cent *annual* desertion level; see: *Crime and Repression*, 80.

[4] These and further examples are cited in Sikora, *Disziplin und Desertion*, 74–80. For more figures, see: Keep, *Soldiers of the Tsar*, 114; Kennett, *French Armies*, 84–5; C. Duffy, *Instrument of War*, 212.

[5] Lynn, *Battle*, 123; M.S. Anderson, *War and Society*, 130–1; Sikora, *Disziplin und Desertion*, 1–2; Martin van Creveld also connects between fear of desertion and insufficient foraging, but argues that the armies were not necessarily constrained to the magazines system as a result, see: *Supplying War*, 37–9.

[6] Frederick the Great, 'Les Principes généraux de la guerre, appliqués à la tactique et à la discipline des troupes prussiennes', in: *Œuvres*, vol. XXVIII, 4–7; see also: C. Duffy, *Army of Frederick the Great*, 57.

hanging for traitors who deserted to the enemy.[7] The Prussian regulations were more explicit. Deserters were to run the gauntlet: a corporal punishment where the culprit was made to walk between two lines of his comrades who would beat him with rods. The deserter would expect to run a minimum of twelve gauntlets of 200 men. Repeated desertion was to be punished by twenty-four or even thirty-six gauntlets, a sentence most contemporaries considered to be equivalent of death.[8]

While some studies examine individual motives for desertion at length,[9] it is generally seen as an indication of the brutal service conditions prevalent in old-regime armies. Describing the ferocious Prussian discipline, Childs remarks that '[t]he trouble with the Prussian reaction to desertion was that the harsh discipline became one of the major reasons why soldiers fled the colours, so creating an insoluble vicious circle'.[10] In other words, the apparent high levels of desertion on the one hand, and the fearful punishments supposedly meted out to deserters on the other, reinforce the conventional image of eighteenth-century soldiers as browbeaten and miserable wretches who were just looking for a chance to escape their ordeal. If this is correct, one has to acknowledge that the despair which provoked these men was remarkable. What extreme state of hopelessness would prompt someone to flee the Prussian service in the period when Frederick the Great boasted that 98 per cent of all deserters from the garrisons of Berlin and Potsdam were caught?[11] Of course, it would hardly be possible to expect that old-regime common soldiers were motivated by anything but coercion and fear of punishment.

This chapter will reconsider this viewpoint. It begins with a short overview of some of the more basic assumptions relating to desertion in old-regime armies. It will show that the overarching argument that those armies suffered from high desertion rates has done much to overshadow many of the finer aspects of what was a diverse phenomenon. Secondly, it

---

[7] TNA WO 71/2 'Rules, etc. Articles of War', Articles of War 1718 art. 10; Kriegsartikel, Articles 23–4, in *Reglement für die sämmentlich-Kaiserlich-Königliche Infanterie*, (1769), 97.

[8] Native-born cantonists would run thirty-six gauntlets after their first desertion attempt, and were to hang if they ever tried to desert again: *Reglement Vor die Königl. Preußische Infantrie*, (1743), 581; C. Duffy, *Army of Frederick the Great*, 63–4. A very similar policy was in force in the Russian army; see: Peter the Great, *Instruksii i artikuli*, (1714), arts. 95–6.

[9] Sikora, *Disziplin und Desertion*, 262–353; Muth, *Flucht*, 95–103. See also: Frey, *British Soldier in America*, 72–3; Brumwell, *Redcoats*, 104–5, Garnham, 'Military Desertion', 93–4; Atwood, *Hessians*, 193–201.

[10] Childs, *Armies and Warfare*, 69; and similarly: Gilbert, 'Why Men Deserted', 553–4; Young, *Fighting Man*, (London, 1981), 114; Atwood, *Hessians*, 192; S.F. Scott, *Response*, 36; Bertaud, *Army of the French Revolution*, 18–9.

[11] Childs, *Armies and Warfare*, 73. See also: C. Duffy, *Army of Frederick the Great*, 66.

will discuss the motives for leaving military service as they appear in the surviving narratives by actual deserters. These demonstrate that the decision to desert would largely be due to specific considerations, and would be more nuanced than a simple by-product of harsh discipline. Lastly, this chapter will present archival data which points to a major alternative factor which influenced desertion rates throughout eighteenth-century Europe.

The view that the rank and file of old-regime armies lacked positive motivation is usually based on the assumption that desertion rates in that century were particularly high. Yet those figures fluctuated, sometimes dramatically, in different times and from army to army. For instance, during the reign of Frederick William I, the Prussian army initially suffered an annual desertion rate of 3.2 per cent; however, from 1727 to 1740, this figure fell to an annual average of 1 per cent. Between 1717 and 1727, desertion was sapping one-tenth of the Saxon infantry. When the totals are adjusted to include lower desertion rates in the cavalry, this meant that Saxony was losing 7 per cent of its troops on an annual basis. In comparison, the annual desertion figures for the entire Saxon army in 1764–7 were about 4 per cent, while during the decade between 1782 and 1792, the highest annual desertion rate from the infantry was 2.5 per cent, and for most years it was below 1 per cent. According to Corvisier, between 1716 and 1749 the French army had an average annual desertion rate of 4.4 per cent, but towards the last years of old-regime France this figure was halved.[12]

Moreover, when desertion rates in old-regime Europe are compared to those in armies from other periods, the results can be telling. Neither popular nor scholarly views of the nineteenth-century US army associate it with mass desertion. Yet in 1830 alone, it had 1,251 deserters from a total force of 5,231 – almost a quarter of the entire army. In 1856, the army numbered fewer than 16,000 soldiers and had 3,223 deserters. A congressional report covering the period between 1820 and 1860 determined that the average desertion rate in these years was 14.8 per cent. Between 1867 and 1891, the US army lost 88,475 deserters from a force whose strength averaged about 25,000 men, and in some of these years over a third of the army made off. Desertion during the American Civil War was comparable if not higher than for most eighteenth-century conflicts. The official figures for the Union vary between 12 and 18 per cent of all soldiers (200,000 to 278,644 cases). Known to be incomplete, the official records for the Confederacy cite some 100,000

---

[12] Fann, 'Peacetime Attrition', 325–7; Kroll, *Soldaten*, Table 17; P.H. Wilson, *German Armies*, 333, Table 9.1; Corvisier, *L'Armée Française*, vol. II, 737.

desertion cases, or about 10 per cent of the Southern army.[13] Another major nineteenth-century force whose situation appears to be rather similar to its eighteenth-century predecessors is the late Victorian army. Between 1862 and 1898 the troops stationed in Britain sustained an annual desertion rate of about 2 per cent, a figure comparable to Sikora's assessment for typical peacetime desertion rates in old-regime Europe.[14] Yet the most revealing comparison comes from the armies of Revolutionary France. In 1793, 8 per cent of its soldiers made off, a total of over 50,000 men! The following year, another 4 per cent of the troops ran away; however, because the army had doubled its size, the absolute number of the deserters remained stable. Some of the French units lost over a third of their men this way, and there were particularly spectacular cases, such as a singularly unlucky battalion from Ruffec whose strength fell from 2,304 to only ninety-four soldiers. Although unrepresentative, its losses alone are comparable to the official figures for the whole French army in 1787.[15]

Moreover, the preoccupation with desertion rates led scholars to overlook the importance of some basic trends which persisted throughout the eighteenth century. For instance, new recruits and foreigners were more likely to desert than veterans and native-born soldiers.[16] There were more deserters in wartime than in peacetime.[17] Units on the march were particularly susceptible to desertion, as were regiments whose soldiers learnt that they were to be sent abroad.[18] Not unlike recruitment, desertion rates demonstrate correlations with economic conditions, or even particular months of the year.[19] Finally, armies whose desertion figures

---

[13] Coffman, *Old Army*, 193, 371; Lonn, *Desertion during the Civil War*, 226–7; see also: Weitz, *More Damning than Slaughter*, 288–94.

[14] Sikora's estimate is between 2 and 3 per cent *per annum*, see: *Disziplin und Desertion*, 74; Skelley, *Victorian Army at Home*, 130–2, 134, Tables 3–6. Old-regime figures also compare favourably with desertion from British garrisons in Canada in the nineteenth century, see: Burroughs, 'Crime and Punishment', 553.

[15] Interestingly, all of the above figures were calculated by Bertaud, who provides one of the more favourable assessments of revolutionary armies compared to its old-regime predecessor; see: *Army of the French Revolution*, 35, 128–9, 259–64, 274–7; This point was already noticed by P.H. Wilson; see his *German Armies*, 333, Table 9.1.

[16] Jany, *Geschichte der Preußischen Armee*, vol. II, 665; Atwood, *Hessians*, 204–5; M.S., Anderson, *War and Society*, 129–30; Steppler, *Common Soldier*, 190–3; Garnham, 'Military Desertion', 94–5; For a detailed breakdown of the figures for native and foreign deserters in the Saxon army, see: Kroll, *Soldaten*, 517–21.

[17] C. Duffy, *Military Experience*, 172.

[18] See, for instance, the precautions taken by the garrison of Gibraltar on the day when one of the regiments was to embark for Jamaica, TNA WO 284/1, entry of 30 September 1735. For another contemporary example: Todd, *Journal*, 62–3; see also: M.S. Anderson, *War and Society*, 129–30; Atwood, *Hessians*, 194–8, Garnham, 'Military Desertion', 94; M. Duffy, 'British Army and the Caribbean Expeditions', 67.

[19] Kroll, *Soldaten*, Table 18.

were examined over a prolonged period reveal that peacetime desertion rates declined as the century progressed. True, this did not occur simultaneously, but was it mere coincidence?

When these trends have been considered, their interpretation is usually a negative one. Native-born soldiers were less prone to escape, as this would expose their families to retaliation from the authorities.[20] Possibly this was the concern of many would-be deserters, yet why discount the possibility that native-born troops could also be genuinely sympathetic to the cause their armies were fighting for? True, younger soldiers were particularly vulnerable to the hardships of military life, yet even if many recruits deserted for that reason, what does it tell us about those who stayed? Moreover, disproportionately high desertion among younger soldiers meant that the army was continuously cleansed of its most reluctant and least prepared human material. Fear and unwillingness to fight and the privations of campaign life undoubtedly contributed to higher desertion rates in times of war. However, this could also indicate that disciplinary controls proved inefficient precisely when they were most needed. Desertion in periods of economic hardship could allude to the miserable condition of the soldiery, but also to the fact that many men considered military service as a form of employment like any other. It is therefore clear that some of the basic assumptions regarding desertion from old-regime armies are either unsubstantiated by contemporary evidence or present a one-sided and mostly negative understanding of old-regime service.

Analysing the decline in desertion levels in the army of Frederick William I, Willerd Fann offers two non-mutually exclusive explanations: institution of successful preventive measures and improvement in the service conditions of the rank and file. The introduction of new regulations in 1727 remedied some of the worst abuses, instituting a fairer recruiting system.[21] This latter part of Fann's argument is in line with those scholars who maintain that the eighteenth century saw a general improvement in the condition of the common soldier, a point which we will return to in the following two chapters. Much of the remaining part of the current chapter will be devoted to the first half of Fann's argument, namely, that soldiers were less likely to desert when subject to effective control mechanisms. Firstly, however, we should pause to consider what old-regime deserters themselves had to say.

---

[20] One common sanction would be to fine the parents of the fugitive or to sequester his share in the family inheritance. See for instance: Bersling, *Der böhmische Veteran*, 474–5; 'Casper Miller's letter to his son' (14 April 1789) in J.P. Miller, 'Papers', 22–4; see also: Nottenbaum, 'Aus Westfälichen Feldpostbriefen', 91.
[21] Fann, 'Peacetime Attrition', 326.

It can be argued that authors of desertion accounts are likely to embellish their narratives. One such example is provided by the exploits of the Saxon Johann Carl Büttner. Sold as an indentured servant in Pennsylvania, Büttner used the outbreak of the Revolutionary War to escape servitude by joining the rebels. Eager to return to Germany, Büttner deserted in his first battle and promptly reenlisted in the Knyphausen Regiment. A few months later, at the battle of Red Bank, Büttner was badly wounded and taken prisoner. Recognised as a former American soldier, Büttner escaped punishment by fabricating a story about how he was forcibly pressed into the Hessian service.[22] Interestingly, this account, which appeared in his published memoirs, was cross-referenced with the papers of James Tilton, the American surgeon who asked Büttner to be pardoned. Tilton repeats Büttner's invented story about his imprisonment and the threats which left him no choice but to enlist with the Hessians. As for his second desertion, however, it appears that Büttner's behaviour was far from heroic, as he feigned death before running over to the Americans.[23] Going back to his published narrative, while ready to admit he was a multiple deserter, Büttner was clearly unwilling to acknowledge cowardice. Moreover, if Büttner, who composed his memoirs in the 1820s, was willing to gloss over some of the less flattering details of his service, what does it say of authors writing closer to the event, or who retained stakes in present affairs? Memoirists who hoped their writings would receive a favourable reception were in a particularly challenging position, which required equally creative solutions. In 1775, Robert Kirkwood, a veteran of the French and Indian War, published his memoirs under the patronage of the officers of the Limerick garrison, probably with the intent to capitalise on renewed interest in American affairs. The modern editors of his account were able to establish that in 1762 Kirkwood was imprisoned for nine months following an unsuccessful desertion attempt; Kirkwood's own narrative for that year states he was serving with his regiment in the Caribbean.[24]

Yet, even if some memoirists suppressed the story of their escape attempts, those admitting their desertion openly still provide a valuable

---

[22] Büttner, 'Narrative', 232–42.

[23] The relevant passages from Tilton's latter are quoted verbatim in Büttner, 'Narrative', 193, see also: De Ortiz, 'German Redemptioners', 294–6; A few months later Büttner, now serving as part of a prize crew on a captured British vessel, helped the captive sailors to retake their ship and take it to New York, where he promptly reenlisted with the Hessians. For this and the remaining part of his military career, see his 'Narrative', 242–50.

[24] See Brumwell's introduction in: Kirkwood, *Through so Many Dangers*, 17, 86–7.

sample of desertion motives. The two desertions of Franz Bersling come closest to the conventional view of desertion, and perhaps of the fate of old-regime soldiers more generally. A Czech conscript, Bersling started his military career as an artilleryman in the Habsburg army, serving during the entire War of the First Coalition, initially in Flanders and then along the Rhine. In early 1797, with no end in sight, the war-weary Bersling escaped into Switzerland, hoping to make it home to Bohemia under a false identity. Lacking the means to support himself, and fearing he might be pressed into the revolutionary French army and then hanged if captured by his old Austrian comrades, Bersling reenlisted into a Swiss regiment in the Spanish service. On its way to Spain, their ship was captured by the Royal Navy, and Bersling, together with the other recruits, was promptly reenlisted into the British Minorca Regiment, in whose ranks he fought in the successful Egyptian Campaign against the French. In 1803, Bersling was granted a formal discharge, but, unable to return to the continent because of the continuing war against France, he reenlisted again, this time in the horse artillery of the King's German Legion. There he was put under the command of an arrogant young officer who took an immediate dislike to the sober orderly Bersling. After enduring his insults for about a year, Bersling deserted for a second time. Upon his arrival in London he was quickly identified as a deserter and was given the choice of being sent back to his old unit or reenlisting. Bersling chose the second option, spending another ten years in the Royal Marines.[25]

Another deserter who was motivated by harsh treatment is the Saxon *fourier* or company clerk Friedrich Christian Sohr, who deserted after receiving twenty-nine flats of a sabre for drunkenness and public disorder. Yet, while clearly resentful of his severe punishment, Sohr had another reason to flee, fearing the imminent regimental muster whose paperwork he had failed to prepare. The harsh conditions of military service also took their toll on Markus Uhlmann, who deserted after serving two months as *fledscher* in the Swiss regiment Lochmann in early 1759. Uhlmann's main concern, however, was not discipline, but disenchantment from life in the army. The service proved unexciting, the food was bad, and so was the company of his uncouth fellow soldiers. Moreover, Uhlmann was disappointed in his hopes to make additional income as a barber-surgeon because only half of his company shaved regularly and he received no patients from the field, as all wounded were sent directly to the main army hospital.[26]

[25] Bersling, *Der böhmische Veteran*, 85–8, 92–103, 123–4, 244–59.
[26] Sohr, *Meine Geschichte*, 89; Uhlmann, *Abwechslende Fortün*, 16–7.

With the exception of these accounts, no other author cites the severity of army life as the primary reason for deserting. Ulrich Bräker was an unwilling recruit, as was Johann Gottfried Seume, who was abducted into the Hessian and then into the Prussian service. Andrew Bryson, who deserted from the garrison of Martinique, was forced into the army as punishment for his role in the Irish Rebellion of 1798, while American sailor Ebenezer Fox enlisted into the British army after spending a number of months on the notorious prison hulk *Jersey*, which was moored in the New York East River. Fox took service not only to escape sickness and hunger, but also in order that he might desert as soon as opportunity arose. Taken to Jamaica to the 88th Regiment, Fox soon gained the trust of his officers and then arranged a daring escape which took him, together with four comrades, to Cuba, and then back to the United States. Another pressed man was Johann Heinrich Behrens, who was abducted into the Austrian army in 1755. However, it was not so much aversion to military service which led him to desert, but the fact that he was being forced to serve a foreign power. After a successful escape, he immediately reenlisted in the army of his native Saxony. Pressed into the Prussian service after the surrender at Pirna, Behrens used the opportunity to transfer into the Prussian Zeithen Hussars where he fought for much of the Seven Years War, until his wounds prevented him from serving further.[27]

William Burke served for over five years as an exemplary soldier who enjoyed the trust of his superiors, not least because during his time as a recruit, he volunteered to lead two search parties deep into the Irish countryside to arrest deserters from his regiment. Even at that early stage, Colonel Monkton suggested that one day Burke might be commissioned as an officer. Monkton's replacement was also kind to Burke, but his death in autumn 1777 dashed Burke's aspirations to be promoted to an officer's rank. Even when a vacancy came up in another regiment, Burke's new commanding officer refused to release him unless Burke could raise two recruits as his replacements. Disgusted, Burke deserted to the Americans a few weeks later. Another deserter with what was originally a good record was the Johann Friedrich Löffler. However, unlike Burke, Löffler was forced into a desertion plot by his own comrades, who burst into his quarters on Christmas night and threatened to kill him unless he joined them. Valentine Duckett also blamed bad company for his initial desertion, although his account, taken from his last statement before he was shot for his third desertion, withholds any specific details. Another

---

[27] Bräker, 'Lebensgeschichte'; Seume, *Werke*, vol. I, 85–6, Bryson, *Ordeal*, 7–15; E. Fox, *Adventures*, 142–5, 160–87; Behrens, 'Lebensgeschichte', 9–19.

man prompted by unfortunate circumstances was Corporal Johann Kaspar Steube of the Swedish Lifeguards, who deserted after wounding an opponent in a duel.[28]

Two deserters openly state that they were acting from what might be termed as ideological motives. The first was Sergeant Sullivan of the British 49th Regiment of Foot. In an appendix added to his journal behind the safety of the American lines, Sullivan tells how, after arriving in Boston, he was so impressed by the American fight for freedom that he decided to help them 'throw away the yoke under which my own native country sunk' (Sullivan was Irish). Sullivan's first attempt to reach the patriots by swimming across the Charles River was unsuccessful, and he had to wait almost three years for another opportunity, when he sneaked away from a British column during the evacuation of Philadelphia. Moreover, Sullivan claims he was prompted to desert for moral reasons: '[the] army in general was a repository of all manner of vice'.[29] Tellingly, although Sullivan's reasons for deserting commence with serious concerns for his freedom and his soul, he admits that his decision was also influenced by more immediate considerations: an insult from his lieutenant colonel, soon followed by a marriage to an American woman. It is much harder to make something of the story of the Quaker Thomas Watson, whose officers are said to have quietly encouraged him to abscond after they learned that he had become a committed pacifist. While this instance might at first strike us as bizarre, as we will see, old-regime officers did not necessarily pursue formal disciplinary action, especially when it could undermine the effectiveness of the military organisation. If he were to continue serving, Watson might convert more of his comrades, while persecuting a devout soldier might result in a scandal. Assuming that his account is correct, Watson was not the only man who deserted with the blessing of his superiors. In autumn 1793, Laukhard was ordered by Prince Hohenloe to desert into Landau in order to arrange the surrender of the fortress to the besieging Prussians. To make his desertion appear believable, Laukhard even started a rumour that he would soon be punished for his supposed revolutionary sympathies.[30]

---

[28] Burke, *Memoir*, 8–10, 17–20; Löffler, *Der alte Sergeant*, 99–100; Duckett, 'Life, Last Words, and Dying Speech', in: Hagist, *British Soldiers*, 85–6; Steube, *Wanderschaften und Schicksale*, 50–60.

[29] Sullivan, *From Redcoat to Rebel*, 221–2. Obviously, the first and much longer part of his journal written while Sullivan was still a British soldier has nothing of that sort, referring instead to the 'tyrannical congress' and is full of admiring descriptions of the heroic feats of the British army and the loyalty of its rank and file; see: ibid., 42–3, 92, 113.

[30] Watson, 'Some Account', 120–2; Laukhard, *Leben und Schicksale*, 322–32.

The last two desertion narratives considered in this study were produced by a totally different type of person: Peter Henly and Johann
Steininger were both skilful bounty-jumpers. The latter deserted fourteen
times, starting with the Piedmontese army, where he initially returned
voluntarily. Shortly afterwards, Steininger deserted again, reenlisting
in his native Württemberg. His first attempt to escape from his new
service failed, and Steininger was to be hanged, but the original sentence
was countermanded, and Steininger ran the gauntlet, providing one of
the few extant descriptions of the practice by the injured party rather
than an observer. Following a spell of hard labour, Steininger was pardoned after volunteering into a contingent destined to serve in Africa.
Deserting during the march, he began a spree of engagements in the
armies of France, Prussia, Austria, Denmark, Holland, the Palatinate
and Bavaria. Steininger's luck ran out again only on his thirteenth
desertion, this time from the Neapolitan army. He was subjected to
a mock execution, an experience Steininger found particularly
unnerving.[31] Henly's record is equally impressive and even more versatile. In addition to deserting from seven different British regiments, Henly
escaped three times from the marines, thrice from indentured service,
twice from the Royal Navy, and had one particularly lucky escape from
the Dutch West India Company. Henly failed only once when attempting
to desert the 60th Regiment and received 200 lashes, a punishment that
Henly himself found ridiculously lenient.[32]

Enlisting in one regiment, collecting the engagement bonus and then
deserting to restart the whole process again was a widespread practice in
old-regime Europe. The French had not one but two terms to describe
such men, *Rouleurs* and *Billardeurs*. A contemporary report from 1712
argues that as many as 30,000 French soldiers, about one-tenth of the
entire army, did nothing but desert and reenlist in regiment after
regiment.[33] Bounty-jumpers were particularly notorious, as their exploits
proved very costly to the recruiting service. Muth has already marvelled at
why men were willing to engage in such a risky practice. If punishments
for deserters were severe already, those reengaging could expect even
harsher treatment.[34] The experiences of Henly and Steininger suggest
a possible answer. It is not only the ease of their escapes which is so
striking, but also the overall impunity with which these were met. When
caught, Steininger either went unpunished, or was spared the worst
possible fate he could initially expect. Interestingly, after coming within

[31] Steininger, *Leben und Abenteuer*.
[32] Henly, *Life*, 30. Henly deserted from the 60th a few days after the punishment.
[33] It is cited in Corvisier, *L'Armée Française*, vol. II, 725–8.   [34] Muth, *Flucht*, 103.

a hairsbreadth of being executed, and seeing two of his accomplices shot at his side, Steininger decided to reconsider his old ways. After deserting one last time, Steininger enlisted in the French army, where he served loyally for almost fifty years, which suggests that, at least in his case, punishment finally did provide a deterrent of sorts. Likewise, Bräker recalls the gauntlets he witnessed in Berlin as the reason why he did not attempt to flee earlier. Nevertheless, fear of punishment did not dissuade him from deserting, but rather cautioned him to choose the moment carefully.[35]

Henly also knew to take his chances well. After enlisting for the third time in the Marines, he was recognised by a former comrade from the 1st Regiment of Foot who denounced Henly in order to obtain the twenty-shillings bounty due to informers. Henly quickly thwarted his designs by declaring he belonged to the 48th Foot. As he had served there before the 1st Foot, the 48th Regiment had priority over Henly and he was sent to rejoin it. Henly, however, was never actually *present* in that regiment, for he escaped from a draft destined to join it some years before while the 48th was still stationed in the Caribbean. After his arrival, its officers were only too pleased to receive a new soldier they had never seen before. For the sake of correct procedure, Henly was quickly acquitted in a sham court martial and then allowed to rejoin his old corps, where he duly remained for the next four months. Declaring oneself as a deserter from another regiment or even a different service was a common ploy, and Henly knew this, for he used the same trick to get out of the Royal Navy by declaring himself a deserter from the army. If the thirty-odd desertions undertaken by Steininger and Henly can be used as a crude sample, desertion did not necessarily lead to arrest, while arrest did not unavoid-ably result in punishment, let alone a very severe one. Likewise in the case of Seume, who was taken on two of his four desertion attempts. The first time, he was pardoned at the preliminary hearing, and the second time his sentence was mitigated at the head of the gauntlet to six weeks' confine-ment on bread and water.[36]

To conclude the second part of the discussion, we have seen that first-hand accounts present a more nuanced image of desertion than its being a mere by-product of harsh discipline. Initial unwillingness to serve among pressed men like Seume and Bryson meant that they would likely

---

[35] Henly, *Life*, 25; Bräker, 'Lebensgeschichte', 447–8, 450. Seume also appeared to weigh the possibilities of success when he refused to join a desertion plot while held in a recruit depot in Hesse and also later when he was rather reluctant to join a friend who was planning to desert and proceed by foot from Halifax to Boston; see: *Werke*, vol. I, 64–5, 95–6.

[36] Henly, *Life*, 16, 25–6; Seume, *Werke*, vol. I, 103–5.

attempt to escape sooner or later. The decision to desert could be provoked by specific concerns, such as the unjust treatment by an officer received by Burke and Sullivan. While nowadays this term has fallen out of favour, combat fatigue might actually well describe Bersling's condition before his first desertion. Bersling served from the age of fifteen, and fought continuously since the age of seventeen. He was been badly burned on one occasion, and had a number of comrades blown to pieces on his side, including a fellow Czech artilleryman who first suggested they might desert together. Alternatively, the decision to desert could be the result of singularly favourable circumstances, as happened to Bräker after his descent from Lobosch Hill, when he noticed there were no Prussian officers nearby. Finally, as seen in the account of the bounty-jumpers Henly and Steininger, even when taken, the deserter could still avoid some of the rigours of military justice. So far, we were able to question the relative height of old-regime desertion rates. Moreover, as seen from the cases of the Prussian, Saxon and French armies, annual desertion rates declined towards the end of the century. The last part of this chapter will aim to provide an explanation for this phenomenon as well as offer an alternative cause influencing levels of desertion: the general inadequacy of the authorities in old-regime Europe to apprehend and punish deserters.

Assuming that old-regime desertion rates were indeed as high as commonly argued, this may actually point to the *failure* of the preventive control mechanisms to provide a viable deterrent. Moreover, if a disciplinary system fails to create the desired effect, what does it actually say of its alleged harshness? Although surviving desertion narratives are insufficient to solve these questions, they are still useful to illustrate a general principle. To rephrase our query, were Steininger and Henly exceptionally lucky in deceiving the authorities for so long, or was their overall success actually representative of what could be expected by a typical escapee? To answer this, we resorted to samples from surviving muster rolls, court martial proceedings and overall desertion statistics drawn from Austrian, British and French military archives. These were examined to determine not only the proportion of apprehended deserters within the overall number of fugitives, but also the percentage of the former who were punished, as well as the severity of their sentences. The information thus proved valuable not only to determine the actual practice of old-regime discipline, but also the deterrent effect it was likely to play.

The decision to rely on muster rolls is not without its difficulties. For instance, it is sometimes argued that desertion from old-regime armies was underreported to save embarrassment to the officers or to allow them to pocket the pay of the missing men.[37] Yet the possibility that muster rolls are skewed towards lower desertion figures only reinforces our argument, for it implies that the effectiveness of military control methods was lower than generally allowed. Moreover, the alleged unreliability of eighteenth-century military records did not prevent historians from reaching the conclusion that desertion was high enough already, and that the primary cause behind it was harsh discipline. A more immediate challenge for a statistical study of muster rolls relates to the temptation to sum up their total figures. Thus, a soldier attempting to desert three times might appear as three individual deserters. Moreover, not every desertion was an irrecoverable loss. Some deserters were apprehended, or returned voluntarily. Thus, desertion rates based on *gross* figures could actually inflate the losses the unit experienced in reality, but *net* desertion figures are even more challenging to calculate. The French muster rolls, for example, consist of notebooks which were renewed as rarely as once a decade. Thus, a *contrôle* is accurate only for the moment when the notebook was filled up. Moreover, as men were continuously shuffled from company to company, the same soldier could appear on records of two or more companies, inflating the total strength of the regiment. The same is true for returning deserters who might be given a new entry and counted as two different individuals instead of one.[38] Compared to the French *contrôles*, the Austrian *Musterliste* are more comprehensive. Renewed in theory at least once a year, they included a separate notebook for every company, to which were appended two monthly tables of all men who joined and left the unit since the last muster. Individual company rolls were further supplemented by a *Mustertabelle*: a large spreadsheet adding up their totals for the whole regiment. The Austrian figures are thus better suited for broader statistical analysis.

As they were updated on a rolling basis, French rolls often contain material on the fate of individual deserters. Their entries would first include the date of escape and then would be amended further if the man was caught and punished. However, if the entry had no other references expect the trial *in absentia*, it can be assumed that the man was not recaptured by the time the roll was completed. British muster rolls mention returning deserters, but give no information about whether they were arrested or returned voluntarily. The rolls also make no reference to punishment, but the National Archives preserve over a thousand court martial records, which have been further studied in detail by Sylvia Frey and Arthur Gilbert. On the other hand, the Viennese *Kriegsarchiv*

---

[37] Kennett, *French Armies*, 80-1, 84; Guy, *Oeconomy and Discipline*, 109.
[38] On the French rolls, see: Corvisier, *Contrôles de troupes*, vol. I, 5–30.

does not preserve trials of common soldiers before the Napoleonic Wars. The rolls mention men executed or sent to hard labour, but without reference to the crime for which they were convicted. Thus, while the records of all the three armies contain evidence on desertion, military justice and discipline, it comes from different types of archival material. Therefore, we utilised those groupings of material in which each archive is the strongest. For Kew, these were the court martial proceedings; for France, general correspondence from the Ministry of War supplemented by samples of court martial verdicts; and for Austria, a large number of rolls combined into a statistical database. Data from the different armies was then compared. The resulting picture is more ambiguous than the clear-cut verdict given by historians of old-regime Europe. Strict codes and harsh justice were prevalent, but, for much of the century, there were ways to circumvent these.

Before 1716, French deserters were to have their nose and ears cropped, branded with hot iron and then sent to perpetual service in the Mediterranean fleet. While formally reinstated that year, the death penalty was not implemented universally. In practice, every three deserters drew lots: one would be executed and the remaining two mutilated and sent to the galleys. This policy remained in force for sixty years, prompting General Rochambeau to argue that desertion was more severely punished in France than anywhere else in Europe.[39] The ordinances of 1716 also codified the pursuit of deserters. The captains were to forward to Versailles the names and descriptions of the fugitives for compilation in special booklets which were distributed every three months to the officers of the military police and the fortress commandants. From 1730, deserters were to be tried *in absentia* and their verdicts also reported to Versailles. If arrested, the deserter would undergo a preliminary hearing before the major followed by a court martial (*conseil de guerre*) consisting of seven officers, presided over by the regimental commander or governor of the garrison. After members of the board received an account of the hearing, the defendant was brought for interrogation. Following this last opportunity to defend himself, the accused was led out and the court proceeded to vote on the verdict. Such a sentence was called *jugement contradictoire*. If the defendant was found guilty, the punishment was to be carried out immediately.[40]

Military justice in old-regime France left the men at the mercy of their immediate superiors. This, together with the severe punishments

---

[39] Corvisier, *L'Armée Française*, vol. II, 694–5, 719–21; Michon, *Justice Militaire*, 8–9; Lynn, *Giant*, 411–4; SHD GR 1 M 1783, item 39, 'Mémoire sur la désertion par le comte de Rochambeau', Strasbourg (8 August 1764).

[40] Corvisier, *L'Armée Française*, vol. II, 716–7; Michon, *Justice Militaire*, 6–7.

prescribed for desertion and other military misdemeanours,[41] appears, at first, to support Rochambeau, as do the surviving court records at Vincennes. Of the 1,522 cases preserved from the Seven Years War, almost all of them deserters, 1,104 men were sentenced to death and most of those remaining to perpetual galleys.[42] In 1759, for instance, out of 252 court cases, 201 were deserters, of whom all but ten were found guilty. Six were pardoned and one was to be sent back to his unit. The rest, however, with the exception of five sent to the galleys, were sentenced to be shot or hanged.[43]

However, 201 trials is not a large figure for an army which lost some 10,000 deserters that year alone. Nor is it sufficient to assume that the majority of court proceedings were lost. Even if Vincennes preserves a mere *twentieth* of actual courts martial records, half of the desertion cases still remain unaccounted for. But the actual fate of many deserters can still be deduced from a few surviving notes juxtaposed inside the piles of surviving verdicts. For instance, on 5 May 1759, a *milice* officer forwarded to Versailles a *jugement contradictoire* of a deserter sentenced to perpetual galleys. According to the sender, this verdict was accompanied by trials *in absentia* of another fourteen soldiers. Major Dramand of the Bourbonnais Infantry Regiment had twenty-two trials *in absentia* attached to a single actual verdict against one of his men.[44] Similarly, Corvisier found that, in 1754, in the whole of the regiment of Royal Cantabres there were ninety-eight trials *in absentia* compared to eight *jugements contradictoires*. Of the latter, the accused were dealt with according to the traditional view of old-regime military justice: five were executed and one sent to the galleys.[45] Nevertheless, the overwhelming majority of deserters went unpunished. Of the 267 surviving court cases for 1760–2 preserved in the archives in Western France, 262 produced death

---

[41] Some of the punishments mentioned in the ordnances of 1727 include death for disobedience to officer, death or corporal punishment when disobeying sergeant, hanging for looting churches, burning for sacrilege and piercing of the tongue for blasphemers. All these punishments were reconfirmed in 1784; see: Michon, *Justice Militaire*, 7–8.

[42] Preserved in SHD GR 1 J 20–29, the totals are calculated in Planchais, *Déserteurs Français*, 11–20.

[43] Men charged with other offences were not better off. Of eleven mutineers all were sentenced to perpetual galleys; from all twenty-three thieves, twenty-two were sentenced either to death or to the galleys. Of the murderers, eight out of nine were executed. Calculations based on the material in SHD GR 1 J 24.

[44] SHD GR 1 J 24 and 1 J 20. The latter note sent on 12 December 1751 is cited by Planchais, who discovered another case of militia regiment of Auvergne which, in the spring of 1757, had thirty-seven trials *in absentia* compared to five *judgement contradictories*, see: Planchais, *Déserteurs Français*, 13.

[45] There was also a militiamen who left his unit to engage in the regiment. His penalty was life service in his old unit which he deserted in order to join the regular army. The last of the eight was acquitted, see: Corvisier, *L'Armée Française*, vol. II, 738.

Table 2.1 *Absolute desertion figures, France 1716–8*

Dates covered	2.7.1716–31.12.1717			1.1.1718–30.4.1718		
	Number	Percentage		Number	Percentage	
Denounced deserters	11,499	100%		1,150	100%	
Arrested	680	6%<	100%	142	<12%	100%
Executed	360		53%	68		48%
Galleys	85		12.5%	11		7.75%
Transferred abroad	34		5%			

sentences, but only twenty-one executions could be ascertained, leading
Bois to conclude that the reality of French military justice was not as
severe as usually portrayed.[46]

Nevertheless, it is hard to reach a definite conclusion, unless one compares the total number of desertions to the number of the men arrested and
punished. Vincennes preserves such statistics for 1716–8, which are summarised in Table 2.1.[47] Again, the fate of the apprehended deserters was
harsh. Over half of the men who were arrested were executed. Adding
those sentenced to perpetual banishment or slavery, over two-thirds were
severely punished. In total, however, less than 7 per cent of all deserters
were actually captured. This table closely resembles the conditions prevailing a generation later. During the Seven Years Wars, most deserters who
were caught were dealt with as harshly, but their cases were a small minority
among the overall instances of desertion. Between 1 January 1757 and 31
March 1761, the army formally reported 18,317 trials *in absentia*, but it is
estimated that at least a third of such verdicts went unreported and that the
actual number of deserters tried *in absentia* during that period was about six
thousand per year.[48] Any conclusion about the severity of French military
discipline up to 1763 has to be tempered by the fact that the great majority
of deserters were able to escape successfully.

Unlike in France, British military justice operated two tiers of courts.
Consisting of five officers, the Regimental Court Martial judged minor
infractions for which corporal punishment could be given. The General
Court Martial (GCM) was to adjudicate capital offences. Thus, desertion

[46] Bois, *Anciens soldats*, 99–100.
[47] SHD GR 1 M 1783, item 2, 'Extrait du quatrième registre des délibérations du Conseil
de la guerre, depuis le 1er Janvier 1718 jusqu'au 24 septembre suivant', fol. 3.
[48] SHD GR 1 M 1783, item 238, untitled; see also: 1 M 1783 item 240 'Etat par généralités
de number des Soldats, Cavaliers et Dragons accuses de desertion qui sont détenus dans
les différents prisons du Royaume et dans cella de l'armeé' (1762).

cases were heard before thirteen senior officers drawn from different regiments. Moreover, the proceedings were led by a deputy judge advocate whose duty was to ensure that the trial was conducted fairly. The summary of the court was to be sent to the Office of the Judge Advocate General (JAG), who then forwarded the verdict for the confirmation of the monarch.[49] Although surviving court martial records for the British army are known to be incomplete, the those that are available still record a substantial number of trials, which provide a more representative picture of the workings of the higher tier of British military courts than any other contemporary source. When compared with the French archival material, it appears that the situation in the two armies was rather similar. Although arrest could lead to a severe punishment, most deserters were able to avoid this fate altogether.

Between 1714 and 1720, Kew preserves a total of 215 desertion cases. At first, they appear to corroborate the severity attributed to old-regime military justice. Of the 198 guilty verdicts, 172 men were sentenced to death, and all but one of the remaining offenders were to be given corporal punishment, usually three gauntlets through their whole regiment.[50] But once the sentences were forwarded to London, the situation changed dramatically. Over half of the deserters under sentence of death were reprieved, while another twenty-nine were ordered to draw lots, producing a further eighteen pardons. On the other hand, from the deserters sentenced to corporal punishment, almost all sentences were confirmed, and only three men were pardoned. Interestingly, under such conditions, a court wishing to ensure a higher probability that its ruling would be upheld was more likely to sentence the accused to corporal punishment than to death. Thus, the royal prerogative put an additional restraint on the courts. Furthermore, the privilege to dispense pardon was absolute. For example, in 1717, after sentencing a deserter to death, a court martial in Berwick-upon-Tweed resolved that, if reprieved, the offender would run the gauntlet; the JAG replied that royal pardons were unconditional.[51] Such a system was not so much merciful as

---

[49] *Rules and Articles,* (1708). arts. 53–7; TNA WO 71/2 'Rules, etc. Articles of War', Articles of War 1718 arts. 17 and 20; Articles of War 1748, section 15, arts. 1–22. This version of the articles which covers the conduct of courts martial remained unchanged till the end of the century. See also the instructions in WO 85/1 'Judge Advocate General's Office; deputation Books, 1751 May 25 – 1768 July 15'. For more on the JAG's role, see: Stuart-Smith, 'Military Law', 481–3.

[50] Only fourteen men were acquitted and another three were to be retried for more minor offences. Calculations based on TNA WO 71/14 'General Court Martial 1710 April–1722 July', fols. 52–290 and WO 71/34 'General Court Martial 1715 Nov–1723 June', fols. 2–350.

[51] GCM of John Leernberg (19 December 1717), TNA WO 71/12, fol. 21 and 71/34, fols. 262–7. This offender eventually received a full pardon.

Table 2.2 *Actual fate of the accused found guilty for desertion at GCMs 1714–20*[52]

		Actual fate of the defendants				
Guilty verdicts for desertion		Executed	Corporal punishment	Pardoned	Other punishment	Totals
Aggravating circumstances	Yes	30–36 (47.5–57.1%)	7 (11.1%)	17–23 (27–36.5%)	3 (4.8%)	63 (100%)
	No	26–34 (19.6–25.2%)	16 (12%)	84–92 (62.2–68.2%)	1 (1%<)	135 (100%)
Total number of cases		60 (30.3%)	23 (11.6%)	111 (56%)	4 (2%)	198 (100%)

capricious. The monarch could reach different decisions in two identical cases, one after the other. This apparently arbitrary and inconsistent behaviour emphasised his right to do as he pleased, without being subjected to any particular imperative.

Even so, some patterns can be discerned in the circumstances under which pardons were granted. The courts could influence the king's decision by recommending mercy,[53] which almost always resulted in reprieve. Of the thirty-two guilty deserters recommended for this favour, thirty were pardoned, and two others had their sentences mitigated. Another distinct trend is seen in confirmation of GCM sentences. A further breakdown of desertion cases reveals that the king was more likely to refuse clemency when desertion was accompanied by additional offences, as demonstrated in Table 2.2.[54]

While twice as likely to confirm the death sentences of those found guilty of desertion with aggravating circumstances, the king reprieved

[52] In this table, men ordered to draw lots are divided between the death and the pardon categories depending on the numbers which were executed and reprieved in every such batch. In cases of mixed batches which included offenders with and without aggravating circumstances, their numbers were added to both categories. Mitigated sentences were added to the relevant category according to the punishment actually inflicted.

[53] In such cases, the court was expected to justify its recommendation. Common explanations included: previous good character of the offender, his youth, stupidity, ignorance of the military law, long service or wounds sustained in recent wars. One soldier was even recommended for mercy on medical grounds, the court noting that the offender 'is sometimes crazy', 'GCM of William Manning' (12 July 1716), TNA WO 71/14, fol. 134 and WO 71/34, fol. 112.

[54] To qualify as such, desertion had to be accompanied by reenlistment, robbery, embezzlement or jailbreak; recurrent desertion was also considered as an aggravated offence.

two-thirds of the men charged with no further offences. Tellingly, even without this subdivision, over half of the deserters were pardoned. Adding in the cases resulting in acquittal, over 60 per cent of the defendants went unpunished. Considering these trends, it can be said that English military justice was not blind or bloodthirsty. It did give out severe punishments, but it then had substantial numbers annulled just as easily. Rather than being unremitting, it was arbitrary and subjected almost every deserter to fear of punishment, rather than inflicting it on each and every one of them.

The comparison between French and British courts martial shows a number of similarities. Apprehended deserters would most probably be sentenced to death. At the same time, most deserters successfully avoided punishment, either because they evaded capture, or through royal pardons. It is clear that the majority of French deserters escaped altogether, while the prospects of those unlucky few who were arrested were worse than in Britain. The proportion of apprehended deserters who were actually punished was lower in Britain than in France. It is impossible to say, though, whether this also means that the British authorities were arresting a higher proportion of their deserters. Circumstantial evidence suggests that desertion at that time hit the British army as heavily as the French. For instance, following the GCM of Edward Seager, his colonel wrote to the JAG asking him to persuade George I to confirm the death sentence, saying that the regiment had lost some 200 deserters in less than a year and that its men were in 'need of example'.[55] During the Seven Years War, the situation in the French army appears to have been similar – recaptured deserters would be severely punished, but the majority of fugitives were never recovered. British figures for that war are insufficient to make a direct comparison, yet, as in the French case, there was a substantial discrepancy between the total number of reported desertion cases and the actual number of surviving trial proceedings. In 1758, there were 613 instances of desertion from the troops stationed in Great Britain, a gross desertion rate of 3.9 per cent. Next year, the respective figures were 475 and 3.4 per cent. In 1759, some 4,000 men deserted from the British army. In comparison, for the whole period between 1756 and 1762, the National Archives preserve 455 desertion cases from all of the marching regiments combined.[56] All this suggests that only a minority of deserters were actually brought before a GCM.

---

[55] TNA WO 71/14 fols. 61–2 and WO 71/34 fols. 4–6. Colonel Pocock was granted his request. For examples of desertion statistics from the time of the War of the Spanish Succession, see also: Scouller, *Armies of Queen Anne*, 293–4; Fortescue, *History of the British Army*, vol. I, 571.

[56] Gilbert, 'Why Men Deserted', 557–8.

In Austria, deserters were first given a preliminary hearing. Unlike in the French and British armies, the board consisted of representatives drawn from every rank, from captain down to private. If court martial was recommended, the jury was doubled to fourteen members, presided over by the major and assisted by the regimental auditor. The verdict was determined by majority of votes, with junior members voting first.[57] Unfortunately, the lack of actual Austrian court records does not allow us to conclude whether the role of enlisted members of the jury was as important as the regulations state. According to Duffy, it was not unknown for the auditor to arrive at the proceedings with the sentence already drafted according to the wishes of the commanding officer.

Despite the wealth of material contained in the Austrian musters, straightforward analysis is difficult because of the discrepancy between the prescribed form of the rolls and their actual contents. Originally, musters were forwarded to Vienna twice a year, in May and November, until the new regulation of 1769 reduced this to one annual submission in springtime or the summer. In reality, however, rolls could be submitted in any month and cover completely random periods of time. Moreover, surviving musters could cover separate detachments, and it is not uncommon to have parts of the same regiment simultaneously covered by two or even three parallel rolls. Therefore, a model had to be devised to integrate data from rolls starting in different months, running for different periods of time and covering whole regiments or only parts thereof.

This was formed by consulting musters from the reign of Empress Maria Theresa, which were utilised to create a single statistical database containing the relative figures for desertion rates, apprehended and returning deserters and the use of the heaviest military penalties. The sample was created by taking at least eight different infantry regiments for every single calendar year from 1740 to 1779. During this period, the Habsburg Empire maintained between fifty and sixty regular infantry regiments.[58] Thus our sample covers at least 12.5 per cent of the entire Austrian army during these years. When one considers the uneven preservation record, with some regiments missing half of their muster rolls, then the size of the current sample as a fraction of the existing archival data is, in fact, even higher. The regiments were chosen at random, but it was ensured that the sample also included Hungarian and Walloon Infantry regiments, which formed a distinct part of the Habsburg army. In these years the Austria endured three separate conflicts: the more

---

[57] *Regulament und Ordnung*, (1737), 99–106; *Reglement für die sämmentlich-Kaiserlich-Königliche Infanterie*, (1769), 155–8.
[58] Hochedlinger, *Austria's Wars*, 301, Table 13.

desperate War of the Austrian Succession; the Seven Years War, which saw the Empire coming frustratingly close to defeating Frederick the Great; and the shorter and comparatively uneventful War of the Bavarian Succession. There were also two relatively prolonged periods of peace. Between 1748 and 1756, the army was reformed in anticipation of a new war against Prussia. Following the Peace of Hubertusburg in 1763, a second set of even more ambitious reforms was undertaken by Emperor Joseph II and his protégée FieldMarshal Lacy. Thus, our database covers substantial phases of wartime and peacetime service.

The basic template employed to organise this material was a single table running from 1740 to 1779, with every year subdivided into months. The values from every *Mustertabelle* were inserted for the relevant month, allowing for rolls covering longer periods to contribute more towards the database. The table was then subjected to horizontal averaging by months. Thus, irrespective of their size, composition and service location, all regiments possessed an equal power factor contributing to the monthly average. The monthly figures were then averaged again for the entire calendar year. The justification for this measure was to downscale the influence of a minority of incomplete rolls which covered detachments rather than entire regiments, while still retaining their contribution to the database. The reason why such partial rolls were not excluded from the database is twofold. Firstly, in wartime, many regiments were subdivided, making complete musters rare. Moreover, because of the random nature of the archival holdings and the inability to anticipate the precise contents of each and every carton, there were instances when not every month was covered by data from enough regiments. The double averaging allowed smoothing over of such instances among the majority of normative cases, when every month was covered by muster rolls from eight regiments or more. The information obtained from this database corroborates the material from the first half of the eighteenth century considered for Britain and France. Up to the Seven Years War, most Austrian deserters had escaped. Nonetheless, there was a gradual decline in absolute desertion figures, which became particularly apparent after 1763. Not only did the portion of arrested deserters grow, there was also a corresponding increase in voluntary returns. This resulted in an even greater decline in net desertion figures because the overall number of annual desertion attempts had fallen as well.

Figure 2.1 is a vertical bar chart representing three different parameters. The overall height of the columns shows the gross annual desertion rate, which is the percentage of deserters from all soldiers who served during the respective calendar year. The lower light part of every bar displays the actual *net* desertion level by indicating share of deserters who were able to

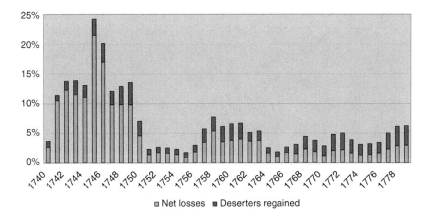

Figure 2.1 – Desertion from the Habsburg army (1740–79): annual rates

escape successfully. The dark upper part of the columns shows the proportion of deserters who reverted back into service. The first point evident from this diagram is that desertion was higher in wartime. From an all-time high during the War of the Austrian Succession, desertion decreased in the early 1750s, only to rise again after the Seven Years War broke out. However, gross desertion rates were only about half the size when compared to the previous conflict. Even more importantly, the fraction of the men who were regained also rose when compared to the War of the Austrian Succession. This later parameter became even more prevalent after 1763. During the 1760s and 1770s gross annual desertion rates had fallen under 5 per cent, but now over half and sometimes as many as two-thirds of all escapees made it back into the army. Consequently, the irrecoverable losses from desertion sustained in the latter half of Maria's Theresa's reign measured at most 2 per cent per year.[59]

Figure 2.2 looks in greater detail at the fate of Austrian deserters. Just like a typical *Mustertabelle* it shows not only the figures for deserters who escaped successfully but also the subdivision between deserters who were detained or arrested and deserters who chose to return to their units or to surrender themselves voluntarily.[60] This diagram confirms further that the

---

[59] Desertion rose again during the two years of the War of the Bavarian Succession, but both its gross and net levels were even lower than during the Seven Years War.

[60] Arrested deserters were indicated on the rolls as *attrapirter* (caught) or *erkanter* (recognised) when they tried to reenlist into another regiment. Fugitives who tried escaping abroad and were sent back to Austria were also grouped with the detained deserters. Returning deserters were indicated on the rolls as *revertirter* (returned) or *selbst gemeldet*.

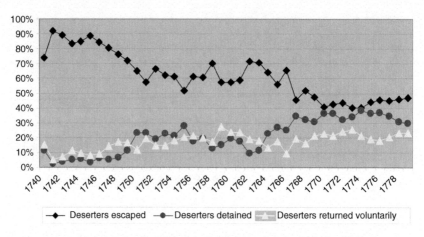

Figure 2.2 – Desertion from the Habsburg army (1740–79): outcome

ratio of successful desertions during the reign of Maria Theresa fell dramatically. During the War of the Austrian Succession, less than one out of ten deserters was taken, but even during the peaceful years of the early 1750s, three deserters out of five would not make it back into the army. This trend reversed during the Seven Years War, but within a decade from 1763, the share of detained deserters increased to at least one third, sometimes even 40 per cent of all deserters. Successful escapes now came to well under half of all desertion cases. This said, the authorities were never able to arrest the majority of the fugitives. The decline in net desertion rates also depended on another factor: the more deserters were taken the more came back themselves. The relation between there two parameters is further confirmed by Figure 2.3. This diagram annuls the chronological factor, with each of the thirty-nine annual figures from Figure 2.1 arranged on axis X according to their absolute value. Axis Y gives the number of deserters returning in that year. This material was then used to create an arithmetic trendline and to calculate a correlation coefficient.[61]

When combined together, the information from the previous three diagrams suggests that the successful suppression of desertion did not require the arrest of each and every fugitive. Even in the 1770s, typically only one out of three deserters was actually captured. Nevertheless, it is evident that when the chances of being caught increased, more men returned

The later term denotes cases when a deserter formally declared himself to the authorities or to members of another military unit.

[61] The correlation coefficient between these two series is equal to the derivative of the arithmetic trendline. It is 0.606765 indicating substantial positive correlation.

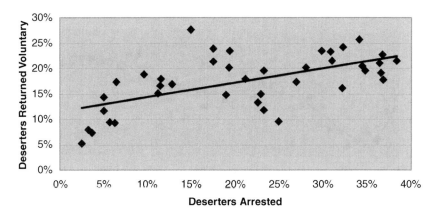

Figure 2.3 – Ratio – deserters detained: deserters returned

voluntarily. In other words, a higher percentage of apprehended deserters exercised a deterrent effect. However, it is known that fugitives who surrendered themselves would be spared the harshness of military law. During the Seven Years War, returning deserters were welcomed back no matter what feeble excuse they offered,[62] and if that was the wartime practice, when desertion was a capital offence, it is unlikely that returning deserters would fare worse in time of peace.[63] As in the French army, it appears that most Austrian deserters escaped without loss of life and limb, either by avoiding capture altogether or by choosing to surrender themselves. Thus, a minority of all cases, that is, only those actually caught, were potentially subject to the full rigours of military penalties reserved for deserters. The question, of course, is how many had actually undergone such punishments. Contemporary opinion considered Austrian military justice to be severe, particularly with regard to the death penalty, which was said to have been inflicted more often than in the Prussian service. The Austrian use of corporal punishment, on the other hand, was not particularly esteemed,

---

[62] According to Christopher Duffy, by the end of the war 'desertion became a thing that was little counted' with swarms of bounty-jumpers switching sides with impunity, see: *Instrument of War*, 214; For an example of deserters asking to be readmitted back into their units, see: Grotehenn, *Briefe*, 48.

[63] According to the company muster rolls, returning deserters would be placed at the end of the list. This meant loss of seniority and, at least in theory, demotion to the status of a recruit. Capitulants, that is men serving under a fixed contract, were also likely to restart their term anew – although even this was not always the case. For instance, the eight-year contract of Private Friedrich Diez, a capitulant at Eder's company of *Infanterie Regiment* 28, was renewed only after he returned from his second desertion attempt, see: ÖStA KA ML 2374.

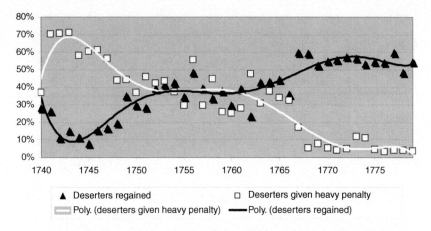

Figure 2.4 – Ratio – deserters regained: deserters punished

and according to one observer (an officer) the Austrian gauntlet was just about sufficient to increase one's blood circulation.[64] Whether this evaluation was indeed correct matters little, however, as Austrian rolls from the time of Maria Theresa make no reference to corporal punishments, leaving this important aspect of old-regime military discipline hidden from the modern researcher. However, the rolls mention in their totals soldiers who were executed or sentenced to hard labour. These figures were used in turn to analyse the incidence of the two severest military penalties to which Austrian deserters could undergo.

This was calculated by dividing the sum of the men executed or sent to hard labour by the total number of arrested deserters, as it appears on every individual *Mustertabelle*. Of course, not every soldier punished like this was a deserter. Instead, these figures provide us with an estimated maximum potential of an arrested deserter to undergo one of the heavy military punishments. Represented as the white series on Figure 2.4, it is seen that the incidence of sentences of capital punishments or sentences of forced labour was the highest during the War of the Austrian Succession. It declined until 1756, rose somewhat after the outbreak of the Seven Years War, but after 1763, the use of those penalties had fallen substantially. By the early 1770s these would befall, at the very most, on

---

[64] Quoted in C. Duffy, *Instrument of War*, 210–1. Muth has questioned this assertion, asking whether there is such a great difference between running thirty-six gauntlets through 100 men and ten gauntlets between 300 men. Muth was referring to the maximum punishments given according to the Prussian and Austrian regulations, respectively, see: *Flucht*, 39, n. 71.

one out of twenty arrested deserters. Interestingly, this overall decline in the implementation of the heaviest punishments corresponds with the decline in irrecoverable losses from desertion seen in the previous diagrams. This is demonstrated further by the black series on Figure 2.4, which represents the sum of the two series for detained and returning deserters, borrowed from Figure 2.2.[65] It appears that the pattern prevailing in the late Theresian army resembles that described by modern criminologists who point out that deterrence is more a function of higher indictment rates than the severity of the sentence.[66] Assuming that Austrian military justice mirrored the practices of its European counter-parts whose records have survived, a defendant taken before a court martial could almost certainly expect a guilty verdict. Consequently, a higher likelihood of arrest increased the chance for surer punishment. The fact that effective abolition of the death penalty for peacetime desertion after 1763 limited it to corporal punishment made little difference. The mutual increase in the percentages of arrested and returning deserters, coinciding with the introduction of more lenient penal procedures, suggests that it was the greater probability of a more moderate punishment, rather than a lesser chance of its being dealt with exemplary severity, which potential and actual deserters found more intimidating.

One of the most evident developments revealed by our database is the sharp decrease in net desertion figures after the end of the Seven Years War. Although this corresponds with the post-1763 reforms, which undeniably improved the conditions of the Austrian soldiery, this change appears to have more sinister roots. Despite the genuine concern for the welfare of the rank and file, the primary aim of the reforms was the creation of a more efficient military force. Enhancing control and surveillance through a programme of barrack-building was one such innovation.[67] Even before 1756, bounties could be paid for the arrest of Austrian deserters. Now, however, this became a standard policy. The new army regulations of 1769 directed that civilians who brought back a deserter were entitled to a cash bounty of twenty-four *florins*. Similarly, if a fugitive was detained by a military party, the captors were rewarded with eight *florins*. Moreover, from now on, the official template for a regimental *Mustertabelle* subdivided the figures between deserters detained by civilians and by members of the military.[68] Evidence from the rolls suggests this policy has been introduced gradually over the previous few

---

[65] The correlation coefficient between the two series in Figure 2.4 measures -0.87113, which denotes a very high negative correlation.

[66] See for instance: Hirsch, *Criminal Deterrence*, 25–7.

[67] Hochedlinger, *Austria's Wars*, 291–325.

[68] *Reglament für für die sämmentlich-Kaiserlich-Königliche Infanterie*, (1769), additional figure n. 2, following page 132.

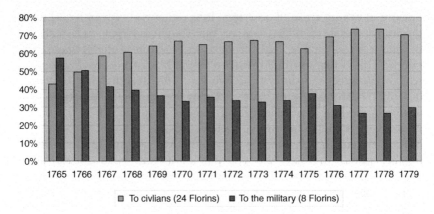

Figure 2.5 – Deserter bounties paid by the Habsburg army (1765–79)

years. The Harsch Infantry Regiment was among the first to put this information on its rolls as early as 1765. During 1766, more and more regiments introduced the subdivision between civilian and military deserter bounties, and by the autumn muster of 1767, the practice has become general for the entire army.[69] Based on this data, Figure 2.5 demonstrates the substantial role which civilians came to play in the pursuit of Austrian deserters.

Strikingly, the decline in desertion from the Austrian service after 1763 owed less to the effectiveness of direct control mechanisms. The practice standardised by the regulations of 1769 essentially privatised the pursuit of deserters. Ironically, to increase control over their troops, the Habsburgs had to resort to the cooperation of their civilian subjects. This is an important point, suggestive of the limits of state power even in the relatively well-managed enlightened absolutist monarchy. What can be said then of the situation in other states which were badly-managed, unenlightened or non-absolutist? Mere offers of bounties for the arrest of deserters were clearly insufficient. In France, a reward of thirty *livres* was promised for the capture of a deserter, but the authorities continuously complained that civilians were more likely to assist runway soldiers rather than to surrender them.[70] Although the unwillingness of the French to betray deserters could be linked

---

[69] ÖStA KA ML 10.466 '50 Infanterie Regiment' (1765). Units which introduced the new measure in 1766 include infantry regiments Marchall (spring muster) and Wied (autumn muster). Kaiser, Hildburghausen and the Karolyi Hungarian infantry regiment introduced this information onto their roll during the autumn muster of 1767, see: ÖStA KA ML 1408 'Infanterie Regiment 18' (1766); ÖStA KA ML 2713 'Infanterie Regiment 28 (1766); ÖStA KA ML 10 'Infanterie Regiment 1' (1767); ÖStA KA ML 528 'Infanterie Regiment 8'; ÖStA KA ML 4388 (1766–7).

[70] M.S. Anderson, *War and Society*, 128–9.

with growing public sympathy towards the plight of common soldiers,[71] one should not overemphasise the power of humanitarian impulses. Without going into the complex issue of historical exchange rates, it appears that the real value of the reward received for their efforts by Austrian civilians was higher. After the Seven Years War, the official enlistment bounty paid to French infantry recruits was 100 *livres* – thrice higher than the reward for captured deserters. As the Habsburgs paid enlistment rates of ten *florins* to an Austrian subject and up to thirty to a foreigner, the Austrian deserters' bounty compares favourably with the equivalent French figures.

Prussia was another state whose civilians were delegated to pursue deserters. Villagers were obliged to place guards as soon as desertion was reported from a nearby garrison. Successful arrests produced a reward of six to twelve *thalers*, while fines of 100 *thalers* could be levied on communities who failed to stop a fugitive from crossing their land.[72] This last measure was clearly intended to get the richer and more influential members of the community more actively involved in the pursuit. A similar situation in a later period might provide a particularly useful parallel here. After the revolution, France suffered not only from absolute desertion numbers which dwarfed all analogous figures from old-regime Europe, but also from massive draft-evasion. After political education failed to leave a mark on the absconders, who sometimes made up as many as 40 per cent of the annual quota, more direct control methods were introduced, only to prove equally ineffective. Swoops by the *gendarmerie*, and even fines meted on the families of designated conscripts, failed to deter men from escaping and then leading a clandestine existence often with the full knowledge and support of their local communities. Then, in 1810, a radical change of policy suppressed this phenomenon within a year. Rather than persecuting the parents of the fugitives who were often too poor to be affected, the authorities shifted the pressure onto the richest taxpayers, who were now forced to sustain the troops engaged in the manhunt for draft-dodgers from their communities. This forceful reassignment of responsibility proved remarkably effective. Mounting pressure from their social superiors, upon whose goodwill they often depended, compelled families to demand their sons to give themselves up, although sometimes this incentive to surrender was sweetened by informal cash bounties raised by the rich.[73]

Although no old-regime state implemented equally forceful policies, some German states likewise succeeded in turning the pursuit of deserters into a public concern. When it could be ensured, the results were

---

[71] Hytier, 'The Decline of Military Values'.
[72] C. Duffy, *Army of Frederick the Great*, 66.   [73] Woloch, *New Regime*, ch. 13.

remarkable. Paradoxically, despite its reputation for disciplinary severity, desertion figures from the Prussian army compare favourably with those of almost any other eighteenth-century army. In the later years of Frederick William I, desertion averaged 1 per cent of all effectives, and there is evidence suggesting that peacetime desertion under Frederick the Great was comparable, if not lower. For instance, between 1740 and 1800, despite covering four major wars, the multi-annual desertion average from the Guards was under 1.5 per cent. The actual ratio between wartime and peacetime desertion can be discerned from the *Regimentsbuch* of the Hacke regiment. During the Seven Years War, it lost on average about one hundred deserters every year, while the short War of the Bavarian Succession cost the regiment 296 deserters. In comparison, in 1783 there were only three deserters, or 0.2 per cent of the regimental strength.[74]

Arguably, low desertion from the Prussian army can be attributed to the loyalty of its native-born recruits. If true, this means that at least some old-regime troops were motivated by patriotic concerns, which would in turn confirm the main argument taken by the current study. However, it should be remembered that cantonists were also easier to trace.[75] Nevertheless, this point still supports the main contention of this chapter, namely that desertion was less a function of patriotism or discipline than of the availability of effective control mechanisms, whose success deterred potential deserters. Nevertheless, just as in the Austrian case, the Prussian success in combating desertion required the active assistance of its civilian subjects. Although the introduction of the cantonal system brought new methods of direct control and surveillance, even eighteenth-century Prussia did not experience a top-down process of social disciplining. The cooperation of local communities was instrumental in ensuring the smooth functioning of the recruiting machine, making it necessary to accommodate their interests and demands. The pursuit of deserters is another example of how the army was forced to rely on the cooperation of the civilian sphere. In states that were unable to ensure the help of their subjects, the fight against desertion remained dependent on direct action from the military or civil authorities. The remaining part of this chapter will try to determine the relative success of these measures in France and Britain.

Although overall statistics for the decade after the Seven Years War are lacking, circumstantial evidence suggests that, on an annual basis, French

---

[74] C. Duffy, *Army of Frederick the Great*, 66; Muth, *Flucht*, 149; Bagensky, *Regiments Buch des Grenadiers Regiments könig Friedrich Wilhelm IV.*, 79, 84–5, 87; For more on this unique document, see: Fann, 'On the Infantryman's Age in Eighteenth Century Prussia'.
[75] P.H. Wilson, 'Social Militarization', 34.

deserters were numbered in their thousands, while the number of arrested deserters did not rise above a few hundred. Surviving quarterly desertion rolls indicate that there were 993 denounced deserters in the first quarter of 1764; 3,105 between April and September 1765; and 1,015 in the first quarter of 1767.[76] In comparison, between 1768 and 1773, in the whole of France the *maréchaussée* convoyed back to their regiments a mere 354 deserters.[77] The tally of deserters arrayed before the *prévôtal*, that is, military police tribunals, does not seem high. For instance, seventy years of such courts in Périgord produced a total of only ninety-seven desertion cases. As before 1763, military justice still caught only a small minority of deserters.[78] The reign of Louis XVI began with a major attempt to confront this situation; its results were, at best, inconclusive.

In 1776, penal measures against deserters were completely overhauled. The death penalty was abolished except for the most grievous cases. Moreover, the regulations introduced two days of grace, when returning deserters would only be punished with two weeks under arrest.[79] However, the core of this new policy was the establishment of a gradated set of punishments. For instance, a deserter who returned voluntarily after an absence of eight days to three months was punished by having the length of his original service contract increased by half. Those who overstayed their furlough by ten to thirty days would serve one extra year; two extra years, if they failed to come back after two months; and three years if they did not return within ninety days.[80] Apprehended deserters were subject to lengthier prolongations and also to corporal punishment. Arrest between the fourth and twelfth month after desertion would result in one extra engagement and ten gauntlets of 100 men. Deserters retaken over a year after their escape would run ten gauntlets of 200 men and serve two additional engagements in the colonies.[81] This new policy posed the following dilemma: either return voluntarily and incur a smaller penalty without corporal punishment, or run the risk of being caught and run the gauntlet, in addition to much longer service.

---

[76] Those quarterly rolls are preserved in SHD GR YA 444. The number of militia deserters was subtracted from the totals.

[77] In the same period, 844 additional men were convoyed from their units to the ports after being sentences for colonial service, SHD GR 1 M 1783, item 239, 'Etat des déserteurs qui ont été conduits a leurs regimens pour y être jugés et ceux conduit aux colonies pendant les années 1768..69.70.71.72 et 1773'.

[78] For instance, out of the 132 surviving judgements for 1772–5 kept in the archives in Brest, 130 resulted in a death sentence but there were only twelve actual executions, see: Bois, *Anciens soldats*, 100; I. Cameron, *Crime and Repression*, 136.

[79] 'Ordonnance du Roy concernant le Désertion' (12 December 1775), art. 8.1.

[80] Ibid., arts. 8.3, 8.4 and 16.

[81] This replaced what was originally perpetual service in the galleys; Ibid, article 9.

The effectiveness of the new measures can be gauged from two parameters: the changes in annual desertion figures and the ratio between voluntary returns and arrested deserters. On the former point, Corvisier estimates that in the last years of old-regime France desertion rates fell to only 2 per cent per year. Moreover, there is circumstantial evidence that more deserters were retaken and punished. Of the 600 court cases preserved in the archives in Brest from the decade beginning in 1776, 450 resulted in a sentence of eight years of hard labour. In the three years that it operated, 888 convicts passed through the hard-labour depot at Metz. Although they included all sorts of offenders, the overwhelming majority were recaptured deserters. According to the regulations, France had three other similar depots.[82] Nonetheless, those pieces of evidence are not as conclusive as they might appear. According to the origins of its convicts, the Metz depot took men from the entire kingdom, including prisoners sent from as far away as the Pyrenees. Markedly, Metz had men sentenced in Strasbourg, which was supposed to have hosted another hard-labour depot. Moreover, when the Metz depot was closed in 1778, its convicts were transferred to Lille, whose citadel was another site designated as a hard-labour depot. It appears that it was opened only in that year, because convicts condemned in Lille in 1776–7 were still dispatched to Metz. If Metz had been the only working depot in those years, the number of deserters sentenced to hard labour in France could not have numbered more than a few hundred per year. Although this data alone cannot denote the overall effectiveness of the disciplinary measures, it is worthwhile remembering that the first eight years of Louis XVI produced 24,838 formal denunciations.[83]

As for the deterrent effect of the new policy, there is a surviving record which proves helpful. It is a table presenting the breakdown of deserters who incurred prolongation of service following a voluntary return, before and after the enactment of the ordinance of 1 July 1786, which modified the length of additional service terms. According to this document, 374 deserters returned before this change, and 478 afterwards. The table also gives the total number of deserters arrested at the same time – 275 cases – punished by longer prolongations of service.[84] It is likely that the table covers one calendar year, because its comparative element would be lost if its two halves cover an unequal time period. Although this document

---

[82] Bois, *Anciens soldats*, 100; SHD GR YA 445, 'Justice militaire: contrôles de déserteurs condamnés à la chaîne'.

[83] SHD GR, 1 M 1783, item 131, Georg Michael von Vietinghoff, 'Etat de Déserteurs d'après les Signalemens envyoés à la Maréchaussée depuis 1776 jusqu'à 1783'.

[84] SHD GR, 1 M 1783, item 135, 'Etat des prolongations de Service prononcées contre des Déserteurs depuis la publication de l'Ordonnance du 1er Juillet 1786'.

remains mute on the two extremes of the new policy – those sentenced to hard labour and those returning during the period of grace – it demonstrates that the policy did produce the desired effect. The offer of a lesser punishment in exchange for voluntary return proved appealing to some deserters. Moreover, following the enactment of shorter additional service terms in mid-1786, the number of voluntary returns increased by a quarter.[85] The reality portrayed in this document fits neatly into Foucault's view on the emergence of modern disciplinary systems intended 'not to punish less, but punish better'.[86] Nevertheless, the impact of the new policy should not be overstated; desertion in late old-regime France still largely paid off.

Assuming that the desertion rate in 1786 was comparable to the official denunciation figures for the first eight years of Louis XVI, it is striking that the number of deserters arrested and punished by prolongation of service that year numbered less than one-tenth of the average annual reported figure for 1776–83. When deserters who incurred service prolongation following a voluntary return are added, almost two-thirds of all deserters remain unaccounted for. True, those figures do not cover those arrested and sentenced to hard labour or executed, although, as argued by Bois, by the mid-1780s such penalties became uncommon. Nevertheless, even if in 1786 as many deserters were sentenced to hard labour as those who incurred additional service, the total would still be less than half of all reported desertion cases. Although this particular observation is suggestive rather than conclusive, it demonstrates that the preventive effect of the new policy had its limits, even when we adhere to the official figures. But what was the actual scale of desertion at that time?

If one believes Baron de Vietinghoff, whose memorial we already cited for the denunciation figures in 1776–83, between half and two-thirds of the regiments failed to report their deserters. This assertion is supported by a statistical model which demonstrates the unequal distribution of denunciations by months and by regiments. Although Vietinghoff's calculations are based on the optimistic assumption that every regiment should have been punctually reporting its deserters to Versailles every calendar month, his basic argument remains correct. For instance, between 1779 and 1783, the six hussar regiments did not denounce

---

[85] Deserters returning before the enactment of the new ordnances were penalised by a total of 1,505 extra years and those returning after by 1,537. The average service prolongation thus fell by nine months. In comparison, those arrested during that time incurred 2,348 extra service years, an average prolongation of eight and a half years.

[86] Foucault, *Discipline and Punish*, 82.

a *single* fugitive. Although the precise scale of underreporting cannot be determined without a more extensive statistical study, it is clear that desertion was higher than the official figures admit. Moreover, all unreported deserters could be considered as good as lost, because their descriptions were not placed on the quarterly deserters' roll, leaving the military police completely unaware of their existence.

However, even when properly denounced, the means to pursue these men remained grossly inadequate. The deserters roll contained their names, place of birth, age, height and usually some other prominent physical features such as eye and hair colour. Yet one can only wonder how the *maréchaussée*, which had thousands of such general descriptions at any given moment, was able to sieve individual deserters from a society otherwise devoid of any formal means of identification.[87] Unless the man returned directly home, it is impossible to know how else he could be detected. The effectiveness of the *maréchaussée* was further impeded by the full extent of its responsibilities and its chronic lack of manpower. Seldom rising above 4,000 agents, the service was also entrusted with maintaining public order in rural communities, patrolling the highways and fighting vagrancy. For instance, the police of Touraine, a province of about 7,000 square kilometres containing some of the major thoroughfares in central France, had at its disposal seventy-seven men in 1766, ninety-three in 1771 and only forty-four in 1780. Their colleagues in Maine and Anjou never had more than 140 agents. As shown by Iain Cameron's study, this situation was indicative of old-regime France as a whole.[88] The effectiveness of the military posts along the borders is also doubtful. For instance, the deserters' cordon in the Western Pyrenees consisted of 168 invalids divided into small detachments spread over one hundred leagues of mountainous terrain. The situation along other borders was not different, and unless the deserter was obliging enough to take a major road, there would be little way of stopping him from escaping outside the kingdom.[89]

The lack of efficient enforcement mechanisms was not the only factor likely to undermine the new policy. For instance, between 1776 and

---

[87] Moreover, those descriptions which were created upon enlistment, were not necessarily brought up to date when the *contrôles* were renewed. For instance, in the four times between 1763 and 1775 when the rolls of the colonel's company of the Boullion Regiment were updated, Lance-Corporal Alexander Dilleman remained continuously young at 25 years of age.

[88] Maillard, 'Maréchaussée et répression', 506; I. Cameron, *Crime and Repression*, 18–20.

[89] Moreover, their presence was deeply resented by the local villagers who were only too happy to aid deserters; see: Bois, *Anciens soldats*, 251–2; see also: I. Cameron, *Crime and Repression*, 121–2. On similar ineffectiveness of the cordons on Russia's Western border, see: Keep, *Soldiers of the Tsar*, 225.

1786, of the twenty-four returning deserters in the Orleans regiment, five had their original contracts prolonged, but fourteen were allowed to reenlist anew, often with the payment of new bounty, while another five were pardoned. Moreover, the number of deserters who were punished remained a small minority. In the same period, four soldiers from the regiment were sentenced to hard labour, and eight more were discovered to be deserters from other units and surrendered to the *maréchaussée*. Thus, a total of thirty-six soldiers from the Orleans regiment encountered the military law against deserters, which is not a high figure considering that during that decade a total of 259 deserters were struck off the roll as irrecoverably lost. The situation in regiments of foreign auxiliaries on the French establishment was probably at least as bad. During the same eight years, the German Boullion regiment was irrecoverably losing over forty deserters every year, compared to a grand total of seven returning deserters and nine more men who were executed, sentenced to hard labour or handed back to their original regiments. On that point, it is worthwhile remembering that, according to the official figures, the supposed annual desertion average in the 135 French infantry regiments in 1776–83 was less than twenty men per year.[90] Those individual *contrôles* not only confirm the inconsistency between reported and actual desertion figures, but also reveal that the stern tone of the regulations would not necessarily apply even to all returning deserters, let alone all fugitive soldiers.[91]

The balance of the available evidence suggests that, despite noticeable similarities to the trends we noticed in Austria, the new penal policy failed to suppress desertion to a comparable effect. The use of the death penalty subsided, and official figures indicate a decrease in annual desertion levels. There are also signs that the later years of the French monarchy saw growth in voluntary returns. Nevertheless, even the minimalist official figures indicate that the proportion of arrested and returning French deserters fell behind the respective figures obtained by Habsburg Austria in 1760s and 1770s. Regulations of 1776 included additional similarities, with Austrian and Prussian measures threatening to fine those who sheltered deserters, as well as tripling the bounty for their arrest. Nevertheless, civilians still refused to cooperate in the pursuit of fugitive soldiers. The weakness of the *maréchaussée*, the only organisation which could have enforced these measures, is indicative of the failure of direct government control in old-regime France, both against the deserters and against

---

[90] Calculation based on SHD GR 1 YC 157 and 1 YC 649.
[91] To quote Bois: 'La justice était plus dure dans les textes que dans la réalité', ['Justice was severer in the text than in reality'], see: *Anciens soldats,* 99.

its civilian population. The military authorities themselves were inefficient, failing to report deserters and undermining the effect of the new
regulations with additional leniency. All this allows us to question
whether the authorities in late old-regime France could combat desertion
to any considerable effect.

The British policy appears to have occupied an intermediate place
between Austria and France. Although it included an element of privati-
sation, the main burden of dealing with deserters fell on the local authorities. The mutiny act of 1708 introduced a bounty of twenty shillings for
informers paid by the local land-tax collector in exchange for a certificate
from the justice of the peace, before whom the deserter was denounced.
For informers, this arrangement operated smoothly and the rewards were
paid quickly; however, it was a totally different matter for the local
magistrates. While the apprehended deserter was imprisoned, his regiment had to be informed so that a party could be sent to collect the man
and also pay for his subsistence during his time in custody. This necessitated circuitous correspondence through the War Office in London,
which could take many months, and the prisoner could further prolong
the process by providing a false name or regiment. This necessitated
a new round of correspondence to establish his real identity, while the
deserter was maintained at the expense of the local borough.[92] Thus, the
denunciation called for a cumbersome administrative procedure which
not only postponed justice, but often allowed the deserter to escape it
altogether. The expenses involved in dispatching an escorting party made
it financially unviable for many regiments to reclaim their deserters. Some
colonels ignored the matter altogether, while others settled the man's
subsistence, but would not bother collecting him. Alternatively, the
deserters could be offered to return independently in exchange for
a pardon. Moreover, from 1742, the mutiny act fixed the amount paid
to the jail-keepers, limiting their expected income. This was unlikely to
make the local authorities any keener to arrest fugitive soldiers. Pursuit of
deserters was a risky financial endeavour, which promised little gain and
the possibility of high loss if the borough ended up with an unwanted
deserter on its hands.[93]

Such considerations were irrelevant for individual civilians, however,
and yet, despite the ease of obtaining deserter bounties, there are
signs indicating that the population was largely unwilling to cooperate.
Samples of the bounty certificates preserved in Kew show that a

---

[92] Scouller, *Armies of Queen Anne*, 296; Steppler, *Common Soldier*, 213–8.
[93] Guy, *Oeconomy and Discipline*, 127; Barrington, *Eighteenth-Century Secretary at War*, 34–5.

disproportionably high number of payments were made to serving and retired soldiers. These probably knew how to identify deserters, and had the assertiveness to challenge them.[94] The rest of society, however, remained more benevolent to the escapees. After his desertion from the 48th regiment, Henly took refuge among Irish miners, and some of his hosts even went to his old regiment and openly challenged the soldiers to come and fetch the fugitive. Lesser magistrates could also place the sensibilities of their communities higher than the interests of the army. For instance, a constable of a Devon village who had been summoned to arrest a deserter instead called upon a group of armed peasants who chased his officer away. Crowds that broke into jails to release smugglers and other offenders would often help detained deserters. During periods of war on the continent, much depended on the goodwill of authorities in the ports through which the deserters re-entered Britain. During the War of the Spanish Succession some, like the mayors of Dover and Harwich, pursued deserters, explaining their zeal in patriotic terms. R.E. Scouller argues, however, that such cases were exceptional.[95]

Desertion levels in late-eighteenth-century Britain remained considerable, and, as in the previous half of the century, there are strong indications that most deserters escaped unpunished. In 1769, for instance, 8 per cent of the troops stationed in Ireland deserted, while during the 1780s as much as one-sixth of its whole establishment would make off in the course of a single year. In 1788, special tribunals were instituted to quickly try and ship such men to the West Indies. John Fortescue remarks that 'according to the numbers transported the penalty held no great terror'. In 1794, for instance, the Irish establishment lost over 2,000 men from a total force of 22,525, with some regiments suffering rates of 20 per cent or more.[96] Compared to those figures, the official desertion statistics for the British troops in North America and the West Indies during the American War of Independence look surprisingly low, mentioning only 3,701 deserters between 1774 and 1780. But even if, as in old-regime France, desertion was underreported, it is still telling that,

---

[94] Goulden, 'Deserter Bounty Certificates', 161–8. See also: Burke, *Memoir*, 8–10.

[95] Frotescue, *History*, vol. I, 567; Scouller, *Armies of Queen Anne*, 298–300. However, many of those who did not wish to depart on campaign did not even leave the country. For instance, the six regiments dispatched from Ireland to Quebec in April 1776 lost some 300 deserters in the week preceding their embarkation; see: Garntham 'Military Desertion', 98–9;

[96] On desertion from the Irish establishment, see: Fortescue, *History of the British Army*, vol. III, 525; Bartlett, 'Indiscipline and Disaffection', 189; On the British army in Ireland, see: Guy, 'Irish Military Establishment, 1660–1776'; Bartlett, 'Army and Society in Eighteenth-Century Ireland'.

compared to these figures, the JAG files preserve only 228 GCM cases from that entire conflict.[97]

The best treatment of desertion in that period, Steppler's micro-study of the First Foot Guards, shows that between 1760 and 1793, up to 8 per cent of its men deserted every year. Actual irrecoverable losses were 4.4 per cent, as about one-third of the deserters were regained; this was still a higher figure compared with contemporary Austrian and Prussian regiments. Furthermore, when put against the number of deserter bounties paid in Middlesex, the county in which the guards were permanently stationed, another interesting point emerges. Between 1783 and 1799, 318 certificates were issued for denunciation of deserters from the regiment, while its monthly returns report 1,781 desertion cases, of which 576 fugitives were regained. Thus, more deserters were arrested in Middlesex than the sum of those retaken in all other parts of Britain together with deserters returning voluntarily.[98] This suggests that if a deserter successfully escaped from his garrison in London, his chances of being arrested fell considerably. Furthermore, as indicated by additional documents, many of the returning men escaped again, often successfully.[99] Although the regimental records of the First Foot Guards do not contain extant GCM records, it is obvious that military justice did not prove a deterrent. The cumbersome mechanisms employed to combat deserters, and the lack of cooperation from the population at large in their pursuit, further explains why desertion from the First Foot Guards in particular, and in Britain in general, did not offer a particularly great risk to life and limb.

Ironically, it was Britain's relatively well-developed administration which further hampered the efficient pursuit of deserters. Despite a designated military police force and well thought-out penal reform, desertion in old-regime France, likewise, did not decline in levels comparable to those in the Prussian or the late Theresian army. Coaxing existing social networks or gratifying the greed of individual civilians proved more effective than a combination of a rational policy and direct

---

[97] BL Add MS 38,375, 'An account of the Men lost and disabled in His Majesties Land Service ... in North America and the West Indies from 1st Novem^r 1774 to the date of the last Returns inclusive'. Tellingly, the statistics from the main British army for 1780 are missing altogether, see also: Gilbert, 'British Military Justice', 24–30; Sullivan claims that after the evacuation of Philadelphia over 800 deserters went over to the American side, see: *From Redcoat to Rebel*, 223–4.

[98] Steppler, *Common Soldier*, 187–9; Grenadier Guards Regimental Archive, London, B09/004 'Monthly Returns'; Goulden, 'Deserter Bounty', 162

[99] William Baylis, for instance, deserted a total of six times between 1776 and 1781. He did not return from his last desertion, see: Grenadier Guards Regimental Archive D3/002, 'Deserter Record 1760–1820'.

control mechanisms. Although there is evidence that their efficiency increased over the century, military and civilian authorities were unlikely to achieve noticeable success against desertion with their own resources. To ensure better control over their soldiers, armies had to resort to relying on the help of civilians. This point is suggestive if we wish to assess the overall limits of government control in early-modern Europe. Other than convicts, soldiers were the only other members of society whose descriptions and whereabouts were kept centrally. Outside camp, every soldier had to carry a pass, and every veteran his discharge papers. And yet, despite these methods of surveillance, which were unprecedented compared with the rest of the population, a very substantial number of soldiers deserted successfully. Moreover, more deserters escaped the most serious forms of punishment through voluntary return. Thus, if a substantial portion of those committing the most serious crime in the most closely-controlled of all social groups escaped unharmed, what does it say about old-regime control methods as a whole? In the framework of this study, this alone should question the singular importance attributed to coercive compliance in the running of eighteenth-century armies.

Moreover, in the cases of pre-1776 France, pre-1763 Austria or the Irish establishment well into the 1790s, desertion meant an easy and relatively risk-free escape from military service. Assuming that the soldiers were as unwilling or indifferent as they have been often portrayed, it is puzzling why *more* men did not desert. The brutality of old-regime military justice fails to provide the explanation here. The discrepancy between the total number of deserters and those actually punished demonstrates that the execution of a few unfortunates carried little weight as long as most deserters escaped with impunity. What did provide deterrence was not the severity of the potential punishment, but a greater possibility of arrest, as clearly seen from the post-1763 Austrian figures. It might even be argued that desertion in old-regime Europe can be seen in terms of a moral economy, whose currency was based on means of control rather than service conditions.[100]

Like any model, the hypothesis presented in this chapter is a simplification of more complex factors. There were probably as many motives to desert as there were individual deserters. Nevertheless, there is enough evidence to show that harsh service conditions were only one of many incentives to escape from military service. Moreover, considering the relative ease and impunity with which it was often done, desertion

---

[100] On the concept of 'moral economy', see: E.P. Thompson's classic 'Moral Economy of the English Crowd'.

figures in old-regime Europe are comparable and sometimes lower than those in armies whose men were supposedly better motivated than their eighteenth-century counterparts. Lastly, the conventional view of desertion fails to answer one major question. Corvisier argues that one in five and sometimes one in four soldiers deserted; but what kept the remaining three or four men with the colours? The remaining part of this study will attempt to answer this question.

3   Discipline and Defiance
A Reciprocal Model

One of the more colourful portrayals of the power of discipline in old-regime armies was penned by Sir Michael Howard:

> It might be suggested that it was not the least achievement of European civilization to have reduced the wolf packs which had preyed on the defenceless peoples of Europe for so many centuries to the condition of trained and obedient gun dogs – almost, in some cases, performing poodles.[1]

The significance of such views, presenting the eighteenth-century soldiery as a closely-controlled and obedient lot, extends beyond the remits of old-regime military history. Social and cultural historians usually see the early-modern armies not only as disciplined but also as a disciplining force which played a major role in bringing the European population under the closer control of their governments. This was a broad process which operated on a number of levels, but at its root lay the growing standardisation of social institutions and mores, replacing tradition with regulation, informality with formality and compromise and negotiation with direct power and hierarchical dictates. Regular armies were not only the product of this development, but also one of its major promoters. However, the role of the military went beyond the coercion of those whose traditional way of life fell victim to the reforming zeal of the authorities. It was argued that the disciplining of the soldiery enabled the social disciplining of the population at large. Their position as the most tightly controlled social institution in old-regime Europe allowed armies to become a testing ground for policies of social management and surveillance before they were implemented on the rest of society, from the introduction of elementary education to a more regularised penal system. Moreover, with their controlled nature, uniforms and drill, armies provided a model for the rest of the society to follow. It can be said that this was also the way in which some old-regime rulers wished to see their

---

[1] Howard, *War*, 76. The next four paragraphs are largely based on Berkovich, 'Discipline and Control', 114–6.

subjects: regulated, predictable and efficient; docile in their obedience, yet ferocious when commanded to execute an order.[2]

Recent studies usually take a more nuanced view of social disciplining and growing state control within the civilian sphere. Rather than being entirely coercive and imposed from above, it was largely based on negotiation and consent, often relying on intermediaries accepted by both the authorities and their subjects. The move towards greater uniformity was also a gradual one. To cite one example, contrary to the argument raised by Foucault in his classic *Discipline and Punish*, the regularisation of the legal system in old-regime France was a slow and measured process, rather than the product of a relatively abrupt upheaval which took place at the end of the eighteenth century. As shown by scholars working on French legal history, the move towards a more procedural, less arbitrary penal system began a century before the revolution.[3]

The traditional view of armies as the most disciplined (read 'civilised') part of society also did not remain unchallenged. For instance, as we mentioned in the previous chapter, Peter Wilson has turned Otto Büsch's classical thesis on its head, arguing that, rather than militarising eighteenth-century German society, it was the constant interaction with the civilian sphere which actually civilised German armies. A number of recent studies covering the conditions of common soldiers arrived at similar conclusions. Brumwell, who studied the British army in North America during the Seven Years War, refutes the traditional view of the eighteenth-century redcoat as a meek, brutalised automaton. Instead, members of the rank and file had a firm perception of their worth and of the rights which they considered due to them. Failure of the military authorities to meet the expectations of their subordinates often provoked varied forms of resistance, including petitions, threats and public displays of resentment. Individual soldiers who felt injured by their officers often deserted, while similar slights to the whole body of the troops could result in equally radical collective action. This happened in the mass mutinies of

---

[2] Roberts, 'The Military Revolution, 1560–1660', 205–6; Nipperdey, 'Probleme der Modernisierung'; Wehler, *Modernisierungstheorie und Geschichte*; Foucault, *Discipline and Punish*, 135–41; Oestreich, *Neostoicism and the Early Modern State*, part 2; Raeff, *Well-Ordered Police State*; A more positive view of this process is taken by Norbert Elias, *Civilizing Process*, vol. I, ch. 2. For an overview of German historiography on the role played by the military in social disciplining with much relevant bibliography, see: Pröve, 'Dimension und Reichweite', 67–71. The French edition of Sabina Loriga's book, whose examination of Piedmontese soldiers is very much in light of this view, is amply titled: *Soldats: un laboratoire disciplinaire*.

[3] Andrews, *Law, Magistracy, and Crime*; Ruff, *Crime, Justice and Public Order*; Silverman, *Tortured Subjects*. For similar developments taking place in other parts of continental Europe, see: Spierenburg, *Spectacle of Suffering*; Evans, *Rituals of Retribution*, 41–50, 109–21.

1763–4, when almost every major garrison in North America rose up after the introduction of excessive peacetime stoppages for food and equipment.[4]

Nonetheless, despite growing understanding of its potential limits, the traditional view of eighteenth-century discipline remains strong. Although he amply demonstrates that old-regime soldiers could take a much more assertive stance to their rights, Brumwell still portrays British military discipline as brutal and unrelenting. Similar arguments regarding the cruel nature of old-regime discipline, and military service more generally, are repeated by numerous other scholars.[5] Similarly to the supposedly high desertion rates from old-regime armies, this definite claim is presented without any comparisons with preceding or subsequent periods. Thus, the accepted wisdom on power relations in old-regime armies does not differ much from the optimal conditions described in contemporary military ordinances. Nevertheless, there is a case to be made for the success of coercive compliance in old-regime armies. While demonstrating its occasional failures, desertion and mutiny were radical forms of resistance which often resulted from extreme conditions and involved only a minority of the soldiers. Was this, perhaps, a sign of the overall success of the disciplinary project of controlling the daily lives of the majority of soldiers most of the time?

Determining the overall success of coercive compliance in peacetime is of great importance if we want to explain old-regime combat motivation. A firefight in a linear formation was won not by physical extermination of the opposing soldiers, but by causing them to break and flee. Battle regulations, therefore, stressed the need to keep men under constant control by their superiors. As the infantry line advanced, NCOs and some officers followed behind the backs of their men, and remained standing there, often locking their halberds, once the firing had started. Nonetheless, even this remarkably direct control method had its limits as, sooner or later, one of the lines broke. Even if we assume that old-regime tactics were based on coercion alone, close supervision in combat was insufficient to ensure military effectiveness. Victory could be achieved if the collective mental endurance of your troops outlasted that of their opponents, but this required preliminary conditioning. Modern scholars

---

[4] P.H. Wilson, 'Social Militarization'; Büsch, *Militärsystem und Sozialleben*. On similar partnership between military establishments and parts of the civilian society in Britain, see: Conway, *War, State and Society*, 39–50; Brumwell, *Redcoats*, 126–37. On the mutinies at the end of the Seven Years War, see: Kopperman, 'Stoppages Mutiny of 1763', 241–54; Way, 'Rebellion of the Regulars'.

[5] Brumwell, *Redcoats*, 101; Keep, *Soldiers of the Tsar*, 140–1, 166–70; Chandler, 'Captain General', 75; Barnett, *Britain and Her Army*, 41–2; James, *Warrior Race*, 303, 307; Atwood, *Hessians*, 83, Hochedlinger, *Austria's Wars*, 134–5.

invoke this rationale to explain the alleged brutality of old-regime military discipline. According to this view, continuous chastisements in peacetime inured the soldiers to prefer the uncertain fate of marching against enemy cannons, rather than face certain punishment at the hand of their superiors, as Frederick the Great himself said. As demonstrated in our examination of desertion, however, the ability of old-regime military authorities to deter, apprehend and punish the most serious military offenders was often inadequate. This suggests that the reality of power relations between eighteenth-century officers and soldiers, in peace as well as wartime, was not necessarily as one-sided as depicted by contemporary regulations and their language of unquestioned obedience. In fact, the example of the linear order provides another telling point, as the soldiers were preceded by a line consisting of more senior-ranking officers than those placed at their back. As for the precise function of these men, it will be considered at greater length in Chapter 6. For the moment, it is sufficient to quote Dennis Showalter's shrewd observation that 'even the rawest and the most arrogant of subalterns was unlikely to rejoice at the prospect of marching into battle in front of a hundred loaded muskets carried by men who hated him'.[6]

Until now, the sources used to examine the effectiveness of old-regime disciplinary mechanisms were military regulations, officers' memoirs and accounts by contemporary civilian observers. No attempt was made, however, to study systematically the testimonies coming from the group whose members were actually subject to all these measures. By looking at accounts left by common soldiers, we are not only dealing with a largely untapped source of evidence, but also with material best suited to assess the practical implementation of the eighteenth-century disciplinary regimen. Were the men subject to the straightforward dominance of their superiors? Did they feel brutalised or victimised by military discipline and its demands? The current discussion begins by providing an overview of the restraints on the ability to exercise direct control in combat and during active campaigning. This chapter also examines the attitudes held by the men towards their own disciplining. According to modern Western sentiments, the mere idea of corporal punishment is abhorrent – but was that also true for the majority of eighteenth-century common soldiers? Did they necessarily consider their lot to be unfair or unjust? This will be followed by considering instances of defiance, both individual and collective, which often fell short of the more radical and better-studied

---

[6] Showalter, *Wars of Frederick the Great*, 23. For the positions of officers in battle line: C. Duffy, *Military Experience*, 219–20; For particular armies, see: C. Duffy, *Instrument of War*, 402–3; C. Duffy, *Army of Frederick the Great*, 84–5; Nafziger, *Imperial Bayonets:*, 77, 87.

mutinies and desertions. Instead of top-bottom disciplining, power relations between officers and soldiers often resembled a continuous tug-of-war in which the men – while always remaining formally subordinate – were able to extract numerous concessions from their superiors. Finally, this chapter brings evidence for the existence of more subtle control mechanisms which preceded, complemented and sometimes replaced the more famous punishments which could be inflicted by old-regime military justice. These were often intended to underscore the legitimacy of the military organisation and its demands. As long as men acted within these basic rules, no heavier coercive methods were invoked. Rather than merely being enforced by terror, the obedience of old-regime soldiers to their superiors was also based on willing consent.

In light of its characteristics, it can be argued that linear combat required the implementation of the most forceful control methods, a point supported by eighteenth-century regulations which instruct that any man turning to flee or even murmuring in the ranks should be killed on the spot. Nevertheless, despite dozens of extant combat descriptions by eighteenth-century common soldiers, and many more by their superiors, there is no concrete evidence of officers employing serious violence against their own men to force them to fight. One exception is provided by some Prussian participants of the battle of Lobositz. *Feldwebel* Liebler reports hearing about an Austrian captain who stabbed *ten* of his own men who attempted to flee, while *Unteroffizier* Klauel claims that FieldMarshal Browne was so angered by the retreat of his Croats that he shot two of them with his own pistol. Ironically, the rumours repeated by the Prussian NCOs ascribe to the Austrians the same control practices occasionally attributed by modern historians to the Prussians themselves. According to Möbius' detailed study of the combat behaviour of Prussian troops during the Seven Years War, although desertion in battle was punishable by death, hitting a running man was often enough to bring him back to his place in the ranks. Such action by a superior would be considered just by the soldiers themselves, but this did not extend to killing one's own men.[7] Moreover, officers who subjected the lives of their subordinates to unnecessary or unjustified danger ran the risk of being killed by their own soldiers. As in modern instances of fragging, direct evidence for officers murdered by their men is rare, but such acts did occur. Duffy mentions a particularly brazen case which involved a British major at the end of

---

[7] '*Unteroffizier* C.G. Klauel to his brother' (6 October 1756) and '*Feldwebel* G.S. Liebler to his wife and relatives' (12 October 1756), in GG, 28, 34; Möbius, *Mehr Angst*, 131–2; Frey, *British Soldier in America*, 126. For an example of an NCO who hit a soldier after action, for failing to react quickly when fellow Russian troops were attacked nearby, see: Popadishev, 'Vospominaniya', 71.

a battle of Blenheim. Seeing the French surrendering, this officer turned around to lead his men into cheer and was immediately shot straight in the forehead.[8]

Although soldiers' writings contain few direct references to the possibility that officers could be harmed by their own men, this theme resurfaces enough to imply that such opportunities were not merely hypothetical. The highly motivated Matthew Bishop states that officers should be careful not to disgust their subordinates by arbitrary or unfair deeds for 'it often proves fatal to them in times of actions'. According to Bishop, if more would follow his advice, 'there would not be such a slaughter among officers as there sometimes is'. Officers of the 30th Regiment clearly had such thoughts on their mind when the regiment was transferred to active service against Revolutionary France. According to James Aytoun, their behaviour, previously petty and tyrannical, underwent a complete metamorphosis as 'the officers found that the men they were in the practice of beating were to be their only defenders'. Superiors could not presume themselves to be safe even in peacetime. According to Seume, a man who was made sergeant after betraying a desertion plot continued to fear for his life despite his promotion. Sergeant James Thompson tells of another sergeant who was attacked by his corporal after reprimanding him for lying down in the guardhouse.[9] Soldiers could also retaliate when they were disturbed by trifles. After the surrender of Yorktown, men of the French contingent were often bothered by requests to stage fake battles to entertain visiting American dignitaries. According to Flohr, such events were rife with 'accidents' because of the anger (*Verdruesslichkeit*) of the soldiery. Flohr remains quiet on the nature of those accidents, but it is clear that the close formation and volleys of the infantry line allowed men to take aimed shots with complete impunity. This is probably the opportunity referred to by the eighteenth-century French soldiers' song 'Soldat Mécontent': 'Ah si jamais nous partions en campagne; Les grands coups de fusil, paieraient les coups de canne'.[10]

Thus, the capacity to control eighteenth-century soldiers was not absolute even when the men stood shoulder-to-shoulder arrayed in linear formation under the direct supervision of their officers. What does this imply, therefore, for instances when such ideal surveillance conditions

---

[8] C. Duffy, *Military Experience*, 136.

[9] Bishop, *Life and Adventures*, 140–1; Aytoun, *Redcoats*, 41–2; Seume, *Werke*, vol. I, 64–5; J. Thompson, *Bard*, 129.

[10] 'Ah, if we ever go on campaign, the musket shots shall repay the blows of the cane'. Eventually, the campaign arrives, and the narrator lives up to his threats killing his own captain, lieutenant and sergeant, and then deserts. See also: Flohr, *American Campaigns*, 59.

were impossible? Despite widespread beliefs about its cumbersome character, the realities of old-regime combat were far more varied than a mechanistic exchange of volleys between blocks of opposing infantrymen. An integral part of the tactics of every eighteenth-century army,[11] bayonet charges usually began with a measured advance, but often turned into a frenzied rush forward. Successful enforcement of direct control under such conditions was impossible. This is exactly what happened to the Prussian left wing at the battle of Lobositz, an opportunity used by Bräker to escape after he noticed there were no officers nearby. For men with different inclinations, however, a successful charge meant continuous advance and pursuit. At the battle of Guilford Courthouse, British and Hessian troops broke through two American lines, chasing the survivors into the undergrowth. According to Sergeant Berthold Koch, men of the von Bose Regiment went so far ahead that they were attacked from their rear. Another participant, British Sergeant Roger Lamb, tells that men advanced and fought as individuals, and soon he found himself essentially alone. George Blennie describes in very similar terms an action fought during the Dutch Campaign of 1799 when his regiment was ordered to advance from the shoreline into the dunes. Formation soon broke as smaller and smaller parties of English and French fought each other from dune crest to dune crest.[12]

Although it could lead to individual combat, the bayonet charge was still considered an integral role of the old-regime line infantry. In contrast, skirmishing is typically seen as the reserve of specialised troops such as Croats or jaegers.[13] However, this division is not as clear as many military historians assume. As shown by Möbius, even Prussian regular regiments adopted an open formation depending on the conditions of the battlefield or the terrain. Although light infantry companies were introduced in 1771, the British already employed light troops in their German

---

[11] Nosworthy, *Anatomy of Victory*, 99–112, 190–2, 316–7; And for individual armies: Möbius, *Mehr Angst*, 44–6; Englund, *Battle of Poltava*, 113–4, 148–50; Upton, *Charles XI and Swedish Absolutism*, 83; Spring, *With Zeal and with Bayonets*, 216–44. Despite this evidence, the view that ruthless bayonet charges were the preserve of the Revolutionary French still prevails, see for instance: Thoral, *From Valmy to Waterloo*, 16–7.

[12] Bräker, 'Lebensgeschichte', 462–4; Kloosterhuis, 'Donner, Blitz und Bräker', 173–81; Koch, *Battle*, 6–9; Lamb, *Original and Authentic Journal*, 361–2; Blennie, *Narrative*, 46; On Blennie's identity, see: Henderson, 'The Irish Rebellion of 1798: Two First Hand Accounts', 34. See also: Surtees, *Twenty-Five Years*, 17–8; Coates, *Narrative*, 52; Nosworthy, *Anatomy*, 114. On the fighting at Guilford Court House, see: Babits and Howard, *Long Obstinate and Bloody*.

[13] C. Duffy, *Military Experience*, 163, 196, 269–79; Gates, *British Light Infantry*, 10–4, who holds a low opinion of old-regime light infantry in general. See also: Wernitz, *Preußichen Freitruppen*, 12; Atwood, *Hessians*, 40.

campaign a decade earlier. The formation of this corps, described by John Tory and Corporal William Todd, was rather informal, with volunteers and drafts drawn from the regular line and re-designated as light infantry-men without any specialised training. The first Russian jaeger units, which were created at the same time, were likewise manned by transferees from the line.[14] On the other hand, British troops stationed in North America were expected to fight as light infantry or skirmishers whenever required. Specific training for this role included fighting in woods with individual soldiers taking cover and firing independently from behind trees. British regular troops continued to employ loose formations during the War of Independence and the Revolutionary Wars. For instance, after the landing in Egypt, the 90th and 92nd regiments were commanded to advance in open order in front of the army. There were also equivalent developments on the continent.[15] Although expected primarily to fight in line, old-regime troops were capable of more versatile tactics, in which direct control by officers was even harder to maintain.

Reading Frederick the Great's instructions against desertion, it might appear that a typical old-regime army operated like a travelling concentration camp. However, the high desertion rates suffered on campaign demonstrate that the precautions described by Frederick could not be enforced in full. Despite the view that eighteenth-century armies subsisted on magazines and convoys, foraging was widespread. This could be done formally, with soldiers sent to secure the supplies in a designated area under cover of cavalry pickets. Men often took matters into their own hands, however, with formal and informal procuring of supplies merging into one. Sent to collect horses for the army, Todd's pioneers entered a German farmhouse and helped themselves to the lunch that was just being prepared. During the 1792 invasion of France, Prussian pickets left their posts at night to plunder, as did soldiers placed on guard within the villages to prevent looting. Shortage of provisions meant that small groups of men would leave camp in search of food and drink without formal approval, but often with the full knowledge of their superiors. Bishop, who returned from one such expedition with a beer barrel of fifty gallons,

[14] Möbius, *Mehr Angst*, 46–8; Todd, *Journal*, 193; Tory, *Journal*, 69; C. Duffy, *Russia's Military Way*, 117, 120–1; Rumyantsev, *P. A. Rumyantsev, Dokumenty*, vol. I, 437–9. On the ad-hoc nature of forming light units, see: Gates, *British Light Infantry*, 18.

[15] Brumwell, *Redcoats*, 191–226, 231–6; Spring, *With Zeal and with Bayonets*, 245–62. For one particular example of training in North America, see: Boscawen, *Capture of Louisbourg, 1758*, 136–41; D. Robertson, *Journal*, 11–2, 31. On the adoption of light infantry in Prussia and its performance, see: Showalter, 'Hubertusburg to Auerstädt', 316–8, 321–2; At the crushing defeat they inflicted on the pursuing French forces at the battle of Muotathal, most of the Russian rearguard fought in open order; see: C. Duffy, *Eagles over the Alps*, 226–36.

'civilly' procured from some Flemish peasants, was complimented by his officers for his concern for his comrades' welfare. Things changed little when the British army campaigned again in the same area forty years later. After another order was issued threatening death to the first pillager, 'to show how little we regarded it', Sampson Staniforth and his comrades plundered four bullocks. On the way back to camp, the party encountered an officer who was perfectly satisfied with the explanation that the animals were honestly bought and paid for.[16] Sometimes, men would even venture out alone. While stationed at Fort Duquesne, Joseph-Charles Bonin continuously went hunting and nut-picking. During the autumn campaign of 1757, Musketeer Dominicus left the quarters of his regiment and went for a stroll until he was challenged by a Saxon officer. Luckily, Dominicus was able to run away and rejoin his unit.[17] What is clear from his case is that, even in the Prussian army on campaign, a man could leave camp whatever the regulations said.

Personal recollections by private soldiers provide further evidence that formal discipline on campaign was not necessarily enforced to the fullest even in cases when it was openly defied. When thirsty British troops from the detachment of Gunner James Field arrived at a well, the men broke ranks, sweeping aside the officers and sergeants who were beating the soldiers with the flats of their swords in a vain attempt to enforce the orders against drinking water from unsavoury sources. Shortly afterwards, the same men arrived at a village where they killed and roasted some hogs. Ordered to advance before the meat was fully cooked, soldiers of the 89th regiment impaled the meat on their bayonets. Attempting to force the men to desist, the major cut it down with his sword, but as soon as it fell to the ground the meat was again raised on the bayonet points, until the soldiers were permitted to keep it. At the beginning of the siege of Yorktown, Flohr reports that the first bread wagons which finally arrived after a long period in which no supplies were brought in were immediately plundered by the hungry troops. Although he declared that such a major breach of discipline deserved exemplary punishment, General Rochambeau proceeded to pardon the soldiers on account of their zeal in building the siegeworks. According to Todd, officers did not punish any of the troops who got drunk on the night they landed in Britain

[16] On another occasion, Todd's pioneers went foraging and presented their officers with some captured fowl, see: Todd, *Journal*, 147–8, 222–4; Laukhard, *Leben und Schicksale*, 226, 229, 240–1; Bishop, *Life and Adventures*, 142–6; Staniforth, 'Life', 327–8; see also: Blennie, *Narrative*, 17–19; Krafft, 'Journal', 65; Shaw, *Autobiography*, 40; NAM 1968-07-260 'Order book of Ensign Chaytor 3rd Foot Guards in Germany' (19 May 1762).

[17] Bibliothèque National, Paris, NUMM-109500, Joseph-Charles Bonin, 'Voyage au Canada', 139–40, 178; Dominicus, *Tagebuch*, 27; more on foraging: C. Duffy, *Military Experience*, 165–7 as well as Chapter 4, 160.

after a raid on the French coast, ordering them to return to quarters instead.[18] In these cases, the exertions the troops had undergone could explain momentary relaxation; however, it is known that this was part of a broader practice to ease formal requirements on campaign. For instance, it was usually acceptable for men to alter their uniforms to the conditions in which they operated. The British soldiers in North America cut the rims of their hats and wore moccasins. Parade ground manoeuvres and appearances were simplified even by campaigning Prussian and Russian troops.[19] This could not be done unless the military authorities themselves were willing to forgo some of their own disciplinary demands.

Another case to illustrate that not every transgression resulted in punishment was the persistence of duelling. Despite being universally forbidden in all regulations, the practice was kept alive, and not only by the officer corps. Jean Rossignol mentions fighting in ten duels preceded by a formal challenge, not including brawls. More interesting for the current discussion, though, was the way his superiors reacted to those exploits. After his first fight, in which he stabbed his opponent in the chest, Rossignol was taken before his sergeant major, who forgave him on account of the defence that a soldier always has to fight when provoked, lest he be dishonoured. On a different occasion, Rossignol was wounded but refused to go to hospital to avoid punishment, and was nursed back to health with a help of another sergeant. Shortly before his discharge, Rossignol's opponents fabricated an accusation that he had refused their challenge, which they sent to his officers. Instead of being praised for this uncharacteristic composure, Rossignol was punished with a daily hour of picketing for the next two months.[20]

The ambiguity of the military authorities towards duelling is also seen in the leniency with which duellists were sometimes treated. McBane had numerous fights, some of them in public, without the least interference from his superiors. On one such occasion, the corporal whom McBane wounded gave him advice on how to escape, while an officer whom McBane met on the way helped him further with money and a letter of recommendation which allowed him to reenlist in a different regiment. After mortally wounding a man while on furlough, Rossignol was absolved by the intervention of an aristocrat who had chanced to see the fight. A sergeant of the Ansbach Regiment who wounded his opponent so badly that the man could not do duty was given forty-one flats of a sabre.

---

[18] J. Field, *Devout Soldier*, 8–10; Flohr, *American Campaigns*, 28–9; Todd, *Journal*, 62; see also: C. Duffy, *Military Experience*, 169.

[19] C. Duffy, *Military Experience*, 107, 286; see also: Surtees, *Twenty-Five Years*, 7.

[20] Rossignol, *Vie veritable*, 14–21, 34–7, 49–50, 56–8.

Similarly, a comrade of Charles-Étienne Bernos, who was originally given a two-week solitary confinement for fighting a duel with sharpened sticks, was pardoned even before the sentence had expired.[21] This is not to say that duelling soldiers were immune from punishment. Todd reports that a man was handed over to a civilian court to be tried for murder after killing an opponent, while Steube deserted after wounding his. Nevertheless, even in these cases, the prohibition on duelling did not deter these men from fighting in the first place. Duelling thus provides a telling example of a prevailing social norm which clashed with formal discipline at the expense of the latter.[22]

As for the zeal with which more trivial regulations were actually enforced, the evidence is largely mixed. For instance, Blennie tells of two soldiers who were punished with extra drill for quarrelling in front of an officer's tent. It was further declared that, for the future, soldiers found to be similarly guilty would be subject to the relevant articles of war, which fined blasphemers one shilling. On the one hand, it can be argued this is a classical case of military disciplining. A different interpretation would be that the threat to implement what was the first section of the British Articles of War, which should have been taken for granted, indicates that these were not fully enforced. On another occasion, Blennie went to a Methodist meeting, despite strict orders forbidding soldiers to attend; unsurprisingly, nothing happened to him. According to Bonin, ordnances forbidding the selling of brandy to the Indians were published by every new Governor of Canada – to no avail.[23] This anecdotal evidence from soldiers' writings is supported, even if indirectly, by official documentation produced by the authorities themselves. For instance, the order books of the Boston garrison, which cover less than a year, contain eleven orders against drunkenness, from forbidding sale by unlicensed vendors to the closing of all 'dram stores'. Some orders introduced preventive measures such as the prohibition of men on furlough leaving camp with their water flasks, lest they bring these back full of brandy. Nevertheless, despite the initial impression that it was rigorously prosecuted, it is clear that the campaign against drunkenness in the garrison largely failed. The number of repetitious orders alone provides an indication that drunken soldiers remained a constant problem. On this point, it is worthwhile recalling Peter Wilson's astute observation that 'as with

---

[21] Donald McBane, 'Expert Swords-Man's Companion', 28, 39, 44; Rossignol, *Vie veritable*, 16, 41; Döhla, 'Tagebuch', (4 July, 1779); Bernos, 'Souvenirs de campagne', 738–9.

[22] Todd, *Journal*, 4; Steube, *Wanderscahften und Schicksale*, 50–3. For more on duelling and soldierly honour, see Chapter 5, 182.

[23] Blennie, *Narrative*, 5, 20–1; Bonin, 'Voyage au Canada', 160.

other areas of legislation in early modern Europe, the very volume of official decrees indicates how poorly they were enforced'.[24]

Moreover, as with duelling, it is hard to speak of a determined attempt to stop drunkenness. As shown by Paul Kopperman, who examined drunkenness in the eighteenth-century British army, the attitude of the military authorities towards alcohol consumption was ambivalent. While drunkenness was obviously seen as a major disciplinary problem, alcohol was often considered beneficial for the men's health. Moreover, it was also a great morale booster. Consequently, officers directed their punitive actions not against drinking but against drunkenness.[25] This was clearly the case in the Boston garrison, whose orders of 8 March 1776, while threatening intoxicated soldiers with 'the most rigorous means', informed the troops that a large quantity of spirit had just arrived on board the fleet. Rather than trying to curtail drinking as such, the orders were aimed to limit it to sanctioned times, while hinting that plenty of rum would be given out. This was a clear acknowledgement that complete control over the troops was not even attempted, let alone possible. It is also confirmed by instances of other disciplinary infractions mentioned in the same order book, which include dismantling fences and houses for firewood, cruelty to animals and an instance when the portraits of a royal couple were defaced. In addition, there were numerous cases of robbery, including the stealing of the governor's own seal. It is worthwhile remembering that all this was happening while Boston was under siege and completely subject to military law. What does this say about conditions in a myriad of other garrisons which were not subject to such extreme circumstances?[26]

According to complaints lodged with their officers, furloughed soldiers from the 9th Infantry regiment, considered among the best in the Frederician army, were guilty of numerous misdemeanours. Those are enumerated in the threatening order issued by their colonel and include opposition to magistrates, requests for preferential treatment, illicit trading, smuggling spirits and importing cloth from abroad rather than buying fabrics from Prussian manufactures.[27] The men guilty of all this were mostly native-born cantonists who occupied an intermediary position between the military and civil sphere. Non-compliance by civilians to regulation, policies and disciplining processes in old-regime Europe is

---

[24] Howe, *Orderly Book*, 11, 14, 33, 44, 54, 95, 111, 182, 203, 228, 229, 231; P.H. Wilson, *War State and Society in Württemberg*, 82.

[25] Kopperman, 'The Cheapest Pay', 445–70; Compare with Todd, *Journal*, 78–9.

[26] Howe, *Orderly Book*, 71, 97, 102, 111, 160, 237. For the disciplinary conditions at another apparently-governable British garrison, see: Berkovich, 'Discipline and Control', 123–30.

[27] *BBS*, 240–1.

a known phenomenon, but there has been no attempt to see whether soldiers were capable of similar practices. Although this subject deserves further research, the evidence considered so far suggests that this was true even of men belonging to one of the better-disciplined European armies. Moreover, the commitment of superiors to the punctual implementation of the disciplinary routine was not always assured, a point which will become even more evident when we come to consider the implementation of eighteenth-century military justice.

Although traditionally seen as capricious, cruel and corrupt, studies of the last generation reveal the diverse and often finer aspects of old-regime criminal law. Recent work on law enforcement, policing and crime in eighteenth-century Britain, for instance, did much to challenge the traditional interpretation of the period as that of the merciless 'Bloody Code'. Rather than terrorising the poor with the unrestrained use of capital punishment, occasionally tempered with sudden bursts of clemency, the practices of the British courts were less arbitrary to begin with. Numerous cases ended with acquittals, and not every indictment meant that the defendant was sent to the gallows, as the authorities often considered the circumstances of the case and the offender. Moreover, legal practices became more consistent as the century progressed. Use of the death penalty declined, but rather than merely being a product of humanitarian concerns, this was largely due to the introduction of incremental punishments, particularly transportation, which caused an increase in indictments.[28] British naval justice, another system which was long blamed for its draconian practices, has been partially rehabilitated by works of scholars like Nicholas Rodger and Markus Eder. Discipline on board was not necessarily oppressive, and the infamous lash was not used at a whim. Moreover, not unlike civil legislation, the system was tempered by its own stated severity. As many offences carried a mandatory punishment, offenders who would otherwise merit a court martial were dismissed with a much lighter summary punishment.[29]

Compared to this more nuanced and generally better evaluation of eighteenth-century civil and naval legal systems, the view of old-regime military justice remains largely monolithic. While some works have argued that eighteenth-century military discipline was not necessarily as oppressive as it has usually been portrayed, this view has penetrated neither general nor specialist scholarship. While its civil counterpart was

---

[28] Beattie, *Crime and the Courts*; For refutation of the bloodthirstiness of British justice in the age of the 'Bloody Code', Beattie, *Policing and Punishment*, 472–5. See also the interesting comparative statistics collected in by Markus Eder in *"At the Instigation of the Devil"*. For a much more foucauldian view of this period, see: Lemmings, *Law and Government*.

[29] Rodger, *Wooden World*, 221–9; Eder, *Crime and Punishment*, 64.

slowly but steadily reforming, few have ventured to examine whether any similar process took place in the military sphere as well. About thirty years ago, Gilbert and Frey debated whether eighteenth-century British military justice became more severe or more lenient,[30] but this discussion was not informed further by any subsequent work. Whatever their disagreements on lash averages and other corporal punishments may be, both Gilbert and Frey agree that military justice mirrored some of the practices of the civilian courts. Both systems concentrated on a single type of offence; the civilian system was largely concerned with crimes against property, the military system with desertion. Other crimes, however, were treated with far more lenience, with the military courts being particularly lenient when dealing with civilian offences such as murder, rape and even robbery. Nevertheless, this suggestion still awaits systematic study, in lieu of which one should not be surprised to encounter statements, such as the one recently made by Peter Way, that British army discipline was based on terror.[31] However, even if we assume that the articles of war were implemented to the last letter of their stated severity, a situation questioned over the preceding pages, one needs to ask whether eighteenth-century common soldiers would necessarily subscribe to the same sentiments.

Before we come to consider contemporary testimonies, it is important to make a number of general observations. The harshness of military discipline, a point considered to be a *sine qua non* whenever the lot of the old-regime rankers is discussed, might not necessarily be that obvious. The perspective of enlightened commentators and the modern historians who follow them, with few of either group experiencing service in the ranks, tells us much about their opinion of the content of old-regime military regulations, which did not necessarily reflect what was actually implemented in practice. Moreover, scholars who reconfirm the harsh stance of the articles of war often do so based on the nature of the surviving archival material. The studies of British military justice cited above are based on the proceedings of the General Courts Martial.

---

[30] Arguments about the more lenient nature of old-regime military justice were raised by Uhle-Wettler, *Höhe- und Wendepunkte deutscher Militärgeschichte*, 27–8; Muth, *Flucht*, 109–12; On possible changes in eighteenth-century British military justice, Gilbert argued it was becoming worse, while Frey made a case for greater humanity; see: Gilbert, 'Military and Civilian Justice', 50–4; Gilbert, 'Changing Face', 80–4; Frey, 'Courts and Cats', *Military Affairs*, 43 (1979), 5–11.

[31] Gilbert, 'Military and Civilian Justice', 45–9, 63–5; Frey, *British Soldier in America*, 90–1; Way, 'Class and the Common Soldier', 480. On the concentration of civil courts on property offences, see: Beattie, *Policing and Punishment*, 458; hopefully, some of the issues described in this paragraph will soon be informed by William P. Tatum's forthcoming Brown University PhD thesis which examines eighteenth-century British military justice as a civilian-influenced imperial institution.

Samuel Scott, who characterised military discipline in the last years of old-regime France as 'very severe', formulated this conclusion based on surviving verdicts of the *conseil du guerre*. In either of these cases, however, these were the papers of the highest tier of military justice that were examined. Interesting as it is, the fate of the most serious offenders which comes across in that material is not necessarily representative of the day-to-day experiences of the overwhelming majority of soldiers. To put military justice into perspective, it should be remembered that eighteenth-century civilians who were occasionally shaken by the brutality of military corporal punishments would gleefully flock to the public execution squares in an atmosphere comparable to a carnival.[32] The position taken by contemporary critics of military discipline appears the more ironic since the use of corporal correction was prevalent not only in early-modern civil law, but was also seen as the legitimate tool of every *pater familias*. It would just as likely to be employed by the master on his workers, the teacher on his students and the nobleman on his tenants and other social subordinates. Steppler, who studied the largely extant records of almost fifty years' worth of regimental courts martial of the First Foot Guards, reminds us that 'physical beatings in one form or another were too prevalent at all levels of society for it to be believed that the common soldier had a peculiar revulsion to the idea of a beating or a flogging'. The question of whether soldiers were necessarily worse off under martial law is a fascinating problem but less germane to the current discussion. For the moment, it is sufficient to refer to Cesare Beccaria, who commended military justice for its rejection of torture thus: 'How strange it must seem to anyone who does not take account of how great the tyranny of habit is, that peaceful laws should have to learn a more humane system of justice from souls inured to massacre and blood'.[33]

Considering the central role attributed to punishment in the daily running of old-regime armies, only a few accounts engage in gory descriptions of floggings and executions. Many authors witnessed military punishments of some sort, which are often described laconically.[34] Personal encounters with discipline, that is, when the author was

---

[32] S.F. Scott, *Response*, 36; Foucault, *Discipline and Punish*, 61; Gatrell, *Hanging Tree*, 56–105, McGowen, 'Making Examples'. For an example of *Schadenfreude* by less enlightened civilians when soldiers were running the gauntlet, see: Löffler, *Der alte Sergeant*, 107.

[33] Steppler, 'British Military Law', 880; see also: C. Duffy, *Army of Frederick the Great*, 68; Hagist, *British Soldiers*, 75–6; Beccaria, *On Crimes and Punishments*, 42–3; Starkey, *War*, 24–5.

[34] See for instance: Todd, *Journal*, 16, 36, 142, 203, Wood, *Gunner at Large*, 39, 97, 121, 134. For more dramatic descriptions of flogging, see: Bryson, *Ordeal*, 93; Coates, *Narrative*, 28–9.

himself punished, are much fewer. This evidence does not lend itself to easy interpretation. If an account does not mention military punishments, does it mean that its author has not seen any or, perhaps, he considered them too trivial to merit a reference? Does the fact that only a small minority of soldier-writers describe undergoing corporal punishment mean that they were the only authors who suffered? Since it is known that some deserters withheld details in their actions, it is very possible that flogged soldiers might likewise wish to keep this unpleasant fact out of their accounts. Quantitative analysis of this evidence is impossible. The diary of Johann Conrad Döhla, for instance, mentions over forty instances of corporal punishment spread over four years of active service. Although he refers only to the two auxiliary regiments from Ansbach-Bayreuth, it is impossible to determine whether Döhla's account covers all corporal punishments which occurred in those units, or perhaps only those that he witnessed.[35] Nevertheless, this and similar first-hand accounts remain valuable. Although Döhla does not provide more than the name of the offender, his crime and the sentence, other authors express their thoughts on what they saw or experienced. Moreover, fragmentary and anecdotal as they might be, their accounts provide the only substantial direct testimony on a point which is otherwise completely lost for the modern researcher. Summary punishments and informal pardons left no trace in the archival records, as was also often the case with lower tiers of military justice. Soldier-authors thus provide a rare perspective on the daily workings of eighteenth-century military discipline. Lastly, as we will see over the following pages, some of the more adamant critics of its brutal practices provide what is actually a positive portrayal of old-regime discipline. The stated preference of their authors thus lends credibility to that particular portion of their accounts.

One of the more iconoclastic sources on the old-regime Prussian military is the recollections of Joseph Ferdinand Dreyer. An Alsatian who enlisted voluntarily in the army of Frederick William I and served in all the wars waged by his more famous son, Dreyer wrote his memoirs shortly after the crushing defeats of 1806. His account of fifty years of happy soldiering in a period long considered the grimmest for Prussian enlisted men even led the otherwise positively inclined Dennis Showalter to remark that Dreyer 'often confuses positive specific experiences with the

---

[35] Döhla, 'Tagebuch', (13 November 1778, 11 August 1779, 20 April 1781, 9 June 1783). In comparison, Stephan Popp, who served in the second Ansbach Regiment, mentions only one disciplinary action, the execution of two deserters, see: 'Journal', 36. For a positive but largely evocative view of old-regime discipline based on Döhla's diary, see: Gaude, 'Military Justice in a "Hessian" Regiment'.

general vigour of lost youth'. Nevertheless, Dreyer's narrative is anything but an old man's ramblings about long-gone glorious days. Although he complains about some of the negative developments brought by modern times, such as the decline in religiosity and the deterioration of old soldierly privileges, Dreyer recognises some recent positive developments. For instance, he praises the new uniforms, which became more practical, lighter and warmer, and acknowledges the benefits for the common soldier now that armies are allowed to live off the land. Likewise, when it comes to discipline, the account provides a complex portrayal. Dreyer openly admits that the proficiency of the army which entered into the Silesian Wars was largely obtained through the abundant use of the cane, although Dreyer himself was usually spared, being a drummer rather than an infantryman. Dreyer underscores, however, that this harshness was in line with the nature of those times, and soldiers were not singled out for worse treatment than the rest of Prussian society. The manoeuvres were not hard, and men who were caned for their mistakes in drill had only themselves to blame. Moreover, soldiers were accustomed to such treatment from their days as peasants, and had no aspiration to be considered equal to their noble officers. Dreyer states further that men should trust their superiors and execute their commands immediately and without question. Nevertheless, military subordination at that time did not entail thoughtless obedience. For instance, if Dreyer noticed his officer was about to lead the detachment on the wrong road, he would be perfectly comfortable pointing out this mistake.[36] Dreyer's account raises three important points regarding corporal punishment and disciplinary practice in general. Firstly, personal encounters with corporal punishment could be reduced and sometimes avoided. Secondly, soldiers did not necessarily consider corporal punishment to be brutal or unjust. Lastly, Dreyer shows that at least some soldiers accepted the prevailing disciplinary system and considered its demands to be legitimate. Each of these aspects will now be addressed in turn.

As already pointed out by Steppler, the evidence regarding the prevalence of summary discipline is not as clear cut: '"manual correction" appears to have been common but how common?' According to some of the surviving narratives, soldiers could serve for a substantial time and never experience or at least avoid its graver forms. Veteran Sergeant John Stevenson says that he 'was never any more afraid of the lash than I was at the gibbet: no man ever comes to that but through bad conduct, just the same as thousands come to the jail and penal settlements'. Bernos' only

---

[36] Dreyer, *Leben und Taten*, 14, 18–23; Showalter, *Wars of Frederick the Great*, 11. See also: C. Duffy, *Military Experience*, 11.

encounter with military discipline in eight years of military service was a short arrest brought about by a genuine misunderstanding regarding alteration to his uniform, and he was quickly released. During the first half of his engagement, Jean Rossignol was not disciplined even once. In the subsequent four years, his rash behaviour led him to various punishments; including confinement, picketing and carrying ten muskets. But, as we will see in the latter part of this chapter, Rossignol was always spared the worst fate reserved for offenders like him. According to reformed Quaker and former light dragoon John Mackellow, he led a wicked life, continuously engrossed in quarrels and debauchery. Unsurprisingly, this behaviour often got him disciplined by his superiors. The punishments endured by Mackellow included picketing, imprisonment in the black hole and a confinement in the barracks chained to a wooden plug.[37] Nevertheless, even for such a troublesome man, disciplining did not necessarily result in brutal caning, flogging or the gauntlet.

It is presumptuous for a modern historian to try to determine the actual physical injury inflicted by corporal punishment. Discussion of lash averages and theoretical comparisons of the physical damage done by the gauntlet and whipping with the cat-of-nine-tails obscures the fact that these were living human creatures who had to endure such ordeals. Nevertheless, it is fair to cite contemporary accounts by men who actually underwent such penalties. Peter Henly's first case of flogging was 100 stripes after a brawl in a public house. According to Henly, this punishment was more intended to please the landlord than to hurt the culprit. After passing without comment a further sentence of 200 lashes for a boxing match, Henly remarks that the offence for which he got his next punishment, 100 stripes for disobedience and disrespect to the sergeant major, was worth at least 300 lashes. An unsuccessful desertion attempt earned him another 200 stripes; a punishment which Henly found to be very lenient. Indifference and even defiance to corporal punishment can also be found in Steininger, whose desertion attempt from the Württemberg army cost him thirty-six gauntlets through 300 men, divided between three separate occasions. Steininger took pride in his own toughness, and agreed to undergo the second run sooner than the other offender who was originally punished with him. The next two runs, however, were a fiasco, as Steininger's comrades were clearly ordered not to strike hard. Some even hit the shirt which Steininger rolled around his

---

[37] Steppler, 'British Military Law', 864–5; Stevenson, *Soldier*, 140; Bernos, 'Souvenirs de campagne', 747; Rossignol, *Vie veritable*, 21; John Mackellow, *Autobiography*, 17–20. See also: Johann Friedrich Löffler, who received his first corporal punishment after six years of service, *Der alte Sergeant*, 97.

waist, something which the officers in charge could not fail to notice.[38] Even when leniency was not invoked, some eighteenth-century soldiers were capable of enormous resilience. Löffler endured ten gauntlets through 300 men in one go. William Surtees tells of a man who broke into the officers' mess and was given 800 lashes in one standing without showing much suffering. Some soldiers even showed open contempt for corporal punishment, such as the Polish soldier who was billeted with von Klöden's family. Occasionally uttering 'Juckt mir wieder mein Puckel so sehr, Muß schröpfen lassen', this man would steal a trifle, and then run the gauntlet. Compared to this more brash case, the resigned acceptance of Friedrich Wilhelm Beeger appears to be a more genuine reaction. Despite being a keen volunteer, Beeger suffered at the hands of his brutal NCO, who punished every minor mistake at drill with three strikes of a cane. 'I suffered', writes Beeger, 'but I chose this life'.[39]

Nevertheless, it is clear that soldiers themselves were not necessarily averse to corporal punishment. In his discussion of Russian military discipline, considered to be the harshest in Europe, Keep cites a case of a hesitant humane officer who was confronted by his men, who requested that a soldier who had dishonoured their company by his negligent behaviour be subjected to the customary gauntlet. This was not a unique instance of soldiers not considering manual correction to be inherently unfair or unjust. Underscoring that soldiers should be treated humanely and that excessive cruelty breeds indignation, Sergeant Lamb concedes, nevertheless, that with some people 'no doubt the lash cannot always be withheld'. Sergeant Stevenson recalls that men sometimes required their officers to discipline drunkards.[40] Moreover, manual correction was occasionally used by the men themselves. Francis Grose's dictionary mentions an informal penalty called 'cold burning', in which cold water was poured down the offender's sleeves. Even more interestingly, on top of such informal practices, soldiers occasionally adopted the practices of their superiors. John Robert Shaw reports such a case when a fellow British prisoner informed the American guards of damage done to the stockade of the camp. The American commissioner proceeded to surrender the man to his own comrades, who held a proper court martial, which sentenced the traitor to receive 500 lashes on his bare posterior.

[38] Henly, *Life*, 12, 28–30. At Steininger's third run, an officer remarked that even school children receive more than this, see: *Leben und Abenteuer*, 52–3.

[39] Surtees, *Twenty-Five Years*, 43; 'My skin itches again, I must have myself bled', Klöden, *Jugenderinnerungen*, 26; Compare with J. Thompson, *Bard*, 149; Beeger, *Seltsame Schicksale*, 24–5.

[40] Keep, *Soldiers of the Tsar*, 225; Lamb, *Memoir*, 63–4; Stevenson, *Soldier*, 166–7. See also: Kenward, *Sussex Highlander*, 79; R. Brown, *Impartial Journal*, 99; Hagist, 'Unpublished Writings of Roger Lamb', 282.

This insistence on proper military formalities was not an isolated incident. Steppler found that in the First Regiment of Foot Guards, soldiers were allowed to hold their own company courts, chaired by a sergeant and assisted by a corporal and three privates. Punishments adjudged by such courts usually involved beating.[41] The fact that men were imitating the judicial practices of their superiors points not only to acceptance but also to the internalisation of the demands of the prevailing disciplinary system. This would be unlikely to happen if the men considered military discipline to be completely unjust.

Much is said about the capriciousness of military justice and discipline in general, a point which comes through in the accounts of the men themselves. It is hard to see much consistency in cases such as that described by Seume, when one mass escape attempt by pressed Hessian recruits was brutally suppressed, while a similar plot shortly afterwards was dealt with merely by admonitions and threats. Use of lots was likewise arbitrary, although one could say that such a practice was blind to personal circumstances.[42] Nevertheless, a number of trends can still be identified. First-time offenders were often pardoned or given a much-reduced punishment. Henly, who sold parts of his uniform to buy food after losing his money at cards, was forgiven by his officer, as was Beeger's first offence. Lamb tells of a first-time deserter whose punishment was remitted after the first seventy-five lashes. Sergeant Stevenson wrote that soldiers are lashed much less frequently then civilians think, and courts would usually pardon offenders a few times before resorting to that method.[43] The severest punishments, including the death penalty, were usually used against hardened offenders after more lenient methods had failed. Rather than being completely random, though, such punishments often came in bursts, which included a combination of threats and amnesties, a few spectacular examples and then more pardons. A representative sequence of this sort is described by James Miller, a survivor of the notorious Jacobite Manchester Regiment, who was pressed to serve against the French in India. After a week in which up to eight men were deserting every night, the troops were addressed by their commander, who promised safe return to England or generous reenlistment conditions with the East India Company. Next week the troops

---

[41] Shaw, *Autobiography*, 49; Steppler, 'British Military Law', 881; Grose, *Classical Dictionary*, q.v. 'Cold Burning'.

[42] Seume, *Werke*, vol I, 64–8; Starkey, *War*, 25; Scouller, *Armies of Queen Anne*, 267; Steppler, 'British Military Law', 876–8. On the use of lots, see: Jonas, *Soldier's Journal*, 26–7; Steininger, *Leben und Abenteuer*, 87.

[43] Henly, *Life*, 7; Beeger, *Seltsame Schicksale*, 21–2; Lamb, *Memoir*, 68; Stevenson, *Soldier*, 150–1; For other instances of pardoning, see: Williamson, *French and Indian Cruelty*, 84, J. Field, *Devout Soldier*, 11–2.

witnessed the execution of two apprehended deserters, while a man who was caught two weeks later was pardoned.[44]

While the pulsating nature of the higher echelons of old-regime military justice was observed by scholars such as Brumwell,[45] one important point went largely unnoticed. As we argued in the previous chapter, higher desertion levels were a product of the failure of existing surveillance and penal mechanisms. It should be asked, therefore, whether more frequent use of corporal punishment in the daily running of armies is actually a sign of weakness and the inability of the prevailing disciplinary system to enforce obedience? To use one example to illustrate this question, let us consider the Regimental Court Martial book of a composite battalion stationed in Boston shortly before the outbreak of the American Revolution. At first glance the situation it describes appears appalling. In less than six months, there were ninety-two trials, in which 95 per cent of the defendants were found guilty, of which over eighty men were sentenced to corporal punishment, all from a force which totalled only 246 men. Steven Baule and Don Hagist, who analysed this source, argue that the situation within the battalion was particularly harsh because the battalion was undergoing a disciplinary crisis after its men became accustomed to lax treatment by their former colonel. Nevertheless, there is an additional way of understanding this data. A third of the defendants were recurrent offenders, and one soldier was even tried four times, implying that the prospect of incurring corporal punishment carried little terror.[46]

The suggestion that too much manual correction actually undermined rather than increased its deterrent effect is supported by an unlikely witness. The memoirs of James Aytoun, who served on the Caribbean island of Domenica following the American War, initially reads as a damning indictment of vicious cane-discipline administered by whimsical, inefficient and corrupt officers. On their arrival on the island, the men were welcomed by ten sergeants armed with rattans, with which they were soon to make an intimate acquaintance. One of the first commands delivered during exercise was 'sergeants draw your canes' which were then used to thrash any man guilty of the smallest error. Nevertheless, the frequent beatings stopped being considered a disgrace, turning instead into a subject for sardonic jokes. Moreover, the men were clearly not overawed by their superiors, whom they lampooned not only in private,

---

[44] James Miller, 'Diary', 222; Compare with Popp, 'Journal', 36. On Miller's former Jacobite unit, see: Oates, 'Manchester Regiment'.

[45] Brumwell, *Redcoats*, 107–10.

[46] NAM 1976-09-3 'Orderly book kept by officer in 18th Regiment of Foot, in North America, chiefly encamped outside Boston 26 Jun 1774–5 Jun 1775'; Baule and Hagist, 'Regimental Punishment Book, 12–3.

but also in public. This could extend to more formal challenges. The ungodly adjutant was successfully confronted on at least two occasions, firstly by a soldier who managed to have his confinement to the barracks revoked and later by a sickly man who lodged a formal complaint after being beaten. To hush up that case, the adjutant was forced to discharge the man with a compensation of forty guineas. An example of another particularly nasty officer demonstrates that at least some of Aytoun's superiors were not all that bad. Although he originally caused a spree of prosecutions and punishments, once it was recognised that the captain-lieutenant was obsessively pursuing every trifle, the other officers began summarily dismissing all the complaints and court cases initiated by him.[47]

This last case shows that, even when described as tyrannical, the actual behaviour of the officers could be far more complex, a point which is amply demonstrated in the writings of another stern critic of old-regime military service. Like Aytoun, future Napoleonic officer Claude Le Roy was stationed in the Caribbean, serving in the colonial garrison of the nearby island of Martinique. Le Roy portrays his superiors, in line with revolutionary stereotypes, as young imbecile nobles who defrauded their own soldiers. A particular injustice which invoked Le Roy's resentment was a summary punishment of fifty flats of the sabre for letting a prisoner escape from arrest. Despite being cleared of all guilt by a subsequent court martial, Le Roy and his two fellow guards were denied the compensation of 300 *livres* due according to the regulations for victims of unjust punishments. Two years later, encouraged by news of the outbreak of the revolution in France, they decided to renew this case. However, the petition, which they proceeded to draft with full endorsement of the entire garrison, also included a long list of complaints about abuses by officers. After publicly receiving this document at a garrison review, the infuriated governor had the petitioners arrested and commanded them to be tried and shot. However, the assembled court martial refused to partake in a judicial execution. The major declared the court incompetent to judge a case which should have been dealt with at regimental level and the jury happily proceeded to dissolve itself. After the governor declared he would write to ask the minister for further advice, the major and the other former members of the court visited the prisoners and encouraged them to hold firm until the answer was received from France. The men were further offered an immediate release if they would ask the governor for clemency. The prisoners refused, but the officers, supposedly shocked by the grim

---

[47] Aytoun, *Redcoats*, for tyrannical behaviour by superiors, see: 8–11, 15–8, 20–1, 25, 32–3, and for defiance by their subordinates, 8, 25–8, 31, 37–9.

conditions of the dungeon, had them released anyhow.[48] Other than proving Le Roy's injustice to at least some of his superiors, his narrative illustrates three aspects which will be discussed in the third part of this chapter. Firstly, resolute defiance by soldiers was possible, while still falling short of mutiny or desertion. Secondly, despite having the men at their complete mercy, officers were not necessarily keen to invoke the whole power of the penal statutes at their disposal, and sometimes even shielded the transgressors from the discipline which they were to enforce. Lastly, and most importantly, such confrontations often included an element of negotiation and compromise.[49]

It is important to understand that even mutiny did not constitute a rejection of the prevailing power relations within old-regime armies. The troops usually rose as a result of a specific grievance, or in the hope of redressing a particular aspect within the disciplinary system. Unpaid wages, undelivered equipment, broken promises or a particularly unpopular officer could cause a mutiny, but this was not equivalent to rejecting military identity. In fact, some mutineers, such as those described by James Miller in Quebec, or the Württemberg troops which partook in the Swabian mutinies of 1757, retained outward signs of military discipline, including marching in formation and maintaining their hold of military insignia. Rather than questioning military authority as such, the mutineers were hoping to win specific concessions through what Eric Hobsbawm called 'collective bargaining by riot'.[50] Rather than responding with violent suppression, the authorities usually reacted with a combination of entreaties and threats, punishing a few ringleaders, while meeting some of the demands put forward by the troops. Armed resistance meant a radical break with these conventions, which could result in far more severe repercussions for the mutineers. In a case described by Samuel Wray, despite being fully armed and possessing artillery, mutineers of the 60th Regiment preferred to surrender when confronted by smaller force. Even when forcibly suppressed, mutinies could still accomplish their aims in the long run. Despite claims to the contrary in John Dayes' memoir, the Duke of Kent did not flee Gibraltar,

---

[48] Le Roy, *Souvenirs*, 45–60.
[49] Some of these ideas have been already expressed by Will Tatum in an excellent paper on authority and negotiation in the eighteenth-century British army; see: 'The Soldiers Murmoured Much'.
[50] Hobsbawm, 'The Machine Breakers', 59; Scouller, *Armies of Queen Anne*, 279–83; Atwood, *Hessians*, 213–5, Emsley, 'Military and Popular Disorder, 103; Way, 'Rebellion of the Regulars', 763; Prebble, *Mutiny*; Centre of Kentish Studies, Maidstone, U1350 Z9A, James Miller, 'Memoirs of an Invalid', 78; see also: Williamson, *French and Indian Cruelty*, 59. For a comparable view of mutinies in the British Navy, see: Rodger, *Wooden World*, 237–44.

nor repeal any of the disciplinary measures which prompted the notorious mutiny in November 1802. Nevertheless, the royal governor was quietly recalled to England a few months later, never to return again.[51] While remaining risky for the individual participant, mutiny was generally a successful device for the soldiery as a whole. Moreover, eighteenth-century enlisted men were also capable of milder forms of collective resistance, which could produce comparable success but without the same strain that a mutiny would cause.

Like mutiny, collective defiance encompassed both prearranged and direct actions. Boycotts and petitions necessitated an element of preliminary planning, and soldiers could take further advantage of external circumstances. The recent arrival of the new commander-in-chief to India prompted the 75th Regiment to complain that the regimental accounts had not been settled for seventeen years. Upon the receipt of their petition, the commander, who was clearly keen to demonstrate his benevolence to the troops at the start of his tenure, immediately forced the officers to settle all existing arrears. The attempt of the governor of Cape Town to pay his men with devalued currency similarly backfired, as the garrison resolved not to pay for anything except with the new copper money. This effectively transferred the cost to the local merchants, who in turn demanded that the governor settle their losses. The men could also rise to address a specific grievance, as happened in the Bayreuth Regiment on its march back from American captivity. After one of their comrades was dragged by his hair to be put under arrest after being unjustly accused of disrespect to the major, the soldiers refused to march further under that officer. Some declared that they would proceed independently to New York to complain to the colonel, while others threw down their uniforms, declaring that since they were no longer treated as soldiers but as slaves they would, therefore, negotiate as criminals.[52] Nor would the men necessarily meekly proceed to acknowledge an order they disliked. According to *Fourier* Sohr, when notified of their disbandment, a unit of Saxon jaegers protested so vocally that more troops had to be summoned to ensure that the men surrender their equipment and receive

---

[51] P.H. Wilson, 'Violence and Rejection of Authority', 8–9, 22–5; Wray, *Military Adventures*, 4–5. For first-hand accounts of the Gibraltar mutiny, see: Dayes, *Memoir*, 7; B. Miller, 'Adventures', 38; and a highly embellished account by Pearson, *Soldier who Walked Away*, 41–3.

[52] Kenward, *Sussex Highlander*, 58–9; Pearson, *Soldier who Walked Away*, 20–1. For a successful boycott of army issued supplies and provisions, see: Aytoun, *Redcoats*, 35–6, 39; Döhla, 'Tagebuch', (13 May 1783). Eventually, some companies continued marching without their officers until the evening when a collective statement was made to one of the captains vouching for the innocence of the arrested man who was immediately released.

their final pay. Soldiers could express their displeasure in a very public manner, as in the case of a review before General Amherst, when all the assembled troops started shouting 'a gill of rum' to protest the withdrawal of this daily bonus to which they were accustomed. Sometimes one man could also brazenly voice the concern of the majority. When the survivors of the Havana expedition were reviewed by General Murray on their return to Quebec, the governor jokingly addressed a grenadier with whom he was familiar: 'You b—r I did not know you, you look so black!' 'We have been on black service, and have got very little white money for it', was the response.[53]

Defiant behaviour on personal grounds could be just as bold. Seume, who was left without any free time after his colonel turned him into a personal secretary, in addition to Seume's responsibilities as a sergeant, protested by going hunting instead of completing the usual paperwork. Seume knew his worth as an educated man, and the gamble paid off handsomely – after a short spell in the guard house, he was released from all military duties and granted extra pay. Soldiers could also occasionally invoke civil justice, as did some of Robinson's comrades, who proceeded to sue their officers for not granting them their promised discharges after the Peace of Amiens. Individual protest, however, did not necessarily entail the rejection of military hierarchy, sometimes quite the contrary. Sergeant Thompson refused to follow a corporal sent by an officer to confine him because he would not be arrested by a junior NCO. After reporting to his lieutenant, Thompson proceeded to the guardhouse independently and confined himself. Thompson thus underscored his unbending allegiance to military discipline *despite* having experienced injustice at the hands of a superior officer.[54]

Defiance could also be covert, as some men were more concerned with hiding transgressions, avoiding punishment or avenging unpopular superiors. Roger Lamb tells how his fellow recruits who sold parts of their kit would borrow each other's equipment before inspection day to keep the loss secret. Whenever Prussian cavalry guardsman Johann Christoph Pickert saw his corporal approaching him with the cane, he would simply avoid him by going down the row of horses and sometimes even climbing under them. Rossignol pursued a more forceful course of action against his sergeant major, putting horsehair into his bedding, drilling holes in his chamber pot and, eventually, by attacking him on

[53] Sohr, *Meine Geschichte*, 78–9; J. Thompson, *Bard*, 218; J. Miller, 'Memoirs of an Invalid', 77–8.
[54] Seume, *Werke*, vol. I, 86; D. Robertson, *Journal*, 37; J. Thompson, *Bard*, 156; For other instances when men put themselves voluntarily under arrest, see: Döhla, 'Tagebuch', (14 March and 10 May 1782).

the street when the sergeant was returning to the barracks from a night visit to his mistress. Bryson avenged himself against an NCO who brought him before a court martial by cutting down his hammock in the middle of the night and pushing it, together with the man, down the hatch of the lower deck. Bersling, whose nasty lieutenant eventually provoked him to desert from the King's German Legion, did not meekly resign himself to enduring the insults of the officer. When the lieutenant attempted to attain the cooperation in a forceful abduction of a young woman, Bersling threatened his superior with a drawn sword. The undeclared war between the two continued. The lieutenant, who served as the unit's riding instructor, would repeatedly miss the horse's feet with his whip, hitting Bersling on the shins, as if by accident. Bersling retaliated by going out in disguise after dark and beating the lieutenant on the street. More senior officers could also be threatened, as in the case mentioned by James Wood, when a captain received an intimidating anonymous letter accusing him of withholding prize money. Although a large reward was promised to anyone who would bring information about this conspiracy, the remaining prize money was paid within a month.[55]

Eighteenth-century regulations typically did not indulge in nuanced definitions. According to the Articles of War published under Queen Anne, mutiny and sedition were punishable by death, as were demonstrations and demands made in a mutinous manner, while officers supporting or ignoring such behaviour were just as culpable. The Imperial articles defined mutiny as four or more soldiers who approached their superior with demands. In Russia, the Petrean regulations allowed soldiers to complain as individuals, but any collective action, even if committed without any ill intent, was punishable by death, as were the officers who tolerated such behaviour. These uncompromising demands, together with the officers' total control over military courts, meant that common soldiers were essentially at the mercy of their superiors. Moreover, failure to act against mutiny formally made them into associates in the crime. And yet officers were not necessarily eager to use their power. Despite the reputation his army had for its unrelenting discipline, Beeger was forgiven his first offence, which included drunkenness, disorderly behaviour, disobedience, escape from custody and attacking two NCOs with snowballs. The pardon, however, was not announced right away, and Beeger was first treated to a long *Strafpredigt* which enumerated all the punishments due to him according to the regulations. Eventually, his captain declared

---

[55] Lamb, *Memoir*, 72–4; Pickert, *Lebens-Geschichte*, 38; Rossignol, *Vie véritable*, 29–31; Bryson, *Ordeal*, 76–8; Bersling, *Der böhmische Veteran*, 248–50, 252; Wood, *Gunner at Large*, 145.

that no court martial would be held, as Beeger was reprieved due to his youth and stupidity by the general under whose window Beeger resisted the NCOs. 'You should write him a thank you note, as soon as we air your uniform', concluded the captain dramatically, while one of victims of yesterday's snowball attack suddenly appeared with a drawn cane. Beeger meekly asked to be punished by another man, and, to the great entertainment of the assembled officers, took a very long time to remove his coat. After tormenting Beeger a bit longer, his captain dismissed him without beating.[56]

Beeger's reprieve was not an isolated instance, as other officers also used admonitions, threats and shaming. Corporal Todd was reprimanded for drunkenness, while Steininger was threatened for squandering his bounty in one night, but no further punishment followed. The master-tailor of Thompson's regiment, who entered Louisbourg after its surrender disguised as a British officer, had the misfortune to bump into his colonel, who was also visiting the town. Colonel Fraser did not say a word, but later that evening he had the tailor summoned to his tent. After a long wait which only reinforced his fears, the tailor was led in front of assembled regimental staff, asked to alter a new coat and then dismissed as quickly. Pardon could also extend to capital offences. Following the rejection of his application for furlough, Rossignol confronted his captain. After the officer refused to explain his decision, Rossignol flew into a rage and accused his captain of being unjust, crying out that the captain's cross of St. Louis was not won but stolen. The infuriated captain attempted to kick Rossignol out of his quarters, but Rossignol continued to resist until eventually he was overpowered by the NCOs. French regulations specified that direct physical assault of a superior was aggravated by an element of parricide and, as such, should be punished by hanging preceded by cutting off the offender's right hand. Fortunately for Rossignol, the regimental priest intervened on his behalf, as did the major, who acted in his capacity as the regimental judicial officer. Nevertheless, Rossignol's fate remained entirely at the mercy of his captain, because pressing the charge in this case meant a certain guilty verdict followed by the prescribed mandatory punishment. The officer eventually relented and agreed that Rossignol should be locked for six months in the black hole instead. Shortly afterwards, the captain visited Rossignol in prison, where the grateful man asked for forgiveness and

---

[56] *Rules and Articles*, (1708), arts. 14–8; *Reglament für die sämmentlich-Kaiserlich-Königliche Infanterie*, (1769), 91 arts. 3–4; Peter the Great, *Instruksii i artikuli*, (1714), arts. 134–5; Beeger, *Seltsame Schicksale*, 19–22. For another soldier who was pardoned for his first offence, see: Bryson, *Ordeal*, 85.

thanked his officer for his generosity. Offered a transfer to the more comfortable guardhouse, Rossignol declared he would stay in the black hole. He was soon ordered to be released, spending a total of twenty-eight days in confinement.[57]

Other than the fact that, just like Aytoun and Le Roy, Rossignol's blank criticism of old-regime military service is unfair, his narrative shows that the resolution of a disciplinary case often occurred before or even without a judicial process. As within other branches of eighteenth-century justice, the mandatory punishment often played a moderating influence, as superiors exercised discretion and opted for more lenient, informal punishments. Thus, as argued by Atwood, the stated severity of military penal discipline actually undermined its own deterrence. Other than the discretion of his superiors, Rossignol's case reveals another important parallel with contemporary justice. Like the defendants described in Peter King's study, Rossignol tried to influence the case against him by declaring his regret and using his contacts with other officers. Accused soldiers could thus play a more active role within the disciplinary process. Moreover, by his formal submission, Rossignol has reconfirmed the legitimacy of the proceedings against him, and thus removed part of the necessity to punish him. Not unlike the acts of defiance described in the preceding pages, this was another device which could be invoked within the framework of power relations between officers and their subordinates. Just as men often stopped short of mutiny, which could overstrain the existing power structure, some officers stopped short of punishment if their authority was no longer questioned. As shown by studies of the early-modern penal system, the elaborate ceremonial aspects of judicial proceedings and executions were intended to provide legitimacy to the existing disciplinary system. Likewise, when military subordination was reconfirmed by the words and deeds of the soldier himself, leniency could be exercised. According to Bräker, soldiers who openly demonstrated their satisfaction with military service were singled out for better treatment, unlike Bräker himself, whose gloomy looks often earned him threats from his officer. Johann Steininger, punished with forty strokes of a cane for hitting his NCO, was addressed the next day by his colonel while another offender was running the gauntlet, and asked whether he deserved one too. 'Ja, Euer Gnaden, Herr Obrest' instantly replied Steininger, saving his back this time.[58]

---

[57] Todd, *Journal*, 129; Steininger, *Leben und Abenteuer*, 40; J. Thompson, *Bard*, 160–2; Rossignol, *Vie veritable*, 23–9.

[58] Atwood, *Hessians*, 174–5; King, *Crime, Justice, and Discretion*; Bräker, 'Lebensgeschichte', 456; Steininger, *Leben und Abenteuer*, 46. For an example of a petition of three soldiers accused of theft, see: BL Add MS 44,084, 'Petition by John Morgain, John Pays and Edward Sanders' (1763), in 'Loudoun Papers', vol. XXII, 121.

However, such extroverted displays of submission were not initiated by men only. Bernos tells of a very illuminating case which occurred while he was marching through Austria in a prisoners' convoy. To entertain a family on which they were billeted, one of Bernos' comrades named St. Etienne changed clothes with the Hungarian cavalryman who had been placed to guard their house. Next morning the men were woken up by the Hungarian officer, who discovered the prank and marched them both to the assembly point as they were, to the great amusement of the convoy and the prisoners. After the French officer discussed the matter with the commander of the escort, the men were finally allowed to change back into their original uniforms. After ordering St. Etienne to rejoin his comrades, the French officer approached the prisoners and suggested they plead mercy for the Hungarian, who was already surrounded by of four of his NCOs. As the punishment was about to begin, St. Etienne went out from the ranks and cried for grace, joined by the rest of the French line. The Hungarian commander graciously relented and forgave his man, although this did not surprise anyone, as the preceding conversation between the two officers had been overheard. What happened was essentially a prearranged show. The potential confrontation was resolved as win-win for all sides, and after demonstrating their severity, the officers also showed their magnanimity. Upholding their moral authority was more important than enforcing the formalities of both Austrian and French regulations which threatened death to anyone requesting clemency for a man undergoing a military punishment. On a different occasion, which involved a similar element of display, a man from Matthew Bishop's regiment called out during a brigade review demanding some unpaid allowance. To pacify the enraged general, the colonel immediately offered to find the culprit and, after quickly turning back to smile at his men, ordered the adjutant to promise a reward to anyone pointing to the man who shouted. Afterwards the colonel proceeded to ride through the ranks brandishing a money purse and, at the same time, smiling and repeating 'don't impeach one another'.[59]

What worked on a public level also worked on a personal level. Rather than forcing them to accept an order, officers were often willing to consider the interests of their immediate subordinates. Upon their arrival in the Hanoverian army, Georg Beß and the other Hessian jaegers were offered the choice whether to serve with the infantry or the cavalry. Sohr's captain asked him whether he could be transferred to another corps, since

---

[59] Bernos, 'Souvenirs de campagne', 684–6; Bishop, *Life and Adventures*, 180–1; Michon, *Justice Militaire*, 7; *Reglament für die sämmentlich-Kaiserlich-Königliche Infanterie*, (1769), 91–2, article 3.

the *fourier* from a different company originally designated for this position could not be as easily spared. On their side, men could approach their officers with similar requests. Todd, who eventually got the post himself, reports that when it became known that the position of pioneer-corporal had become vacant, many corporals went to their captains and asked not to be selected. Comparable informal requests by the men could include more mundane matters, ranging from asking for extraordinary passes and furloughs to disciplinary matters. Mackellow, who was ordered to drill with the recruits, asked his adjutant to revoke this punishment, arguing that no one had ever been punished before in that manner. Likewise, soldiers could occasionally solicit pardons for their comrades. This could be done directly, as in the case of Corporal Todd, who asked for one on behalf of his sergeant, but also as part of a collective action which could involve additional parties. After Rossignol was arrested for going absent without leave, his comrades from a different regiment applied to his captain for pardon. After meeting with initial rejection, they approached their colonel, who in turn persuaded Rossignol's captain to release him. After *Fourier* Knoll was demoted, the regiment interceded for him with the colonel and Knoll was promoted corporal.[60]

Moreover, rather than merely accepting or rejecting each other's requests, both sides could also negotiate. After being passed over in promotion in the light company of the 56th Regiment, Surtees applied to transfer to the rifle corps, which prompted his officers to offer him a corporal's post in a different company. Surtees did not concede and transferred anyway. Later, his new colonel made him corporal, to persuade Surtees not to take advantage of a discharge successfully solicited by his parents. Sergeant Thompson tells an anecdote of a fellow highlander, Sergeant Duncan McPhee, who took as a trophy the rapier of a captured French officer. Although Duncan's disregard of accepted gentlemanly conventions threatened his colonel with major embarrassment, he could not simply order it to be returned. Instead, Colonel Fraser ridiculed Duncan for taking such interest in a silly twig, offering him money instead. Duncan, who had already tied the rapier near his more menacing broadsword, declared he cared not about money but honour! It took more persuasion and ten crowns before the rapier was returned to its original owner. Moreover, as happens in negotiations, the subsequent position of the enlisted man could be reinforced by a degree of initial defiance. Bernos twice ignored a summon to go to see the regimental

---

[60] Beß, 'Aus dem Tagebuch', 193–4; Sohr, *Meine Geschichte*, 34–5; Todd, *Journal*, 139, 142; Staniforth, 'Life', 338; Mackellow, *Autobiography*, 64–5; Rossignol, *Vie veritable*, 54–5; see also: Döhla, 'Tagebuch', (1–5 June 1783); Bernos, 'Souvenirs de campagne', 738–9.

adjutant, who wanted to appoint Bernos as his assistant. Eventually, arriving after threats of arrest and being further reprimanded for insubordination and ingratitude, Bernos replied that he saw no viable prospects in the position. Firstly, this was a sergeants' post, but Bernos did not want to be promoted as it would add three more years on top of his original service contract. Nor did he consider relief from all other duties to be an advantage because it was wartime, and transfer away from his company would see him branded as a coward. Bernos proposed to help the adjutant, but only in winter quarters or during rear service, an offer which was accepted.[61]

Just as men could argue their cases assertively, officers could attempt to exert their power by subtle means. After Corporal Todd was confined by Lieutenant-Quartermaster Burlow for supposedly failing to provide him with enough wood, Todd's pioneers collected twice as much wood and then offered to petition the major on his behalf. Todd dissuaded them, declaring that he preferred to be relieved from duty as corporal instead. On his side, Burlow tried to resolve the matter by sending a sergeant who enquired whether Todd would make a written submission, but the corporal refused. Since no agreed compromise was achieved, the case passed up the military hierarchy into the hands of the major, who released Todd and informally reprimanded Burlow. Officers could also attempt to win defiant soldiers over to their side, as did the captain who originally attempted to arrest Thompson in a case we described earlier this chapter. Despite drink invitations and other overt marks of friendship, Thompson remained cold, understanding this sudden outburst was due to his popularity with the men and good relations with the colonel.[62] Nevertheless, the fact that confrontations between superiors and subordinates could sometimes turn into informal haggling is revealing of the actual nature of the power relationship prevailing in eighteenth-century armies.

This chapter has tested the assumption that the success of coercive compliance in combat could be achieved through successful conditioning of the men with rigorous formal discipline during the sustaining stage. As demonstrated in the above pages, the eventual obedience of the men to their superiors might just as well be a product of compromise. Moreover, even battles were not immune to an element of negotiation. As demonstrated by Möbius, rather than using brute force, Prussian officers led their men by example and also by persuasion, using moral exertions, jokes and appealing to the men's sense of honour. Moreover,

---

[61] Surtees, *Twenty-Five Years*, 41–3; J. Thompson, *Bard*, 147–8; Bernos, 'Souvenirs de campagne', 747–8. Negotiations could also take place at enlistment, see: Butler, *Narrative*, 28–9.
[62] Todd, *Journal*, 208–10, 216; J. Thompson, *Bard*, 192.

soldiers were capable of making their voices heard, and good officers would not force them to fight beyond the limits of their endurance. The reality described by Möbius is that of a balance of power based on consent rather than upon a strict hierarchy. A point which escapes Möbius, however, is that sometimes these were the soldiers who clamoured for action while their superiors initiated negotiation in the hope of avoiding it. Hearing the noise of battle in front of them, men of David Robertson's regiment requested loudly to be formed into a battle line, continuing to shout until the order was finally given. When Beß's jaeger detachment was surprised on the march by French cavalry, it was none other than Beß's lieutenant who suggested that the men surrender. As senior NCO, Beß remonstrated, suggesting a ruse to keep the attackers at bay and save the detachment. Beß makes it clear that the men supported his proposal and that the lieutenant relented, but officers could press for surrender more assertively, as did Pickert's commander during the retreat from Jena. Informing his troops that they were surrounded by the French, the officer asked whether they wished to break out or capitulate. Since the soldiers initially asked to fight on, he then told them that the only available road they could take was in a bad condition and already covered by enemy artillery. The men simply replied that if the road were bad it should not be used, and the commander quickly proceeded to surrender.[63]

This last example of a Prussian general who felt obliged to convince his men to allow him to surrender presents old-regime soldiers in a very different light from the one in which they are typically portrayed. Nor does it appear that enlisted men felt disempowered by their officers, whom they defied on numerous occasions. The assertiveness of the soldiers stemmed in part from the concrete restrictions placed by the conditions of war and peacetime service upon the control mechanisms available to their superiors. What Lars Behrisch fittingly defined as the early-modern paradox of overregulation and under-government[64] applies just as well to old-regime armies. Moreover, even when they were able to enforce discipline without restraints, the officers often chose to forgo many of its penal aspects. Although their men were also capable of harming them, this ambiguous stance of the superiors can best be explained through immediate pragmatic considerations. Confrontation

---

[63] Möbius, 'Kommunikation'; D. Robertson, *Journal*, 16–7; Beß, 'Aus dem Tagebuch', 203–4; Pickert, *Lebens-Geschichte*, 48; For more examples when soldiers pressured their officers to stop fighting, see: Flohr, *American Campaigns*, 40; Beß, 'Aus dem Tagebuch', 236; For a recent studies which underscore the consensual nature of military discipline in modern warfare, see: Smith, *Between Mutiny and Obedience*; Audoin-Rouzeau and Becker, 'Violence et consentement', Cochet, *Survivre au front*.

[64] Behrisch, 'Social Discipline in Early Modern Russia', 332.

strained the military organisation, whose complete breakdown was even less desirable to the officers than to their men. Compromise, on the other hand, would be a safer option, and also drew the soldiers closer into the disciplinary system. By accepting concessions, men also reaffirmed the basic legitimacy of their superiors and the organisation in whose name they acted. Besides, the fact that negotiations were held and resolved within the army is indicative that the men had internalised many of its institutional aspects and, consequentially, demands.

This interpretation of power relations within old-regime armies is largely at odds with received wisdom. Nevertheless, in line with the case made in the previous two chapters, the preceding pages show that eighteenth-century enlisted men were active actors rather than passive subjects. Moreover, despite the availability of desertion as a clear alternative, many men preferred to defy the military system while remaining an integral part of it. Instead, the men employed subtle forms of resistance which, to use James Scott's words, could be described as 'a tactical choice born of the prudent awareness of the balance of power'. Soldiers also had much to lose from a confrontation with their superiors. Consequently, the military authorities and their subordinates resorted to what might be termed a dialogue. Authorities played a more conspicuous part by announcing rules and sometimes implementing them. The men, on their part, answered either by obeying as desired, or not. In the latter case, measured shows of dissatisfaction were sufficient to provoke a reaction which, whatever its rhetoric, was often a conciliatory one. This, rather than formal negotiation between equals, lay at the heart of the consent which characterised old-regime military discipline, and, some would say, every disciplinary system. Nevertheless, despite remaining a rigid hierarchical system, the power relations within eighteenth-century armies had an element of reciprocity. Moreover, considering the daily practice of old-regime armies, it is clear that their disciplinary regimen was intended not so much to control as to contain. Combined with our findings regarding desertion, this chapter questions the central role of coercive compliance, both in the sustaining and combat stages. This alone points to the role of the other two levers of compliance in the running of eighteenth-century armies.[65]

---

[65] J.C. Scott, *Domination and the Art of Resistance*, 183; These last two paragraphs were also informed by Certeau, *Practice of Everyday Life*.

4   Why Did They Enlist?

In his memoirs, written some forty years afterwards, Ensign of the Invalids, James Miller describes his enlistment in the British army at the start of the Seven Years War. Impressed by the writings of Plutarch and Nepos as well as his schoolmaster, a proficient sportsman and prizefighter, young Miller acquired an idealistic view of life. Hearing a drumbeat for the first time 'set [his] heart on fire'. After failing to impress a number of recruiting parties, Miller's wish to join 'the first of mortals' and guardians of the realm was gratified after he encountered a crimp, one of the civilian recruiting agents notorious for their semi-legal activities. However, no strong-arm methods were necessary with Miller, who happily believed in the glories of soldierly life and in promises of gold and honour. After he was whisked away with a few other boys on the very next morning without being given a chance to bid farewell to his family, Miller began to doubt his choice, but it was too late.[1] Miller's account appears as an archetypical story of enlistment in an old-regime army. The image of a silly youngster whose romantic notions were exploited by unscrupulous recruiters was widely accepted at that time. While such men could be excused for their foolishness, another group of likely recruits had far more sinister motives. Contemporary discourse pointed to the army as a refuge for all kind of drunkards, troublemakers and idlers. Although mentioned less often than stupidity or delinquency, eighteenth-century observers pointed to a third motive for taking the bounty. It was neatly put by Daniel Defoe, who remarked that 'in winter the poor starve, thieve or turn soldier'.[2]

A combination of these three motives is typically cited in modern historical writings as well. General scholarship still tends to present a largely negative portrayal of eighteenth-century recruits. Lawrence James, for instance, writes that British recruits included hungry derelicts

---

[1] Centre of Kentish Studies, Maidstone, U1350 Z9A, 'Memoirs of an Invalid', 5–9. For more on James Miller, see: Way, 'Memoirs of an Invalid'. On crimps and their activities, see: Gilbert, 'Analysis'; Steppler, *Common Soldier*, 8, 18. For another first-hand account of an encounter with the crimps, see: Matson, *Indian Warfare*, 15–6.

[2] Defoe is quoted in: Chandler, 'Captain General', 75.

and bored youths, but the majority simply enlisted while in a drunken stupor. When the material factor is emphasised, it is also often painted in grim colours. Richard Holmes describes typical recruits as poor and hungry, with few alternative choices in life.[3] In other words, while not necessarily being criminals or dupes, potential recruits were driven primarily by desperation. This argument usually builds on a growing body of specialist studies that point to the relation between macro-economic conditions and enlistment levels. For instance, many of the victims of the decline of the traditional weaving industry in Britain found their way into the military. Periods of crisis or famine tended to be most fruitful for recruiting. One such instance was the harsh winter of 1708–9, when many flocked to the colours of the French army, if only in the hope of being fed. Moreover, recruitment tended to go better during winter months, when demand for unskilled labour was at its lowest.[4]

As with the social character of the recruits, specialised scholarship went further, to offer a more positive interpretation of financial considerations for enlisting and underscoring the pragmatic motives of the recruits. The pay of eighteenth-century common soldiers was usually equivalent to that of an unskilled labourer. However, compared to the latter case, the soldier could be certain he would be paid relatively regularly, whatever the conditions on the job market. Soldiers could further be ensured that they would be clothed, housed and fed, perhaps inadequately, but still better than many among the social classes from whence they came. Moreover, the army provided its members with a modicum of welfare. Rudimentary medical care was guaranteed, and those fortunate to serve for long enough had the prospect of a pension or help finding employment as minor officials. Moreover, as shown by Corvisier, under certain conditions, enlistment could prove a sensible investment. Bounty, especially in wartime, could amount to a substantial sum, and not every recruit proceeded to squander it in a drunken frenzy. If set aside for the future, a soldier who managed his affairs well could turn it into a small stock, which could ensure him a modest living upon his discharge.[5]

---

[3] James, *Warrior Race*, 292–4; Holmes, *Redcoat*, 135; see also: Bell, *First Total War*, 39.

[4] Frey, *British Soldier in America*, 53; Corvisier, *L'Armée française*; Loriga, *Soldati*, 115–22; For the beneficial effect of famines on recruitment, see: Girard, *Service militaire*, 72; Lynn, *Giant*, 151, 352, 389; Chandler, *Marlborough*, 245; Robson, 'Raising of a Regiment', 108–9. For enlistments rates in particular months of the year, see: Loriga, Fig. 4; Ingrao, *Hessian Mercenary State*, 131. The best recent work examining the links between economic conditions and recruitment is Edward Coss' study of Wellington's Peninsular army. Although it deals with a later period than the current study, many of its conclusions are relevant for the eighteenth-century as well, see: *All for a King's Shilling*, 244–63.

[5] Showalter, *Wars of Frederick the Great*, 170. For similar consideration to enlist in the Hessian army, see: Ingrao, *Mercenary State*, 131. Similarly, although without much evidence to support this assertion, Frey, *British Soldier in America*, 119.

Compared to the widely accepted role of material factors, idealistic motives are not given much prominence. Scholars like Duffy or Showalter who cite the genuine appeal of a military career are in the minority.[6] While not discarding this factor entirely, other historians usually attribute it only to very specific cases, such as soldier's sons or discharged veterans. When first-hand accounts cite such motives, they are typically treated with suspicion, and often considered as later rationalisations by the authors, who were either aiming to gratify their readers or to mask their folly in enlisting in the first place. Another point noted by eighteenth-century observers, and repeated by modern historians, is that the army offered a chance to radically change one's circumstances. However, this is also interpreted negatively. Those likely to take advantage of this option thought more about escaping the burden of responsibility or routine rather than suddenly discovering anything particularly appealing in life as a soldier. Apprentices enlisted to avoid drudgery and hard work, husbands and lovers to be rid of their partners and offspring, minor offenders to dodge the law.[7] Contemporaries were well aware of this set of motives, and it was invoked in sources ranging from George Farquhar's comic play to legal proceedings with the civil authorities. For instance, in reply to a petition filed by a master craftsman whose apprentice enlisted in the British regiment known as the Green Howards, the recruiting officers stated that: 'If apprentices and Servants weary of their master's service, Husbands of their wives and any sett of People inclining to change their present conditions of lif, can't enlist, ther's an End of Recruiting the army since no Man is born a soldier, but enters into it at the Time he's found fit and willing for service.'[8]

And yet, even this example is indicative of a broader phenomenon. Not every wayward youngster, philanderer or drunkard in old-regime Europe chose to enlist. Those wishing to escape their current circumstances could try their luck in a large city, join the throngs of migrant workmen and vagrants, or even offer themselves as indentured labourers in the colonies. The fact that military service was likelier to attract certain types of individuals already demonstrates that it could exercise an appeal which went beyond practical considerations. Likewise, the possible financial benefits of enlistment were not necessarily all that apparent to every recruit. For

---

[6] C. Duffy, *Military Experience*, 91–2; Showalter, *Wars of Frederick the Great*, 101. Another scholar to mention idealistic motives for enlistment, although without further elaboration is S.F. Scott, *Response*, 7.

[7] Guy, 'Army of the Georges', 92–111; Brumwell, *Redcoats*, 79–81; Pröve, *Stehendes Heer*, 37–8; Hurl-Eamon, '"Youth in the Devil's Service"', 168–70.

[8] Farquhar, *Recruiting Officer*; Green Howards Regimental Museum, Richmond, M 383 'Counter Petition on behalf of Ensign Lemisden and George Clark Apprentice'.

instance, the young age of many of the soldiers makes it unlikely that they considered such long-term schemes, as described by Corvisier, when they first took the bounty. Hence, while it is impossible to deny the significance of the army as a potential resort for those desiring change or those wishing to improve their material status, it appears that there were further factors that can explain the initial motivation of old-regime soldiers.

The discussion in this chapter is informed by an influential model formulated by American sociologist Charles Moskos, who argues that the army is a social organisation which moves between two opposite poles: institutional and occupational. According to Moskos, an institution 'is legitimated in terms of values and norms, that is, a purpose transcending individual self-interest in favour of a presumed higher good'. Material considerations play a secondary role in this social environment, especially since the pay of its ordinary members is likely to be low. Instead, '[m]embers of an institution are often viewed as following a calling; they generally regard themselves as being different or apart from the broader society and are so regarded by others'. In an institution, general societal norms would often be subordinate to specific norms, many of which are not only informal but would sometimes go further than the declared official norms of the organisation itself. In comparison, an organisation where the occupational element prevails 'is legitimated in terms of the marketplace'. Instead of selfless principles on behalf of the organisation and their fellow associates, individual members would be steered by material elements expecting 'monetary rewards for equivalent competencies'.[9]

Moskos' main argument that the abolition of the draft and the transformation of the US military into a professional all-volunteer force shifted its organisational premise from institutional to occupational was not without its critics.[10] More generally, Moskos' model came under scrutiny for its dualistic nature. Later researchers argue that its two components are separate dimensions whose level could vary independently of one another.[11] Nevertheless, none of these critics has questioned the existence of both institutional and occupational considerations in the

---

[9] Moskos, 'From Institution to Occupation', 41–3; Moskos, 'Institutional/Occupational Trends in Armed Forces: An Update'; Moskos, 'Institutional and Occupational Trends'.

[10] For instance: Faris, 'Economic and Noneconomic Factors'; Moore, 'Propensity of Junior Enlisted Personnel'; Segal, Freedman-Doan, Bachman and O'Malley, 'Attitudes of Entry-level Enlisted Personnel', 207; Sackett and Mavor, *Attitudes, Aptitudes, and Aspirations of American Youth*, 202–12; Eighmey, 'Why Do Youth Enlist?'.

[11] Stahl, McNichols and Manley, 'Empirical Examination'; Cotton, 'Institutional and Occupational Values'; Manigart and Prensky, 'Recruitment and Retention of Volunteers', 104–7; Segal, 'Measuring the Institutional/Occupational Change Thesis', 354–8; Woodruff, Kelty and Segal, 'Propensity to Serve and Motivation to Enlist'.

motivation of individuals to join and serve in the military. Thus, while the precise relation between the aspects of Moskos' theory is continuously debated, its basic premise remains intact.

To use the terms adopted by the current study, Moskos' distinction between institutional and occupational motives for enlisting corresponds with normative and remunerative compliance. When his views are applied to the prevailing scholarly interpretations of old-regime initial motivation, it becomes clear that previous research dealt largely with the occupational aspect of eighteenth-century military service. The initial motivation of recruits is largely seen in material or practical terms. Very few, however, have considered the institutional appeal which the eighteenth-century army could have exercised on its potential recruits. The main aim of this chapter is to fill this gap by considering surviving testimonies of those common soldiers who describe the reasons, thoughts or circumstances which led to their enlistment. By scrutinising this evidence, it is hoped not only to verify the existence, but also to determine the overall significance of normative factors in the recruitment of old-regime soldiers. A crucial point in answering this question is not only to see what alternatives, if any, were available to would-be recruits, but also whether their narratives take more of an institutional or an occupational view of military service. A shorter point to be considered in the later part of this chapter is the role of remunerative compliance in the sustaining and combat stages. Again, this will be done by considering the writings of common soldiers and examining the importance they attribute to pay and booty.

Before we consider the views held by potential recruits towards military service, it is important to weigh up how old-regime armies were likely to present themselves to their prospective soldiers. Whatever dodgy methods the recruiters might occasionally use, eighteenth-century armies preferred to man their ranks with genuine volunteers. Moreover, as shown by recent studies, there were enough such men to provide the bulk of the rank and file. Even in the Prussian army, which resorted to the cantonal system, the number of native-born conscripts in a typical peacetime year did not exceed a few thousand. In wartime, armies could rely heavily on the conscription of native subjects. Many of the Prussian regiments towards the end of the Seven Years War were made up mostly of cantonists. Drafts from the *milice* contributed about a third of the French manpower in the same conflict. The impressment acts in Britain provided a substantial portion of the recruits during the War of the Spanish Succession.[12]

[12] P.H. Wilson, 'Social Militarization', 18–21; Girard, *Service militaire*, 167–74; Kennett, *French Armies*, 80; Scouller, *Armies of Queen Anne*, 374–5; Gilbert, 'Army Impressment', 702; Middleton, 'Recruitment of the British Army', 229–30. However, as shown by Stephen Conway, the contribution of impressment to British manpower in later

Nevertheless, with the exception of the Russian army, no old-regime force would be able to function without relying on volunteers. Such men also provided the backbone of the active army in peacetime after the *miliciens* were discharged and the cantonists sent home on extended leave. However, in order to draw such men, the armies had to make themselves appealing. How was this done?

Other than demonstrating that there were enough literate would-be soldiers to justify the printing of such documents, eighteenth-century recruiting posters provide the best indication of the public face worn by the armies not only vis-à-vis their recruits, but also for society at large. Even allowing that their content included substantial embellishments, the choice taken by their creators is an important one. The aim of the posters was to draw recruits, and this would have been impossible if their message had been completely irrelevant or unappealing.

Interestingly, the enlistment bounty, whose attraction is typically emphasised in modern studies, does not figure prominently. In most of the twenty-five posters from old-regime France collected by Albert Dépreux, the recruits are promised *bon* and even *tres-bon engagement*, a clear reference to the bounty, but none actually cites any specific figure. A few regiments, like the Laval Infantry, mention the officially mandated daily subsistence rate paid to the recruits between their engagement and their departure to the unit. Although it could come to 40 *sous*, close to five times the daily pay rates in the French infantry,[13] this was not part of the recruitment bonus, whose official rates could be a hundred *livres* or more. Likewise, with the exception of advertisements to enlist in the artillery corps, no reference is made to other financial benefits such as pay, pension or future employment opportunities. The recruits were promised that they would be taught reading and writing and given schooling in arithmetic and draughtsmanship. The prospect of promotion to commissioned rank was underscored, as artillery regiments had over twenty officer vacancies set aside for deserving rankers 'distinguished by their talent and good conduct'.[14] However, such promises were an exception

---

eighteenth-century Wars was 10 per cent or below; see: 'Mobilization of Manpower' 392–3; On impressments of vagabonds in Electoral Saxony, see: Kroll, *Soldaten*, 95–8.

[13] Depréaux, *Affiches*, pl. 7 Laval Infantrie (1747), pl. 20 Strasbourg Artillerie (1784–5), pl. 23 Roussilon Cavalerie (1786). More generally on French recruiting posters, see: Girard, *Service militaire*, 76.

[14] 'on leur donnera toutes les connaissances nécessaires pour parvenir aux vingt-une places d'Officiers que le Roi a créées dans ledit Régiment d'AUXONE, pour les canonniers, qui, par leur talens & leur bon conduite, se distingueront'. Soldiers unable to earn a commission were promised upon retirement preferment to positions in garrison cities, militia and the commissary service, some worth 3,000 *livres* per year, see: ibid., pl. 15 Auxone Artillerie (1769–70), pl. 16 Corps Royal Artillerie (1770), pl. 20 Strasbourg Artillerie.

for the corps which required the most specialised and skilful manpower. An advertisement for the new elite heavy cavalry regiment of carabineers, printed shortly before the revolution, was the only other placard to cite the teaching of literacy as an incentive to enlist. Promotion, but only to NCO rank, is mentioned by the Royal Cuirassiers and the Orleans Cavalry Regiments; the latter also tried to lure recruits by promising the opportunity of future transfer into the guards. Some regiments advertised for professional craftsmen like the artillery, again citing actual pay figures rather than just mentioning the skill required.[15] However, when considered together, such practical or material inducements are entirely surpassed by incentives of a completely different kind.

A typical French placard would combine flattery with promises of thrills and honour. Headings such as *Avis a la brilliante* or *belle Jeunesse* were not a particularly subtle insinuation as to what type of character should consider taking military service. This set the tone for the remaining part of the poster, which usually underscored the agreeable, joyful and honourable facets of military service. The Royal-Piedmont Cavalry Regiment, for instance, invited men to acquire glory and be crowned with the laurels of victory, while the La Fère Artillery Regiment informed its potential recruits that they could expect to dance three times per week, play tennis twice a week and spend the rest of their time bowling, playing skittles and doing some drill. The liberated nature of a soldier was further underscored by fancy uniforms, whose written descriptions on some posters were longer and contained more specific details than the customary vague references to pay and bounty. A placard of the Bourges Provincial Regiment described its uniform down to the pink lapels and monogram on the buttons, while the carabineers emphasised that their men wore distinctive braided uniforms and silver-trimmed hats.[16] References to uniform could also mention additional marks of merit, as underscored in the posters of the Royal Cuirassiers: 'the only unit of French cavalry equipped with BREASTPLATES which they bore with honour since their creation'.[17] Less-detailed posters still portrayed their regiments as good, distinguished or honourable, as well as underscoring references to elite status. A placard of the Guyenne Infantry mentioned that the regiment had recently been augmented by a grenadier and

---

[15] Ibid., pl. 16 Corps Royal Artillerie, pl. 9, Penthiévre Infanterie (1752–6), pl. 10, Orleans Dragons (1757).

[16] Ibid., pl. 24 Royal-Piemont Cavalerie (1780–3), pl. 12 La Fère Artillerie (1766), pl. 11, Regiment de Bourges (1764–5), pl. 25 Corps de Carabiniers (1789).

[17] 'LES CUIRASSIERS DE ROI sont la saule Troupe de Cavalerie Française qui sont armée de CUIRASSES & cette Armure, qu'ils ont protées avec l'honneur depuis leur création, a toujours distingué ce Corps dans les Armees & dans de batailles', Ibid., pl. 13 Cuirassiers de Roi (1767–76).

a *chasseur* (light infantry) company, a message further highlighted by crude images of men from both companies in their distinctive bear and leather caps. A poster of the Chasseurs de Vosges only included but a short bilingual notice about the unspecified advantages of serving in that corps, and a very detailed representation of two grenadiers, together with a file of sharp-looking musketeers and a troop of horse. The high quality of that engraving demonstrates that the mere look of a soldier could prove alluring, for otherwise it would be hard to explain why the recruiters would commission such work to begin with.[18] Another non-material element of military service mentioned in some posters was the ability to serve the king. The poster of the Strasbourg artillery regiment, otherwise containing the most detailed description of the practical benefits of enlistment, begins its appeal to those desirous of acquiring glory in the service of their *fatherland*, showing that the loyalty of the would-be recruit could extend beyond the immediate person of the monarch.[19]

Promotional material from Great Britain, where recruiting advertisements were also often placed in local newspapers, conveys very similar messages. There are few advertisements dealing only with the financial benefits of enlistment, such as that of the 56th Regiment of Foot, which promised bounties from one-and-a-half to two guineas, depending on the height of the recruit, plus a gift of another guinea from the Earl of Northumberland, or an advertisement of the Royal Artillery which promised its enlistees a daily pay of one shilling and four pence. An advertisement for the Royal Wagon Train, another corps where pay was relatively high, dryly elaborates on the desired qualifications ('Farmers' Servants or such young men who have been accustomed to Horses are the description of the people wanted') but, again, this is an exception. Some horse regiments, like the light dragoons, required saddlers and collar-makers, while foot regiments could tempt literate recruits with the promise of immediate promotion to NCO.[20] Nevertheless, such practical considerations were usually merged into more uplifting language. A 1766

---

[18] Ibid., pl. 19 Guienne Infanterie (1782–8), pl. 21 Chasseurs des Vosges (1785); On possible appeal of service with the grenadiers, see: C. Duffy, *Instrument of War*, 196–7.

[19] Both those consideration would be united by the carabineers who underscored that their crops will not take vagabonds or foreigners but only loyal Frenchmen who could be trusted by the king for such type of service, see: Depréaux, *Affiches*, pl. 20 Strasbourg Artillerie, pl. 25 Corps de Carabiniers.

[20] Burrows, *Essex Regiment, 2nd Battalion (56th)*, 3–4; Royal Artillery, A.W. Haarman quoting verbatim from the *New York Gazette* of 7 April 1777, in *JSAHR*, 48 (1970), 61; Royal Wagon Train (1800), G.O. Rickwood quoting verbatim from the *Nottingham Journal* (15 February 1800), *JSAHR*, 31 (1953), 36; Royal Light Dragoons (1759), quoted verbatim from the *Leeds Intelligencer* (3 July 1759) in *JSAHR*, 34 (1956), 45; 94th Regiment of Foot, quoted by G.O. Rickwood from the *Ipswich Journal* and *Chelmsford Chronicle* dated August to November 1779, in *JSAHR*, 29 (1951), 42–3;

advertisement for the East India Company mentions the pay figure of ten pence per day, the bounty and the free equipment, as well as the possibility of making a great fortune in the orient. The notice, however, begins by inviting those '[w]hose ambition is above Slavery and Mean Employment, or to be subject to Masters or Mistresses Tempers' to hurry 'with the noble spirit of a gentlemen' to meet the recruiting captain and 'the usage they will receive[...] will remind them of what they will have when they join the company in India, which is well known to the world to be both honourable and genteel'.[21] Promises of making one's fortune could also be laced with patriotic language, such as that of the 100th Regiment of Foot, whose placard was headed with the phrase 'LOYAL RANGERS, A Spanish War makes an Englishman's Fortune'. The 44th Regiment of Foot, whose newspaper advertisement mentioned the prospect of a daily pension of one shilling for discharged veterans, emphasised the distinction won by the regiment in the recent American War and appealed to [a]ll clever young fellows [..] ambitious of becoming gentlemen'.[22]

Less-detailed or flamboyant advertisements still flattered the recruits by referring to them as 'gentlemen volunteers', 'brave enterprising youths', 'young men of spirit' or 'dashing lads'. Some posters underscored that the recruits must be of 'good character' while the Prince of Wales' Dragoon Guards declared that 'to save unnecessary Trouble, none need apply whose Character and Figure are not unexceptionable'. It was hinted that those endowed by such attributes might have further incentives to enlist. The same advertisement concluded by inviting recruits to 'enter a Life of ease and Jollity ... [y]oung Man troubled with Inquietude of Mind, from Connections with the Fair Sex, or any uneasy Circumstance whatever'. The Lincolnshire Regiment of Foot was more straightforward, informing that 'Spirited Lads of Size, Character & Qualifications, may acquit themselves of all Women Labouring with Child and young Children & enter into the direct road

---

125th Regiment of Foot or Loyal Stamford Volunteers, quoted by G.O. Rickwood from the *Nottingham Journal* (6 September 1794), in *JSAHR*, 31 (1953), 39–40.

[21] East India Company (1766) quoted verbatim by G.O. Rickwood in *JSAHR*, 21 (1941), 149; For very similar language, see more notices for the same service from the *Worcester Journal* (14 February 1771) and *Norwich Mercury* (7 November, 1778) in: *JSAHR*, 25 (1947), 137 and *JSAHR*, 31 (1953), 179–80.

[22] 100th Regiment of Foot (1780), placard brought verbatim in *JSAHR*, 24 (1946), 146; 44th Regiment of Foot (1786) notice from the *Ipswich Journal* (22 July 1786) in Burrows, *Essex Regiment, 1st Battalion (44th)*, 26–7. For other examples of regiments who refer to their wartime achievements, see: NAM 1980-12-21 'Recruiting poster for the King's Light Dragoons' (1779); NAM 1975-11-30 'Recruiting poster for the 6th (1st Warwickshire) Regiment of Foot (1795)'.

to Honour & Preferment'.[23] More exalted ideals were attributed to the would-be highland recruits of the Black Watch, who 'have withstood, immovable as a rock, all the assaults of surrounding luxury and dissipation'. Although this advertisement referred to a bounty of five-and-half guineas, more prominence was given to a personal appeal to the courageous highlanders from Britannia, who was insulted by her 'inveterate foes' France and Spain.[24]

Comparable patriotic language was already present in advertisements from the Seven Years War. In 1759, the dean of Gloucester offered to top up the bounty and offer a free flannel coat to proficient marksmen from the nearby Forest of Dean who would 'compose a Body of Light Infantry the most capable of annoying our enemies in their present Desperate design against the Protestant religion, and British Liberties'. Placards from the American War of Independence mention the deluded American brothers who had to be saved from the clutches of the tyrannical congress. Nevertheless, the main ire was again reserved for the French and Spanish, whose perfidy and treachery challenged the liberties of old England.[25] This message could be reinforced with artwork, as in the case of the Sussex light dragoons, whose placard shows one of its troopers trotting over two vanquished foes while another two enemy soldiers beg for mercy on their knees. Their lanky and ridiculous appearance could be directly inspired by the figures from Hogarth's Gate of Calais.[26] Adverts from the beginning of the Revolutionary Wars contained similar tirades about serving 'king and country' and chastising the perfidious French, but soon a new tone appeared. The 6th or the Warwickshire Regiment of Foot, which had just returned from the West Indies where it had been

---

[23] As well as getting rid of the drudgery of servitude and 'exchange their whips for Laced Coats and Silver hilted swords', the placard of the Lincolnshire Regiment of Foot (1793) is quoted verbatim in Leetham, 'Old Recruiting posters', 132; Prince of Wales' Dragoon Guards, notice from the *Ipswich Journal* (8 December 1770), reprinted in *JSAHR*, 2 (1923), 99–100. For more flatteries addressed to the recruits, see the advertisement of the 106th Regiment of Foot, Black Musketeers, quoted from the *Leeds Intelligencer* (8 December 1761), in *JSAHR*, 34 (1956) 46; Horse Grenadier Guards, notice quoted from the *Ipswich Journal* (25 October 1766), in: *JSAHR*, 22 (1943–4) 169; Third Regiment of Foot Guards (1795), Bodleian Library, Oxford, G.Pamph. 2850 (2); First Dragoon Guards (1803), notice quoted verbatim in *JSAHR*, 20 (1941), 116.

[24] 42nd Regiment of Foot Watch, Notice copied by J. Paine from the *Scots Magazine* for August 1779, in: *JSAHR*, 29 (1951), 41.

[25] 85th Regiment of Foot, notice quoted by R.M. Grazebrook from the *Gloucestershire Journal* (2 October 1759), in *JSAHR*, 27 (1949), 137; NAM 1950-10-9 'Recruiting Poster for 88th Regiment of Foot'; NAM 1969-07-17 'Recruiting Poster of the 1st Battalion of Pennsylvania Loyalists'; 86th Regiment of Foot, original notice in *Nottingham Journal* (21 August 1779), quoted in: *JSAHR*, 34 (1956), 137–8; 94th Regiment of Foot (1779), in: *JSAHR*, 29 (1951), 42–3.

[26] NAM 1992-07-261 'Sussex Light Dragoons' (1779–80). For Hogarth's characterisation of the French, see: Colley, *Britons*, 33–5.

decimated by yellow fever, appealed to 'A FEW GOOD RECRUITS' by praising its victorious war record '*over that most execrable and detestable banditti,* THE FRENCH [w]hose cruelties and infamy in murdering their KING and QUEEN with the innumerable other barbarities they have been guilty of, make them most justly detested and abhorred by all civilised nations, and by every honest man'. The Midlothian Light Dragoons combined patriotism with material benefit, citing their recent employment 'in exterminating the Croppies' and at 'present eating their beef, bread and potatoes (which by the way are not got for nothing) in peace and comfort in one of the most delightful, plentiful and cheapest Counties in Ireland'.[27]

Comparing French and British advertisements clearly shows that recruiters in both countries appealed primarily to institutional rather than occupational considerations. Although not ignoring them altogether, material factors were usually subsumed into the more exalted language of gallantry and even patriotism. Not unlike their modern counterparts, the adverts tried to flatter young men into accepting a challenge, while occasionally also offering to make them some money in the process. The relative downscaling of the latter factor is unsurprising, though, considering the actual value of military wages. Nevertheless, it is telling that even professional corps, where pay was relatively high, stressed what were normative considerations: the honour, the challenge and the joy of military service. One cannot fail to notice the irony in the summons to accept what was, essentially, the yoke of military discipline, often expressed in terms of embracing freedom.

The question still remains, though: how likely were such messages to attract potential recruits? One should not be too naïve about the precise wording of the advertisements. Considering the slow penetration of English into the Scottish highlands, it is unlikely that many of the individuals so highly praised in the above-mentioned notice of the Black Watch could *read* Britannia's call for arms, even if they did have access to the Edinburgh-based *Scots Magazine*, where the appeal was originally printed. Moreover, there is additional evidence that the advertisements were intended for a broader audience than the recruits themselves. Almost every French and British placard or newspaper notice offered rewards for persons helping to bring recruits, a clear invitation for third parties to try and procure enlistees. Nevertheless, assuming that the recruitment advertisements were also intended to provide guidance and

---

[27] Lincolnshire Regiment of Foot (1793) and Seaforth's Highlanders (1793) and Midlothian Light Dragoons (1798) in: Leetham, 'Recruiting Posters', 119–20, 132–3; 125th Regiment of Foot (1794), in *JSAHR*, 31 (1953), 39–40; NAM 1975-11-30 'Recruiting poster 6th Foot 1795'.

a possible template to entice potential recruits via an educated intermediary, their choice of language is important. The consistent stress on the exciting nature of military life rather than any practical benefits, as well as the use of artwork which depicted soldiers in fancy uniforms rather than coffers of money, is an indication of the way the army was perceived in the popular imagination. In other words, although it is impossible to quantify its precise strength, it is clear that the old-regime militaries were aware of their appeal as institutions. Its use demonstrates that normative considerations in the initial motivational stage cannot be ignored.

Recruitment was conducted along similar lines in almost every European army. It was carried out by small detached parties, usually consisting of an officer, a sergeant or two, a few trusted soldiers and a drummer. These would tour fairs and market towns, but also larger cities, where there was an even greater likelihood of encountering throngs of idle young men. The drummer would beat a ruffle, and the sergeant would entreat the assembled folk to enlist, pointing them to the quarters of the recruiting officer, usually conveniently located in one of the local taverns.[28] What happened next is often associated with the drunken farce satirised by Farquhar. Sobering up next morning, the young dupes would be informed that they were duly enlisted, after having voluntarily taken the bounty.

While such practices did undeniably take place,[29] old-regime recruiting could not be sustained by deceit or strong-arm methods alone. The recruiters could not operate without the cooperation of local authorities, who could retaliate if they exceeded their powers. Likewise, the crowd could take matters into its own hands, liberating the unwilling men. Most importantly, the ability to attract recruits was often a function of a good reputation.[30] Bräker tells how the business of the five Prussian officers based in Schaffhausen completely dried out after it became

---

[28] C. Duffy, *Army of Maria Theresa*, 48; C. Duffy, *Military Experience*, 89; C. Duffy, *Instrument of War*, 196–7; Steppler, *Common Soldier*, 8 13.

[29] Sometimes the recruiters would also be assisted by civilian agents and women who lured unsuspecting victims to the tavern; see: Laukhard, *Leben und Schicksale*, 72–5; Pearson, *Soldier who Walked Away*, 14–5; Bräker, 'Lebensgeschichte', 414–7, 420–3. The Prussian recruiters in the time of Frederick William I were particularly notorious for their unfair means, which included the kidnapping of foreign subjects; see for instance: 'Soldat Johann Schultze, an seine Verwandten, Arneburg' (13 August 1723), in: *BBS*, 282–4; For a contemporary fictional account of their practices, see: *List und Lustige Begebenheiten derer Herren Officiers auf Werbungen*. The view of old-regime recruitment as a largely deceitful business still prevails in some generalist studies, for instance: Hippler, *Citizens, Soldiers and National Armies*, 15–8, 21–3.

[30] Ex-Prussian and Austrian Sergeant turned playwriter, Gottlieb Stephanie puts a similar suggestion into the mouth of a recruiting officer in: 'Die Werber', in *Stephanie des jüngern sämmtliche Lustspiele*, vol. I. 50.

known that a local man who enlisted in Prussia was not granted his discharge. What is true for a whole army is also true for a single recruiting officer.[31] Moreover, the recruiting parties often spent many months on the road, sometimes passing through the lands of different states. This offered reluctant recruits numerous possibilities to abscond, with the recruiting officers liable to pay the expenses in all such cases. Put together, these were not insignificant considerations for ambitious young officers, for whom the recruiting service was one of the few ways open in peacetime to make a name for themselves, and also gain some revenue to purchase the next commission.[32] Officers wishing to succeed in this activity were advised to provide a steady intake of decent recruits, and they were more likely to achieve this if willing men could be attracted.

To succeed, first the party had to engage the attention of the potential recruits. This could include making references to material benefits, just as the Second Battalion of 79th Highlanders did when they commissioned a banner promising recruits a bounty of sixteen guineas. Nevertheless, as with the recruiting posters, these were usually subsumed in what Steppler called 'an atmosphere of general merriment', aimed to demonstrate that the army was a fun, prosperous and exciting place to join. Regulations recommended that enlisted men assigned to recruiting service were chosen from the best-looking soldiers and, if possible, issued with new uniform or eye-catching accessories.[33] Civilian musicians could be engaged to augment the drummer, and some officers attempted to reinforce the message by flamboyant displays of military bravado and, in wartime, by patriotic speeches. A recruiting rally which took place in Dublin shortly after the outbreak of the American War of Independence provides a good example of this practice. The officer who organised the event paraded with a large sack of gold but his cortège also included a hired wind orchestra playing 'God Save the King' and a cart laden with barrels of beer, which was distributed freely. The assembled spectators were then addressed with rousing words, exerting them to show their loyalty and save the rebellious colonists who, 'like unnatural children, would destroy

---

[31] Bräker, 'Lebensgeschichte', 429. On civilians attempting to release recruits and attacking recruiters, see: Girard, *Service militaire*, 113–24; *BBS*, 33–9.

[32] Gilbert, 'Military Recruitment and Career Advancement'. Recruitment could also be a way of demonstrating loyalty by officers from suspect political groups; see: Mackillop, *More Fruitful than the Soil*, 31. For a German study which doubts the overall importance of forceful recruitment: Pröve, *Stehendes Heer*, 43. A more middle point is taken by Huck, *Soldaten gegen Nordamerika*, 75–6

[33] Mackay 'Recruiting Flag of the 2nd Battalion 78th Highlanders'; Esterhazy de Gallantha, *Regulament und unumänderlich gebräuchliche Observations-Puncten*, (1747), 311, Bräker, 'Lebensgeschichte, 435; Lawrence, *Dorset Soldier*, 17; Shaw, *Autobiography*, 13. See also: Steppler, *Common Soldier*, 14–5.

their ever indulgent Parent, forgetting the Torrents of Blood spilt, and Heaps of Treasure expended for their Preservation'. The recruitment of William Pell on a Northamptonshire country-road was a much less sumptuous occasion, but the message conveyed to him was essentially similar. The off-duty sergeant of the First Regiment of Foot Guards who enlisted him mentioned some practicalities such as the duty and pay of the guards, but also described their privileges, and gave a lengthy account of the many curiosities to be seen in London.[34]

Moreover, the challenges experienced by the recruiters did not end when a man was convinced to take the bounty. A typical party did not have enough members to see individual enlistees to their units. Instead, the recruits stayed with the party for weeks and even months at a time before enough were assembled either to be dispatched under escort, or for the whole party to return to the regiment. Furthermore, it was not uncommon for a party to split its recruiters between numerous localities, with one or two men in each, and a successful recruiting sergeant could thus end with a number of recruits on his hands. Likewise, when the whole party was on the march, the recruits could easily outnumber their escorts. Although additional armed guards could sometimes be provided, and recruits could be secured overnight in a local gaol, most recruiting parties resorted to a different method to control their men. Instead of coercive compliance, the recruiters tried to keep their men content.

When possible, the merriments of the initial day of enlistment were prolonged. After he was hired as a valet to a Prussian recruiting officer, Bräker describes the following six months as a never-ending thrill of dancing, travelling and jollity. Moreover, as a youngster who just descended from a mountain hamlet, he received his first ever instruction in polite manners. It was this lifestyle which prompted Bräker to remain with his new master, despite warnings that he might end up pressed into Prussian service.[35] There were no disguises in the case of John Robert Shaw, who enlisted in the 33rd Regiment of Foot. Shaw remained with his party for the next few months, furnished and 'treated like a gentleman'. Moreover, Shaw and his fellow recruits were clearly encouraged to take to their new identity as soldiers, being exercised in running, jumping and 'learning to walk, straight'. Rather than being a mere hanger-on, Shaw was treated as an active member of his party, joining it

---

[34] *Dublin Journal* (August 1775) reprinted verbatim by J.J. Crooks in *JSAHR*, 2 (1923), 146–7; see also: Shaw, *Autobiography*, 11; Grenadier Guards Regimental Archive, London, E6/003, William Pell, 'Narrative', part 1, fols. 3–5.
[35] Bräker, 'Lebensgeschichte', 423–5, 427; see also Chapter 5, 165.

whenever it advertised for recruits. He was clearly not the only recent recruit to have done so willingly.[36]

Another point made clear by Shaw's account is that supervision of the new recruits could be very relaxed. He himself was granted an eight-week furlough while still attached to the recruiting party. Other than having to report to his recruiting sergeant once a day, Alexander Alexander was essentially left to his own devices during the three months until his party finally left Glasgow to join their regiment. After enlisting in Paris, Jean Rossignol and his fellow recruit were allocated a travel allowance and sent independently to their new regiment stationed in Dunkirk. After recruiting alone for five months in his native Beverly, Corporal Todd was ordered to rejoin his regiment in Ireland; the only recruit whom he enlisted accompanied him the whole way. One of the recruiting parties joined by bounty-jumper Peter Henly had thirty-five recruits and three overseers – a captain, a sergeant and Henly himself, who was quickly promoted on account of his former military experience. Henly was the only man who deserted from that party.[37] This apparent laxness cannot be explained by efficient control mechanisms for, as mentioned already, few European states had anything of the sort. A more feasible interpretation would be that these recruits were simply trusted. This would not be the case, however, unless they had enlisted of their own accord.

Moreover, potential recruits sometimes approached recruiters on their own initiative. Claude Le Roy enlisted himself at the office of the famous Parisian recruiter Dagobert, while Dreyer walked directly at the door of the Prussian recruiting house in Aachen. Alexander Alexander first hinted at his intention to enlist to a highland sergeant but, after being misunderstood, directly approached a recruiter for the Royal Artillery. Friedrich Christian Sohr applied for the position of *fourier* through the offices of a friend. After deciding to enlist, Henry Grace sought the first recruiting party which came to Winchester.[38] Furthermore, all these men made the

---

[36] Arriving in Leeds with the intention to enlist, the first military man he met was another recent recruit who immediately took him to the recruiting officer; Shaw, *Autobiography*, 11–5. Other instances when recruits prompted others to enlist include, Bishop, *Life and Adventures*, 123–33 and Burke, *Memoir*, 10. Sometimes recruits would employ similar deceitful methods as experienced recruiters would; see: Todd, *Journal*, 109. Bräker was continuously asked to help his master with recruiting; see: 'Lebensgeschichte', 429.

[37] Shaw, *Autobiography*, 15; Alexander, *Life*, vol. I, 77; Rossignol, *Vie veritable*, 12; Todd, *Journal*, 6–7; Henly, *Life*, 22.

[38] Le Roy, *Souvenirs*, 42; Dreyer, *Leben und Taten*, 12–3; Alexander, *Life*, vol. I, 71–4; Sohr, *Meine Geschichte*, 29–31; Grace, *History of the Life and Sufferings*, 3–4. See also: Bishop, *Life and Adventures*, 120–4; Lamb, *Memoir*, 61–2; J. Dorman, 'Interesting Memoir', 132; Highlander Donald MacLeod has offered himself to a party of the Royal Scots, although this particular part of his memoirs is likely to be wholly made up, see: *Memoirs*, 28–9; Brumwell, *Redcoats*, 303–4.

choice to take military service in advance, following some initial reflection. At least in their case, enlistment was a deliberate act, rather than the product of spontaneous fancy or a drunken whim.

Also interesting is the determination to enlist shown by some of the recruits. Although it is true that old-regime armies were not particularly selective in regard to their potential enlistees, it does not mean that every person who approached a recruiter was guaranteed to be taken. If a man was rejected by the colonel upon arrival at the regiment, the officer who enlisted him had to cover from his pocket whatever expenses were incurred, as well as paying for his return journey back home. Although some regiments provided concise instructions to avoid bad characters, it is usually agreed that recruiters seldom enquired too deeply into the morals of their would-be soldiers.[39] Youth and feebleness were a different matter, however. Teenagers like Shaw and Rossignol, who were initially told that they were too young, insisted to the recruiting officer that if they were not be enlisted by him, they would go and find another regiment. Despite numerous rejections, Samuel Hutton continued approaching recruiting parties until finally taken by the 12th Regiment of Foot. After being refused by his father's artillery unit for being too frail and ignorant, Beeger happily took the offer to enlist in an infantry regiment, although even there he almost had to beg the doctor to approve him.[40] Likewise, recruits sometimes actively resisted the attempts of their disgruntled relatives and friends to buy them out of the army. Laukhard, whose enlistment shocked the university community in Halle, wrote a number of letters to his friends and colleagues asking them to desist from trying to procure his release. Simon Stainforth, who was bought out once by his mother, proceeded to reenlist into a different regiment.[41]

The evidence regarding the willingness, or even the determination, of some of the recruits demonstrates a broader principle. Recruits could be active and assertive agents of their enlistment and not the infantile victims of crafty recruiters, as they are so often portrayed. Nor were they necessarily the passive recipients of the joyful impression which the recruiters attempted to convey. William Cobbett decided to enlist after noticing

---

[39] Steppler, *Common Soldier*, 23–9; Nevertheless, Peter Henly was rejected more than once, including an instance when he was suspected to be a deserter, *Life*, 24–5.

[40] Shaw, *Autobiography*, 11–2; Rossignol, *Vie veritable*, 11–2; Hutton, *Life*, 39, 74–5; Beeger, *Seltsame Schicksale*, 16–8. See also: Bibliothèque National, Paris, NUMM-109500, Joseph-Charles Bonin, 'Voyage au Canada', 35–6; Payne, 'Life', 437, W. Griffith, 'Memoirs', 152; Shipp, *Memoirs*, vol. I, 21–4.

[41] Laukhard, *Leben und Schicksale*, 144–6; Staniforth, 'Life', 325. See also: Jonas, *Soldier's Journal*, 1–2; Shaw, *Autobiography*, 13–5; Alexander Alexander rejected the suggestion of his foster brother to desert, *Life*, vol. I, 79. See also: Macdonald, *Autobiographical Journal*, 33.

a recruiting poster for the marines which promised riches and glories to be won at sea. It was not this bravado which appealed to Cobbett, who was badly bored with his work in the Inns of Court, but the offer of extreme change and travelling. After taking the bounty, Cobbett discovered that he was deceived, and that he actually enlisted into a marching regiment, the 54th Foot, whose sergeant major he became within a few years.[42] The success of the dubious methods of his recruiters as well as Cobbett's surprisingly smooth acceptance of his new destiny are less important here. Cobbett's case shows that the promotional material or the show put on by the recruiting parties, if not intended for those already converted, at least targeted those initially inclined.

Some modern research on recruitment can prove valuable in understanding this point. Studies on enlistment into the American army published over the last generation have demonstrated the existence of a vocational propensity to serve among a noticeable fraction of recruits. For instance, a multi-annual study of the attitudes of young people conducted by Bachman and his colleagues found that recruits who exhibited a strong association with the military had acquired this before their enlistment. Moreover, follow-up examination of survey respondents who expressed a high desire for a military career demonstrated that most had actually enlisted within the next few years. In other words, recruitment needs to be understood, in part, as a self-selection process from a small pool of predisposed individuals, who contribute a disproportionately large number of enlisted personnel. Moreover, it is clear that it is values rather than practical considerations which define the positive views of this group towards military service.[43] The second part of this chapter will argue that a similar model of recruitment applies just as well to the old-regime armies.

Although the reasons for voluntary enlistment into eighteenth-century armies have been discussed in some previous works, no serious attempt has been made to consider in depth the available recollections of the recruits themselves, of which the current study has located close to fifty. This wealth of diverse material does not lend itself to easy categorisation.

---

[42] Cobbett, *Autobiography*, 24–5, 31.

[43] Bachman, Sigelman and Diamond, 'Self-Selection, Socialization, and Distinctive Military Values'; Bachman, Segal, Freedman-Doan and O'Malley, 'Does Enlistment Propensity Predict Accession?'; Bachman, Freedman-Doan, Segal and O'Malley, 'Distinctive Military Attitudes among U.S. Enlistees'; Bachman, Segal, Freedman-Doan and O'Malley, 'Who Chooses Military Service?'; see also: J.E. Dorman, 'ROTC Cadet Attitudes', 203–16. For propensity to serve among recruits into the Belgian and German militaries, see: Manigart and Prensky, 'Recruitment and Retention of Volunteers', 109–10; Jackson, Thoemmes, Jonkmann, Lüdtke and Trautwein, 'Military Training and Personality Trait Development'.

The same author would often give a number of reasons for pursuing military service, without necessarily indicating which one provided the key incentive. Nevertheless, it is possible to identify a number of basic trends. Material inducements such as pay and bounty do not figure prominently. Moreover, these and other practical concerns are seldom mentioned alone. Instead, they are usually laced with immaterial or institutional considerations. On the other hand, an initial predisposition for military service or a craving for some of its aspects forms the single most common cause for enlisting.

Although often mentioned by modern scholarship, which sometimes delves into establishing its actual financial value, the bounty does not figure prominently in first-hand accounts. Some narratives do mention its size, but it is rarely invoked as an incentive for enlistment, let alone the sole one. William Crawford mentions the bounty as one of the reasons for joining the 29th Regiment of Foot, but also the appeal of the uniform and that of military life in general. According to Jonas, some men do enlist for bounty, although he himself enlisted to satisfy his 'rambling curiosity'. Runaway teenage apprentice William Lawrence joined the soldier who offered him a bounty of sixteen pounds. After arrival at the 40th Regiment, the colonel cut the offer to only two-and-a-half pounds, but Lawrence enlisted anyway as it was his second escape from an abusive master to whom he had not the least inclination to return. James Bristow, who was given a single shilling for his enlistment in the East India Service, clearly states that he enlisted not for the money, but to see the world. Robert Butler, who originally began his military service as a substitute in the militia, received twenty-two pounds from the man whom he replaced. Butler, who knew he might soon be balloted anyhow, thought it would be a good idea to take advantage of the well-paid replacement bounties. Nevertheless, his main reason for taking military service was to pursue a personal passion. The military was the only place where Butler could receive proper instruction in playing the fife. In his later decision to transfer to a regular infantry regiment, Butler was tempted by the prospects of higher pay, but again, this was not his only motive. He was offered a position of fife major in a regiment which was about to go on foreign service, and Butler took this opportunity to satisfy his long-standing desire to see the world.[44]

Likewise, although it is argued that it could prove a sensible future investment, again, only a few authors mentioned making any long-term financial choices regarding their bounty. Laukhard left his eight *Louis-d'ors*

---

[44] Crawford, 'Narrative', 318; Jonas, *Soldier's Journal*, 1–2, 188; Lawrence, *Dorset Soldier*, 18, Bristow, *Narrative of the Sufferings*, 16; Butler, *Narrative*, 18–9, 27–8.

with his captain, drawing from this sum for the next four years. Pell similarly decided not to collect his bounty after the enlistment, but to retain it for future use. Alexander mentions that his refusal to drink away the whole bounty enticed the ire of the other recruits.[45] The latter case also makes clear what it was most common to do with one's bounty. Bonin says he was lucky to get a gift on top of his bounty, which allowed him to retain some money after he marked his 'bien venue selon l'usage etablie' (welcome, according to the established custom), which procured him numerous friends. After enlisting in Württemberg, Steininger spent the whole of his bounty of seven *florins* on good wine on his very first night.[46] According to these accounts, the bounty was more of a bonus to celebrate one's enlistment and to ensure initial socialisation into the military. The only two other references to actual use of bounty money come from Löffler, who re-tailored his uniform to make it look more elegant, and Le Roy, who gave half of his engagement money to a friend who helped him to travel to Paris.[47]

Although it is generally agreed that the pay rates of the old-regime rank-and-file were simply inadequate to induce enlistment, it is also typically argued that, to quote Frey, low and erratic as it was, a soldier's salary was still an 'acceptable substitute to a chaotic existence'. In other words, pay, along with whatever additional benefits were offered by military service, was an important consideration in the initial motivation of those recruits who were unemployed, poor or lacking any prospects of making a living. Nevertheless, it is possible to argue that need alone was insufficient to explain initial motivation on an individual level. As noted by Steppler, only a small fraction of the unemployed actually enlisted.[48] In Britain, the necessity to enact press acts that essentially sanctioned the forcible enlistment of any able-bodied man without visible means of maintenance further demonstrates that even vagrants and the most economically destitute were not necessarily keen recruits.[49] Most importantly, even when soldier-authors cite material need as a reason that prompted them to enlist, it is often clear that military service was not the only alternative available to them.

---

[45] Laukhard, *Leben und Schicksale*, 142; Pell, 'Narrative', part 1, fols. 15, 33–4; Alexander, *Life*, vol. I, 77.

[46] Bonin, 'Voyage au Canada', 16; Steininger, *Leben und Abenteuer*, 40. See also: Lawrence, *Dorset Soldier*, 17; J. Dorman, 'Interesting Memoir', 133, Shaw, *Autobiography*, 56–7. On recruits spending their bounty on celebration, see: Hale, *Journal*, 6–7; Steppler, *Common Soldier*, 21.

[47] Löffler, *Der alte Sergeant*, 31–2; Le Roy, *Souvenirs*, 41.

[48] Frey, *British Soldier in America*, 53; Steppler *Common Soldier*, 29–30.

[49] Besides, as shown by Gilbert, only a token of the men originally taken by the constables were actually delivered to the army; see: 'Army Impressment', 697–700; Gilbert, 'Analysis', 39; Gilbert, 'Charles Jenkinson and the Last Army Press', 11.

Suspected of being a runaway apprentice, William Kenward had difficulties finding work after abandoning his first master, but after obtaining a new employment, he found it dull and eventually enlisted in the 75th Highland Regiment, which was then raised for the Indian service. Having to support himself after his arrival in Quebec, Bonin determined to take military service and applied to the artillery, due to its higher pay. Although it is clear that he would have preferred a better job, Bonin left for the colonies from what was a secure, if low-paid, position as a clerk. Another reason which prompted him to try his luck abroad was 'l'envie de voyager'. Sohr and Le Roy failed respectively to find work as a scribe and a hatter, but neither was in penury. In the latter case, Le Roy speaks of his adventurous spirit, which had already led him to flee from home at the age of fourteen to join the French navy during the American War of Independence. This puts into perspective his decision to serve in the army. Even Laukhard, who had incurred heavy debt due to his extravagant lifestyle, made his initial resolution to enlist after falling envious of the cheerfulness of some soldiers whom he saw carousing in a tavern. Despite an element of financial hardship, none of these cases shows the utter desperation which is often attributed to old-regime recruits. Moreover, these were their own attitudes and preferences which either prompted these authors to enlist or at least contributed towards the conditions which made their enlistment a far likelier option.[50]

One feature that stands out in many of the recruiting accounts is the unwillingness or inability of their authors to adjust to the life path for which they were destined. Some were unhappy with their current circumstances, which could include cruel masters as in the cases of Lawrence or of Hutton, who escaped from two apprenticeships, spending five years as a child vagabond. Rather than outright abuse, however, soldier-authors who initially studied a trade complain of unsatisfactory conditions and, even more, of boredom. Originally bound to a tobacco spinner, Donald McBane enlisted after his mistress started saving on his subsistence, but also makes it clear that 'I was always wild [. . .] and full of anything but work'. John Haime preferred a freer employment to his father's work as a gardener, and after trying himself as a button-maker and a tanner, eventually joined the Queens' Regiment of Dragoons. Future gunner Benjamin Miller spent three years as a servant,

[50] Kenward, *Sussex Highlander*, 2–3; Bonin, 'Voyage au Canada', 9–10; Sohr *Meine Geschichte*, 25–9; Le Roy, *Souvenirs*, 3–6, 41; Laukhard, *Leben und Schicksale*, 139–40. See also: Conway, 'Mobilization of Manpower', 393–4.

a position which he disliked as much as his subsequent apprenticeship to a glove maker, which was also badly paid.[51]

Interestingly, Miller identifies himself as 'being rather of a roving disposition', a term which appears, with a few variations, in a number of other recruitment accounts. Another former apprentice, Jonas, explains his enlistment as a product of his 'rambling disposition', as does John Macdonald, who worked as a teacher and tutor to children of the Sutherland gentry. This was a happy time and, according to Macdonald, 'I might live so all my life only for my rambling disposition', which prompted him to enlist, 'let the consequences be what it would'. The use of this term in English narratives denotes that their authors had either accepted or at least recognised the prevailing negative attitudes towards men who took military service. Henly, for instance, refers to his exploits as 'my wicked rambling life';[52] however, it is actually his case which cautions against replicating eighteenth-century stereotypes that present the enlistees not only as incapable of decent productive work, but also as unsteady and fickle. Men unable to accept any type of stability could be expected to desert as quickly as they enlisted, as demonstrated in Henly's own case, as well as that of fellow bounty-jumper Johann Steininger. Higher desertion rates among younger soldiers certainly account for such cases, as well as those who failed to adjust to military life for whatever reason but, as we have seen, most recruits remained with the colours. Taking the bounty could and often did mean a radical break with one's previous life, but it did not necessarily mean the denial of authority or discipline as such. Rather than being the mere outcome of childish hedonism, enlistments could also be the result of a desire to find an alternative to a system which some recruits considered as dull or without prospect.

This is not to say that recruits did not include individuals whose reasons are in line with a more stereotypical view of enlistment. Sent by his family to Winchester College in the hope that he would become a priest, Grace describes himself as an idler who neglected his studies, incurring the wrath of his teacher and fellow students, 'wherefore I took the resolution to enlist as a soldier'. Another soldier-author who regretted his licentious youth is Crawford, who admits to a fondness to racing and the fair sex.

---

[51] Hutton, *Life*, 34–9, 59–74; Haime, 'Life', 210–2; McBane, 'Expert Swords-Man's Companion', 25; B. Miller, 'Adventures', 12. The biographers of MacLeod, *Memoirs*, 12–8, and J. Field, *Devout Soldier*, 2, also identify them as unsatisfied apprentices. See also: T. Brown, *Plain Narrative*, 3. However, the most telling case of dissatisfaction with one's life is the fate of Hutton's former second master: 'heartily weary of his wife, and weary, perhaps of beating her, he had undertaken to beat the French'. The wife was avenged, however, as the man was soon killed; see: Hutton, *Life*, 41,75.

[52] Jonas, *Soldier's Journal*, 1–2; Macdonald, *Autobiographical Journal*, 33, Henly, *Life*, 31. See also: Plummer, *Journal*, 1; Greenleigh, *Veteran Soldier*, 26–7; Hurl-Eamon, '"Youth in the Devil's Service"', 165.

It is clear from both these accounts, however, that their authors were aiming to elicit compassion from a respectable audience. Crawford wrote his memoir as a death-row inmate and Grace as a destitute invalid who returned to England after more than a decade of captivity with the North-American Indians and French Canadians.[53] Nevertheless, this is not a reason to discard their testimony, just as there is no reason to discard automatically such accounts which describe more positive motives for enlisting, even if their authors were likewise moved by a sense of youthful rebellion. Joseph Ferdinand Dreyer explains he was prompted to escape from home after growing bored of his small Alsatian town, desiring to see the world further and to try provide for himself independently. A similar motive also comes out in Alexander's account. The bastard son of a well-to-do Glasgow lawyer, Alexander rejected plans to set him up in the colonies and decided to enlist to prove that he could advance in the world without his father's help. Another enlistment prompted by filial disobedience was that of von Klöden's father, who escaped from home after his initial request to pursue a military career was rejected.[54]

As seen from the above cases, some men saw military service as a vehicle for self-fulfilment, a challenge or at least as an alternative of a sort. On one end of this spectrum of self-perceived adventurous freedom-loving young men there are cases like Shaw who, after misbehaving and incurring his father's displeasure, followed the advice of his friends to enlist, 'be clear from work and [become] gentlemen at once'. On the other side stands the unique case of Matthew Bishop. Bishop claims to have served in the navy, which he joined in the hope of making a fortune and possibly procuring advancement. Although little came out of these plans, Bishop was not dissuaded and, inspired by news of the battle of Blenheim, decided to try himself in land warfare. In other words, Bishop craved adventure. Although the authenticity of this account still inspires controversy,[55] similar motives are repeated by other soldier-authors. Although usually expressed in less brazen terms, desire to travel, if not

---

[53] Grace, *History of the Life and Sufferings*, 3–4, 55–6; Crawford, 'Narrative', 315–6. For more recruits who enlisted to avoid mishaps with the law, their employers or their family, see: J. Andrew, 'Last Speech', 175–6; Berrepo, 'Letter', 74, R. Young, 'Last Words', 140; Mackellow *Autobiography*, 15. See also: Bernos, 'Souvenirs de campagne', 681–2; Bräker, 'Lebensgeschichte', 429.

[54] Dreyer, *Leben und Taten*, 11–2; Alexander, *Life*, vol. I, 17, 34, 71; Klöden, *Jugenderinnerungen*, 10–2. See also the case of the Thrupp brothers, both of whom enlisted shortly after the older brother had a dispute with the father: NAM 1992-12-146 'A Short Account of the Life and Transactions of James Thurpp', 3–4.

[55] Shaw, *Autobiography*, 9–11; Bishop, *Life and Adventures*, 5, 45–6, 80. On the latter account, see: Carter, *Matthew Bishop of Deddington in Oxfordshire*, Also available online (Last accessed 7 October 2016): www.deddington.org.uk/_data/assets/pdf_file/0005/29 39/Bishopcomplete.pdf.

providing the sole reason, at least provided a catalyst for signing up in many of the enlistment accounts.

Military service was not the only option available to men of humble background who craved to see the world outside their immediate communities, but it was a more obvious choice for those desiring distant travel or visits to exotic places. This was the main motive of Thomas Sullivan, who thought 'by that means that I would be enabled to satisfy an inclination, so strongly bent upon rambling; especially by entering into a regiment that was going abroad'. Rambling disposition could just well be a genuine desire to see the world, and there is no necessary reason to interpret it negatively. In 1759, despite a secure position back in Zurich, Markus Uhlmann's desire to feel fresh air and see new lands led him to travel to northern Germany, where he enlisted as a surgeon's mate in a Swiss Regiment in the French service. In the very same year, Thomas Payne, who was similarly inclined, decided to enlist, first offering himself to the light dragoons. Although it is not stated in his account, it is worthwhile mentioning that this regiment was then campaigning in Europe. Rejected for being too short, Payne remained undeterred in his desire to travel far from home and joined the East India Service, spending the next few years in the garrison on St. Helena. Henly's rambling disposition led him not only to a string of desertions, but also enlistments. After escaping from indentured service in Pennsylvania, Henly arrived in Philadelphia, where he was quickly to enlist in the first battalion of the Royal Americans, stationed in Quebec. Henly agreed, explaining that this 'would be a good opportunity for me to see the country'.[56]

In addition to these men, as well as Jonas and Bristow, whose accounts we considered above, an urge for travel could also make the eventual choice to enlist a likelier outcome, even when it was not the initial thought crossing the mind of the would-be traveller. Military service could become a more obvious alternative for someone like James Green, who was left penniless in London after running away from home in February 1772. Cobbett's ultimate decision to enlist is less surprising if one considers that before moving to London, he had already escaped twice from home, including an unsuccessful attempt to sign up as

---

[56] Sullivan, *From Redcoat to Rebel*, 3; Uhlmann, *Abwechslende Fortün*, 4; Payne, 'Life', 437; Henly *Life*, 28. Travelling even proved interesting for men who did not join the army of their free will. For instance, Stephan Popp, who served in one of the Bayreuth regiments hired by the British during the American Revolution did not share the grief of these soldiers who lamented when the order for departure came, 'for I had long wanted to see something of the world'. Popp mentions he was not the only one thinking that way, see: 'Journal', 27. For similar attitudes, see: Seume, *Werke*, vol. I, 63–4, 66; Alexander, *Life*, vol. I, 93.

a seaman.[57] A similar experience was the lot of future soldiers Dreyer, Mackellow, Bonin, Le Roy and Rossignol, who escaped from home and travelled in France as an apprentice and hired hand for over a year before returning to Paris, where he enlisted shortly afterwards. Löffler's *Reiselust* led him to leave his native Schweidnitz in 1785 to try his luck finding work as a weaver. After two years of travels through Prussia, Poland and the Habsburg Empire, Löffler eventually arrived in Vienna jobless and ill. As he wandered around the streets, Löffler was approached by a sergeant, who apparently did not need much effort to persuade him to enlist in the Deutschmeister regiment, even before treating the weakly young man to his first proper meal in a long time.[58]

Although his case might first appear as a classic example of enlistment under material duress of the type commonly cited by modern scholars, it is important to remember that Löffler would have been unlikely to end up in the Habsburg army without his pre-inclination for travelling. Löffler's story, therefore, should be seen as a case where initial predisposition increased the likelihood to take up military service for financial reasons. Men longing to try their luck outside their communities could likewise fall prey to forceful recruitment. Urged by a dubious character who worked with his father, Ulrich Bräker decided to leave home and try his luck finding employment as a valet, a choice whose outcome was described in Chapter 1. Although he was duped into joining the army, Bräker's case is relevant to our discussion of potential vocational predispositions because of his aspirations to try a radically new and, ideally, better and more gentlemanly life. If Bräker had been content with his fate back home, he would have been far less likely to end up pressed into the Prussian service. Travellers also made likely candidates for impressment, as happened to Johann Gottfried Seume and Johann Heinrich Behrens. Stirred by stories of distant travels as a boy, Johann Carl Büttner decided to become a barber-surgeon rather than a priest. Extensive travels as a journeyman eventually brought him to Amsterdam, where after failing to obtain a post with the East India Company, he was sold into indentured service in North America. This eventually led to his enlistment into the continental army, followed by desertion to the Hessians, as described above.[59]

---

[57] NAM 1972-01-36 (1), 'Account of American service and letters by James Green'; Spater, *William Cobbett*, vol. I, 11–5; Ingrams, *Life and Adventures of William Cobbett*, 4–8. For other men who ended up in the army after trying first to go to sea, see: Coates, *Narrative*, 18–9; Watson, 'Some Account', 106.

[58] Rossignol, *Vie veritable*, 4–10; Löffler, *Der alte Sergeant*, 4–5, 12–4, 29–30.

[59] Bräker, 'Lebensgeschichte', 414–7; Seume, *Werke*, vol. I, 63; Behrens, *Lebensgeschichte*, 11; Büttner, 'Narrative', 206–14.

Steppler, who has considered most of the surviving accounts by British soldiers who served between 1760 and 1793, remarks that their authors appear as restless souls, interested in adventure, who got into the army through some kind of hardship.[60] Steppler's observation should be amended. Firstly, as we have seen, dislike of stability did not necessarily continue once the man became a soldier. Furthermore, desire for travel and adventure could itself be an incentive to enlist. This provides an additional proof that normative compliance played a major role in initial motivation. Moreover, one cannot ignore underlying normative attitudes, which increased the probability for some coercive and remunerative outcomes. There is, therefore, a case to be made that vocational predisposition was as relevant for enlistment in old-regime Europe as it is in modern armies. Old-regime recruits were likely to come from the poorer working-class, but this is too general a factor to explain why some men chose to enlist voluntarily. Rather, men desirous of travel and adventure or those who were otherwise willing to challenge their current circumstances had a higher chance of ending up as soldiers. As demonstrated in the discussion of the recruiting posters, the military had an institutional appeal, while the narratives considered so far point to the existence of normative considerations. This leads to the question of whether a military career itself could also exercise genuine appeal. Were some men drawn directly to military service as such, rather than seeing it is as a vehicle for adventure or an escape from boredom? The answer, according to most accounts, is yes.

Predisposition for military service could begin at home. Beeger, an orphan of a Prussian artillery officer who was commissioned from the ranks, was brought up by his grandfather, a former hussar NCO. Despite the latter's harsh ways, young Beeger made up his mind that he wanted no other career but the military, going as far as refusing offers to learn a trade. Von Klöden's father, Joachim Friedrich, came to a similar conclusion, despite his own father's opposition, after being inspired by his upbringing as a young nobleman and the glorious stories of the recent war. Sampson Staniforth acquired his inclination for the army after keeping company with soldiers. Roger Lamb had a brother killed in a sea battle, and was further excited by his father's conversations about naval matters. According to Lamb, he possessed a 'natural and inherent love of military Life'.[61] Moreover, further authors, while not providing a clear reason for their origin, clearly acknowledge that they held similar attitudes.

---

[60] Steppler, *Common Soldier*, 33–4.
[61] Lamb, *Memoir*, 7–8, 47–8; Beeger, *Seltsame Schicksale*, 6–7; Klöden, *Jugenderinnerungen*, 6–11; Staniforth, 'Life', 325. See also: Wright, 'Life', 318; Butler, *Narrative*, 18; Shipp, *Memoir*, 6–9; Greenleigh, *Veteran Soldier*, 23–7.

In Britain, there was a constant movement of men from the militia into the army, the former providing a testing ground for the military-inclined youth, as in case of Surtees, who joined the Northumberland Militia. Surtees resolved that he would leave the service should military life not prove to be to his taste, but after liking his new experience, he volunteered to transfer to the 56th Regiment. David Robertson, who found service in the militia to be too dull, first moved to the Caithness Fencibles and, after finding that they proved no more exciting, transferred into the 92nd Regiment. Although his journal gives no account of when and how he joined to the line, Corporal Todd was another man who began his military career in the militia, as was John Dayes, who initially served as a militia substitute for two-and-half years.[62]

Dayes' account of his later service with the 5th Regiment provides a further interesting point, which sheds light on the motives of men who volunteered or transferred from the militia during the emergency of the 1790s and early 1800s. Learning that their regiment was not to be sent on the Egyptian expedition because it was manned by many drafts from the militia, whose oath extended to serve only in Europe, the soldiers volunteered in bulk, declaring their willingness to serve anywhere in the world.[63] According to Dayes, the men were motivated to uphold the reputation of their regiment, but it is possible that some were also looking to try active service. Modern research shows that some servicemen looked forward to and even actively requested a transfer to an active theatre, in the hope that this would provide them with a challenge to prove their worth, or a right of passage into becoming real soldiers. It was even suggested that Moskos' classic model should be augmented by a third pole, which Fabrizio Battistelli called 'post-modern' and whose motivation centred on the desire for adventure and self-development.[64]

Arguing that some old-regime soldiers enlisted in order to fight might prove a step too far, unless more accounts such as that of Bishop are uncovered. Nevertheless, other accounts do state that active service

---

[62] Surtees, *Twenty-Five Years*, 1–2; D. Robertson, *Journal*, 1–2; Todd, *Journal*, 1–2; Dayes, *Memoir*, 5; Samuel Wray, in contrast, volunteered directly into the army, *Military Adventures*, 4. For more militia men who chose to transfer into the regulars, see: W. Green, *Where Duty Calls Me*, 43; Morley, *Memoirs*, 6–7; Hale, *Journal*, 5.

[63] The commander-in-chief thanked the troops, but this request is not granted Dayes, *Memoir*, 6–7. According to John Vardin, his regiment has also volunteered for the Egyptian Campaign, see: NAM 1976-06-16 'Manuscript letter by John Vardin of the 86th reg, of foot' (30 April 1802).

[64] H.C.B. Rogers, *British Army of the Eighteenth Century*, 62; Moskos, *American Enlisted Man*, 161–2; Battistelli, 'Peacekeeping and the Postmodern Soldier', 468–70. A very similar argument, however, was made earlier in Gorman and Thomas, 'Enlistment Motivations of Army Reservists: Money, Self-Improvement, or Patriotism?', 591–2. See also: Erik Hedlund and the sources he cites in 'What Motivates Swedish Soldiers'.

proved attractive for their authors. Despite enjoying a pleasant time with the Light Dragoons in Ireland, Crawford volunteered to be drafted into the 20th Regiment destined for America in order 'to satisfy [his] ardent disposition for adventure'. According to Johann Christoph Döhlemann, when his regiment was ordered to the American War, while some officers and men attempted to procure a discharge, many others came forward asking to join. A successful drill corporal in a colonial depot, Le Roy could have easily remained in France, but requested to be sent to the Caribbean. The comrades of von Klöden's father looked forward to campaigns, if only to curtail the monotonous experience of garrison life. Even the pressed Seume was disappointed that his service in North America ended without any military action.[65] In our discussion of self-selection, we saw that some eighteenth-century recruits had an initial predisposition for military service, often as a product of attitudes formed before enlistment. It is not unfeasible that, at least in some cases, the craving to experience adventure and travel could extend one step further into a craving to try oneself in combat.

On the other hand, there are only three first-hand accounts which mention enlisting to serve the cause of an ongoing war. Although enlistment was not part of his original plans, when loyalist Stephen Jarvis escaped to British-held New York, he was soon informed that the Americans had murdered his father, and 'this melancholy news determined me for a military life'.[66] Peter Williamson joined the rangers to avenge the Indians and French, whose raiders had killed his family and at whose hands he had endured a cruel captivity. Soon afterwards, he volunteered to join the pursuit of some marauding Indians: 'never did I go to any enterprise with half that alacrity and cheerfulness I now went with this party'. Williamson was further prompted to enlist because he had lost his whole property in the raid, and the memories of what he endured made him reluctant to restart his life anew on his destroyed farm. Association with war aims is attributed to some of the recruits into the Dutch service during the War of the Spanish Succession. According to John Scot's poem, while some men enlisted 'for want of bread', others signed up 'to serve a good cause'. Scot's own motive also invokes loyalty, although of a different type, as his family were tenants to Lord Loudoun, whose son was the captain in whose company Scot had enlisted. Scot's

[65] Crawford, 'Narrative', 318; Döhlemann, 'Diary', 10; Le Roy, *Souvenirs*, 43; Klöden, *Jugenderinnerungen*, 36–7; Seume, *Werke*, vol. I, 94–5. This last point was already noticed by P.H. Wilson in *War, State and Society in Württemberg*, 81. See also the cases of MacLeod, *Memoirs*, 74–5 and B. Miller, 'Adventures', 22.

[66] Jarvis, 'An American's Experience', 197. Luckily, it later turned out that Jarvis' father was only plundered.

case demonstrates a wider phenomenon – namely, landowners using their influence and patronage networks to prompt recruitment into units owned by their family members. The personal nature of Scot's enlistment is underscored in his poem, as is the material benefit which he hoped to draw upon, having been promised to be set up in into some business after his discharge. Nevertheless, patronage, like poverty, is a constant, and cannot explain by itself why a particular tenant enlisted, while so many did not. In Scot's case, there is a good possibility of vocational predisposition, as his recruitment took place in a fencing school.[67]

Other accounts which mention patronage likewise show that it was usually laced with other factors. Pipe-Major John Macdonald was prevailed to transfer into the marching regiment by an offer of 'very good terms', which included a bounty of twenty guineas. That said, it was already mentioned that it was Macdonald's rambling disposition which prompted him to take up military service in the first place. Likewise, Uhlmann's acquaintance with some officers prompted him to join the Lochmann Swiss Regiment, but his original reason for trying military service was his desire for *frische Luft*. James Thompson joined up as gentleman volunteer to serve under his friend Captain Bellanie, partly due to personal attachment and partly because he hoped to secure a commission. In 1720, Sergeant Donald MacLeod bought his discharge from the Royal Regiment of Scotland to join as a private in the newly formed independent highland companies. His reasons, as given in his biography, were his fondness of highland dress and a desire to serve both with his compatriots and under Lord Lovat, who was married to MacLeod's distant relative.[68] Although his motives for enlisting are unknown, it is telling that André Amblard's company in the Soissonais Regiment included two more men from his home village and another five from the surrounding region. The authorities, on their side, were well aware that servicing together with acquaintances or immediate countrymen would be appealing to some, a point which comes out in the accounts of Surtees and Todd, who were sent to recruit in their home counties.[69]

---

[67] Williamson, *French and Indian Cruelty*, 38, 43–4; Scot, 'Remembrance', 313–4, 318; Hippler, *Citizens*, 15–4; Conway, 'Mobilization of Manpower', 395–7; Pröve, *Stehendes Heer*, 38–9; For a recent study of this phenomenon in Scotland, see: Mackillop, '*More Fruitful than the Soil*'.

[68] Macdonald, *Autobiographical Journal*, 35–6, 40; Uhlmann, *Abwechslende Fortün*, 14–5; J. Thompson, *Bard*, 116, 143–4; MacLeod, *Memoirs*, 41–2, 44.

[69] Amblard, 'Histoire des campagnes' in 'De Lussas vers l'aventure I', 188, 195–8; Todd, *Journal*, 6–7; Surtees, *Twenty-Five Years*, 50–1; D. Robertson, *Journal*, 36–7. Also see the poster advertising for the Seaforth's Highlanders (1793) in: Leetham, 'Recruiting Posters', 133.

Such cases suggest that joint service by men who knew each other before their enlistment could provide an incentive even in the initial stage.

As mentioned in the introduction, initial motivation leads to a single decision to undertake military service. The only possibility for an individual to return to that stage was when a discharged soldier made a decision to reenlist. Some modern scholars consider such men to be the only group which acquired a genuine taste for military life. Although this argument does not contradict our basic point regarding the existence of vocational predisposition, this point requires further explanation. Some reenlisting veterans were repeating the same pattern which led to their original enlistment. Dreyer, who was pressed into the Austrian army after being taken prisoner in 1745, was bought out and taken as apprentice by a rich goldsmith whose house he helped to save from a fire. Despite these excellent material prospects, the old ways proved stronger and Dreyer returned to the Prussian army, preferring the cheerfulness and vigour of military life. Trumpeter Johann Schimmel was forced to retire from the Prussian army because of pains in the chest. After his health recovered, Schimmel, who did not like 'playing for the peasants', wished to resume military service and was soon able to reenlist in the Red Hussars.[70] Secondly, and more importantly, however, the situation of veterans was not dissimilar to that of men who were either unwilling to settle or predisposed for travel. Previous military service made reenlistment likelier, and sometimes it was the only available resort. Former ranger Thomas Brown, who acquired his discharge after returning from Canadian captivity, fell ill on his way back home. Being penniless and without friends, he agreed to join the light infantry in exchange for a promise that his new unit will provide for him. Macdonald agreed to reenlist in the 25th Regiment, as he made no provisions for his future. Jonas' account also implies that material considerations prevented him from settling back home, and he reenlisted in his old corps, hoping to be sent back to the Caribbean. Returning deserter Sohr, who lived in poverty following his pardon and dishonourable discharge, attempted to reenlist in his old company, but his application was denied. Duncan Cameron reenlisted because he was unaccustomed to hard labour, although he also hoped that travel would help to dispel his grief after the death of his mother and sister.[71]

What unites these accounts is that all these men decided to rejoin the military for concrete, usually material, reasons, rather than the influx of

[70] Dreyer, *Leben und Taten*, 17; Schimmel, 'Kurze Lebensbeschreibung', 192–3.
[71] T. Brown, *Plain Narrative*, 26; Sohr *Meine Geschichte*, 169–72; Macdonald, *Autobiographical Journal*, 62–3; Jonas, *Soldier's Journal*, 168; D. Cameron, *Life*, 10. See also: Payne, 'Life', 442; Löffler, *Der alte Sergeant*, 72.

positive attitudes gained during their service. Just as in modern armies, the balance of evidence on initial motivation as a whole suggests that self-selection was a major factor which prompted enlistment. This is not to say that socialisation was unimportant. In fact, much of the next chapter demonstrates how this was instilled actively, by the military authorities, and informally, by the soldiers themselves. Moreover, it can be said that these two factors complement each other well. If a substantial proportion of recruits possessed attitudes which predisposed them towards military service, this means that many of the socialisation methods which came into play during the sustaining stage would fall on fruitful soil. Even if military service was not the original intent of the recruit, choices which made him likelier to end up in the army also brought him closer to individuals directly pre-inclined for military service. A craving for adventure, a rejection of obvious and respectable civilian mores, as well as the tendency to end up in trouble, could provide an initial bonding effect. As far as the military authorities were concerned, one of the aims of the drill was to mould the recruit into a new type of character. This chapter argues that the initial basis for the creation of such a type was already formed beforehand.

The role of remunerative compliance in sustaining and combat motivation deserves a detailed discussion in its own right, especially in view of the abundant material available in the recollections of old-regime common soldiers. Although their writings often allude to pay, subsistence and, occasionally, booty, this evidence still awaits systematic consideration. Unlike the issue of normative compliance in the initial stage, however, the material conditions of the troops have been examined by modern scholars. Rather than looking at the testimonies of the men themselves, studies of eighteenth-century enlisted men have usually concentrated on the value of their pay, often comparing it to the economic conditions within the social groups from which the troops were recruited. It is generally agreed that pay, being low and subject to substantial deductions, could not provide an incentive to serve except for the most economically desperate. Moreover, official pay rates remained unchanged for generations at a time, taking no account of inflation and periods of economic dearth. Although towards the end of the century there were attempts to regularise, limit and even remove some of the deductions, a soldierly wage remained barely sufficient to guarantee anything but the most basic living standard.[72] Booty, which is often considered as a major incentive for the

---

[72] See: Guy, 'Army', 95; Scouller, *Armies of Queen Anne*, 137–32; Steppler, 'British Army', 14; Keep, *Soldiers of the Tsar*, 107, 110–4, 175 180–7; S.F. Scott, *Response*, 43–4; Hochedlinger, *Austria's Wars*, 131–2, 314. In the latter case, C. Duffy argues that the

mercenaries of the sixteenth and seventeenth centuries, was of little relevance for regular soldiers of old-regime Europe, even in wartime, as chances to pillage became few and far between. As shown in the following short overview, these conclusions are in line with the descriptions found in the writings of the soldiers themselves.

Direct testimonies on the living standards of the men are not one-sided. Some soldier-authors were clearly making a decent living. This, nevertheless, was often the product of side-earning, unique talents or conditions. Cobbett sent his fiancée 150 guineas, which he amassed after about four years of service, but he was a regimental sergeant major. Le Roy was very content with the material conditions on Martinique but the pay of colonial troops was three times higher than in France and the food cheaper. Aytoun, who was serving at the same time on the nearby island of Dominica, made about thirty pounds, while John Matson, who served in the 100th Regiment of Foot during the Second Mysore War, lost some twenty pounds-worth of equipment in a shipwreck on his way back to Britain.[73] Qualified craftsmen could earn well in their free time, as could educated men who hired themselves out as teachers or helped with the regimental paperwork. As in the latter case, some additional income could be made in a semi-official capacity, for instance by musicians giving public performances, by artillerymen for arranging fireworks and by pioneers for fetching firewood for the officers.[74] However, even these examples demonstrate the comparative meagreness of soldierly pay. Rossignol remarks that when he was stationed in the port city of Le Havre, soldiers could earn over three *livres* per day, about a *third* of their official monthly wages. Beeger, who helped a gentleman to carry a heavy chest, was tipped with eight *groschen*, an equivalent of five days' pay. Moreover, according to Beeger, since the majority of men did not have a profession, their prospects of earning in their spare time were usually limited to offering themselves for hire, standing at one of the bridges or by post offices. Beeger eventually succeeded in securing decent pay as a gardener and theatre extra, but, as his account makes clear, he was

late Theresian army had a good record of paying its men punctually, see: *Army of Maria Theresa*, 55, *Instrument of War*, 206–7.

[73] Cobbett, *Autobiography*, 38; Le Roy, *Souvenirs*, 44; Aytoun, *Redcoats*, 40; Matson, *Indian Warfare*, see also: Lamb, *Original and Authentic Journal*, 435; MacLeod, *Memoirs*, 15; Rossignol, *Vie veritable*, 33–4; Bonin, 'Voyage au Canada', 74, 176–7, 180–2, 186; J. Dorman, 'Interesting Memoir', 134; Archives Nationales, Paris, Mar/B4/288 Jacques Gruyer, 'Letter to his father', (17 January 1782).

[74] Bräker, 'Lebensgeschichte', 443, 449; Seume, *Werke*, vol. I, 86; Todd, *Journal*, 134–5, 215; Sohr, *Meine Geschichte*, 77–8; Döhla, 'Tagebuch', (29 June and 4 July 1783); Lamb, *Memoir*, 57; Macdonald, *Autobiographical Journal*, 34; Bonin, 'Voyage au Canada', 40–1; Stang, 'March Routes', 35; Cranfield, *Useful Christian*, 14; Steppler *Common Soldier*, ch 3.

luckier than most of his comrades. Pell spent some of his free time from his duties with the First Regiment of Foot Guards, hiring himself as an auxiliary farmhand or working on the London waterfront. When Pell's exemplary conduct in the regiment earned him a quick promotion, this proved at first to be an unwelcome development, as his new duties limited his ability to earn for a living. However, he was soon able to remedy the situation by securing an evening job at the Drury Lane theatre.[75] For Pell, working in his off-duty hours was not a bonus, but rather a necessity.

Those subsisting on their pay alone were likely to remain vulnerable. In Britain, the soldiers were entitled to a daily subsistence rate of six pence, from which they were also to cover service related expenses such as cleaning utensils and laundry. Moreover, officers sometimes made their men buy additional items which were not required by regulations. Jonas complained that as much as half of the pay was spent on such trifles. Staniforth complains that his pay was so small that he often went hungry, as did Cobbett, who claims during that his first year in the army he and other recruits were on the brink of starvation. Corporal Todd remarks that, in time of shortage, the soldiers had many 'Banyan days', that is, days without meat. According to Surtees, during the famine of 1799–1800, all of his pay was spent on food, and he was even forced to rob a vegetable garden. Similar complaints are voiced by men serving in other European armies. Like Cobbett, Beeger was still a growing lad, and could not satisfy his hunger from his eight *groschen*. Seume's pay in Halifax was similarly mostly used up on food. Uhlmann complains that neither his pay nor his rations were sufficient.[76] A different voice is provided by Sergeant Stevenson, who claims that 'we always looked on soldiers as being in better circumstances than any country labouring men, and we have considered ourselves to as much better off than we should have been if we had remained at home'. This was not necessarily an exaggeration. When his regiment was stationed in Ireland, Stevenson was billeted with a man who had to support six children on a daily wage of ten pence. Stevenson's host was astonished by the rations of bread and meat received by the soldiers. A similar case is reported by Todd, whose hosts, a German peasant family, were stunned to see that British soldiers were issued white bread. Soldiers were thus sometimes better off than the poorest members of the populace. Moreover, military authorities

---

[75] Rossignol, *Vie veritable*, 33–4; Beeger, *Seltsame Schicksale*, 25, 29–30; Pell 'Narrative', part 1, fols. 29–30, 39–40. On soldiers working in ports, see also: Seume, *Werke*, vol. I, 97.

[76] *Soldier's Journal*, 172–5; Cobbett, *Autobiography*, 24–5; Staniforth, 'Life', 326; Todd, *Journal*, 39; Surtees, *Twenty-Five Years*, 38–9; Beeger, *Seltsame Schicksale*, 28–9; Seume, *Werke*, vol. I, 68; Uhlmann, *Abwechslende Fortün*, 16–7. See also: Klöden, *Jugenderinnerungen*, 41–2; Bräker, 'Lebensgeschichte', 442–3 and 449–50.

occasionally made an effort to ease their lot in time of need. Nevertheless, this rarely exceeded the provision of basic necessities.[77]

In wartime, troops could hope to earn something through booty. According to Todd, officers and men departing on a raid to France hoped to make some money there. The prospect of free loot was a morale booster in its own right, as reported by Sergeant John Wilson, who states that Marlborough decided to thank the troops for their heroic storming of Donauwörth by allowing free pillage in Bavaria. Dominicus reports a similar case when Frederick the Great allowed the troops to loot a village whose peasants had concealed some Austrian soldiers. The king's order was carried out enthusiastically, and after all movable possessions were taken, the village was burned to the ground. Dominicus' account further describes numerous foraging forays in which locals were forced to supply men with food, drink and money. Moreover, the troops often did not spare the houses, sometimes dismantling them for firewood, or simply destroying them out of sheer vandalism. A similar attitude is expressed by McBane, who writes on the army's march through the enemy country, 'we did as we pleased and led a jolly life'. Friendly civilians did not fare much better, as happened at the Great Siege of Gibraltar, where the British defenders happily looted the abandoned civilian properties in the town they were defending.[78] Such behaviour was prompted not only by material considerations, a point which will be considered in greater length in the next chapter. For the current discussion, though, it is more important to determine whether there was any actual substantial material benefits to be gained from imposing the tax of violence on defenceless people, friends and foes alike. According to the soldierly accounts, it provided troops with badly needed food and drink, new clothes and, possibly, some cash. Moreover, as clearly shown by Dominicus, sometimes this was the only way to ensure one's survival in a devastated war-zone. As in the case of side-earning in peacetime, plundering civilians was at worst a necessity at best – a welcome supplement to meagre subsistence. However, it offered little prospects for genuine enrichment, a point which is also true for booty taken in combat.

---

[77] Stevenson, *Soldier*, 33, 140; Todd, *Journal*, 256; Barrington, *Eighteenth-Century Secretary at War*, 331–2. Soldiers were clearly better off than civilians in war-devastated areas; see: Grotehenn, *Briefe*, 94, 126; 'Feldwebel G.S. Liebler to his wife and relatives' (12 October 1756), in GG, 35.

[78] Todd, *Journal*, 21; J. Wilson, 'Journal', 46; Dominicus, *Tagebuch*, 11, 14, 21, 23, 27, 33–5, 72–3; McBane, 'Expert Swords-Man's Companion', 37; For similar instances of foraging, see: Todd, *Journal*, 94, 147–8; Bishop, *Life and Adventures*, 146; 'Journal of the Expedition up the River St. Lawrence', 4; Ancell, *Circumstantial Journal*, 114; Macdonald, *Autobiographical Journal*, 51; see also: Aytoun, *Redcoats*, 6–7, Büttner, 'Narrative', 232; Keep, *Soldiers of the Tsar*, 218–9.

Although all soldiers were entitled to the possessions of killed or captured opponents, it was mostly cavalrymen and light troops who could take advantage of this opportunity. For instance, horses captured by Georg Beß' jaegers were granted to his detachment, while he himself received as booty the horse of a captured enemy hussar whom he defeated in single combat. Dreyer headed a small free corps which often helped itself to captured enemy supplies and the purses of captive Austrian officers. Johann Gottlieb Allfärty was unhappy when his father requested him to transfer into the dragoons because he thought his prospects of obtaining booty were higher in the grenadier free corps to which he had been originally attached. Dominicus even reports a particularly lucky coup by the Prussian Red Hussars, who captured an Austrian paymaster with 25,000 *thalers*, an amount so large that the money was divided by hatfuls.[79] Linear formation, however, offered few comparable prospects for individual killing or capture. A soldier would be lucky to encounter an officer, as did Sergeant MacLeod, who had a singular success collecting 175 ducats from the pockets of a French colonel he killed at Fontenoy. Breaking ranks to plunder was forbidden, but, whenever possible men returned to the battlefield to rummage through dead bodies, with officers' possessions again being particularly valued.[80] Nevertheless, the only serious prospect for a regular infantryman to make a major gain was during the storming of a besieged city. Contemporary observers were shocked by the sacking of Bergen op Zoom, so vividly described by Charles-Étienne Bernos, whose account also provides many details of the rich booty taken by the grenadiers who headed the French assault columns. However, this exceptional case points to the rule of eighteenth-century siege warfare. Rather than a bloody *coup de main* followed by a breakdown of discipline and an unrestrained rampage by attacking troops, most eighteenth-century fortresses surrendered, following an elaborate ritual which usually guaranteed the safety and belonging of the inhabitants.[81] Even when the town was subject to a contribution, this largely went into the pockets of the officers. In one of the more notorious

---

[79] Georg Beß, 'Aus dem Tagebuch, 212, 219; Allfärtty, *Friedrich des Großen letzter Dragoner*, 18–9; Dreyer, *Leben und Taten*, 32–33, 39–40, 47; Dominicus, *Tagebuch*, 72–3; see also: Todd, *Journal*, 143. Alternatively, for a case of the free corps cavalryman who has lost a fortune, see: Cura, 'Tagebuch', 40.

[80] MacLeod, *Memoirs*, 66; Bonin, 'Voyage au Canada', 147–8; Büttner, 'Narrative', 240.

[81] Bernos, 'Souvenirs de campagne', 754–60; C. Duffy, *Fire and Stone*, 151–3; On the storming of Bergen op Zoom: C. Duffy, *Fortress in the Age of Vauban and Frederick the Great*, 107–10; Browning, *War of the Austrian Succession*, 319–21; M.S. Anderson, *War of Austrian Succession*, 173–4; For another example of troops on rampage in a stormed city, see: Kenward, *Sussex Highlander*, 30; according to Löffler, Austrian troops in Belgrade were better behaved *Der alte Sergeant*, 58.

instances, the capture of the great Spanish port of Havana netted the British commander a sum of 132,000 pounds, while the common soldiers received less than two-and-a-half pounds. Moreover, sometimes it took a few years before men were paid their share. It is only fair to agree with Frey that opportunities for looting were too few and far between to provide a stable incentive in wartime.[82] A remark by Prussian participants of the bloody battle of Prague says more about the actual role of remunerative compliance in combat than any price comparison. Corporal Nikolaus Binn writes that, although some hussars got plunder, 'ich halte doch meine beute beßer, nehmlich die gesundheit'. Binn was just happy to stay alive and in one piece.[83]

Gratuities were occasionally given out to the troops after battles or other strenuous exertions. Often coming from the commander's own purse, these were more of a symbolic gesture, and the men's accounts often recognise it as such. In absolute terms, however, it was very little. Following the battle of Kunersdorf, Frederick the Great personally paid his troops two *groschen*, while Dominicus' regiment was lucky to receive another four from its colonel-proprietor. After their return from captivity, General Coote awarded every man who was captured with him in Ostend one shilling. British troops who raided Dorchester heights during the siege of Boston were given new shoes and stockings. Otherwise renowned for his stinginess, the Duke of Marlborough presented the British troops who fought at Blenheim a gratuity of up to two pounds, an equivalent of about two months' worth of wages.[84] Exceptionally brave action by individual soldiers could merit a substantial reward, or even a commission. One very famous case was that of the grenadier who was ennobled by Frederick the Great for being the first to scale the walls of Prague in 1744. This unique case made such a strong impression on contemporaries that some Prussian soldier-writers were still invoking it in 1757. Sergeant John Johnson tells of a similar instance when Wolfe offered an ensign's commission to a sergeant who extracted a detached party from a French

---

[82] J. Miller, 'Memoirs of an Invalid', 69–74; M. Duffy, 'British Army and the Caribbean Expeditions', 68; Frey, *British Soldier in America*, 113–4; For more complaints about officers limiting opportunities for plunder and unfair distribution of prize money, see: Kenward, *Sussex Highlander*, 31–2; Todd, *Journal*, 80.

[83] For the last quote, see: 'Corporal Nikolaus Binn to his wife and family', (8 May 1757), in Liebe, 7; For a very similar view taken by other soldiers, see: Glantz, *Auszüge aus Briefen*, 27, Grotehenn, *Briefe*, 124.

[84] Dominicus, *Tagebuch*, 58, 66; NAM 2004-03-75 (1), 'Two manuscript letters written by Private James Morgan, Coldstream Guards to his father'; Sullivan, *From Redcoat to Rebel*, 33; McBane, 'Expert Swords-Man's Companion', 32, 43; see also: Scouller, *Armies of Queen Anne*, 148; For more examples of gratuities, see: Sohr, *Meine Geschichte*, 66; Döhla, 'Tagebuch' (25 March 25 1777), Tory, *Journal*, 57, 60; Löffler, *Der alte Sergeant*, 48–9.

ambush. A point highly praised by Johnson is that the NCO refused the promotion, asking only to be allowed to retire as a master gunner in his hometown once the war was over.[85] More formalised rewards were instituted for men who captured enemy standards or cannon, and it was common to top up the pay of men engaged in particularly hazardous duties. Soldiers might sometimes be presented with gratuities in peacetime, such as the ten *florins* paid to Steininger and his comrades for playing their role well when the Duke of Württemberg fooled *Tsarevich* Paul of Russia by presenting him with the same men over three consecutive days wearing the uniforms of different regiments. Soldiers would often be offered free food or drink for their officers' health, but again this was largely a symbolic acknowledgement.[86] Truly generous gratuities were rare and granted to a few, while general ones were more of a tip, even if given to men who had risked their life in combat.

The balance of evidence on material incentives suggests that remunerative compliance remained at best a stable and, at worst, a declining factor in the motivation of eighteenth-century common soldiers. Pay and subsistence, while often providing a decent living standard compared to the poorest members of society, was just enough to provide for the basic needs of the soldiery. Moreover, the military wage failed to provide men with a safety net, not only against unforeseen economic circumstances such as famine and inflation, but even against apparently trivial incidents. After his grenadier cap was ruined by another soldier, Beeger went hungry for five days to pay for a replacement, while a lost half-penny once cost Cobbett his supper. Jonas, whose book concludes with a long complaint on the conditions of the soldiery, points to the hardships caused by the need to cover for more and more extravagant uniform accessories. To make things worse, drill sessions, which were originally intended to teach the men, now became an end in their own right, leaving soldiers no time to work to supplement their meagre pay. Although Jonas might also have been influenced by the all too common human tendency to glorify older days, it is interesting that very similar observations are made by Dreyer on the Prussian army after the Seven Years War. These testimonies are reinforced when one considers the empirical evidence that the purchasing power of the eighteenth-century military wage was steadily declining.[87] Chances to make a quick gain through looting similarly

---

[85] 'Anonymous soldier from Prague to his wife and family' (10 May 1757), in GG, 54–5; J. Johnson, 'Memoirs of the Siege of Quebec', 116.

[86] *Reglement Vor die Königl. Preußische Infanterie*, (1743), 349; Todd, *Journal*, 170–1, 201, 217; Tory, *Journal*, 64; Steininger, *Leben und Abenteuer*, 47–8; Scot, 'Remembrance', 350, 369, 391, 398–9, 432–3, 562–3. See also: Flohr, *American Campaigns*, 30, 39.

[87] Jonas, *Soldier's Journal*, 169–78; Dreyer, *Leben und Taten*, 20–1.

declined, partially due to more restrained modes of warfare, partially due to growing regularisation which allowed the authorities to keep a greater share of the prize money. Eighteenth-century soldiers could live off the land as well as revolutionary Frenchmen, but this could not be a stable source of income; nor could gratuities and prizes which depended on chance, luck or extreme circumstances.

Considering the material prospects of their common soldiers, it is nothing short of remarkable that old-regime armies succeeded not only in drawing a sufficient number of volunteers, but also retained enough men to ensure the smooth functioning of the military machine. Moreover, desertion always provided an outlet for the unsatisfied, whether they were unwilling or disenchanted recruits, or veterans unhappy with their financial conditions. While many soldiers took advantage of this opportunity, many more did not. The case of Ensign Miller, whose enlistment we recounted at the beginning of this chapter, provides a fitting conclusion for the present discussion. Miller makes clear in his account that his original romantic notions of military service did not survive for long. Moreover, his education offered good prospects outside the army. Nevertheless, Miller remained in the ranks for over a dozen years, and later rejoined the army as a loyalist officer at the beginning of the American War of Independence. Considering his options and his background, Miller's choices cannot be explained as a simple by-product of his youthful folly or of a yearning for material benefit. As demonstrated by the current chapter and the previous two chapters, neither coercive nor remunerative compliance can explain why Miller formed a lasting attachment to the military profession, as did most other old-regime soldiers. This points to the importance of normative compliance, whose significant role in initial motivation we have already touched. The following two chapters will discuss its role in the sustaining and combat motivation.

5   A Counter-Culture of Honour

Shortly after he hired himself to Lieutenant Marconi, Ulrich Bräker underwent a complete transformation. Not only had the master bought a set of elegant clothes for his new valet, but he also instructed the country boy how to hold himself in style. '[M]ußt du hübsch grävitatisch marschieren', Bräker was told. Soon afterwards, Marconi presented his protégée with a sword and taught him the intricacies of proper hairstyle, attaching the first pigtail to the back of Bräker's head. Bräker was also encouraged to dance and to behave more assertively in the presence of women. When sent to Berlin, Bräker was given a full marching kit, including a gun.[1] In light of these actions, Bräker's later assertion that the lieutenant originally intended to keep him as a servant, rather than hand him over into the Prussian army, appears highly improbable. Marconi was following the practice of the time to set recruits apart from their old milieu by altering their appearance and remoulding their behaviour. Bräker's socialisation into a new role as a soldier had begun even without his knowledge.

When more honest enlistment practices were employed, the recruit was often given some visible token, such as cockade or a ribbon, to mark him out from the general populace. Although men were occasionally provided with some items of military equipment, the uniforms were usually issued only when the recruit arrived at the regiment, which often happened months after he took the bounty. Although originally introduced to ensure basic clothing standards throughout the army, the functionality of uniforms soon became subordinate to fashion. Modelled on elegant gentleman's dress, uniform was not only the most evident sign separating soldiers from the rest of society, but also provided a unifying aspect between the enlisted men and their superiors. The higher social class to which soldiers supposedly belonged was further reinforced by carrying swords which 'may have been a tactically useless piece of ironmongery,

---

[1] Bräker, 'Lebensgeschichte', 423–5, 436, 446; Marconi's instructed Bräker to 'walk in a nice well-measured pace'.

but they symbolized the common soldiers' link to a higher class and a higher calling'.[2] In the French army, the new life taken up by the recruit was emphasised by giving him a name. The so-called *nom de guerre* was usually of a cheerful note and was intended to denote a new beginning, irrespective of the man's previous circumstances.[3]

Drill was another outward method which encouraged men to embrace their new military identity. Just like the uniform, which retained a practical role in making soldiers easily distinguishable and helping to hinder desertion,[4] drill also had an important functional role to fulfil. The collective proficiency which made possible the complex geometrical manoeuvres lying at the heart of old-regime tactics would have been impossible without individual proficiency. Recruits were first taught to march separately, then in small groups, by files and by ranks, and only then as part of platoons and companies. The whole process was repeated again after the recruit had mastered his musket drill. This slow gradual learning process was not only a function of combat efficiency but of basic safety. Unless men were fully proficient in the use of their firearms and knew their precise place within the formation, a volley from a closely-packed infantry line could prove deadlier to the men who discharged it than the opponents facing it.[5] It is unknown whether old-regime military drillmasters were also aware of the possible cohesive effects of collective movement in unison.[6] What is clear, though, is that the initial stage of the drill was intended to achieve much more than instructing the recruit in the principles of cadenced step or manual of arms, whose mastery would allow him to be integrated into training with larger bodies of men.

[2] Showalter, *Wars of Frederick the Great*, 101; C. Duffy, *Military Experience*, 89, 105–9; Lynn, *Battle*, 116–8; Füssel, 'Wert der Dinge', 105–11; Allmayer-Beck and Lessing, *Die kaiserlichen Kriegsvölker*, 214; Todd, *Journal*, 112; Alexander, *Life*, vol. I, 76–7. The Russian practice of marking new recruits gave rise to the expression *pobrit v rekruti* (to shave into a recruit), which denotes conscription.

[3] Corvisier, *L'Armée française*, vol. II, 848–61; Bois, *Anciens soldats*, 131–3; For personal examples of how the *nom de guerre* was given, see: Bibliothèque National, Paris, NUMM-109500, Joseph-Charles Bonin [Joulicoeur], 'Voyage au Canada', 35–6; Rossignol [Francouer], *Vie veritable*, 12. For reference to the uniform as the king's coat, see: Beeger, *Seltsame Schicksale*, 22.

[4] On uniforms as methods of control, see: Füssel, 'Wert', 107–8; Uhlmann, *Abwechslende Fortün*, 15; see also: Lamb, *Original and Authentic Journal*, 400–1; Steininger, *Leben und Abenteuer*, 19; See also the entries in the orders of the Gibraltar Garrison' in: TNA WO 284/3 (6 December 1748) and 287/7 (19 April 1785).

[5] On the rationale of eighteenth-century infantry drill, see the illuminating description in Showalter, 'Tactics and Recruitment'. For other types of realistic training, see: Ancell, *Circumstantial Journal*, 44; Bense, 'Brunswick Grenadier', 428; Centre of Kentish Studies, Maidstone, U1350 Z9A, James Miller, 'Memoirs of an Invalid', 18; Surtees, *Twenty-Five Years*, 3.

[6] On 'muscular bonding' see: McNeill, *Keeping Together in Time*. For more on the potential role of the drill in the creation of regimental culture, see: Lynn, *Battle*, 157–8.

The training of the individual recruit began with teaching him the proper posture – how to stand, walk and hold himself in line. This was more than a matter of mere physical aptitude, as regulations were clearly aimed at producing not just a professional soldier but also a reformed individual.

The Prussian infantry and cavalry regulations of 1743 specified the dressage which the new *Kerl* (fellow) was to undergo to give him the air of a soldier and remove that of the peasant. The head was to be held vertically with the eyes looking straight ahead; legs were to be kept unbending at the knee. Men were not to hunch, but keep their bodies upright, with the chest brought forward. Influenced by contemporary Prussian practices, future Russian Generalissimo Alexander Suvorov began his first regimental instructions on training by explaining the correct martial posture to be mastered by the recruits prior to being admitted to drill in the ranks. In addition, recruits were to be untaught certain habits such as 'vile guise' and 'peasants' talk', and it was recommended that their future contacts with the *muzhiks* be kept to minimum lest the soldiers readopt once again 'their looks, manners, tricks and talk'.[7] Austrian regulations likewise required that private soldiers should not to be 'ein in Soldatenkleidern verhüllter Bauer'. Instead, they were to have a free and unconstrained appearance and speak with reason and modesty. It was also expected that soldiers would achieve a modicum of polite accomplishment. In France, privates learned fencing and dancing. Although it was not a formal requirement in Britain, enlisted men were expected to have similar aspirations and were often referred to by their recruiters and, occasionally, by their superiors as 'gentlemen soldiers'. Rather than merely turning into a military craftsman, the old-regime soldier was remoulded as a new individual. He was not only supposed to appear different, but also to hold himself apart from the members of the classes from which he came. He was to appear sharp, speak briskly and perceive himself not only as more refined but also as more free than his civilian counterparts.[8] By becoming a soldier, men were now to take orders only from their noble superiors, headed by the monarch himself, rather than subjecting themselves to their social equals whose authority

---

[7] *Reglement Vor die Königl. Preußishce Infanterie*, (1743), 42–3; *Reglement Vor die Königl. Preußische Cavallerie-Regimenter*, (1743), 31; 'Polkovoije Ucherezhdenie (1765)' in: Suvorov, *Dokumenty*, vol. 1, 86, 145. For more on the sources which influenced Suvorov's early military writings, see: Rogulin, *'Polkovoie Ucherezhdenie' A. V. Suvorova*.

[8] *Reglement für die sämmentlich-Kaiserlich-Königliche Infanterie*, (1769), 8. On dancing and fencing as part of the French soldiers' exercise, see: Bernos, 'Souvenirs de campagne', 675. More generally on the connections between dance and drill, although concentrating on the higher classes, see: M.D. Field, 'Middle Class Society and the Rise of Military Professionalism'; McCormack, 'Dance and Drill'. On the supposed contrast between refined Prussian cantonists and other German peasants, see: *BBS*, 335.

was merely a product of greater age or professional skill. In this way, perceptions of soldierly freedom were reconciled with the demand for unwavering obedience.

As in the case of disciplinary regulations, the wishful language of the ordnances did not necessarily correspond with reality. Nevertheless, considering evidence coming from the men themselves, it is clear that at least some old-regime soldiers were not only aware that they were undergoing a formally induced process of socialisation, but that some actively embraced it. Upon his arrival at the regiment, the author of the *Soldier's Journal* was fitted out with 'all necessary to make me a gentleman soldier' and, after quickly learning to walk properly, moved to train with the firelock. Roger Lamb was also first taught to 'to walk and step out like a soldier', before moving to drill twenty-one days later. After being promoted to the rank of corporal and put in charge of other recruits, Lamb remarks that 'it is indeed surprising how soon an awkward young man becomes well disciplined, performs his evolutions with neat agility and handles his arms in graceful dexterity'. After six months in Chatham, Shaw and his fellow recruits learned their drill so well that they challenged the rest of the garrison. Le Roy's willingness and agility earned him promotion to corporal within six months of enlisting. After learning to fence, he became one of the top men in his battalion. Even the unwilling Bräker, who left some sour descriptions of Prussian drill sessions, recalls with pride that he was chosen to march with his regiment when the Seven Years War broke out, while many older soldiers had to remain in Berlin with the training battalion. Later in life, Samuel Hutton recalled with pleasure how, after becoming one of the best-looking men in his regiment, he chanced to meet one of the captains who had originally rejected him when Hutton was still a clumsy teenager.[9]

When successful, this transformation left a lasting mark. After Bräker returned home, his own family did not recognise him, so manly had he become; Shaw was not recognised by his own father only a few weeks after his enlistment. Guards placed at the city gates of Berlin were to question any apprentice or workman who was stoutly built or had the air of a soldier. The agents of the *maréchaussée* were to act likewise when they encountered soldier-like individuals travelling in civilian dress. After

---

[9] The captain expressed regret; Hutton, *Life*, 75; Jonas, *Soldier's Journal*, 10; Lamb, *Memoir*, 62, 89; Shaw, *Autobiography*, 17; Le Roy, *Souvenirs*, 43; Bräker, 'Lebensgeschichte', 453; For other soldiers who liked the drill or were proud of mastering it quickly, see: B. Miller, 'Adventures', 16; Surtees, *Twenty-Five Years*, 2–3, 41–2; Rossignol, *Vie veritable*, 12–3; Aytoun, *Redcoats*, 6; Grenadier Guard Regimental Archive, London, E6/003, William Pell 'Narrative', part 1, 27–9; For NCOs equally proud of their work, see: Cobbett, *Autobiography*, 31, Hagist, 'Unpublished Writings of Roger Lamb', 282.

escaping from captivity, Beeger took a long detour around a city occupied by Napoleonic troops, for otherwise he would have been easily recognised on account of his 'militärische Haltung'.[10] Unconscious physical absorption of the military bearing was only one of the products of this process. Some men also internalised the values which it promoted. Those who did not possess the air of soldiers were mocked. Lamb complains that the captive troops of Burgoyne's Convention Army who were allowed to work were very industrious, but lost that 'animation which ought to possess the breast of a soldier'. Bernos refers to the Croats who guarded him during his time as a prisoner of war as riffraff (canaille) because they wore greased shirts instead of military uniform. The British and their German auxiliaries remarked disparagingly on the looks of the continental army, a point repeated later against the Revolutionary French. Corporal Todd mentions an order given to the British troops during a coastal raid on France not to waste any ammunition on the cowardly militia, while Sergeant Johnson refers to the Canadian militia as nothing but savage cowards. Low regard was also reserved for the free battalions operating on the periphery of regular armies, not least because of their disregard of accepted honourable conventions. Good Jaeger Georg Beß refers to the French Fischer Chasseurs as Canallien, while Todd concludes his description of free troops by stating that these were universally despised for plundering the wounded.[11]

The proceeding discussion illustrates the socialisation of soldiers into broader military culture. In this particular case, the process was initially induced from above by the officers and NCOs who drilled the recruits, acting as primary socialising agents. However, once new members of the organisation had accepted its desired identity, they turned into agents of socialisation themselves. Thus, rather than being just a top-down process, military socialisation also operated on a horizontal level. Moreover, if drill can be considered an element of social disciplining, the willing association with proper military bearing denotes the existence of social control. Adhering to accepted institutional values was not only admirable in the eyes of one's peers, but also a practical choice to make; failure to follow these norms would result in disapproval, isolation or worse. The rest of

---

[10] Bräker, 'Lebensgeschichte', 469; Shaw, Autobiography, 12–3; Witzleben, Aus alten Parolebüchern, 19; I. Cameron, Crime and Repression, 121–2; Beeger, Seltsame Schicksale, 51.

[11] Lamb, Original and Authentic Journal, 398; Bernos, 'Souvenirs de campagne', 688; Shaw, Autobiography, 42; Popp, 'Journal', 247; Grenadier Guards Regimental Archive, A03/03, George Darby, 'Account of the Capture of Valenciennes' (13 August, 1793); D. Robertson, Journal, 23–4; J. Johnson, 'Memoirs of the Siege of Quebec', 134–5; Beß, 'Aus dem Tagebuch', 194; Todd, Journal, 89, 196–7.

this chapter will further examine the workings of this phenomenon by scrutinising soldierly narratives for evidence of the absorption of other normative factors. Firstly, we shall consider the culture of honour which, despite recent arguments to the contrary, was deeply internalised by the rank and file. Although some of its norms ran contrary to the official aims of the military organisation, perceptions of martial honour drew the individual soldier to accept other military values. This is followed by an overview showing how old-regime soldiers adopted external signs of military identity such as specific jargon, as well as group standards which, in turn, contributed to the creation of distinct corporate attitudes. Soldiers perceived themselves not only as gentlemen, but also as romantic anti-heroes whose values often clashed with those of civil society. Lastly, this chapter considers *esprit de corps*, less through its external manifestations, such as regimental traditions or ceremonies, but rather through evidence for the creation of personal attachment developed by individual soldiers to their units. Although all of this material is mostly concerned with the workings of normative compliance in the sustaining stage, its findings also contribute towards an understanding of combat motivation. Moral involvement in their immediate surroundings is commonly seen as one of the reasons why soldiers agree to fight. In other words, active association with shared military values formed in the sustaining stage would contribute towards greater combat cohesion.

As in the case of the supposed moral qualities of their subordinates, there is a substantial difference between what old-regime commanders stated in private and how they acted in public. Both Frederick the Great and James Wolfe are good examples here. Frederick stated that his men were incapable of honour and ambition, while Wolfe's private correspondence occasionally refers to his soldiers as scum. When addressing their men, however, both adopted a totally different type of language. Before the battle of Leuthen, after underscoring that the Prussians would attack a much stronger enemy holding a defensive position, Frederick threatened to disgrace regiments failing to do their utmost. Marks of public dishonour invoked by Frederick included taking away the regimental standards and soldiers' swords and cutting off the braid from the hats of officers and NCOs. Three years later, Frederick meted out this punishment on the Anhalt-Bernburg Regiment, which had broken during a sortie of the Austrian garrison of Dresden. Depriving its men of a few external marks of military honour proved spectacularly effective. In its next major battle, the regiment spearheaded a bayonet charge in what was one of the few occasions in Western warfare when a cavalry force was overthrown by attacking infantry in a regular field engagement. Wolfe did not have to call upon collective shaming, but often appealed to his men's honour and sense of duty.[12] If either of these commanders truly thought that their soldiers were totally indifferent to honour, they would have used some other means to encourage them into action.

Official dispensation of public marks of honour and shame are similarly mentioned by the men themselves. For instance, the anonymous grenadier who served in the Bourbonnais Regiment during the American War of Independence tells of two diametrically opposed cases which occurred during an Atlantic sea battle. A fellow grenadier, who was manning one of the cannons on the exposed forecastle, refused to leave his post despite his wounds, earning praise from General Rochambeau. A soldier from a different regiment, however, who bragged about his prowess before the battle, demanded to see the surgeon as soon as the first shot was fired. Despite being rebuked by his NCO, who remarked that no illness other than fright appears so suddenly, the man managed to be excused to fetch his sabre, and then proceeded to hide inside a cooking cauldron. Discovered there after the fight was over, the soldier was taken to his captain, who ordered one of his moustaches to be cut off. He further commanded that, should there be another sea battle, the coward was to be tied to the mainmast, armed with a foil to parry the cannon balls flying at him. Men who disgraced themselves in some way had to be ceremonially purified, usually by passing under the regimental standard. In the Austrian service, this was an elaborate ceremony in which the man, surrounded by his comrades, had to beg forgiveness three times. Aytoun and Rossignol mention that soldiers who committed light offences could be ordered to wear their coats inside-out, a punishment which could also be sentenced by a British company court martial.[13] On the other hand, Sergeant Thompson noticed that French soldiers from the La Reine Battalion who distinguished themselves were allowed to wear a shell in their buttonhole as a sign of honour. In 1776, the French army formally adopted a veteran's badge in shape of a heart with two crossed swords, given to men who had served more than twenty-four years.[14] All these gestures were unlikely to be invoked if the men were indifferent to them.

---

[12] C. Duffy, *Army of Frederick the Great*, 176, 193–4; C. Duffy, *Frederick the Great: A Military Life*, 147, 204–5; C. Duffy, *By Force of Arms*, 255–6; Brumwell, *Paths of Glory*, 266. Compare with Todd's description of Granby's address to his troops at Vellinghausen and Höxter, *Journal*, 164, 181; see also the collective punishment meted on the light company of the 57th Regiment in 1779: Dornfest, 'Unusual Case of Discipline', 65.

[13] Library of Congress, Washington, 'MCC 1907 Milton S. Latham Journal', 16–9; Steininger, *Leben und Abenteuer*, 55; *Regulament und Ordnung*, (1737), 114–5; Aytoun, *Redcoats*, 26–7; Rossignol, *Vie veritable*, 28, 59. See also: Chartrand, 'Punishment for Cowardice, Quebec, 1759', 186; Brumwell, *Redcoats*, 102–3.

[14] J. Thompson, *Bard*, 197. See also: Todd, *Journal*, 193. For an introduction to the Order of Merit in the British 5th Regiment of Foot, see: Brewis, 'Order of Merit'. For

Further evidence that honour was not only a recognised but also a desired concept is denoted by its frequent occurrence in the men's writings. For instance, it was evoked to describe successful military actions, especially when it was achieved against great odds. Describing the battle of Rhode Island, Johann Conrad Döhla writes that the German and British regiments won much honour and fame when they held an exposed position against much superior force and despite coming under heavy artillery fire. Guardsman John Tory, some of whose phraseology was borrowed by Corporal Todd, describes how his detachment marched through rain and mud for ninety-six miles without tents and food to save an isolated Prussian force. On another occasion, after two days of continuous marching and skirmishing, the British forced a much larger and fresher French force to retreat from a narrow defile: 'We gained much honour and they nothing but disgrace'. What worked for the collective also worked for individual soldiers. Before embarking on a campaign, veteran artillery Corporal George Robertson wrote to his family that 'I don't expect to come off as cleare as I did last war, But it is death or honour. I exspeck to be a Gentleman or a cripel [sic]'. Sergeant Lamb refers to his own sense of honour when he decided to escape from Burgoyne's Convention Army since the Americans were the first to break their word by refusing to parole the British prisoners. More generally, Lamb remarks that although the army did contain some bad individuals, and while others were tempted to commit ill, readers should not think that soldiers were indifferent when it comes to honour. Joseph Ferdinand Dreyer writes that Prussian soldiers in the time of King Frederick William I and the early reign of his son were motivated by a love of honour, which was further reinforced by the preference given to soldiers vis-à-vis the other estates. According to Sergeant Johnson, despite initial failures against Quebec, the British common soldiers were as resolute as ever to continue the siege, inspired by gentlemen at their head and desiring glory as much as their generals were. James Miller states that commanders who failed to acknowledge their men's sense of honour damaged themselves. For instance, General Burgoyne undermined the confidence of his army by stating publicly that soldiery was composed from the scum of the nation. According to Miller, the army might be composed of young ignorant boys who knew no other life than that of a soldier, but they did care 'when slandered and treated with contempt'.[15]

a suggestion of how to increase positive competition between regiments with the help of music, see: Dreyer, *Leben und Taten*, 51–3.

[15] Döhla, 'Tagebuch' (29 August 1778); Tory, *Journal*, 41–2, 57; Todd, *Journal*, 158; G. Robertson, 'Two Letters', 23; Lamb, *Memoir*, 105, 234; Dreyer, *Leben und Taten*, 20; J. Johnson, 'Memoirs of the Siege of Quebec', 101; J. Miller, 'Memoirs of an Invalid',

Just like the desire for honour, fear of shame provided not only a powerful incentive, but also a value in its own right. Rossignol, for instance, claimed that after his arrest for striking his captain, he was ready to commit suicide rather than have himself dishonourably hanged. Failing at first to earn any money during his off-duty hours, a hungry Beeger was almost driven to begging, but as he was about to approach a well-dressed passer-by, Beeger backed off, ashamed what people would think of 'a soldier in the royal uniform, a son of a brave officer and a beggar'. For the same reason Beeger refused his first job offer – cleaning sewers. Questioning their honour could also propel men into action which they were otherwise reluctant to follow. Although von Klöden's father was a veteran of twenty-four years and entitled to a pension and exemption from all further active service, he still rejoined his regiment at the start of the campaign of 1792. Susceptible to honour, he could not resist his fellow sergeants, who said that he could not stay behind now that their country was in danger. This also included shaming men into action, as was done by Georg Beß, whose raiding detachment initially refused to follow him after learning that 200 Croats had taken position nearby. Beß harangued his men, who were mostly recent recruits, by telling them that 'Vogel friß oder stirbt! Ehre oder Schande [. . .] Wer ein braver Jäger seyn wollte, sollte mir folgen', further underscoring that he intended to go forward, alone, if necessary. Matthew Bishop similarly used a combination of shaming and flattery to impel a group of soldiers to cross a deep river. After fording it first, Bishop addressed his comrades, who all happened to be taller than him, proclaiming 'you are gallant men and afraid of nothing'.[16]

While these examples show that they were concerned for their individual reputation, soldiers also felt stung if they became associated with failure which occurred through no fault of their own. After the unsuccessful expedition against Rochefort, Miller reports the dismay of the returning troops who were cheered on their departure, but were now insulted by the mob 'as if answerable for the conduct of their superiors'. Similarly, Peter Williamson considers the journey of British troops to Oswego and back in 1755 to be a disgrace.[17] Surrendering troops could also be deeply

---

134–5. For other instances when authors clearly took pride in their side achieving success against great odds, see: 'Journal of the Expedition up the River St. Lawrence', 10; Wray, *Military Adventures*, 11.

[16] Beeger, *Seltsame Schicksale*, 28–9; Rossignol, *Vie veritable*, 24–5; Beß's address can be translated as 'Eat or be Eaten! Honour or Shame! [. . .] Whoever wants to become a brave jaeger, will have to follow me', 'Aus dem Tagebuch', 209. For instances of shaming men into action, see: Bishop, *Life and Adventures*, 142; Laukhard, *Leben und Schicksale*, 327–8.

[17] J. Miller, 'Memoirs of an Invalid', 17; Williamson, *French and Indian Cruelty*, 81; see also: Laukhard, *Leben und Schicksale*, 270.

moved by their experience. According to Löffler, when it became known that Landrecies was to surrender to the Revolutionary French, soldiers of the Deutschmeister regiment, many of whom were veterans of the Turkish and even the Seven Years War, broke their weapons. Even Johann Christoph Pickert, whose account purposefully avoids all reference to martial honour, tells of the distress when his detachment surrendered to the French. Many men cried, and Pickert himself felt ashamed when he had to give away his weapons. An officer who witnessed the evacuation of a small isolated French fort surrendered to the British at the end of the Seven Years War wrote that although the garrison was made of old soldiers and invalids:

When the Sentries were relieved and the Guard just ready to march off, the French colours were pull'd down. Upon sight of this those Honest Old Veterans were greatly chagrin'd. They could not help venting their Indignation, by shrugging their shoulders and declaring when they had fought under Marshals Berwick Saxe and Lowendale, no such dishonour was then ever seen.[18]

Precisely because of the disgrace involved on such occasions, some soldiers tried to preserve their pride as much as possible. Bräker remarks that many Saxon prisoners clearly looked embarrassed during the surrender of Pirna, but others put on a defiant air. Bernos reports that his detachment defied its Austrian captors; its men maintained their military bearing despite being taunted and paraded between the victorious enemy troops. Daniel Krebs sees such behaviour, as well as the clauses intended to preserve the dignity of the surrendering troops often inserted into capitulation articles, as a sign that the culture of honour, traditionally associated with the officers only, filtered down to their subordinates.[19]

Studies on the concept of honour usually distinguish between its internal and external aspects. In the former case, the individual follows his own inner principles and he is the sole judge of the morality of his actions. In the latter case, honour is measured publicly, and the individual is judged by his adherence to an accepted code of behaviour. Excelling in this grants respect in the eyes of one's peers, while failure to obey will impinge on one's reputation. To feel shame, however, one has to be

---

[18] Captain Thomas Stirling quoted in Kirkwood, *Through so Many Dangers*, 100; Löffler, *Der alte Sergeant*, 124; Pickert, *Lebens-Geschichte*, 48; Döhla, 'Tagebuch' (19 October 1781). For examples when surrendering troops were taunted or shamed, see: Dominicus, *Tagebuch*, 77–8; Deane, *Journal* 41, Englund, *Battle of Poltava*, 177–81.

[19] Bräker, 'Lebensgeschichte', 458; Bernos, 'Souvenirs de campagne', 674; Daniel Krebs, 'Making of Prisoners of War'. For more on the experience of captivity in the eighteenth century, see: Voigtländer's annotated anthology, *Vom Leben und Überleben in Gefangenschaft*.

seen by an audience who shares the same values and in whose view one's behaviour is disgraceful. Gabriele Taylor calls these 'mini-honour groups', a notion which bears a striking resemblance to primary groups, not only in its definition but also in the way it operates. The separation between the private and public faces of honour is not that obvious, though. Individual principles often reflect societal ones, and it is hard to distinguish whether their origin is within the individual or represents his subconscious internalisation of socially acceptable values. Moreover, consistency in following what is originally a personal code of honour can be enforced by external factors, as demonstrated in the example of George Blennie. When he enlisted, Blennie was averse to swearing and reprimanded his comrades who engaged in it. Corrupted by military life, Blennie eventually stopped caring about blasphemous talk, but still refrained from swearing, as he feared to become a laughing stock for failing to follow his own professed principles. This study, therefore, adopts a more general definition of honour – the desire for respect – or, as Frank Henderson Stewart puts it, 'the right to be treated as having a certain worth'. The accounts considered over the preceding pages, and also the assertive stance occasionally put up by enlisted men against their superiors discussed in Chapter 3, demonstrate that members of the rank and file had developed a strong sense of self-esteem, both as individuals, as well as part of a larger military collective. As far as the available material stands, it is highly unlikely that they would have agreed with Armstrong Starkey's recent verdict that '[t]here is little evidence that the rank and file embraced the culture of honor'.[20]

Soldierly bearing was officially promoted; soldierly honour was an acknowledged value, even if some superiors doubted it in private. More specific signs that men were deeply socialised into their new identity as soldiers included their acceptance of a large set of customs and norms, which denotes the existence of an active culture which ran independently and, occasionally, contrary to formal regulations. Its most evident sign was the use of military slang. Soldiers often did not walk or travel but marched, even when journeying alone or on private business. Use of nicknames was common, although when referring to persons and places, these usually measured somewhere between innocent and ticklish. Bernos and his fellow French prisoners christened the commanders of their Hungarian and then Croatian guards as Sancho Panza and Monsieur Rondeux. Due to an incident which happened during the

---

[20] On the dualist definition of honour, see: Robinson, *Military Honour and the Conduct of War*, 2, which contains much useful bibliography; Taylor, *Pride, Shame and Guilt*, 63; Blennie, *Narrative*, 4; Stewart, *Honor*, 145; Starkey, *War*, 92.

fighting retreat at the battle of Sainte-Foy, Major Irvine of James Miller's regiment became known to his men as 'damn the old wig'. According to Williamson, the soldiery at Oswego informally referred to Fort George as Fort Rascal, in honour of the lieutenant who built it.[21] Use of sarcastic terms was widespread. Enemies could be *visited* but, if they ventured to attack first, their soldiers could expect to be given a *warm reception*, greeted with *salutes, compliments* and even *dancing*.[22] Some of the figures of speech bordered on the macabre, such as sending a few *winter plumbs* at the backs of fleeing Frenchmen evoked by John Marshall Deane, or curing the toothache of the unruly London mob mentioned by William Calder. Punishments could also be referred to ironically. Extraordinary labour in the Gibraltar garrison was named after a local spirit; sleeping under a bed in Frederick William I's army was alluded to as 'standing' under it. The Fraser Highlanders considered flogging as a type of back-scratching.[23]

On top of language came humour. Jokes retold by men in their accounts are biting and often sardonic. They could be relatively simple elaborations on the themes already touched on above, as in the case of Sergeant John Hall, who writes that at Malplaquet, 'We had but an indifferent Breakfast, but the Mounseers [sic!] never had such a dinner in their lives'. Soldiers also sometimes made use of verbal puns. Friedrich Christian Sohr, who fell off his bench while discussing with his comrades whether he should transfer into a Free Corps, quickly rose to declare it was a sign that 'ich einer mit von den ersten seyn werde, der in des Feindes Land einfällt!'.[24] Less innocent were the remarks made by the

---

[21] For instances of marching, see: Beeger, *Seltsame Schicksale*, 39; Williamson, *French and Indian Cruelty*, 77, 82; Todd, *Journal*, 6–7, 114–6; Bräker, 'Lebensgeschichte', 423, 437. For nicknames given to persons and places, see: Bernos, 'Souvenirs de campagne', 675, 689; Steininger, *Leben und Abenteuer*, 84; Aytoun, *Redcoats*, 27; J. Miller, 'Memoirs of an Invalid', 38, 64; Deane, *Journal*, 26; McBane, 'Expert Swords-Man's Companion', 38; and to weapons: Scot, 'Remembrance', 435. See also: Grose, *Classical Dictionary*, q.v. 'Camp Candlestick', 'Tilt', 'Toasting Iron', 'Whinyard'.

[22] Deane, *Journal*, 7, 11, 60, 97; J. Wilson, 'Journal', 50, 84; Kenward, *Sussex Highlander*, 25; Beß, 'Aus dem Tagebuch', 195, 197, 216–7; Dominicus, *Tagebuch*, 17; BL add MS 45,662, Richard Humphrys, 'Journal', fols. 12, 48; D. Robertson, *Journal*, 13, 17; '*Unteroffizier* from the Anhalt Regiment to his father' (6 October 1756), in GG, 21; 'Musketeer Jakob Angerstein to his wife' (24 April 1757), in GG, 39; '*Feldwebel* G.S. Liebler to his wife and family' (7 May 1757), in GG, 47; Linn, 'The Battle of Culloden', 22; Cura, 'Tagebuch', 36.

[23] Deane, *Journal*, 91; NAM 1986-11-1 'Letters of Sergeant Calder (American War) 1778–5' (19 June 1780); Linn, 'Battle of Culloden', 22; Grose, *Classical Dictionary*, q.v. 'Black Strap'; Johann Schultze, 'Soldat Johann Schultze, an seine Verwandten, Arneburg, 13. August 1723', in BBS, 283; J. Thompson, *Bard*, 149; McBane, 'Expert Swords-Man's Companion', 29.

[24] Hall, 'Letter to Sergeant Cabe' (26 September 1709); compare with Koch, *Battle*, 19; Bishop, *Life and Adventures*, 160, 204–5; Flohr, *American Campaigns*, 33. Sohr

comrades of Private Johann Ullrich Teufel, who drowned during the crossing of Hell Gate tidal strait to the east of New York. Sergeant Thompson mentions, without quoting them verbatim, the jokes made by his comrades after an Indian sharpshooter was killed with a lucky shot through the groin. When at the battle of Rhode Island, a party of American troops was chased into the sea, Döhlemann compared them to a herd of sheep or hogs that were trying to swim. Unfortunately for them, 'with head shots one after another forgot about swimming'. On another occasion the corpses of the dead rebels were thrown into the water with rocks around their necks, 'in proportion to their weight'.[25]

Jokes could also be made at the expense of the narrator and his comrades. Sohr recalls how well armoured he was in his first battle, because of the clerk's briefcase hanging on his chest. Guardsman Deane tells that the soldiers were receiving such a measly allowance in the navy that men were growing as fat as whipping posts. Rather than a matter of self-deprecation, however, such jokes were likely to provide comic relief in what were highly unpleasant situations. Johannes Reuber mentions how jokes and high spirits in general diverted the Hessian troops during their first days at sea, during which the men where constantly vomiting from sea sickness. James Field's biographer similarly tells how, despite the dreadful conditions of the winter of 1794–5, the men were, nevertheless, entertained by the icicles dangling under the moustaches of their comrades. When their officers left Flanders for England on recruiting service, Bishop relates that his comrades used to say that 'they are going in order to bring over those that were killed in the last campaign'. According to Bishop, such statements 'created Mirth and Diversion, which is the only thing a soldier had to keep up his Spirits'.[26]

The customs which the men were supposed to follow presents another aspect of the way that soldiers perceived themselves. The overt manifestation and occasional enforcement of the ideals for which these customs stood demonstrates the normative element of their culture. One such value was generosity. As mentioned in the previous chapter, recruits were expected to spend their bounty to treat their new comrades. Bonin procured himself numerous friends in his company by spending a month's worth of pay to celebrate his enlistment. New NCOs were

announced that his fall was a sign that 'I will be among the first to befall upon the enemy's land!, *Meine Geschichte*, 35.

[25] Döhla, 'Tagebuch' (20 June 1778); Stang, 'March Routes', 33; J. Thomspon, *Bard*, 149; Döhlemann, 'Diary', 13–24; see also: Kenward, *Sussex Highlander*, 49; Surtees, *Twenty-Five Years*, 15.

[26] Sohr, *Meine Geschichte*, 38; Deane, *Journal*, 55; *Royal Dragoon*, 16; Institut für Stadtgeschichte, Frankfurt am Main, S1/367 Johannes Reuber, 'Tagebuch' (17–8 April 1776); J. Field, *Devout Soldier*, 19; Bishop, *Life and Adventures*, 174

likewise expected to mark their promotion. When he was made *Gefreiter* during one of his stints in the Austrian service, Steininger went on to celebrate with his new colleagues 'according to the common usage'. Corporal Todd writes that it was customary to spend about a week's pay on such occasions. Men were expected to continue treating their comrades whenever an opportunity arose. During his furlough in Paris, which he was given after his return from Austrian captivity, Bernos was left with little money because of frequently inviting comrades for drinks. As with enlistment bounties, when men happened to get their hands on large sums of money, there was a good chance these would be spent merrily and quickly. On a more serious note, William Cobbett wrote that generosity was a product of the men's sense of responsibility to each other.[27] Generosity was clearly a virtue to be proud of. Authors mentioned instances of kindness extended to fellow soldiers on the enemy side. Pastor Täge witnessed a moving scene after the battle of Zorndorf when a wounded Prussian grenadier shared his loaf of bread with a hungry Russian prisoner, saying 'you must be a fine chap like me!' During the campaign in Spain an anonymous royal dragoon captured an Irishman who was serving with the French. The prisoner said he had nothing but one single piece of silver, which the dragoon refused to take.[28]

If gaining a reputation for open-handedness was socially helpful, allegations of miserliness were a sure way to become generally disliked. Bräker tells of a fellow soldier named Bachmann, whose stinginess prevented him from blending in with the other men. While serving in the Halifax garrison, Seume managed to save some money, but his comrades quickly persuaded him 'to put it back into circulation' after threatening to break Seume's 'dead face with heavy gold pieces'. Men who had more money clearly invoked jealousy, and if they happened to be socially astute, they would quickly remedy the situation. After overhearing complaints that the officers tipped him more than the other recruits, Bishop declared that he was actually given a bonus to be divided between all men so they could drink to the officers' health. The middle way between such munificence and affronting your equals was sharing. In fact, there is evidence

---

[27] Bonin, 'Voyage au Canada', 37; Todd, *Journal*, 136; Steininger woke the next morning already *after* being demoted and received a further twenty-five canes for drunkenness, *Leben und Abenteuer*, 72–3; Bernos, 'Souvenirs de campagne', 746; Kirkwood, *Through so Many Dangers*, 86; J. Dorman, 'Interesting Memoir', 125, Cobbett, *Autobiography*, 45.

[28] It turned out the dragoon was cheated as a less scrupulous guard later despoiled the said prisoner of thirty gold pieces; see: *Royal Dragoon*, 20; Täge, *Lebensgeschichte*, 193–4; For another instance of generosity to prisoners, see: J. Wilson, 'Journal', 88–9; Starkov, *Raskazi*, 286. For instances of generosity towards enemy non-combatants, see: Blennie, *Narrative*, 14, 17–9; 'Feldwebel G.S. Liebler to his wife and relatives', (12 October 1756), in GG, 35; J. Thompson, *Bard*, 150.

that this was occasionally considered to be a formal obligation. Büttner's knowledge of English helped him to obtain more patients than the other Hessian surgeon's mates. His attempt to ignore the agreement made between them to share all their income equally almost led to a duel. Todd's pioneers contributed all of their extra-earnings to the benefit of their mess, and the same was true for booty they found on the battlefield. Such arrangements also included an element of mutual responsibility. For instance, when Todd was under arrest, his messmates continued to bring him his share of the common meal.[29]

The expectation of sharing was not limited to members of one's immediate outfit. After squandering their pay, Samuel Hutton and a comrade went into London in hope of finding some money to buy supper. As they were rambling through the streets, they were joined by another man from their regiment. Soon afterwards, Hutton was lucky to find a shilling lying on the ground, which he quickly picked up and hid before the other two soldiers noticed. Hutton explained that if he had announced the discovery, he would have had to share it with the third man who joined them halfway. Returning from a foraging expedition, Bishop shared what he found with the other men. According to Blennie, it was common for comrades to buy refreshments together, usually taking turns on different days. A very similar arrangement was made by Todd and his fellow corporals who instituted a formal club, whose rules not only specified that the weekly meetings would be hosted by every corporal in turn, but also the maximum amount of money to be spent on such occasions. Attempts to divide booty fairly could sometimes descend into the macabre. After annihilating an Indian raiding party, men from Peter Williamson's detachment had to cast lots since there were not enough scalps to give as trophies to every ranger.[30]

Whether formally or informally prompted, such rudimentary forms of fairness suggest the existence of horizontal loyalty among the soldiery. As we will see in the next chapter, malingering was particularly detested. Nevertheless, Blennie's fellow patients, although very unhappy that one of their number was scratching his skin in order to stay longer in the hospital, did not expose the fraud. Reporting on one's comrades to the authorities was not only unacceptable, but also dangerous. According to Seume, a man who betrayed a desertion plot continued to fear for his life even after he was promoted and transferred to a different

---

[29] Bräker, 'Lebensgeschichte', 445–6, 467–8; Seume, *Werke*, vol. I, 97; Bishop, *Life and Adventures*, 140; Büttner, 'Narrative', 247; Todd, *Journal*, 157–8; 169, 209, 214.
[30] Hutton, *Life*, 60; Bishop, *Life and Adventures*, 193, 198–9; Blennie, *Narrative*, 6; Todd, *Journal*, 14; Williamson, *French and Indian Cruelty*, 43–4; see also: Hall, 'Letter to Sergeant Cabe' (26 September, 1709).

regiment.[31] Solidarity between men could also continue after death. Revolted by the lack of decent burial arrangements, soldiers of the British garrison of Dominica raised a subscription to pay for decent funerals for their dead comrades. Sergeant Kenward similarly tells of subscriptions arranged to pay for a monument to the dead of his regiment. Separated from its sister ship by a tempest, Bonin's ship arrived at France much later than expected. After disembarking, Bonin and the other paroled prisoners of war learned that a mass had already been arranged on their behalf by their comrades from the other ship, who thought them to be lost at sea. Moved by this gesture, Bonin and his fellow passengers treated all the soldiers who travelled on board the other vessel to a feast which lasted a whole day.[32] In this episode, the norms of soldierly solidarity, generosity and also jollity all merged together.

In his autobiography, *Magister* Friedrich Christian Laukhard says that the liveliness of soldiers reminded him of students. Members of both groups often had to borrow, pay debts and be crafty. They were also lively and spent much time drinking, wenching, arguing, quarrelling and, occasionally, brawling. After spending time as a French prisoner and a Dutch marine, Löffler ended up in a polyglot unit garrisoning British Jamaica. Although he enjoyed neither drinking nor quarrelling, his honour as a soldier and as a German impelled him to compete against his comrades. The nature of these competitions is revealed by Löffler's admission that the English were usually unsurpassed in drinking and blaspheming, the French excelled in dancing and courtly behaviour and the Spaniards were the best cursers. Sergeant Thompson recalled with pride how he went to a ball immediately after a forced march of eighty-one miles. Saxon surgeon's mate Johann Georg Schreyer, who travelled to Frankfurt with a contingent of Swiss guards to represent their elector at the Imperial coronation, took pride in the prowess of his comrades. After spending an evening in a tavern where more bottles of wine were drunk than there were men in his detachment, cheered by the locals, Schreyer remarked: 'you see what we did here for our honour against the other nations!' On the other hand, when reformed Quaker John Mackellow declined to

---

[31] Blennie, *Narrative*, 105; Seume, *Werke*, vol. I, 64–5. On the unpopularity of snitchers, see: TNA WO 284/2 (22 May 1746); Scot, *Remembrance*, 37–8; Bishop, *Life and Adventures*, 180–1. For a soldier who was unwilling to report on his officers even to the cost of his promotion, see: Jarvis, 'An American's Experience', 206–7, 209–11.

[32] Aytoun, *Redcoats*, 23–4; Kenward, *Sussex Highlander*, 55; Bonin, 'Voyage au Canada', 226. For examples of soldierly solidarity, see: McBane 'Expert Swords-Man's Companion', 39; J. Miller, 'Diary of James Miller, 1745–50, 222; Compare with Popp, 'Journal', 217.

drink toasts in the public house where he was lodging, everyone was surprised. Soldiers who refused drink were apparently uncommon.[33]

As mentioned by Laukhard, there was also an expectation that soldiers would be successful when it came to dealings with women. Many of his comrades lived by the motto 'ein ander Städtchen, ein ander Mädchen' and when a hundred soldiers arrived at a new place, there would be twenty-five soldiers' sweethearts within four days. Some soldier-authors claim to have used their appeal on that front to gain unfair advantages of different kinds. Samuel Hutton and James Andrew were able to extract some money on the pretext of an imminent marriage, as did Donald McBane, who even arranged for a sham wedding to be performed. When imprisoned in an American gaol after an unsuccessful attempt to escape from captivity, Crawford decided to regain his freedom by seducing the daughter of the sheriff. He succeeded in this endeavour by using skills acquired during previous military service in Ireland. After returning to his regiment after an abortive desertion attempt which included running through a forest to escape from pursuing peasants, Steininger was asked why he had green marks on his knees. Steininger's reply that he was in the woods with a girl and that 'all went well' satisfied his superiors, and he was let off without any further questions. The practice which Steininger falsely alluded to is known in English by the term 'to give someone a green gown'.[34]

The alleged achievements of the soldiers with the 'bottle and lass', to quote a contemporary British recruitment poster, should be understood as part of a broader notion of military masculinity. Although the gender identity of enlisted personnel in other periods has been widely studied, the few works on this phenomenon in old-regime armies deal primarily with their officers or, in the case of Jennine Hurl-Eamon's recent excellent study, with the women with whom the soldiers interacted.[35] The one

---

[33] Laukhard, *Leben und Schicksale*, 150–1, 179,181; Löffler, *Der alte Sergeant*, 308; J. Thompson, *Bard*, 122; Schreyer, *Wahl und Krönung*, 30–2; Mackellow, *Autobiography*, 60. See also: Steininger, *Leben und Abenteuer*, 64–5, 78–80.

[34] Laukhard, *Leben und Schicksale*, 286; Hutton, *Life*, 41; J. Andrew, 'Last Speech', 175; McBane, 'Expert Swords-Man's Companion', 41; Crawford, 'Narrative', 316, 322–3; Steininger, *Leben und Abenteuer*, 71–2; Oxford English Dictionary, qv 'green gown'. For other examples of soldiers as ladies' darlings, see: J. Thompson, *Bard*, 150, Young, 'Last Words', 140; Wood, *Gunner at Large*, 32; Schimmel, 'Kurze Lebensbeschreibung', 191–2.

[35] NAM 1969-07-17, 'Recruiting Poster of the 1st Battalion of Pennsylvania Loyalists'; Hurl-Eamon, *Marriage and the British Army*; McCormack, 'Dance and Drill; Kennedy, 'John Bull into Battle', in: Hagemann, Mettele and Rendall *Gender, War and Politics*. The other essays in this volume say much about military masculinities of citizen-soldiers but not of their opponents. For studies of military masculinity in other periods, see: Rogg, '"Wol auff mit mir, du schoenes weyb"'; Hughes, *Forging Napoleon's Grand Armée*,

scholar who has investigated the self-perception of these soldiers as men is Möbius. His study of letters by Prussian soldiers during the Seven Years War demonstrates that the terms honour and courage were closely associated with manly behaviour. In other words, being a man meant possessing these qualities, and Möbius sees this as part of the broader military ethos which helped to sustain men in combat. This interpretation is close to modern understandings of military masculinity, as put forward in studies on combat motivation. In this context, manly behaviour is associated not only with courage but also with aggressiveness, toughness and resilience.[36] Old-regime soldierly memoirs also cite these values as desirable. One obvious example of such manly behaviour, which also demonstrates the internalisation of the culture of honour, is duelling. Duels among the lower ranks clearly followed the customs of their established elite counterparts. This included the presentation of a formal challenge, setting the conditions and the presence of seconds and witnesses. Moreover, the whole practice was governed by an informal code of honour. Soldiers mindful of their reputation could not fail to react to an affront. Shaw's messmate tried to provoke him to fight and, after being initially ignored, insulted Shaw in public. Told by his sergeant 'You whip him or I'll whip you', Shaw was left with no choice but to fight. After responding to an opponent who made fun of him during a game of cards, Johann Kaspar Steube was challenged to a duel. Before he could decide how to proceed, Steube was relieved to learn he was ordered to transfer to a different garrison. But instead of forgetting the whole matter, his comrades laughed him off as *fruchtsamer Hase* (a cowardly hare). Returning to Stralsund five months later, Steube was immediately approached by the challenger, who summoned him again. Their encounter the next day led to a bloody fight and Steube's desertion.[37]

Withstanding hardships was a point of pride. Aytoun tells how he witnessed a man who was peacefully smoking a pipe while his hand was amputated. According to Samuel Wray, despite the gruelling desert

---

108–35; Hagemann, *Mannlicher Muth und Teutsche Ehre*; Streets-Salter, *Martial Races*; Orna Sasson-Levy, *Zehuyot be-madim*, [Rights in Uniform].

[36] Möbius, '"Bravthun", "entmannende Furcht" und "schöne Überlauferinnen"'; Shils and Janowitz, 'Cohesion and Disintegration', 293–4; Stouffer et al., *American Soldier: Combat*, 130–3; Moskos, *American Enlisted Man*, 154–5.

[37] Shaw, *Autobiography*, 36–7, Steube, *Wanderschaften und Schicksale*, 50–2. Another soldier who unwillingly accepted a challenge in order to save face was McBane, see: 'Expert Swords-Man's Companion', 39. For more on duelling soldiers, see: Lorgnier, *Maréchaussée*, vol. II, 49; Kiernan, *Duel in European History*, 133; On connections of duels and masculinity, although almost entirely in elite context, see: Frevert, *Man of Honour*; on the spread of duelling practice among the lower orders, see: Spierenburg, 'Knife Fighting and Popular Codes of Honour'; Cuénin, *Le duel*, 292–3

march from Suez to Cairo, the British soldiers scorned the chance to complain. After heavy wind blew sand into his haversack, Sergeant John Stevenson remarked that the food inside became 'actually past eating, except to a soldier'.[38] In some British regiments it was a point of honour not to 'nightingale', that is, cry out during flogging, which gave rise to the expression 'to chew a bullet'. Public displays of weakness ran against the prevailing ethos of toughness. When leaving Halle on campaign against France, many soldiers of the Anhalt Regiment were clearly distressed when they took farewell of their families, but few cried. According to Laukhard, it was inappropriate for soldiers to convey such feelings, and those who could not restrain their tears were ridiculed by their own comrades. Winning respect meant being manly, that is, being strong and bold, and flaunting this openly. In addition to extroverted displays of drinking and quarrelling, this included more risqué activities. Before scaling down the walls of Tortona in his third desertion from the Piedmontese army, Steininger paused to inscribe a disparaging verse on the wall of the sentry booth. During the Great Siege of Gibraltar, Thomas Cranfield sat down with a fishing rod on a rocky outcrop in full view of the enemy – and calmly remained there even when one of the Spanish cannons fired at him directly. On another occasion, after his detachment had successfully completed some fortification works under heavy artillery fire, Cranfield mounted on the parapet and shouted three cheers.[39]

Displays of bravura could also take place with the full blessing of the military authorities. During a lull in the fighting during the Flanders campaign of 1746, the French soldiers staged a mock battle between two armies equipped with wooden sabres, blunt sticks and barrels of water. The event was announced by a drumbeat with the permission of Marshal de Saxe, who honoured the battle with his presence. After successful manoeuvres led by their own general, a sergeant in the regiment of Champagne who rode a richly adorned mule, the 'French' troops broke through the 'Austrian' line, capturing a redoubt and 200 prisoners. The marshal congratulated both armies and suggested that the soldiers retain their daring against the common enemy. His gift of 100 *Louis d'or* was used to pay for the celebrations of the peace treaty which was

---

[38] Aytoun, *Redcoats*, 35; Wray, *Military Adventures*, 11; Stevenson; *Soldier*, 39; see also: Butler, *Narrative*, 30; Coates, *Narrative*, 65. Some narrators saw their deprived or tough upbringing as a good preparation for military service; see: Beeger, *Seltsame Schicksale*, 2–5; Hutton, *Life*, 77, Dreyer, *Leben und Taten*, 9, 14.

[39] Grose, *Classical Dictionary*, q.v. 'Nightingale'. 42; Laukhard, *Leben und Schicksale*, 197; Steininger, *Leben und Abenteuer*, 82; Cranfield, *Useful Christian*, 16–7; On resilience during corporal punishment, see Chapter 3, 112–3.

formally signed in a sutler's tent.[40] This soldierly carnival contained clear elements of mockery directed both against their superiors and the military experience in general. Nevertheless, not unlike duelling, it exalted courage, a value which the military organisation was actively promoting. By engaging in daring displays, the soldiers demonstrated that they had internalised this concept, and were thus more likely to follow the behaviour it dictated.

On the most trivial level, soldier-writers simply used the term 'brave' when referring to themselves, irrespective of context. The giant grenadier Johann Ernst Hoffmann, upon going to see Frederick William I to ask for a pay rise, justified his request by telling the king that 'I promised to serve you as a "brave soldier"'. Being allocated to an active field battalion at the start of the Seven Years War, Bräker refers to himself as 'einen fertigen dapfern Soldaten'. Such use of the term suggests that bravery was seen as a quality that was supposed to be inherent to their status as soldiers. Nevertheless, the place to demonstrate their courage and their manliness was in battle. Manly courage is mentioned a few times in John Scot's poem, while Deane, describing the battle of Odenarde, tells that men fought as it befits gentlemen and soldiers. For Deane, bravery was clearly a universal soldierly virtue. On another occasion, he praised the Bavarian garrison of Donauwörth, who put up a 'brave defence and a bold resistance against us as brave loyall hearted gentlemen souldiers ought to do for there prince and countrey [sic]'. Other writers likewise invoke compliments supposedly received from the enemy side. Satisfied by the disdain of the Yorktown garrison at the speed with which its French besiegers constructed their fieldworks, Georg Daniel Flohr claims that the British commander attributed this success to the intervention of the devil. An anonymous British artilleryman writing home after the victorious battle of Minden tells that the French army hoped to surprise the allies. Instead, the attackers had the misfortune to fall on the 'hardy English, or, as they sometimes call us, English devils'. Edward Linn says that the Jacobite prisoners taken in Culloden said that their English victors fought like madmen.[41] References to the preternatural and even madness when describing their fighting prowess denote that soldiers considered themselves capable of achievements which were beyond the

---

[40] Bernos, 'Souvenirs de campagne', 749–50; For more references to bravado, see: ibid., 759; Dreyer, *Leben und Taten*, 14. For an example of knowingly making a false positive impression, see: Klöden, *Jugenderinnerungen*, 34–5.

[41] Hoffman, 'Letter to his mother', 171; Bräker, 'Lebensgeschichte', 453; Scot, 'Remembrance', 332, 492; Deane, *Journal*, 7–8, 61–2; Flohr, *American Campaigns*, 30; 'Battle of Minden-1 August, 1759', 126; Linn, 'Battle of Culloden', 23. More on madly courage, see: Bernos, 'Souvenirs de campagne', 754.

reach of ordinary people. This leads to another important aspect of soldierly culture, its antipathy towards civilians.

When dealing with civilians, soldiers often behaved awfully. This did not only include pillaging their goods, as described in the previous chapter, but also being purposefully rude and destructive. According to Bräker, the Prussian soldiers not only plundered the inhabitants of Köpenick, the last town before the Saxon border, but also behaved in an incredibly foul manner. Homeowners whose supplies the soldiers helped themselves to were also cursed and mistreated, often within full view of the officers, some of whom behaved even worse than their men. According to John Frederick Whitehead, Swedish soldiers comported themselves as if peasant dwellings were their own. Resisting the unwanted visitors ended, in lucky cases, with gross abuse, but the soldiers occasionally destroyed the whole property and burnt the houses. British soldiers who marched through Princeton destroyed the library of the local college. Arriving at a small Bohemian estate, Saxon troops immediately proceeded to smash the glasshouse. According to Dominicus, Prussian troops occasionally broke the windows in villages through which they were marching. Convoyed through a burnt French village whose inhabitants have just returned, John Stevenson and the other British prisoners were almost lynched by the infuriated peasants. This led Stevenson to remark that 'such is the effect of warfare on the morals of soldiers, that an act which, in time of peace, would have been shuddered at as a revolting crime, is perpetrated without remorse, or regarded merely as a mischievous joke'.[42] In fairness it must be said that civilians, whichever side they were on, were not at all toothless. During the siege of Tournai, some Hessian and Hanoverian marauders were taken and mutilated by French peasants. According to Thomas Bartlett, 'soldier baiting was a favourite blood sport in both England and Ireland'.[43] Nevertheless, rather than being merely a by-product of wartime brutalisation, this mutual dislike had much deeper roots.

Assuming the new identity of a soldier upon enlistment meant a rejection of the old civilian one. Basically, this meant an active change

---

[42] Bräker, 'Lebensgeschichte', 454–5; Whitehead, 'Life', 61; Sullivan, *From Redcoat to Rebel*, 97; Sohr, *Meine Geschichte*, 40; Dominicus, *Tagebuch*, 11; Stevenson, *Soldier*, 10–1. For examples of senseless destruction of property, see: J. Field, *Devout Soldier*, 9–10; J. Miller, 'Memoirs of an Invalid', 15; Laukhard, *Leben und Schicksale*, 224–5; Nottenbaum, 'Aus Westfälichen Feldpostbriefen', 88; see also: C. Duffy, *Instrument of War*, 220.

[43] Deane, *Journal*, 86; Bartlett, 'Army and Society in Eighteenth-Century Ireland', Hagist, *British Soldiers*, 190; Grose, *Classical Dictionary*, q.v. 'Houghing'. When fire broke out in the English cantonments in Lille, Deane remarks that it was put out quickly, fortunately without any damage 'but wch. The boors sustained', *Journal*, 69

in one's appearance and manners. From the very beginning, Bräker was told to address Lieutenant Marconi as 'Herr Lieutenant'. After Bräker expressed qualms about serving a Prussian recruiter, Marconi instructed him to address him with the civilian 'Ihr Gnad'. When meeting him a few months later in Berlin, Bräker was again told to use the military form of address. Even before, when he met his Prussian comrades for the first time, Bräker was told off after addressing one of them as 'Herr Zittmann'. Being associated with civilians was an insult. After a complaint he lodged against Mackellow was dismissed by their colonel, his sergeant still had his revenge by calling Mackellow publicly a 'bad rider' and 'tailor'. During a furlough in Paris, Rossignol's dispute with another soldier, who called him *mouchard* and said that Rossignol did not have an air of a soldier, resulted in a deadly duel.[44] This external demarcation against civilians allowed soldiers to define themselves. Soldiers were generous, but civilians were greedy, as argued by Döhla. Soldiers knew what sacrifice meant, compared to armchair generals who campaigned through newspapers and bulletins. Learning that some civilians in Britain were complaining about the long time it took to reduce Lille, Deane sneered at the 'Coffee house warriors' who did not know that besieging a place like Lille takes time. Soldiers took issue with what they perceived as lack of patriotism and loyalty. During the Jacobite Rising of 1745 when news arrived of victories won by the government forces, soldiers stationed in a number of Scottish towns went on to smash the windows of houses that were not illuminated. Similar behaviour reoccurred during the American and the French Revolutionary Wars. Laukhard tells of a brawl which broke out between Prussian soldiers and Hessian civilians after the latter doubted the justice of the war against Revolutionary France.[45]

Nevertheless, as shown by another episode described by Laukhard, when it came to the destruction of property, the soldiers were not particularly ideological. Asking a fellow soldier why he was smashing the kitchen set of a parson's wife, Laukhard received the reply 'and why should I not? Those damn patriots! It is their fault we hate them so much'. Despite referring to the French by the correct political term which denoted members of the revolutionary party (and also leaving Laukhard to wonder what patriotism actually meant), this and other

[44] Bräker, 'Lebensgeschichte', 427, 440, 445, 454; Mackellow, *Autobiography*, 61–2; Rossignol, *Vie veritable*, 35.
[45] Döhla, 'Tagebuch' (31 October 1783); Deane, *Journal*, 66; Humphrys, 'Journal', fols. 59–60; Pickert, *Lebens-Geschichte*, 5; NAM 2001-02-400, Major George Nicholson, 'Transactions in the Buffs', 9; NAM 2002-07-251 'Statement re: Riot committed by soldiers in Aberdeen'; Asteroth, 'Diary', (27 March, 1781); Atwood, *Hessians*, 174–5; Frey, *British Soldier in America*, 76; Emsley, 'Military and Popular Disorder', 109; Laukhard, *Leben und Shicksale*, 199.

Prussian soldiers did not bother to distinguish between those on the right and wrong sides. War offered a chance to mistreat civilians with relative impunity, and when this opportunity arose, friendly civilians could suffer just as badly. Stephen Conway, who analysed similar behaviour of British troops during the American War of Independence, argues that this was the result of antipathy to civilians in general and rebels in particular. Besides, soldiers saw loot as a fair compensation for their hardships. But a basic cause missing from this interpretation is revenge. As discussed in the previous chapter, enlistment was often a by-product of failure in integrating into, or outright rejection by, civilian society. Moreover, civilians had a low regard for soldiers, seeing them as insubordinate sons, absconding apprentices or simply idle and debauched good-for-nothings whose mere existence was both a rebuff and a threat to the decent hard-working ways of a proper family and community. This explains why not only, to quote Dennis Showalter, many soldiers took 'revenge against the social system that offered too many of its sons no respectable place', but also failed to respect them in their alternative choice. Again, soldierly behaviour boiled down to honour. Not unlike modern gang members, soldiers were not devoid of it. Rather their code of honour was based on a rejection of civil society and its values. It is a classic case of counter-culture.[46]

However, soldierly culture was not just based on abstract notions like honour or negative reconfirmation of its identity vis-à-vis the civilian. Soldierly memoirs abound with references to their units, usually their regiments. This could include mentioning elements of material culture, such as the violet facings of the British 56th Regiment of Foot, which earned it the nickname 'Pompadours'. After the 33rd Foot distinguished itself in the battle of Long Island, Shaw reports that a new ribbon was added to the regimental standard, while its recruits, who were still languishing in Yorkshire, got new cockades. Flohr tells how a mortar captured during the storming of a British redoubt was presented to his regiment as a badge of honour. According to Flohr, King Louis had reconfirmed the privilege, and further allowed the mortar to be paraded in front of the regiment whenever it was on the march. Whether or not they resulted in similar rewards, men clearly took pride in the martial accomplishments of the units to which they belonged. André Amblard quotes the order of the day in which General Rochambeau complimented the grenadiers of his regiment after a sea battle in March 1781. In his

---

[46] Laukhard, *Leben und Schicksale*, 225; Conway, 'Great Mischief', 376–85; Showalter, *Wars of Frederick the Great*, 12, Hurl-Eamon, '"Youth in the Devil's Service"', 164–5; see also: Emsley, 'Military and Popular Disorder', 109–12; Keep, *Soldiers of the Tsar*, 218–9; For a modern comparison, see: Bourgois, *In Search of Respect*, ch. 4.

description of the British raid on Saint Malo, Sergeant Porter mentions that his grenadier company was among the first to land on French soil. Corporal Robertson tells that his battery caused more damage to the enemy than all the other allied troops employed at the siege of Valenciennes. Reference to regimental achievements could also be made through innuendo. For instance, Deane, in his description of the battle of Ramillies, says that the French Royal Regiment of Foot had to beg for mercy and surrender its colours – a clear contrast to the performance of its English counterpart in which Deane was serving.[47]

Like other types of success, however, regimental achievements were worth little unless put into some kind of comparative perspective. Disputes between old-regime officers regarding the standing and seniority of their respective regiments are well documented. Their subordinates could be just as mindful regarding their regiments' reputation, often with references to other units. When telling how his regiment was sent to occupy some French forts, Robert Kirkwood first informs his readers of the defeat of the 22nd Regiment, which was sent beforehand on the same mission. Referring to the brave fight put up by the British guards at Malplaquet, Bishop remarks that they fought 'to save their honour', that is, to justify their unique privileges. Nevertheless, in order not to give them too much credit in the eyes of the reader, Bishop adds that the guards were notorious for robbing their own dead comrades. Disputes between different regiments could be resolved in a relatively good-natured way, as in the case of an argument between the 28th Foot and the Irish Artillery over some captured French cannon.[48] However, as with duels, invocations concerning reputation and honour could only be truly resolved by fighting. During their furlough, Bernos and his Parisian comrades from the Limousin Regiment often quarrelled with royal guardsmen who snubbed them for belonging to a junior corps. Bernos and his friends retorted by referring to their opponents as 'Canards du M[a]in', to remind the guards of their ignominious escape from the battlefield of Dettingen. The insistence of Rossignol's colonel on frequent mandatory prayer sessions had led soldiers from other units to refer to the

---

[47] Surtees, *Twenty-Five Years*, 3; Shaw, *Autobiography*, 15; Flohr, *American Campaigns*, 38; Amblard, 'Histoire des campagnes' in 'De Lussas vers l'aventure II', 248,250; NAM 1959-02-46, 'Account of the raid on St. Malo by sergeant Porter of Grenadier company, 23rd foot', (5 June 1758); G. Robertson, 'Two Letters', 23; Deane, *Journal*, 36; see also: D. Robertson, *Journal*, 13; For a case of a regiment appropriating a royal badge, see: Chartrand, 'Britannia Badge of the 9th Foot', 189.

[48] Kirkwood, *Through so Many Dangers*, 101; Bishop, *Life and Adventures*, 210; J. Field, *Devout Soldier*, 18. See also: Dayes, *Memoir*, 6–7; BL Mss Eur B296 Samuel Hickson, 'Letters' fols. 121, 129. For a colonel who cared about the good name of his regiment, see: J. Thompson, *Bard*, 166;

Royal–Roussillon as the Capuchin regiment. This led to numerous con-frontations, resulting in killed and wounded men on both sides. A dispute between the different British regiments, which began as a disagreement over seniority and deteriorated into mutual recriminations regarding former defeats, resulted in another defeat at the battle of Montmorency, as some troops rushed in to attack too soon. Regimental rivalry extended into the supposedly indifferent ranks of the Prussian army. In Frederician Potsdam, for instance, it was dangerous for royal guardsmen to stray into parts of town where other regiments were quartered.[49]

Some modern scholars doubt the existence of a genuine regimental *esprit de corps* in eighteenth-century armies. In peacetime, regiments were often dispersed in small detachments in the countryside. Regional recruit-ing, which makes such an important contribution to the identity of some modern British units, was uncommon. Regiments were instead recruited all over the country, and sometimes further supplemented with foreign recruits. Lastly, in wartime, it was common to draft men from units stationed at home to regiments on active service. This meant that soldiers could go to combat side by side with men whom they barely knew, and as part of a unit for which they had had little time to form an attachment. John Lynn takes a more positive approach, suggesting that the bonding role of drill and the exclusion of women and children from regular regi-ments led to the creation of unique military communities. Characterised by Lynn as 'standardized, permanent and male', regiments commanded the loyalty of their men as their new and only home. Neither interpreta-tion is fully satisfying. Firstly, Russian, Prussian and Austrian armies maintained regional recruitment. In fact, in Prussia these were not only the regiments which were allocated cantons, but often each individual company was also assigned a specific district of a few villages. As for Lynn's argument, although there is clear evidence that soldiers appre-ciated manly virtues, these were associated not with particular units, but with the whole soldierly class. Besides, the perception of the regiment as one's new home would not apply to many conscripts who did have a real home to return to once their training was over. The best and simplest definition of *esprit de corps* still comes from the pen of Frederick the Great: persuading the men that their regiment is the best in the world.[50]

---

[49] Bernos, 'Souvenirs de campagne', 745; Rossignol, *Vie veritable*, 58–9; Brumwell, *Redcoats*, 114–5; 'Extracts from Journal of the Particular Transactions during the Siege of Quebec', 176; P.H. Wilson, *German Armies*, 334.

[50] Guy, 'Army of the Georges', 95; For a forceful argument that regimental culture is largely a modern phenomenon, see: French, *Military Identities*; Lynn, *Battle*, 156–7; On regional recruitment, see: *BBS*, 66–9, 84–5; Frederick the Great, 'Das militärische Testament von 1768' in: *Werke*, vol. VI, 233; For a much more longer and complex, albeit contemporary definition of *esprit de corps*, see: *Reglament für die sämmentlich-Kaiserlich-Königliche Infanterie*,

The examples cited in the previous paragraphs demonstrate that old-regime common soldiers would probably concur.

Attachments to one's immediate unit, however, did not rule out other horizontal loyalties. Grenadiers and light infantrymen, who enjoyed elite status and were often brigaded together rather than serving with their units, clearly had their own ethos. A French grenadier captured by Samuel Hutton proclaimed that he was glad to have the honour to be taken by a fellow grenadier. Beß praised the achievements of the Hessian jaegers. For instance, he claims that they had established such a firm reputation that the mere distinct whistle of their rifle bullets was enough to dishearten their French opponents. However, as in the case of regimental pride, the definition of who you were could also be based on who you were not. According to Sergeant Sullivan, Beß's successors who served in America were held to such a high professional standard that if any of them missed his target, he was immediately sent down to the infantry. Demotion to the infantry was one of the most grievous punishments mentioned by the Austrian artillery regulations. The infantrymen, for their part, occasionally retaliated. James Miller characterises the disgraceful performance of the British gunners at Charlestown as diametrically opposite to 'the pompous parade on Woolwich warren'. According to the NCO of the Anhalt regiment, following the failure of the Prussian cavalry attack at Lobositz, his colonel encouraged the regiment to advance, saying 'Was die Kavallerie verdorben hat, das werden die Herrn Infantristen verbessern' ('What the cavalry has spoilt will now be put right by the Gentlemen of the infantry'). According to Scot, during the defence of Tongeren, the cavalry escaped in a disgraceful manner, headed by its own general, whose carriage stopped only when he reached Maastricht some twenty kilometres away. Left alone against a French army of 60,000, the two infantry regiments resisted so fiercely that even the French commander was impressed.[51]

Moreover, despite all their squabbles, members of different regiments and army branches were ready to unite forces against greater enemies.

(1769), 139. For an example of regional attachment at least in one British regiment, see: Shaw, *Autobiography*, 15–6. A group which could have seen their regiments as their home were children born to serving soldiers. James Gee fondly remembers his father's regiment to which he was attached 'as most people are to their native place'; Gee, 'Memoirs of an Eighteenth-Century Soldier's Child', 222; For an autobiography of another *enfant du crops*, see: Dillon, *Short Account*.

[51] Hutton, *Life*, 41; Beß, 'Aus dem Tagebuch', 195, 212, 214; Sullivan, *From Redcoat to Rebel*, 61; *Reglement für das Kaiserlich Königliche gesammte Feld-Artilleriecorps*, (1757), 9; J. Miller, 'Memoirs of an Invalid', 106; 'Letter of an *Unteroffizer* from the Anhalt Regiment', (1 October 1756), in GG, 3–4; Scot, 'Remembrance', 335; On rivalry between line infantry and jaegers, see: Döhla, 'Tagebuch', (10 March 1777).

This included sailors and soldiers from allied armies. In the former case, contacts between the two groups were relatively limited and usually occurred within the specific context of a sea voyage. Sailors are described in men's accounts as a rowdy lot, playing practical jokes and feeding fish stories to the honest soldiers whom they were transporting on board.[52] Since many eighteenth-century wars were fought by coalitions, there were many more opportunities for interactions with allied soldiers. The trend of regimental rivalry now repeated itself on a grander scale, but the basic principle remained the same: fights against individuals and disparaging remarks about the collective. McBane's account is full of brawls and duels fought with members of other armies, particularly the Dutch. While they were typically instigated by mundane affairs, such as disagreements over booty, and also McBane's own criminal enterprises, some fights bore a distinctly national character. Soon after landing in the Netherlands, English soldiers started being mocked by Swiss troops in the Dutch service, who called them 'beardless boys'. After a few English soldiers were murdered after dark, their comrades, with the full blessing of the officers, formed a self-defence squad which killed so many Swiss soldiers that their regiment had to be transferred to another garrison. Karl Wilhelm Friedrich Flemming tells of a fight which broke out between Saxon and Prussian soldiers after the latter had demanded to be given priority in the use of a road because they were 'royal troops', implying that the Saxons were merely serving a prince elector. Swords and other weapons were employed, and it took the officers much trouble to separate the men. Referring to the numerous quarrels between British and Hessian troops in North America, Atwood writes that '[t]hey were nothing more than what was to be expected between men of various nations, ignorant of one another's customs and language, particularly when armies were composed of the lowest and most pugnacious element of the populace'.[53] The point missed from this otherwise concise description is reputation and honour. These elements explain both the incentive for an individual brawl and for the more general derogatory statements by which soldierly narratives refer to allied armies as a whole.

---

[52] Reuber, Tagebuch (9 July, 13 August, 4–5 September 1776); Jonas, *Soldier's Journal*, 15; Flohr, *American Campaigns*, 71–2; Bonin, 'Voyage au Canada', 17–8; J.R., 'Journal', 31; For witty remarks at sailors' expense, see: J. Thompson, *Bard*, 150, Ancell, *Circumstantial Journal*, 250–1; For fights and disputes, see: Rossignol, *Vie veritable*, 46–8; Sullivan, *From Redcoat to Rebel*, 12–3; Hickson, 'Letters', fol. 111; Coates, *Narrative*, 27–8.

[53] McBane, 'Expert Swords-Man's Companion', 30, 33, 39 and 43–44; Flemming, 'Aus dem Tagebuche', 19; Atwood, *Hessians*, 155. For brawling between men from different contingents in a peaceful time, see: Schreyer, *Wahl und Krönung*, 56–7.

Just like civilians, allies were viewed critically merely for being who they were; although such comparisons were usually developed further to reflect negatively on their moral character. A member of Rochambeau's corps unflatteringly compared the shabby looks of the American soldiers to the excellent military bearing of the French troops. Surtees states that although it is a sad recompense as such, the Russian troops who landed in the Netherlands looked even worse than the British ones. Although both willingly admit that the actual relations with allied Prussian troops had been cordial, Yakov Starkov describes their over-elaborate, impractical uniforms, which made them appear passive, while Ilya Popadishev claims that the Russian soldiers were far more alert and stronger. According to Scot, prompted by greediness, captive Dutch soldiers willingly reenlisted with the French. Members of the Scottish Brigade remained true to their oath, and the few who reenlisted did it because of dire necessity. Corporal Robert Brown tells of how, during the Flanders campaign, allied Austrian and German troops plundered mercilessly, while the British were strictly forbidden to do so. Sergeant George Darby, who fought in the same campaign, remarks with glee that Austrians had great antipathy for the French because of their defeats in the previous year. In his next letter, Darby tells how the cowardly Dutch failed to capture the position at Lincelles, which was later taken by a much weaker British force. The English victors then generously sent captured Dutch cannon recovered from the French fortifications back to their original owners. David Robertson remarks with disdain that the Turks were cowardly in battle, but would then come out to butcher defenceless French prisoners once the fighting was over.[54]

Allies were also blamed for more concrete issues. Joseph Coates complains that the bread provided by the Turks to the British troops in Egypt was as hard as flint. Bernos tells of how, during its stay in Bohemia, the allied army was weakened by desertion *particularly* among the Bavarians. Prussian troops attributed their failure against the French at Valmy, among other things, to the late arrival of the allied Austrian contingent. According to Corporal Fox, after Burgoyne's army was surrounded at Saratoga, the general requested all colonels to ask their men whether they would agree to fight one more time. All British regiments replied with three cheers. The Germans, on the other hand, refused even when offered three guineas per man, leaving the army no choice but to

[54] Starkov, *Raskazi*, 71–2; Popadishev, 'Vospominaniya',74–6; 'Milton S. Latham Journal', 46; Surtees, *Twenty-Five Years*, 8–9; Scot, 'Remembrance', 326–7; Darby 'Capture of Valenciennes', (13 August, 1793), and 'Account of the Battle of Lincelles', (26 August 1793); R. Brown, *Impartial Journal*, 19–22, 24; D. Robertson, *Journal*, 23–5. See also: B. Miller, 'Adventures', 31.

capitulate.[55] Such negative portrayals of allied troops stand in stark contrast to positive remarks about enemy soldiers, who are often praised for their courage and resolution. Edward Linn describes how at Culloden the Jacobite Scots pressed boldly to attack the British, sword in hand. Sergeant Wilson praises the French for the courageous resistance of the garrison in Blenheim and for a daring sortie during the siege of Ghent. According to a Prussian NCO writing home after the battle of Lobositz, the Austrian troops resisted heroically; nevertheless the Prussians still won the day. When referring to enemies in such terms, 'soldiers saw them as reflections of their own virtues'.[56] Victory won against courageous enemies and, occasionally, in spite of useless allies, multiplied their achievements and, consequently, their honour.

The success of a military organisation in making its men internalise its values is best measured when no formal enforcement mechanisms are available. A good illustrative example is provided by prisoners of war. Unlike most of their regiment, which capitulated on another occasion, the surrender conditions of Bernos' detachment did not bind it to remain under French military discipline. Nevertheless, its men continued to exercise daily, including the customary lessons in fencing and dancing. Brunswicker Johann Bense tells of how the prisoners from Burgoyne's army held weekly parades and provided their own guard to hinder desertion. According to Corporal Fox, who also spent time in the Convention Army, its camp was arranged as a proper military encampment with pickets and church parades. The prisoners also maintained their drill using sticks instead of muskets. Celebration of national holidays and the birthdays of the sovereigns were marked by both German and British troops. In the latter case, it was clearly done to irritate the Americans. For instance, Döhla says that the British prisoners celebrated St. George's Day 1783 by shouting loudly 'hurrah for King George' the day after the peace treaty was officially declared.[57] Even more tellingly,

[55] Coates, *Narrative*, 68; Bernos, 'Souvenirs de campagne', 671; Glantz, *Auszüge aus Briefen*, 12–3; Laukhard, *Leben und Schicksale*, 246–7; G. Fox, 'Corporal Fox's Memoir', 160; For a rare compliment to allied troops for heroic battlefield action, see: Grotehenn's description of the British and Hanoverian infantry regiments at Minden, in: *Briefe*, 73.

[56] Linn, 'Battle', 22; J. Wilson, 'Journal', 51, 68; Ancell, *Circumstantial Journal*, 98; 'Unteroffizier J.S. Liebler to his wife and family', (3 October 1756), in GG, 19; James, *Warrior Race*, 291. See also: Scot, 'Remembrance', 363; Döhla, 'Tagebuch', (23 June and 18 August 1780); J. Miller, 'Memoirs of an Invalid', 22, 29; Lamb, *Original and Authentic Journal*, 343–4; Hoppe, 'Wahrhafte Schilderung', 194; Starkov, *Raskazi*, 39, 290, 301; Grotehenn, *Briefe*, 46. For modern parallels, see: Moskos, *American Enlisted Man*, 151–2.

[57] Bernos, 'Souvenirs de campagne', 675; Bense, 'Brunswick Grenadier', 436, 440–3; G. Fox, 'Corporal Fox's Memoir', 163–4; Sampson, *Escape in America*, 62; Döhla,

despite deserting, Bräker and Seume kept their uniforms. Bräker later cleverly sported it in the local church, while Seume's attachment to his old outfit got him recognised as a former deserter and pressed into the Prussian army. It is highly unlikely that Seume – already a victim of forceful recruitment once before – was unaware of the risk involved in crossing Germany without a pass and wearing an old Hessian coat. Nevertheless, he kept it. On this point it is worthwhile remembering that winning and keeping desired status symbols lies in the heart of normative compliance.[58]

Finally, it is important to note that some soldiers found happiness in their military life, a happiness which they could not replicate after their discharge. Samuel Hutton's brother and niece both confirm that soldiering was the only period of his life which Samuel truly enjoyed. While Sergeant Kenward's earlier surviving letter home deplores his decision to enlist, in a much later message he expresses no desire to change his state as a soldier. William Calder's letters underscore that he was happy with his service in the Scots Guards. One of his later surviving notes states that 'I am very happy at my station and want for nothing. Thank God for it.' When he came back to his mountain hamlet, Bräker was put to work in a saltpetre manufacture. Recalling his hard and dirty time there, Bräker admits having second thoughts about his return home. Despite his tough service as a soldier, he had many happy days in the army and, more importantly, he was not a *Schweinskerl*. In the end, Bräker chose to remain in Toggenburg. Nevertheless, even an unwilling soldier like himself clearly formed an association with some of the stated values of soldierly culture such as its aspiration for freedom, honour and higher social status.[59] These values contributed towards the creation of a unique corporate identity which would not have existed unless the majority of soldiers had accepted it. This demonstrates that old-regime soldiers could develop a deep personal involvement in their immediate social surroundings. The existence of such associations is a major prerequisite when one finally comes to consider why the overwhelming majority of them also agreed to fight.

'Tagebuch', (30 November 1781, 24 February and 23 April 1783); Popp, 'Journal', 252; Reuber, 'Tagebuch', (June 1777), fols. 94–5. For more examples of soldiers defying and otherwise refusing to cooperate with their capturers, see: Todd, *Journal*, 228, 232–3; Williamson, *French and Indian Cruelty*, 98; Bristow, *Narrative of the Sufferings*, 26; C. Duffy, *Instrument of War*, 218–9.

[58] Bräker, 'Lebensgeschichte', 469–70; Seume, *Werke*, vol. I, 102–3.

[59] Hutton, *Life*, 39–40, 42 75, 77; Kenward, *Sussex Highlander*, 103–4, 108–9; NAM 1986-11-1 'Letters of Sergeant Calder (American War) 1778–5', (30 March 1778, 12 February 1779, 26 May 1784); Bräker, 'Lebensgeschichte', 470–1. Compare with Dreyer, *Leben und Taten*, 17; see also: C. Duffy, *Army of Frederick the Great*, 68

6   Networks of Loyalty and Acceptance

After describing the victorious battle of Crown Point, Sergeant Roger Lamb digresses in order to explain to his readers what prompts soldiers to do their duty in combat. Lamb mentions three basic reasons: 'personal bravery, hope of reward, and fear of punishment'. While the first two aspects apply equally to first-timers and veterans, the last one distinguishes between them. Since soldiers are taught to believe that those running away are likely to be shot by their own comrades, even a young coward would be prompted to fight. Unlike the inexperienced, who see danger everywhere, veterans know much better when and what to expect. When actual danger looms ahead, they would 'approach it without thinking'. Lamb explains that the disturbing thought that their lives will soon depend on mere chance instils a sense of emotional numbness which helps men to withstand the ordeal of combat and, particularly, the shock of seeing their comrades being killed or wounded. Once the fighting is over, the excitement subsides and an upsurge of emotions takes over. By that time, however, men can afford this, since their lives are no longer in danger. Lamb further adds that the unpredictability of one's fate also provides solace of a sort. Although such thoughts are not necessarily shared by each and every soldier, many perceive their destiny as part of a divine plan. Since the will of God cannot be avoided, the men are thus reconciled with their fate, whatever it might be.[1]

Another old-regime soldier who presents his views on combat motivation is the Jaeger Georg Beß. According to Beß, while the repute won by their corps was encouraging enough, the main reason for the bravery of individual jaegers was a mixture of camaraderie and status. Firstly, the jaegers combined a friendly competition to outdo each other in acts of courage with the genuine desire to support their comrades in combat. Moreover, the contempt earned by those who failed to perform well often prompted such men to attempt to regain their reputation by some exceptional act of bravery. Men also expected courageous performance

---

[1] Lamb, *Memoir*, 175–7.

not only on the part of their peers, but also from their officers and NCOs. On a personal level, Beß remarks that he drew consolation from the belief that he had God's aim to fulfil. The understanding that nothing would befall him without the express wish of the Almighty gave him courage. Lastly, Beß was convinced that if he were to be killed, his death would be followed by honour and rest.[2] These thoughts bear a number of remarkable parallels with Lamb's ideas. Both authors divide their observations between general principles which apply to the soldierly collective, and specific coping strategies employed by individual soldiers to surmount their fear. This approach is strikingly similar in both accounts, and can be described as a combination of fatalism and optimism. Despite recognising their inability to influence their fate, the men continued to believe no ill would come to them without the express will of heaven. Neither Lamb nor Beß explain why they found this resignation so reinforcing. The most likely reason lies in their religious convictions. The mere thought that God could possibly want you dead must have been very unnerving to Lamb and Beß who, like the overwhelming majority of religious people, were likely to take their personal salvation for granted.

Even if the precise nuances of their arguments are impossible to recreate, the ideas expressed by Lamb and Beß remain significant. In a period when superior officers often attributed their men's performance to instinctive reactions, like bravery, or thought that soldiers should be led into battle by discipline and fear, two of their subordinates formed distinct views on combat motivation. Moreover, their observations share much in common with modern studies on the subject. The three basic incentives to fight, as put forward by Lamb, are essentially identical to the three levers of compliance. Beß's portrayal of the jaegers bears striking resemblance to the workings of primary group cohesion. Both describe how soldiers make use of a sophisticated psychological defence mechanism that reminds some of the coping strategies mentioned by Stouffer's study.[3] Moreover, Lamb and Beß are not alone, as more old-regime soldiers left testimonies about their motivation, both in combat and, more generally, in wartime. Matthew Bishop, who survived the bloodbath at Malplaquet, says he fought for honour and self-preservation. As he was travelling back from hospital to the front, Johann Friedrich Löffler states he wanted to take revenge on the Turks for his wounds and the atrocities committed against his comrades. Moreover, Löffler claims he wanted to help the imperial army to regain

---

[2] Beß, 'Aus dem Tagebuch', 195–6, 238–9.
[3] Stouffer et al., *American Soldier: Combat*, 188–91; Also compare with the coping strategies described in the excellent study by Alexander Watson, *Enduring the Great War*, 85–107.

its honour after its initial setbacks. Just before the battle of Kunersdorf, Corporal Binn wrote home about the barbaric crimes of the Russian invaders and entreated his family to pray earnestly for the success of the Prussian army. In his sermons, Methodist John Haime encouraged his fellow soldiers that they were fighting for a good cause, for their king and in defence of their country. Moreover, those who were killed were already with Jesus. Sergeant Calder, who was part of the troops who quelled the Gordon Riots, writes that unless the army had intervened, the mob would have probably destroyed the whole of London. Not that he was particularly happy to fire at rampaging civilians, but this was his duty and 'we must do it and say nothing'.[4]

Furthermore, soldier-authors occasionally described the motivation of their counterparts who fought on the opposing side. Although such portrayals are somewhat more negative, the overall range of enemy motives proves markedly similar. James Miller acknowledges that the French Canadians fought in defence of their country. John Scot tells us that at Ramillies the French arrived with the intent of avenging their previous defeats, while in one of the subsequent sieges, the garrison went on sortie 'To gain their honour in the martiall houre, expecting a large recompense'. On a different occasion, Scot claims that French troops reinforced their courage with brandy.[5] Enemy troops could also be prompted by religious fanaticism, draconian discipline or simply because they wanted to survive. The Prussian soldier Andreas Christoph Glantz attributes the ferociousness of the French attack at Pirmasens to the threats to guillotine the revolutionary generals should they delay their offensive any longer. According to McBane, the French defenders of Liege fought much harder after witnessing how some of their comrades, who surrendered to the English troops, were then massacred by the second wave of Dutch attackers.[6] While not as

---

[4] Bishop, *Life and Adventures*, 209; Löffler, *Der alte Sergeant*, 44; 'Corporal Nikolaus Binn to his family' (20 July 1759), in Liebe, 22; Haime, 'Life', 224; NAM 1986-11-1 'Letters of Sergeant Calder (American War) 1778–5', (19 June 1780 and 10 February 1781); see also: J. Johnson, 'Memoirs of the Siege of Quebec', 101; Kirkwood, *Through so Many Dangers*, 64–6; Surtees, *Twenty-Five Years*, 26, 30; Sullivan, *From Redcoat to Rebel*, 98; Dominicus, *Tagebuch*, 35; 'Journal of Captain's Cholmley's Batman', 29–30.

[5] Centre of Kentish Studies, Maidstone, U1350 Z9A, James Miller, 'Memoirs of an Invalid', 33; Scot, 'Remembrance', 325, 376, 529; see also: Koch, *Battle of Guilford Courthouse*, 19; 'Letter of an *Unteroffizier* from the Anhalt Regiment' (1 October 1756), in GG, 5; Bersling, *Der böhmische Veteran*, 86.

[6] Glantz, *Auszüge aus Briefen*, 26; McBane, 'Expert Swords-Man's Companion', 33. See also: '*Unteroffizer* C.G. Klauel to his brother' (6 October 1756) in GG, 28; '*Feldwebel* G.S. Liebler to his wife and relatives' (12 October 1756), in GG, 34; Löffler, *Der alte Sergeant*, 54; NAM 1987-10-7 'Manuscript letter written by Corporal Samuel Blomeley, Coldtstream Guards describing their voyage in Ireland (2 July 1798)'; Todd, *Journal*, 180–1.

sophisticated as the models formulated by Lamb and Beß, these examples demonstrate that at least some eighteenth-century soldiers had a very
clear sense that fighting was done for a reason. Moreover, even if we
agree with scholars like Klaus Latzel that the actual fighting was done
in detached delirium, such a state requires explanation. As we saw
already, coercive compliance, both in and out of combat, not only had
its limits, but was rarely enforced up to its full potential. Consequentially,
the hypothesis which attributes combat motivation to successful disciplinary inoculation in the sustaining stage cannot stand. As long as men
agreed to enter combat, it must be assumed that they had an active reason
to do so.

However, to explain combat motivation, it is insufficient to consider
combat performance alone. Combat motivation should be seen as a
combination of two basic factors. On the one hand, it is the product of
a long preparatory process in which training, previous experiences and
attitudes, some inherent and some gained, would come together to
prepare the soldier for an ultimate test. On the other hand, combat
behaviour is influenced by the immediate conditions prevailing on the
battlefield and individual coping strategies. This chapter considers the
first of these two aspects. It follows the previous chapter in examining
the connections formed between eighteenth-century soldiers and their
broader political and social milieu. So far, the association formed
between soldiers and a military culture of honour has been demonstrated. However, this was not the only form of loyalty of which the
men were capable. The discussion begins with an overview of national
references as they appear in soldierly narratives. The aim here, though,
is not to enter the heavyweight battle between modernist and primordi-
alist interpreters of nationalism, but rather to understand whether old-
regime soldiers were capable of forming allegiances to their cultural and
religious groups, their polities and their dynastical rulers. Another type
of loyalty to be considered is that towards officers from the commander-
in-chief to the subaltern. If personal attachment to direct military superiors existed, it was likely to legitimise their authority and the orders they
gave. The last basic type of military loyalty examined in this chapter is to
one's comrades. The role of the mess as a basic social institution, as well
as a potential enforcer of group standards relevant for combat, will also
be discussed.

According to their writings, old-regime soldiers were aware of national
and religious differences. In fact, they relished them. Positive traits, most
typically courage, were obviously associated with the side of the narrator.
British narrators often spoke of 'British courage', 'British play', giving the
enemies a 'British reception' or simply described their fellow soldiers as

behaving in a manner befitting British troops.[7] Just as they were about to land in America, comrades serving together with Johann Conrad Döhla were all burning with the desire to demonstrate the military prowess of the German race, especially the Franconians. Bonin writes that at Quebec the army went into battle 'autant courage que d'ardour en l'impétiosité françoise'. An NCO writing home soon after the battle of Lobositz began his letter by declaring that one Prussian was worth three Imperial soldiers. Beß speaks of 'our brave German troops', describing a successful bayonet assault against an entrenched Swiss regiment at the battle of Krefeld.[8] However, such references were usually outnumbered by disparaging remarks about the other nations, their culture and religion. This could involve simple curses and cynical references. British writers occasionally refer to their Spanish and French enemies as 'Dons' and 'Monsieurs'. Beß refers to the French as *Schurken* and *Lumpenkerls* (rogues and scum). *Feldwebel* Liebler tells us that the victory in Prague was achieved over the 'enemies of the gospel', and Löffler refers to the Turks as the 'hated enemies of Christianity'.[9] Protestant soldiers were prejudiced against Catholicism, which they associated with all sorts of superstitious practices and bigotry.[10]

More specific stereotypes are also invoked. British narrators, from participants of the War of the Spanish Succession up to soldiers who fought in the revolutionary wars, are consistent in their prejudice against the French. They are portrayed as braggarts and cowards who first boast about their martial prowess but refuse to face their enemies honestly in

---

[7] Lamb, *Original and Authentic Journal*, 303–4; Ancell, *Circumstantial Journal*, 22, 27, 61, 136; Macdonald, *Autobiographical Journal*, 47; Stevenson, *Soldier*, 60, 70; Coates, *Narrative*, 52; Grenadier Guards Regimental Archive, London, A03/03 George Darby, 'Account of the Battle of Lincelles' (26 August 1793).

[8] Bibliothèque National, Paris, NUMM-109500, Joseph-Charles Bonin, 'Voyage au Canada', 196; Döhla, 'Tagebuch', (3 June 1777, 24 February 1783); 'Letter of an *Unteroffizier* from the Anhalt Regiment' (1 October 1756), in GG, 1; Beß, 'Aus dem Tagebuch', 201. For more references to German and French armies and nations, see: Grotehenn, *Briefe*, 95, 121; Flemming, 'Aus dem Tagebuche', 19.

[9] Hall, 'Letter to Sergeant Cabe' (26 September 1709); Jonas, *Soldier's Journal*, 10; D. Robertson, *Journal*, 26; Ancell, *Circumstantial Journal*, 146–7, 273; Scot, 'Remembrance', 320; Beß, 'Aus dem Tagebuch', 200, 214, 217; Löffler, *Der alte Sergeant*, 33; '*Feldwebel* G.S. Liebler to his wife and family' (7 May 1757), in GG, 45.

[10] Jonas, *Soldier's Journal*, 101–2; Deane, *Journal*, 4, 29; Scot, 'Remembrance', 468–71; Tory, *Journal*, 36; Bristow, *Narrative of the Sufferings*, 86; Kenward, *Sussex Highlander*, 46; R. Brown, *Impartial Journal*, 96; B. Miller, 'Adventures', 18–21; Lahatt, 'Autobiography', 47, 60; Flemming, 'Aus dem Tagebuche', 12. For more expressions of religious prejudice, see also: Crawford, 'Narrative', 325; Plummer, *Journal*, 5, 16–7; For more examples of religious slandering, although not of enemy soldiers but of Jews, see: Dominicus, *Tagebuch*, 79–80; Laukhard, *Leben und Schicksale*, 219–20; Coates, *Narrative*, 36; Schimmel, 'Kurze Lebensbeschreibung', 198; Lamb, *Original and Authentic Journal*, 293, 323.

the open, either refusing combat altogether or hiding behind fortifications. The French are also occasionally portrayed as carriers of silly cultural mannerisms, foppery and popery, and subjects of political despotism. John Marshall Deane combines both labels, saying 'We are not to be bugbared by any of those genteele fopps or ruffled monkeys who once thought themselves the Hectors of Europe & sol Governours of Christendome [sic]'. Such biased views of the French were not limited to the British. Döhlemann writes that the French were frivolous and irresponsible dandies. While nominally allied with the French immigrants, their pretensions to cultural superiority, promiscuity and general silliness meet a scathing rebuke from Laukhard and his Prussian comrades, many of whom refer to them as 'französische Spitzbuben Armee' (Rogue French army).[11] French narrators accuse the British of arrogance and false piety. Döhla says that while they maintained a splendid military bearing, British troops excelled in blaspheming, thieving and whoring. Seume remarks disparagingly about British food.[12]

The soldiers were occasionally called upon to uphold their national honour. According to Bonin, the dying Montcalm encouraged his troops to defend the honour of France. Moreover, men's individual honour could be entwined with the country or monarch whom they served. When asking his mother to inform the parents of a comrade who had been disembowelled alive by a cannon ball, Sergeant George Slater says this man, who fell in an action 'which will ever be remembered as glorious to the British arms', was 'a good soldier and a credit to his country'. Describing how his brother Benjamin expired from wounds, Johann Christian Riemann writes he died a true warrior, who gave his life for the honour of his king, his *Vaterland* and countrymen. On a more general level, collective martial success looked more impressive when put into perspective. This could be historical, as in case of Guardsman Deane, who states that the English army took Donauwörth,

---

[11] Deane, *Journal*, quoted 116–7, but see also: 51, 60, 65, 89, 102–3, 107, 129; Scot, 'Remembrance', 330–1; 335; 378; 385, 453; Millner, *Compendious*, 28, 127; Bishop, *Life and Adventures*, 224; NAM 1976-07-40 'Manuscript letter written by gunner James Hardcastle addressed to Hardcastle's father' (1743); Tory, *Journal*, 10; J. Johnson, 'Memoirs of the Siege of Quebec', 101; Kirkwood, *Through so Many Dangers*, 84; Ancell, *Circumstantial Journal*, 53, 87–8; Darby, 'Battle of Lincelles'; Döhlemann, 'Diary', 26–7; Laukhard, *Leben und Schicksale*, 208–9; see also: Bersling, *Der böhmische Veteran*, 18.

[12] Amblard, 'Histoire des campagnes' in 'De Lussas vers l'aventure II', 252; Library of Congress, Washington, 'MCC 1907 Milton S. Latham Journal', 50; Seume, *Werke*, vol. II, 369. For other instances of gastronomic patriotism, see: Döhla, 'Tagebuch', (16 July 1777); Schreyer, *Wahl und Krönung*, 66; Döhlemann, 'Diary', 12. For a German soldier from Waldeck vilifying the Dutch, see: Steuernagel, 'Brief Description', 100.

and that the pass had withstood fourteen attacks since the days of Gustavus Adolphus. Richard Humphrys says that the capture of Havana was the most serious defeat inflicted by Britain on Spain since the Armada.[13] Achievements could be further magnified when contrasted to the indifferent performance of one's allies. Sergeant Stevenson attributes statements to enemy prisoners that favourably compared British martial prowess to that of the Russians and the Turks. A French officer, captured in an unsuccessful enemy counterattack near Texel, says he had just arrived from the batteries captured at the Rhine 'but was told that those batteries were not defended by Britons, "No" he said "they were not"'. Corporal George Robertson says that once Valenciennes surrendered, it was taken only by the British forces and no other, concluding his letter with a wish 'May the British flag ever flourish over the world'. Narrators also occasionally considered such gains within the immediate framework of the ongoing conflict. Humphrys takes pride in the final reduction of Canada, achieved by three completely independent British armies that converged on Montreal within a few days of each other. Writing to his wife from the recently captured island of Guadeloupe, Johnston Abercromby states that not only was it a great achievement that the troops disembarked without any losses despite a strong French cannonade, but 'in the space of 3 months we have added to England 5 Islands, more than ever was known to be gained in so short a space before'.[14]

Instead of seeing them as passive participants, the military authorities clearly encouraged their men to become concerned with the success of the ongoing conflict. Victories were celebrated with *feu de joie*, involving three rolling salvos discharged along the line by the whole army as it was arranged in battle order. Such occasions were obviously intended to increase morale. For instance, Surtees found it very uplifting when the British reinforcements bound for the Netherlands performed it just before their embarkation. Hessian Valentin Asteroth was similarly excited when the garrison of Charlestown marked the news of a recent victory with *feu*

[13] Bonin, 'Voyage au Canada', 196; Slater, 'Egypt 1801', 118; 'Two Letters by Musketeer Johann Christian Riemann to his Family and Friends' (16 June 1762 and undated, summer 1762), in Liebe, 32, 34; Deane, *Journal*, 7; BL add MSS 45,662, Richard Humphrys, 'Journal', fol. 125.
[14] Stevenson, *Soldier*, 41, 45, 61; G. Robertson, 'Two Letters', 23; NAM 2001-01-611 'Letter from Johnston Abercromby, 3rd Battalion Grenadiers, to his Wife Betsy, Describing the Capture of Various French West Indian Islands' (27 April 1794); see also: Shaw, *Autobiography*, 31; McBane, 'Expert Swords-Man's Companion', 37; Millner, *Compendious Journal*, 99–100. For more expressions of dynastic loyalty, see: Ancell, *Circumstantial Journal*, 42, 223, 253; Tory, *Journal*, 14. For cursing enemy monarchs, see: *Royal Dragoon*, 51; Jurikson, 'Russkije voijnoplennie v Visinge', [Russian Prisoners of War in Wisingsborg], 205.

de joie and illuminations. In Marlborough's army, in addition to the more conventional rolling fire, soldiers also threw their hats into the air, cried 'huzza', and shouted obscenities at the French.[15] British overseas victories offered numerous opportunities for celebration for the beleaguered allied army in Hanover, which fired *feu de joie* to mark the captures of Quebec, Montreal, Belle Île, Pondicherry, Dominica, Martinique and Havana. Moreover, if the enemy lay close nearby, the celebration assumed elements of psychological warfare. Dominicus' diary mentions three such examples. Firstly, Daun's Austrian army shot a *feu de joie* in front of the Prussian army to celebrate the French success at Saint Cast. Shortly afterwards, the Russians did the same to mark the defeat of a small Prussian covering detachment. The Prussians retaliated the next year by firing a *feu de joie* in honour of the victory of Minden, as the Russians were digging in on the nearby heights of Kunersdorf.[16] In addition, soldiers were also kept updated on the war progress on other fronts and in their individual theatres. According to John Tory, after the victory at Vellinghausen, the British troops were informed of the operation undertaken by their allied troops in other sectors of the battlefield. Moreover, sometimes such news was clearly intended not only to inform, but also to shape. According to Tory, over the course of a few days the details of the capture of Zornburg, mentioning the officers and the men who distinguished themselves, were advertised in the orders of the allied army. While this was intended to inspire by example, other orders directly appealed for the men's involvement. According to Corporal Todd, on one occasion soldiers were commanded to be diligent because the enemy was spreading false rumours of peace, hoping to undermine the alertness of the allied army. On 7 June 1794, the Duke of York issued an angry proclamation lambasting the recent resolution of the French National Convention ordering its armies to grant no quarter to British and Hanoverian troops. According to Corporal Robert Brown, the statement was publicly read to the men, together with additional comments over the course of the next few days.[17]

[15] Surtees, *Twenty-Five Years*, 4–5; Asteroth, 'Diary', (26–7 March 1781). See also: Scot, 'Remembrance', 353, 357, 459–60; 454

[16] Glasgow City Library, Ms. 72, John Burrell, 'Account of the Allied Army's Travels & Actions', (25 June 1761); Grotehenn, *Briefe*, 75, 95, 111, Todd, *Journal*, 175; Tory, *Journal*, 30, 64, 76; Dominicus, *Tagebuch*, 44, 54, 58; For some examples of *feu de joie* fired in honour of victories won elsewhere, see: Popp, 'Journal', 33, 38; Ancell, *Circumstantial Journal*, 238–9; Deane, *Journal*, 43, 114. For more examples of *feu de joie* shot in the presence of the enemy, see: Scot, 'Remembrance', 390; Tory, *Journal*, 51; Todd, *Journal*, 170; Institut für Stadtgeschichte, Frankfurt am Main, S1/367 Johannes Reuber, 'Tagebuch', (15 August 1776).

[17] Popp, 'Journal', 37; Amblard, 'Histoire des campagnes' in 'De Lussas vers l'aventure II', 252; NAM 1959-02-46, 'Account of the raid on St. Malo by sergeant Porter of Grenadier

Although the mere existence of an official policy should not be taken as evidence of its ultimate success, these measures were at least partially effective. Judging by the quotations in their memoirs, enlisted men were often willing consumers of official dispatches or uplifting sermons. Moreover, some soldier-authors went further than simply passively internalising formal discourse. While they were prisoners in the hands of the Americans, Döhla and his comrades read newspapers to remain updated on the progress of the war. Todd tells us that he discussed current affairs with one of his officers. According to Laukhard, during the 1790 tension with Austria, his comrades often debated whether Prussia should go to war. Some of these debates ended in fights. Clear association with the aims of the conflict was formed by the British prisoners who were languishing in Burgos at the end of the War of the Spanish Succession. According to one of them, when its preliminaries were declared, the men just could not believe that their country had agreed to sign a peace treaty without succeeding in securing the Spanish throne for the Habsburg claimant. Sergeant Darby refers to the 'king-killing' spirit of the French inhabitants of Valenciennes, who turned away when a British military band began playing 'God Save the King'.[18]

Some opponents were singled out for special resentment. The defeat suffered at the hands of the Russian barbarians in Kunersdorf must have proven very disturbing to a good Prussian like Dominicus, who claims that Russian troops were actually defeated, and the battle was only lost because of the sudden intervention by Austrian reinforcements. This unwillingness to recognise Russians as worthy opponents appears to have been widespread. A contemporary Prussian soldiers' song attributes the allied success at Kunersdorf entirely to the role of the Austrian General Laudon. Musketeer Hoppe claims that the earlier Russian victory in Gross-Jägersdorf was an accident which happened only because two Prussian columns lost their way in the forest and started firing at each other. Berthold Koch similarly argues that the surrender of Yorktown took place only because of French reinforcements and that the Americans themselves were incapable of achieving similar success.[19] According to

company, 23rd foot', June 5 1758', (26–9 June 1757); Tory, *Journal*, 25–6, 63 Todd, *Journal*, 162, 169–70; R. Brown, *Impartial Journal*, 156–63.

[18] Döhla, 'Tagebuch', (12 August and 25 December 1782); Todd, *Journal*, 138; Laukhard, *Leben und Schicksale*, 179; *Royal Dragoon*, 56, 138; Darby, 'Capture of Valenciennes'; see also: Scot, 'Remembrance', 319, 407–8; Humphrys, 'Journal', fol. 87.

[19] Dominicus, *Tagebuch*, 64; Ditfurth, *Einhundert historische Volkslieder*, 50–1; Hoppe, 'Wahrhafte Schilderung', 194. Koch, *Battle*, 9. For other cultural feuds, see: Keep, *Soldiers of the Tsar*, 214–21; For a view that such feuds lived more in the minds of enlightened observers rather than frontline soldiers, see: Möbius '"Haß gegen alles, was nur den Namen eines Franzosen führet"?'.

Conway and Spring, the antagonism against the 'rebels' formed by the British and Germans had much to do with the Americans' lack of military demeanour and their disregard for accepted military conventions. Not only British and German generals, but also their subordinates, were bitter about American guerrilla tactics. In a letter written back to their relatives in Hesse, Jung Heim Steller and his comrades complain that the Americans fought like robbers and thieves, while Private Thomas Plumb of the 22nd Regiment characterised the rebels as 'cowardly rascals [who] will not stand their ground But watching all Oppertunitys by lying in Ambush behind some trees [sic]'.[20] Similar views were formed by some British soldiers serving in Ireland during the Rising of 1798. According to Corporal Samuel Blomeley, the rebels lacked not only military discipline, but also shoes and stockings, while they also fought drunk and committed all sorts of depredation. George Blennie portrays the rebels as bigoted Catholics who, although they took the oath of the United Irishmen, immediately begin molesting Protestants. Moreover, they refused to drill as they were unwilling to be 'like redcoat slaves'. Blennie calls such liberty disingenuous bigotry and a mere excuse for hedonism, not missing the irony that the Irish allied themselves with the atheist French, taking arms 'for France and the blessed virgin'.[21]

Some of the anger directed at the other side probably had to do with the fact that these people had to be fought against in the first place. According to Laukhard, when Prussian troops who assembled in the Rhineland learned of the storm of Tuileries, they were infuriated and proclaimed that the damn 'patriots' should be hanged and broken alive, because the allies were now left with no choice but to march on Paris. But the enemy could also be accused of specific atrocities. After his arrival in America, Amblard remarks on the pitiful state of the country after three years of English ravages. Another member of Rochambeau's expedition similarly reports that the British forces committed heinous atrocities, including crucifying women on barn doors and torturing men to death. British narrators could hold an equally dim opinion of their French opponents. According to Sergeant Wilson, after taking the English camp at Arleux by surprise, the French proceeded to torture the prisoners and to mutilate the female camp followers by cutting off their tongues and breasts. Such descriptions could also contain a comparative element. Telling how

---

[20] Conway, 'Great Mischief', 378–9; Spring, *With Zeal and with Bayonets*, 124–36, Atwood, *Hessians*, 158–70; Steller, 'Letters', 1; Plumb, 'Letter to his Brother' (22 February 1777), available online on http://redcoat76.blogspot.com/2013/01/thomas-plumb-22nd-regiment-of-foot.html (Last accessed 7 October 2016).

[21] NAM 1987-10-7 Samuel Blomeley, 'Letter', (2 July 1798). See also: Blennie, *Narrative*, 22–4; Stevenson, *Soldier*, 35.

retreating Austrian troops had drunk many barrels of mead and destroyed all those that could not be taken to prevent them from falling into the hands of the advancing Prussians, *Feldwebel* Liebler says that the Austrians behaved badly, 'in a way we never would'.[22] British participants in the War of Independence accused Americans of using poisoned balls and slugs that caused particularly grievous wounds. Dominicus sounds uncharacteristically modern when he claims that the enemy artillery at Kunersdorf employed ammunition 'not allowed in war', including chain-balls, chunks of pig iron and particularly deadly canister.[23] Some British soldiers in North America resented the fact that the French employed Indian allies, whose barbarities sometimes left them no choice but to retaliate. According to Sergeant John Johnson, after the murder and scalping of the first British soldier from the expeditionary force sent against Quebec, Wolfe unsuccessfully remonstrated with Montcalm. Since the murders continued, Wolfe reluctantly allowed the men to avenge themselves on the French by tolerating 'some irregularities' committed during forage expeditions in outlying Canadian villages. Similar righteous responses could occur if rumours circulated that the enemy had ordered its troops to give no quarter.[24]

The alleged enemy crimes could be linked further with the immorality of those capable of such actions. To demonstrate to his family what kind of fate would await them if the enemy army should invade Prussia, Barthel Linck cites a few episodes of the Austrian conduct at the battle of Lobositz. After surrendering his sword, watch and purse to the lieutenant who captured him, Prince Lobkowitz proceeded to fire at the man with a hidden pistol. When taken prisoner, Colonel Esterhazy blasphemed so terribly that a Prussian grenadier, who could not hold back his righteous anger, shot him dead on the spot. After the battle, the burial of the fallen was interrupted by a Croat sniper, who killed a Prussian soldier standing by the open grave. McBane writes that at Malplaquet the French started

---

[22] Laukhard, *Leben und Schicksale*, 224; Amblard, 'Histoire des campagnes' in 'De Lussas vers l'aventure II', 246; Flohr, *American Campaigns*, 18; J. Wilson, 'Journal', 83, 'Feldwebel G.S. Liebler to his wife and family', (7 May 1757), in GG, 46; see also: Beeger, *Seltsame Schicksale*, 35–7, Dreyer, *Leben und Taten*, 43–4; Dominicus, *Tagebuch*, 54.

[23] Sullivan, *From Redcoat to Rebel*, 20; J. Miller, 'Memoirs of an Invalid', 175; Dominicus, *Tagebuch*, 61, 64. For more on 'illegal' ammunition, see: Bersling, *Der böhmische Veteran*, 205

[24] J. Johnson, 'Memoirs of the Siege of Quebec', 81–2, 89–91. See: Williamson, *French and Indian Cruelty*, 36–7. For supposed issue of enemy orders to grant no quarter, see: 'Barthel Linck to His Wife and Family', (3 October 1756), 13; 'Feldwebel G.S. Liebler to his wife and relatives', (12 October 1756), GG, 34; Kirkwood, *Through so Many Dangers*, 82. For allegations of murdering prisoners, see: Scot, 'Remembrance', 494; Tory, *Journal*, 68.

cannonading the British troops while they were still praying. During
the Great Siege of Gibraltar, the enemy shot at a priest in the middle of
a burial ceremony. Moreover, the Spanish were also capable of great
cruelty to their own men, at least according to Samuel Ancell, who claims
that their artillery fired at English gunboats while these were helping to
evacuate Spanish sailors caught up in the burning hulks of their own
floating batteries. Some of the Prussian and Austrian troops who fought
against revolutionary France believed that French civilians served poisoned food to the allied soldiers. John Burrell, who fought as farrier of the
Scots Greys during the Seven Years War, tells of treasonable conspiracies
organised by the clergy and the Catholic inhabitants to help the French
army. During the siege of Münster, the locals guided a French raiding
party into the allied camp in the middle of the night to murder soldiers in
their sleep. On another occasion, monks concealed French troops inside
their monastery, from which they would sally out at night to massacre the
allied patrols. This scheme was discovered by the allied commander-in-
chief, Prince Ferdinand of Brunswick, who went undercover into the
convent disguised as a beggar. The next day allied troops thoroughly
plundered the place, and would have burned the monastery with everyone
they found inside, if not for the mercy of the prince.[25] These accounts are
important not so much because the actions they describe did or did not
occur, but rather because they demonstrate that old-regime soldiers could
adopt a highly hostile view of their opponents that, in turn, could easily
lead to objectification and revenge. Moreover, an order to fight against
such people would be considered legitimate.

According to Alan Guy's important study of British military administration during the reign of the first two Georges, officers viewed their men
as 'commodities: human resources to be recruited, drilled and exercised,
managed as an investment, discharged when worn out, or drafted from
one regiment into another'. This is an unsurprising conclusion considering it was drawn from the surviving correspondence, papers and accounts
in what was still a time of proprietary command. Nevertheless it is
a partial picture, for it ignores how men viewed their relationship with
their superiors. Moreover, private papers and public actions can present
totally different portrayals of the same individual. To use the example of
Frederick the Great, the surviving writings of native Prussian troops
present him as a vigorous, trusted and, at the same time, concerned
leader. Before battle, the king rode out to encourage the troops, in

---

[25] 'Barthel Linck to his wife', (3 October 1756), in GG, 14; McBane, 'Expert Swords-
Man's Companion', 42; Ancell, *Circumstantial Journal*, 26, 264; Löffler, *Der alte Sergeant*,
90–1; Laukhard, *Leben und Schicksale*, 231–2; Burrell, 'Account', (unpaginated). See
also: Bell, *First Total War*, 81.

Plattdeutsch, if necessary. At Kunersdorf, according to Dominicus, the king led his troops in person, but once the battle was clearly lost, Frederick himself ordered retreat to save their lives from needless slaughter. Despite the defeat, Frederick ordered that every soldier should be paid two *groschen* in appreciation of their courage. If a battle ended well, however, the king toured the army, stopping in front of every company to thank the soldiers in person. Moreover, *unser weiser König*, as his men occasionally refer to him, went on reconnaissance, made careful battle dispositions and arranged for supplies and provisions despite the lurking Croats. Frederick is also said to have shared the hardships of his troops, occasionally even sleeping on the bare ground.[26]

As far as the testimonies of his soldiers are concerned, Frederick comes out very differently than he does in some of his better-known statements regarding his own army. Interestingly, when an old-regime enlisted man makes reference to bad officers, they are usually criticised for lacking the very virtues praised by Frederick's soldiers. Officers failing to demonstrate personal example or show concern for their men like General Shirley, who refused to winter with his army at Oswego, or the French officers who escaped from the sinking ship while their soldiers were still aboard, drew enraged comments. Lack of familiarity undermined trust. According to Surtees, the 1799 expedition to Holland was compromised before it even began, because the troops were assembled too quickly. This resulted in a situation where the officers did not know their men, while the soldiers did not have confidence in their superiors. On a personal level, lack of trust or a cynical joke could prove equally discouraging. One of the reasons that prompted Steininger to desert from Württemberg was a remark by the Duke when he ordered Steininger not to pursue an escaped horse, saying 'my horse will return and you might not'. Moreover, soldier-authors rejoiced when fate punished an unjust officer. For instance, one of Wray's superiors went mad soon after unfairly condemning a man at a drumhead court martial.[27] However, even when

---

[26] Guy, 'The Army of the Georges', 94; For a generally negative interpretation of officer-men relations in old-regime France, see: Lynn, *Bayonets*, 67–8; 'Barthel Linck to his wife', (3 October 1756), in GG, 12; Dominicus, *Tagebuch*, 46, 59, 64–5; 'Franz Reiß to his wife', (6 October 1756), in GG, 31; 'Letter of an *Unteroffizier* from the Anhalt Regiment', (1 October 1756), in GG, 1–2; 'Feldwebel G.S. Liebler to his wife and relatives', (12 October 1756 and 7 May 1757), in GG, 33–4, 46; Hoppe, 'Wahrhafte Schilderung', 193; Schimmel, 'Kurze Lebensbeschreibung', 189.

[27] Surtees, *Twenty-Five Years*, 5; Flohr, *American Campaigns*, 21–3, 74–5; Williamson, *French and Indian Cruelty*, 59; 'Letter from a Musketeer in the Anhlat Regiment', (8 May 1757), in GG, 52; Beß, 'Aus dm Tagebuch', 218–9; J. Thompson, *Bard*, 177–80; Henly, *Life*, 10–1; Steininger, *Leben und Abenteuer*, 49; J. Miller, 'Memoirs of an Invalid', 134–5; D. Cameron, *Life*, 8; Wray, *Military Adventures*, 8–9. See also: Steuernagel, 'Brief Description', 197–9.

augmented by the highly critical but somewhat suspect portrayals of the entire officer class by Le Roy, Rossignol and Aytoun, such cases are considerably outnumbered by positive descriptions of involved and courageous superiors.

On the most basic level, officers took care to ensure that their men were decently provided for. Accounts by Todd and Tory contain numerous references to the generosity of the Marquess of Granby, who issued his troops with additional supplies paid from his own pocket. Deane praises the French governor of Douai, who ran up into high personal debts to feed his garrison. *Fourier* Sohr mentions with gratitude a Prussian general who ordered his men to share their forage with the Saxon troops attached to his corps during the war of the Bavarian Succession. During the famine in Ireland, Surtees' major changed the supply arrangements to allow the men to receive more nutritious foodstuffs.[28] Individual soldiers could also benefit from such concern, including from relatively senior officers. When Corporal Todd fell ill, his colonel sent him fresh meat and ordered a lieutenant to visit Todd every day until he recovered. Similarly, Grotehenn's sick cousin was put into the quarters of their regimental proprietor, Lieutenant General von Imhoff. While blatantly criticising the incompetence and corruption of some Prussian officers during the miserable retreat from France in the rainy autumn of 1792, Laukhard also tells of a captain who gave over his tent to be used as a workshop by the regimental cobblers. Although the spiritual welfare of eighteenth-century soldiers is usually associated with mandatory prayers, at least one officer chose to approach the matter differently. Since most of the soldiers in his garrison regiment could not be trusted to leave the citadel, Steininger's colonel arranged for weekly dances to which women from the nearby town were invited. On occasions when not enough guests arrived at the fortress, the colonel ensured his men were provided with enough dance partners by ordering all garrison wives to partake in the festivities, irrespective of their husbands' wishes.[29]

Patronage benefited individual soldiers as well as whole units. Direct superiors helped their men to secure promotion, pension or even protection from punishment. Beeger, whose pay was insufficient to buy food,

---

[28] Todd, *Journal*, 170, 191, 220; Tory, *Journal*, 24, 43, 49; Deane, *Journal*, 110–1; Sohr, *Meine Geschichte*, 43; Surtees, *Twenty-Five Years*, 39. See also: Jonas, *Soldier's Journal*, 179–80; D. Robertson, *Journal*, 9; Hoppe, 'Wahrhafte Schilderung', 180. For another British commander who was known to care about the welfare of his men, see: Chandler, 'The Captain General', 89; Scouller, *Armies of Queen Anne*, 287–8.

[29] Todd, *Journal*, 24, 66; Grotehenn, *Briefe*, 40; Laukhard, *Leben und Schicksale*, 263–4; Steininger, *Leben und Abenteuer*, 42–3. See also: Hall, 'Letter to Sergeant Cabe', (26 September 1709); Löffler, *Der alte Sergeant*, 44; Lamb, *Original and Authentic Journal*, 396; Burke, *Memoir*, 12; Lahatt, 'Autobiography', 58.

was often fed by his captain, who also forgave Beeger's first disciplinary offence, arranged his first off-duty job and obtained him a promotion to battalion drummer. Colonel Fraser saved his regimental master-tailor from court martial after the man, who disguised himself as an officer, got drunk and punched a real officer from another regiment. Officers sometimes intervened to shield a soldier from their junior colleagues or NCOs. Laukhard's captain summarily dismissed a number of petty complaints by his *Unteroffizier*. After Laukhard was unjustifiably reported as a thief, the captain conducted an investigation, and once the accusation was proven false, ordered the NCO to receive twenty-five flats of a sabre for disparaging the character of his own subordinate.[30] Officers could also help men against the civil authorities. The lieutenant of trooper Hermann Heinrich Wiemer, who was engaged in a long inheritance dispute, wrote to the judge to ensure his man got his due. Moreover, when the favourable verdict was pending, the judge was contacted again and this time warned that any further delays would incur the displeasure of Wiemer's regimental *Chef*, the king's brother, Prince Henry of Prussia. British officers could not act as assertively against civil justice, but could still attempt to help their men. For instance, Colonel Fraser, whose sergeant was charged with murder, first tried to prevent his surrender to a civilian court. Failing to do so, he acted as attorney and translated from Gaelic the favourable witness statements of the man's comrades, many of whom barely spoke English. Officers defended their regiment's reputation, like Hessian Colonel Rall, who prevented a general from taking away a standard captured by Rall's grenadiers. There were even strange cases of patronage, such as the one mentioned by Ludwig and Martin Otte, when their regiment was pulled out from a battle line by the Prince Henry of Prussia because of his attachment to that unit.[31]

Recorded by the enlisted men themselves, all these examples show that men of the line took notice when officers showed genuine concern for their needs. This does not necessarily mean that officers were personally attached to their subordinates. Nevertheless, precisely because the eighteenth century was still a period of proprietary command,

---

[30] Beeger, *Seltsame Schicksale*, 17, 19, 21–2, 23; J. Thompson, *Bard*, 127, 130–1, 169; Laukhard, *Leben und Schicksale*, 152. See also: Todd, *Journal*, 136; Beß, 'Aus dem Tagebuch', 226; D. Robertson, *Journal*, 36; Lamb, *Original and Authentic Journal*, 436; Kenward, *Sussex Highlander*, 53; For a case of an NCO defending his man against punishment, see: TNA WO 71/12, fols. 212–3.

[31] 'Trooper Hermann Heinrich Wiemer to Judge Kaspar Dietrich Marck in Schwerte', (7 February 1741), in: *BBS*, 246–8; For a similar instance of patronage, see: 'Letter from Grenadier Kaspar Hülsenberg to his wife', (21 January 1745), in: *BBS*, 289–9; Reuber, 'Tagebuch', (21 August 1776); 'Letter from Prague by Ludwig and Martin Otte', (10 May 1757), in GG, 57.

officers had a strong practical incentive to treat their men well. The soldiers remained, to an extent, the property of their captains and colonels, but profitable ownership required careful management. Mistreated, unpaid or disgusted men were more likely to desert or to defy their superiors. As we have already seen, such a possibility was not hypothetical. If such incidents occurred, the financial and career prospects of the officers could be seriously hampered. Under such conditions, maintaining authority necessitated not so much felt but *demonstrated* concern. The informality with which old-regime soldiers approached their senior officers is stunning by modern standards. Grenadier Hoffmann saw King Frederick William I twice to ask for a pay raise. Johann Heinrich Beherns personally asked General Ziethen to be transferred into his hussar regiment. Steininger mentions a number of encounters with the Duke of Württemberg, who knew many of his soldiers by name and reputation. After being abducted into the British army, Andrew Pearson was able to complain in person to his general and two governors. Although his requests were not granted, it is still telling that he could approach them all directly.[32] Men also made reference to what they perceived as clear instances of just behaviour. After a disagreement with his captain over a furlough that almost got him hanged, Rossignol refused to apply for furlough the next year. Nevertheless, his captain issued him one anyhow. While he was in jail, Steininger asked to transfer some money for his father. After learning that it had not been delivered, he approached the commandant in person, who arranged for the money to be returned so that Steininger could resend it. On another occasion, Steininger's colonel prevented his captain from taking away charity money given to Steininger after he had endured a mock execution.[33]

Moreover, in addition to its utilitarian aspects, the contractual obligation which bound officers and men had a moral element to it. The relationship between them was not egalitarian. The officers were not only their men's military but also social superiors, but along with the authority to which this entitled them also came responsibility. The connection between them is best understood as a relationship between patron and client. The officers enjoyed not just military but paternal authority, a practice

[32] Hoffman, 'Letter to his mother', 171; Behrens, *Lebensgeschichte*, 17–8; Steininger, *Leben und Abenteuer*, 49, 56; Pearson *Soldier who Walked Away*, 15, 18–9. See also: Löffler, *Der alte Sergeant*, 46–7; Beeger, *Seltsame Schicksale*, 23–4; Surtees, *Twenty-Five Years*, 51–2.
[33] Steininger, *Leben und Abenteuer*, 54–5, 88. See also: Rossignol, *Vie veritable*, 33–4. On the paternalistic nature of eighteenth-century officer-men relations, see: Frey, *British Soldier in America*, 120; Brumwell, *Redcoats*, 70–1; Hurl-Eamon, '"Youth in the Devil's Service"', 174–7.

best demonstrated in the German and Russian armies, where men addressed their superiors as 'father'. Frey mentions how the higher social status of the officers could have contributed to the combat motivation of their men. Officers led from the front while taking the same, if not greater, risks as their subordinates. Thus, their social authority was further reinforced by a moral one. This is an important point which further underscores the consensual nature of old-regime military and combat service. The idea that soldiers were meek appears unlikely, considering the more reciprocal reality of the power relations in old-regime armies. Moreover, while not all men who joined the military were rebels, voluntary enlistment usually meant an earlier defiance towards immediate superiors in one's original family or community. Deferent men willing to submit to any type of power were less likely to end up in a situation where they would desire or be forced to take the bounty. Such men were even less likely to be submissive than the early-modern lower orders from whence they were drawn; orders that, as we are now aware, often resisted and defied their social superiors. Subordination in peacetime and willingness to follow officers into combat can be explained neither by coercion nor by the preconditioned inoculation of military obedience. Interestingly, as demonstrated by Stouffer, a better indication of effective leadership is not the fearlessness of the officer but his personal concern for his men.[34]

Officers, however, were not just administrators and benefactors, but also combat leaders. James Green, who was commissioned from the ranks during the American War of Independence, explained in a letter to a friend the duties of an officer in combat. These included a control element 'to see that [men] do their duty properly – level and fire well' and 'keep them from breaking and confusion'. Another important responsibility was '[to] assist them with his exhortations to inspire them with courage'. As shown in Chapter 3, few men describe witnessing direct action against reluctant soldiers. On the other hand, their accounts abound with references to the encouraging role of their superiors. Speeches before combat were common. One contemporary officers' manual even offered a template for such an address, that promised respect and recognition for the brave and censure and disgrace for the cowardly. Linn reports how the Duke of Cumberland rode before the British line before the battle of Culloden 'desiring us not to be afraid'. Before the battle of Lobositz, the Duke of Anhalt arrived at his regiment and directed his men to behave as 'righteous fighters'. Other commanders spoke of country and honour, or invoked some national attributes. John Stevenson

---

[34] Sylvia Frey, *British Soldier in America*, 123–6; Stouffer et al., *American Soldier: Combat*, 123–4.

mentions how, when ordered to remove their greatcoats before approaching the enemy, a British Guards officer remarked 'That's right, my lads, show them your colours'. Some superiors chose to discharge the tense atmosphere with a joke. Before the storm of Seringapatam, General Baird issued the parole 'Tipoo or no Baird', further asking the troop to follow and help him 'shave the tyrant!'[35]

Soldiers mention the personal example of commanders-in-chief, general officers and regimental colonels, who often held higher army ranks, who fought with their troops or encouraged them by riding along the line or placing themselves in a conspicuous spot. Scot reports that, at Malplaquet, Prince Eugene personally led the Dutch troops into battle, despite suffering a wound early in the engagement. At Prague, the battalion of *Feldwebel* Liebler was led by Prince Henry of Prussia. Humphrys tells us that after landing at Montmorency, General Wolfe was among the first to rush into a French battery, spiking one of its cannons with his own bayonet. According to Thomas Sullivan, at the battle of Bronx, 'General Howe stood in the rear of the Cannon, and his undaunted courage and resolution animated the troops, seeing themselves commanded by so bold and prudent commander'.[36] In addition to making their presence known, officers of all ranks tried to encourage men to press on despite initial setbacks. After enquiring why his regiment had stopped firing and learning that its ammunition had ran out, the Duke of Bevern exclaimed 'What? Don't you have bayonets? Go on and skewer the dogs'. After his battalion was ordered forward once the initial Prussian attack at Kunersdorf was stalled, Dominicus reports that its adjutant rode by and called 'hold a bit longer children, you held well so far, and if anyone in front of you thinks of retreating, shoot their heads off!'. Döhla tells us of a grenadier captain whose hand was shattered with grapeshot, who insisted on staying with his men. After taking a mortal wound in the chest, the captain not only continued to encourage them to fight on, but also consoled his grenadiers who were clearly distressed by his fate.[37]

---

[35] NAM 1972-01-36 (1), 'Account of American service and letters by James Green'; Linn, 'Battle of Culloden', 23; 'Barthel Linck to his wife', (3 October 1756), in GG, 12; Stevenson, *Soldier*, 6; Todd, *Journal*, 181; Shaw, *Autobiography*, 31; Dominicus, *Tagebuch*, 15; Kenward, *Sussex Highlander*, 28; For another general who, on the contrary, promised not to shave himself until victory is won, see: Bishop, *Life and Adventures*, 228.

[36] Scot, 'Remembrance'. 477–8; '*Feldwebel* G.S. Liebler to his wife and family', (7 May 1757), in GG, 47; Humphrys, 'Journal', fol. 46; Sullivan, *From Redcoat to Rebel*, 69. See also: *Royal Dragoon*, 35; J. Johnson, 'Memoirs of the Siege of Quebec', 102; J. Miller, 'Memoirs of an Invalid', 21; Todd, *Journal*, 166, 205; Amblard, 'Histoire des campagnes' in: 'De Lussas vers l'aventure III', 186.

[37] 'From the Letter of Mr. Kistenmacher, Secretary to the Duke of Bevern', (2 October 1756), in GG, 10; Dominicus, *Tagebuch*, 59–60; Döhla, 'Tagebuch',

Officers also continued to demonstrate concern for their men's well-being and reputation in wartime. Sergeant Thompson recalls how Wolfe made sure to make daily visits to the highlanders' camp, although it lay three miles from the general's headquarters. According to Grenadier Reuber, the mortally wounded Colonel Rall continued to think about his troops until his very last breath, earnestly pleading General Washington to ensure that the Hessian prisoners taken in Trenton were treated decently. According to the dragoon who fought at the battle of Brihuega, his squadron retreated, following the bad example of its own captain. When asked to provide an explanation by General Pepper, the captain claimed that his men would not stand the enemy. Hearing this, the general called the captain a liar, and personally led the squadron back into combat. Private James Morgan tells how, after their return from the French captivity, the men of the Ostend detachment were welcomed by their former commander General Coote, who praised their performance and assured them that they had successfully preserved their honour despite the eventual surrender.[38] The moral responsibility which officers were expected to bear towards their men is, perhaps, best demonstrated when the formal demands of the military organisation were gone. Officers who were taken prisoner with their men helped to ease the lot of their captive subordinates by providing the necessary credit, or paying the local suppliers upfront from their own means. Officers of the captured German auxiliary troops provided their men with clothes, blankets, provisions and basic pay. Bernos' detachment, which surrendered at discretion and was thus ineligible to be paid by its Austrian captors, was relieved through the efforts of its major, the Chevalier de Nancourt. The major persuaded the other prisoners to forfeit part of their subsistence, and added much from his own resources, which allowed all captive French troops to receive basic pay. This irregular arrangement later got Nancourt a reprimand from the commissioner for the French prisoners.[39]

After victory, commanders proceeded to congratulate the army. According to Sergeant Wilson, after Donauwörth and Blenheim, the Duke of Marlborough rode from battalion to battalion to thank the men

(6 October 1777). See also: Williamson, *French and Indian Cruelty*, 96; Reuber, 'Tagebuch', (17 November and 25 December 1776), Lamb, *Original and Authentic Journal*, 361, Allfärtty, *Friedrich des Großen letzter Dragoner*, 21–2; For troops discouraged by the death or wounds of their superiors, see: Humphrys, 'Journal', fols. 68, 71; Sullivan, *From Redcoat to Rebel*, 50; D. Robertson, *Journal*, 18–9.

[38] J. Thompson, *Bard*, 154–5; Reuber, 'Tagesbuch', (25 December 1776); *Royal Dragoon*, 46–7; NAM 2004-03-75 (1), 'Two Manuscript Letters Written by Private James Morgan, Coldstream Guards to His Father'.

[39] Döhla, 'Tagebuch', (28 February and 13 March 1782); Bense, 'Brunswick Grenadier', 442; Bernos, 'Souvenirs de campagne', 676, 687.

for their performance. An anonymous soldier from Barrel's Regiment of Foot writes that, after the battle of Falkirk, an unnamed brigadier congratulated the regiment for turning the tide of the battle, and stopped to kiss some of the men in the first rank. Expressions of gratitude would also go all the way up the military hierarchy. The British participants of the battle of Bunker Hill were first thanked by their direct commander General Howe, then by General Gage, the commander-in-chief in North America, and finally by King George. In Rochambeau's corps, a translation of King Louis XVI's message was prepared for the benefit of the German speakers of the Deux-Pont (Zweibrücken) Regiment.[40] Troops were also thanked for good performance on reviews, for reacting quickly to an alarm and sometimes even for unspecified reasons. Individual soldiers could be marked for special favour. After Dreyer's successful raid on Tratenau he was invited to meet General de la Motte Fouquet, while one of his later escapades earned a quick audience with Frederick the Great, who called him a brave soldier and awarded him a symbolic sum of money. After his escape from American captivity, Sergeant Lamb was paid a bounty. Although it was not specified who paid for it, Lamb suspects it was the commander-in-chief who provided the money from his own pocket.[41] The reference to such cases in soldiers' narratives makes it unlikely that old-regime troops considered their superiors to be indifferent to their exertions.

What is clear, though, is that old-regime soldiers could see their relationship with their superiors in much more positive terms than those described by Guy or Lynn. Moreover, some soldiers refer to their officers, if not with open fondness, then at least with attachment. Corporal Todd said he had lost 'two friends' after his sergeant and captain-lieutenant were promoted into different regiments. After transferring to another unit, Todd uses the same term when speaking of his new lieutenant, as does Sergeant Kenward, referring to one of his captains. Wolfe is called a 'soldiers' friend' by a number of his subordinates, including a pressed

---

[40] J. Wilson, 'Journal', 46, 57; 'Letter from a Private Soldier in Barrel's Regiment at Edinburgh, dated Jan. 19', (1746), 42; Howe, *Orderly Book*, 3, 9–10, 97; Flohr, *American Campaigns*, 53–4. See also: Linn, 'Battle of Culloden', 23; 'Franz Reiß to his wife', (October 6 1756), in GG, 31; Tory, *Journal*, 42, 45; Todd, *Journal*, 169–70, 185; Lamb, *Original and Authentic Journal*, 111; Sullivan, *From Redcoat to Rebel*, 109; Amblard, 'Histoire des campagnes' in 'De Lussas vers l'aventure II', 248; Ancell, *Circumstantial Journal*, 177, 279, 289; Darby, 'Battle of Lincelles'.

[41] Todd, *Journal*, 133, 145; Tory, *Journal*, 3; Döhla, 'Tagebuch', (10 May 1780); Howe, *Orderly Book*, 131, 214, 257; Dreyer, *Leben und Taten*, 35, 45; Lamb, *Original and Authentic Journal*, 262; For a recommendation to officers by a former sergeant major to award unique acts by their men, see: Astley, *Remarks*, 17; On Philip Astley's career after his discharge, see: Bulloch, 'Soldiering and Circuses'.

man.[42] Soldier poet William Vernon dedicated one of his verses to his grenadier captain. Löffler shared with his officers some of the booty he took in Belgrade. There is evidence that at least some superiors reciprocated. Berthold Koch says that Cornwallis cried when biding farewell to his army after the surrender of Yorktown. Lamb says that the friendship between officers and men continued for life. The obituary read by his captain at the funeral of Musketeer Dominicus still survives:

Rest in peace deserved by you through many brave and Christian deeds, noble Dominicus! Rest until summoned for the final roll call [i.e. last judgment]. Long live the king and the land which has such brave Christian soldiers as was Dominicus. His memory is an example to our children.[43]

In addition to willing association with their officers, whose role as direct superiors further legitimised the demands of the broader social, political and cultural system on whose behalf armies operated, soldiers were part of another important loyalty network. Not unlike the culture of honour, camaraderie was initially promoted by official means. The smallest formal unit to which every eighteenth-century common soldier belonged was not a tactical but an administrative one. On the most basic level, the mess comprised soldiers who took their meals together. Messes could number anything from a few men to fifteen soldiers or more, although the actual number was often the by-product of lodging arrangements. According to the regulations, subdivision into messes and the responsibility for their overall management was in the hands of the captain, who was also to ensure that new recruits were allocated a mess when they arrived to their company. When provisions were given out, these were issued to the messes rather than to individuals. Soldiers were also quartered according to the same principle, with an individual mess often corresponding to one or two tents. There is also evidence of forming ad-hoc messes in cases such as sea journeys. While clearly intended to relieve the organisational burden of their superiors, enlisted men were also supposed to benefit from this arrangement. Pooling their pay allowed messmates to save on foodstuffs. The mess could also provide itself with communal utensils such as cooking pots, and some even had a horse to carry its property, as well as the equipment of its individual members.[44]

---

[42] Todd, *Journal*, 16, 134; Kenward, *Sussex Highlander*, 73–4; J. Thompson, *Bard*, 143–4, 152–3, 186; 'Letter from Quebec', (7 October 1759). See also: Grotehenn, *Briefe*, 90; BL Mss Eur B296/1 Samuel Hickson, 'Letters', fol. 87.

[43] Löffler, *Der alte Sergeant*, 58; Vernon, *Poems on Several Occasions*, 93–6; Koch, *Battle*, 22; Lamb, *Original and Authentic Journal*, 436; Dominicus, *Tagebuch*, vii. See also: Döhla, 'Tagebuch', (7 June 1780).

[44] Esterhazy de Gallantha, *Regulament und unumänderlich gebräuchliche Observations-Puncten*, (1747), 444; *Reglement für die sämmentlich-Kaiserlich-Königliche Infanterie*, (1769),

Nevertheless, as far as the official requirements of the military organisation were concerned, the mess was an economic and administrative institution, a point that also comes across in soldiers' accounts. Reporting that the sender is now serving together with his *artel* is one of the archetypal phrases used by the scribes who wrote the letters on behalf of illiterate Russian soldiers in the siege of Narva in 1700. Bernos often mentions the *ordinaire* through which French soldiers got their provisions and quarters, an arrangement that remained unchanged after his unit was taken into Austrian captivity. Embarking on ships bound for America, Sullivan's company was divided into messes of six men and given one platter and bowl to share. The provisions in Shaw's regiment were similarly allocated to prescribed groups of six soldiers.[45] Nevertheless, these and other narratives also make clear that the messes played an important social role as well. Messes clearly aimed to enforce a rudimentary form of equality between their individual members. In Jonas' mess, in which all the members slept together in a single tent, all blankets were sewn together to ensure no man enjoyed more space. There was also an elaborate arrangement when the mess divided its food. The first member carved the meat, the second pointed at the different pieces and a third, whose back was turned to the rest, named the member who was to have it. Men contributed from their pay equally towards the maintenance of the common table, while cooking chores were divided by rotation or paid for from the common purse. Disillusioned Swiss surgeon's mate Markus Uhlmann remembers with disgust the division of chores in his mess of eleven men. Uhlmann was able to avoid cooking by paying another soldier to do this duty, but still had to collect wood and hay for his messmates. Outward formal fairness was also maintained between different messes. For instance, allocation of places on board ships could be done by a lottery. Seume and Le Roy, who were former heads of their messes, write that it was a respected post, since its bearer was assumed to be an honest man. As for its potential bonding effect, it is worthwhile remembering that one of the longest surviving legacies of military messing in most European languages is the term 'comrade', originally denoting 'roommate'.[46]

19, 24, 26; Tuch'kov, *Voienji Slovar*, q.v. *Artel* and *Artelshik*; Webb-Carter, 'Colonel Wellesley's Standing Orders', 75; C. Duffy, *Army of Frederick the Great*, 59; Harari, *Renaissance Military Memoirs*, 139.

[45] See the letters of Danila Larionov, Nikita and Brothers Alexander and Philip Gerasimov; in Kozlov 'Okopnie Pisma', 204, 205, 210; Bernos, 'Souvenirs de campagne', 672, 684, 748–9; Sullivan, *From Redcoat to Rebel*, 9; Shaw, *Autobiography*, 40. See also: J. Wilson, *Journal*, 64; Bräker, 'Lebensgeschichte', 458; Lamb, *Original and Authentic Journal*, 396; Lamb, *Memoir*, 64–5; Kappes, 'March Route', 8; Lahatt, 'Autobiography', 58.

[46] Jonas, *Soldier's Journal*, 4, 10–3; Reuber, 'Tagesbuch', (29 May 1776); Bishop, *Life and Adventures*, 33; Seume, *Werke*, vol. I, 70–1; Uhlmann, *Abwechslende Fortün*, 16–7;

The social contacts of individual soldiers were not limited to their messmates only. As they are described, personal friendships could evolve based on some common characteristic such as rank, or national and regional origin. *Fourier* Sohr befriended a fellow regimental clerk of a different company who helped Sohr to adapt in his early days in the Saxon army. Alexander Alexander befriended another 'dictionary man' whose education and social aspirations made him unpopular with other artillerymen. When hungry, Grenadier Hoffman was often helped by another Mecklenburger, a sergeant, who shared his pay with him. Often short on money, Bräker was assisted by another Swiss recruit, who was receiving an extra allowance. Bräker refers to this man, whose name was Scharer, as his *Herzenbruder*. Kenward was likewise attached to a friend and fellow sergeant, with whom he made a pact never to part. Kenward lived up to this promise when he arranged a transfer into his friend's regiment when it was ordered to return from India to Britain. Personal friendship could also survive initial separation, as in the case of Bernos, who was transferred away from his original messmates into another Austrian fortress. Although Bernos quickly made new friends, he was very happy to meet his old comrades again when he chanced to visit their encampment as assistant to the Austrian prisoners' commissioner. Surtees tells of a personal friend, William Sutherland, whom he first met while serving in the same militia company. Both were of the same height and had similar sounding names, which often got them placed by each other's side in the same rank. This continued after both men volunteered together to transfer into the regular army. Sampson Staniforth's friend, Mark Bond, prompted him to leave his bad ways and become a good Christian. At the battle of Lauffeld, Bond was wounded while they fought together side by side. Bond could not keep up in the subsequent retreat and had to be abandoned, to Staniforth's great personal distress.[47]

A more general sense of camaraderie comes out in the writings of William Cobbett, who claims that '[t]o the army, to every soldier in it I have bond of attachment quite independent of any political reasoning. I was soldier in that time of life when feelings of attachment are best formed'. A similar view is expressed by Staniforth, who, after returning from detached service, was welcomed back not only by his Methodist

---

Bernos, 'Souvenirs de campagne', 682, 748–9; D. Robertson, *Journal*, 22; Le Roy, *Souvenirs*, 51–3; Grose, *Classical Dictionary*, q.v. 'Comrade'. For an example of stealing on behalf of one's mess, see: Henly, *Life*, 8–9; Surtees, *Twenty-Five Years*, 38–9.

[47] Sohr, *Meine Geschichte*, 85–6; Alexander, *Life*, vol. I, 173–4; Hoffmann, 'Letter to his mother', 171; Ulrich Bräker, 'Lebensgeschichte', 445–6; Kenward, *Sussex Highlander*, 73–4; Bernos, 'Souvenirs de campagne', 738, 741; Surtees, *Twenty-Five Years*, 3–4; Staniforth, 'Life', 328–31, 339, 342.

friends but by the whole company, 'for I have frequently remarked, there is a kind of affection in the army toward one another, which is hardly to be found elsewhere'. After being written off as incurable, flux-ridden Peter Henly was sent to rejoin his regiment. He reports that when he arrived, his comrades were very happy to see him, despite his condition. Retaken again after Yorktown, multiple escapee Sergeant Lamb was welcomed and helped by his old comrades from the 9th Regiment of Foot, with whom he served until 1777.[48] Being left alone, on the other hand, was a frightening prospect. According to George Blennie, 'coming to a new place with a lot of people is distressing for there is no one to trust and confide too'. Despite falling badly ill during the campaign in Bohemia, Sohr asked not to be sent to hospital, but to stay with his regiment. Learning that his unit was about to leave Portsmouth, the hospitalised Corporal Todd asked his lieutenant colonel to be allowed to march out too, explaining that staying alone in hospital would kill him.[49] Soldierly solidarity also continued in action. When forming their free corps to fight against the Austrians, Franz Karl Cura and his comrades took an oath never to forsake one another in danger. After he was hit in the leg, Beß was carried to safety by his fellow jaegers. James Miller tells of how he and the other wounded were supported by their comrades during the retreat back to Quebec from the battlefield of Sainte-Foy. If a man was lost, his friends might also take revenge. After a corporal was murdered by Hindu robbers, his old comrades, including Sergeant Kenward, caught the men and hanged them without trial. After a confrontation with Dutch civilians that left a number of British troops killed and wounded, the infuriated soldiery set alight to the house from which the shots had been fired. One man fled but another was taken. The soldiers continued to shoot and mangle him for a while, and finally left his corpse to hang as an example for others.[50]

According to their own words, eighteenth-century soldiers were clearly capable of forming an attachment to their peers, of helping, caring and, occasionally, even killing for them. With such a balance of evidence, the possibility that these men also fought for their comrades, to use the modern terminology of primary group cohesion, does appear plausible.

[48] Cobbett, *Autobiography*, 45; Staniforth, 'Life'; Henly, *Life*, 10; Lamb, *Original and Authentic Journal*, 397–8. See also: Bishop, *Life and Adventures*, 156; Kirkwood, *Through so Many Dangers*, 59; Stevenson, *Soldier*, 29, Plummer, *Journal*, 31.

[49] Blennie, *Narrative*, 108–9; Sohr, *Meine Geschichte*, 47; Todd, *Journal*, 35–6. For enforcement of solidarity by formal means among Russian recruits, see: Keep, *Soldiers of the Tsar*, 157.

[50] Cura, 'Tagebuch', 32; Beß, 'Aus dem Tagebuch', 215; J. Miller, 'Memoirs of an Invalid', 37. See also: Williamson, *French and Indian Cruelty*, 58; Dominicus, *Tagebuch*, 75–6; Kenward, *Sussex Highlander*, 54, R. Brown, *Impartial Journal*, 198–201. A similar case described by Sullivan, *From Redcoat to Rebel*, 107–8.

Nevertheless, the question of whether primary group cohesion is a relevant concept for old-regime warfare is a complex one. Lynn and Spring cite the mess as a potentially equivalent institution, which could play the role of a primary group. Their argument is not without problems, however. Firstly, unlike the squad or company, which doubles as the primary group in modern armies, the mess had no tactical role to fulfil. Although regulations drawn in the later half of the century referred to the *Corporalschaft*, the Russian *kapralstvo* and even the French *ordinaire* as a tactical unit headed by a corporal, its actual combat role is unclear. The platoon still remained the basic tactical unit, often cutting across existing companies, of which existing messes were a part. Moreover, in battle it was rare to arrange troops in individual formations smaller than battalions. On the other hand, unlike in modern warfare, where one's immediate combat partners can be dispersed over a wide area, old-regime formations were closely concentrated. The frontage of a Prussian battalion averaged about one hundred metres. The physical proximity to one's comrades, considered an important reinforcing factor in modern studies of combat motivation, would still apply to old-regime combat formations, even if messmates were allocated to different platoons. Under such conditions, one did not have to be arrayed shoulder to shoulder with immediate messmates in order to be seen by them. Moreover, in this situation, hiding one's personal performance would probably prove impossible.[51]

It can be argued, however, that the relevance of primary groups for old-regime combat motivation is largely conceptual. Although rarely interpreted in such terms, primary group cohesion presents a classic example of active social control enforced by one's peers. Although the basic loyalty prevailing within a primary group is to one's immediate combat partners, the actual values it promotes, such as courage, camaraderie and mutual responsibility, are advantageous for the official goals of the military organisation. However, in order to prove effective, members of the primary group have to be involved within their immediate military milieu. The reason for this is based on two non-mutually exclusive factors. The first is willing association with the prevailing values, which makes their pursuit worthwhile in itself. The second factor is the reluctance to pay the social price for going against the accepted social norms which operate within that setting. As demonstrated above, this aspect clearly applies to old-regime soldiers who willingly associated with their comrades and their officers. Moreover, they have internalised an institutional culture based on a specific understanding of honour.

[51] Lynn, *Giant*, 440–2; C. Duffy, *Army of Frederick the Great*, 69–70, 84.

Lastly, some of them were clearly not indifferent to the broader social and political framework within which they served. Consequently, determining the actual eighteenth-century equivalent of the modern primary group becomes less relevant. It is important to understand whether old-regime armies had group standards of behaviour that were relevant for combat situations. If the answer is positive, one needs to see if and how were they enforced.

The Second World War US troops interviewed for Stouffer's study reported guilt when they were out of combat while their comrades were either fighting or were about to be sent into battle. Old-regime troops clearly shared similar sentiments. Rather than rejoicing at the prospect of safe and comfortable service, Russian soldiers detached from their units during the Kościuszko's Uprising to guard the estates of the loyalist Polish nobility cried with despair and begged to remain with the field army, which was marching towards the enemy. After Gibraltar was invested by the Spanish, regimental tailor Thomas Cranfield requested his commander 'to allow him to take his share in the duties and dangers of the private soldier, from which, by his employment, he was exempt'. Besides, men suspected of knowingly avoiding combat could be accused of cowardice. After he was discharged from hospital, Lamb, whose regiment had already left Dublin on its way to Canada, was offered to go to England on recruiting service. However, Lamb thought it was 'incompatible with spirit of a soldier to avoid service in time of war while his comrades were fighting', and quickly left for Cork where he caught up with his regiment just before it embarked. Two years later, after his first escape from captivity, Lamb was offered the opportunity to return to Britain, but asked to stay serving in North America. The survivors of the flank companies of the 22nd regiment, which numbered only eighteen men out of the original 210 after the two first attacks on Bharatpur, participated in the third storm despite orders to remain in camp. The ropemaker in whose house James Thompson was billeted during his first winter in North America took a liking to his lodger and offered to take Thompson as a business partner, procure his discharge and marry him to his daughter. Thompson rejected this generous proposal, explaining that he would be branded as a coward if he left service before any fighting has taken place. On another occasion, Thompson, who had just reported to the guardhouse following a disagreement with an officer, learned that his company was to be sent that night into the trenches. Fearful for his reputation, Thompson quietly eloped from under arrest and rejoined his men. Staniforth's wife, who married him on the understanding that he would soon leave the army, was disappointed when Staniforth was sent back to his regiment in Flanders. Reminded of his original promise,

Staniforth replied that because a big battle was soon expected, applying for a discharge would make him a laughing stock in the eyes of his comrades.[52]

Lingering in hospital could prove equally suspicious. Thompson tells of a fellow sergeant who, on hearing of a coming battle, left hospital, being afraid he might be considered as a 'skulker', a term which was already widely used to denote soldiers who deliberately avoided their duty. News of upcoming action could exert a miraculous healing effect. According to a British surgeon serving in the disease-ridden Caribbean, while new patients were arriving at the hospital every day, not a single man reported when the regiment was ordered to attack Demerara. Moreover, while many men genuinely recovered just before the battle, others escaped the hospital, fearing the doctors would not discharge them. According to Sergeant Johnson, ill and hungry men abandoned the hospitals and fell in with their regiments as they were marching out of Quebec to fight against the French at Sainte-Foy. Löffler concealed his weakness from the doctors so he could be sent back to the army as soon as possible.[53] Some wounded soldiers refused to leave their posts. John Haime tells how at Fontenoy fellow Methodist William Clemens refused to evacuate to the rear despite his broken arm, saying he could still hold his sword in his second hand. James Miller, whose neck was scratched by a musket ball during the British capture of Martinique, remained with his company until the next day. Some men stayed on despite being entreated to retire by their own superiors. A grenadier from the Bourbonnais Regiment, attached to a naval gun crew, refused to abandon his post despite being grazed by a cannon ball which burnt his skin and lodged numerous splinters in his leg. During the march of the British army along the Nile to Cairo, the exhausted Joseph Coates initially rejected the offer of being put on the barge which was conveying the sick men. Coates explains to his readers that 'honour is much more valuable to a soldier, than a precarious life of toil and privation' and that he would take every sacrifice rather than being suspected of avoiding his duty. Only after he was given a formal order by his captain and after his

---

[52] Stouffer et al., *American Soldier: Combat*, 136–7; Starkov, *Raskazi*, 21–2; Cranfield, *Useful Christian*, 14–5; Lamb, *Memoir*, 107; Lamb, *Original and Authentic Journal*, 262–3; Kenward, *Sussex Highlander*, 68–9; J. Thompson, *Bard*, 128–9, 156; Staniforth, 'Life', 340; For the firsthand account of the sergeant who led the forlorn hope at Bharatpur and who had to cheat the doctors in order to be allowed to participate in the fourth and last storm of the fortress, see: Shipp, *Memoirs*, vol. I, 195–205.

[53] J. Thompson, *Bard*, 203–4; M. Duffy, 'British Army and the Caribbean Expeditions', 73; J. Johnson, 'Memoirs of the Siege of Quebec', 120; Löffler, *Der alte Sergeant*, 44; See also: Todd, *Journal*, 255–6; Grose, *Classical Dictionary*, q.v. 'Skulker'.

comrades pleaded with him did Coates agree to go by boat – but for *one* day only.[54]

Fear of stigma was not the only reason why men insisted on remaining at their posts. Seeing that Blennie was hit in the ankle, his officer called on him to fall out, but Blennie refused and later explained that he did it for his comrades: '[n]ot that I loved to stay in a place of danger; but I did not want to leave them in the time of it'. This sense of mutual responsibility could be further reinforced by the sense that risk or exertions were shared equally. After complaining of the very hard work he endured while building a Canadian fort, Henry remarks that 'as I had as much as another, it reconciled me a little'. This could also be promoted officially, as in the French army in front of Yorktown, where soldiers were formally forbidden to exchange with or pay another man to replace them for their spell of duty in the siege trenches. When one of Bernos' comrades questioned the order by which men were allocated to the pickets during the siege of Bergen op Zoom, the soldiers took the matter to captain for resolution. Interestingly, although he knew that his comrade pretended to misunderstand the duty roster, Bernos tells that the issue was discussed 'without bitterness'. This suggests that arguing too assertively for one's rights in such a situation might appear suspect. In addition to a sense of fairness, soldiers could also be guided by an individual sense of duty. Sergeant Thompson tells of fellow Sergeant Duncan McPhee who, when posted as a sentry near Louisbourg, refused to 'quit his post' when the tide came in. McPhee almost drowned before an officer formally ordered him to move to dry land. This uncompromising punctuality in the execution of his orders won McPhee personal approval from General Wolfe.[55]

As we have already shown, cowards could be shamed publicly, but such men could also be dealt with informally without the intervention of the military authorities. Corporal Todd summarily dismissed one of his pioneers who failed to return promptly after being sent to escort a wounded comrade to the rear. At the battle of the Plains of Abraham, as the highlanders were preparing to attack, their regimental piper, whose music was supposed to encourage the men, was nowhere to be found. The charge succeeded anyhow, and the disgraced piper was ostracised by the soldiers. According to Thompson, he was compelled to draw his provisions independently, as no mess would take him. After his music

---

[54] Haime, 'Life', 222–3; J. Miller, 'Memoirs of an Invalid', 56–7; 'Milton S. Latham Journal', 16–7; Coates, *Narrative*, 73. See also: Bishop, *Life and Adventures*, 21–2; MacLeod, *Memoirs*, 65; B. Miller, 'Adventures', 17.

[55] Blennie, *Narrative*, 93; Grace, *History of the Life and Sufferings*, 10; Flohr, *American Campaigns*, 30; Bernos, 'Souvenirs de campagne', 753; J. Thompson, *Bard*, 150–1; see: ibid., 182, for another sergeant who insisted on punctual adherence to military protocol.

helped to rally a broken regiment at the battle of Sainte-Foy, the piper recovered his reputation and, consequentially, his messmates. According to Yakov Starkov, an identical arrangement existed in the Russian army, where 'if the soldiers noticed that one of their comrades was disorderly or lazy, they would make his life miserable. Such a man would neither have voice within the circle of his companions, nor hear a kind word from them; this would inevitably force him to improve'.[56] In such cases, the sanction and the reinstatement in favour were both accomplished informally, without any action on the part of the military superiors. Loss of reputation and the public contempt it brought was not a negligible matter. Steininger, who rejoined his Piedmontese regiment after voluntarily returning from his first desertion attempt, was goaded as a coward. Fighting with a number of men who joked at his expense proved useless, prompting Steininger to desert again. A similar reason was cited by John Blacknell of the 8th Regiment of Foot at his court martial. After returning from hospital, Blacknell failed to complete his drill, which earned him a kick from his captain, who further called him out loud a 'malingering scoundrel'. After the men 'frequently reflected on him for it', Blacknell deserted. After spending two months there, Alexander Alexander left hospital before making a full recovery because he was unable to bear any longer the rowdy jokes of the other soldiers, who deemed him a malingerer.[57]

Alexander's military career also illustrates the social price to be paid by men who were unable or unwilling to adhere to the prescribed group standards. An illegitimate son and former overseer of slaves in the Caribbean, Alexander enlisted in the hope of obtaining a quick promotion to a commissioned rank. According to his account, Alexander's refusal to drink away his bounty immediately earned him the scorn of the vulgar drunkards with whom he enlisted. Moreover, as an aspiring gentleman himself, 'I had wants they dreamed not of', and Alexander's insistence on bring provided with separate billets did not make him any more popular. Occasionally treating these ragamuffins to a drink did not soothe them either. The same story repeated itself after he joined his regiment. Every mistake at drill was ruthlessly mocked by the privates and NCOs who, instead of praising Alexander for his sober conduct, turned out to be

---

[56] Todd, *Journal*, 169; J. Thompson, *Bard*, 185–6, 200; Starkov, *Raskazi*, 23. On another occasion Starkov tells a story which implies that cowards who dishonoured their units in battle could be killed by their own comrades, see: ibid., 223–5.

[57] Steininger, *Leben und Abenteuer*, 24–5; Helen C. McCorry, 'Desertion and Discipline', *JSAHR*, 71, (1993), 47; Alexander, *Life*, vol. I, 127. For more sneering on cowards, see: Bräker, 'Lebensgeschichte', 464–5', NAM 1959-02-46, 'Account of the Raid on St. Malo by Sergeant Porter', (June 7 1757); Büttner, 'Narrative', 239.

a crew of petty tyrants. Ridiculed for being the only man in his room who owned a trunk, Alexander's plan to pacify everyone by giving away the trunk and its contents to the NCOs brought no relief. He only made new enemies among those who received no gift. Alexander's education and occasional work as a clerk made him a target of further puns as 'skulker'. Most importantly, his demeanour while enduring these insults appeared only to provoke his tormentors further.[58] Alexander's experience was completely different to that of *Magister* Laukhard. Former professor at the University of Halle, Laukhard began his military service by heading directly to the largest tavern in town and drinking *Bruderschaft* with all the soldiers who were there. According to Laukhard, his successful subsequent integration into his regiment owed greatly to the fact that his new comrades were impressed that Laukhard, despite his higher social standing, always treated them as equals.[59]

Alexander's snobbery did not have to be manifest to alienate his fellow soldiers, while Laukhard's social refinement and education, which he never compromised or vulgarised, did not prevent him from winning the respect of his comrades. Their different experiences can be summarised by one term – acceptance. Not only success but even basic social functioning within the military society was based on acknowledgement of institutional norms and established group standards. Although some were promoted officially, it was their internalisation by the rank and file that made them truly effective. Rather than witnessing tension, old-regime armies presented an actual symbiosis between social disciplining and social control. The former aimed to involve men within the ongoing war and the authority of their superiors. The latter was based on attachment to one's immediate comrades, but also to the military collective in general. Formal and informal value systems often corresponded, rarely clashed and, all in all, contributed in parallel towards the overall goals of the military organisation. Judging from the available evidence, men accepted both. Whether the basic motive of an individual to abide by the standards of either system was idealistic or practical is less important here. Likewise when it came to combat. Successfully sown during the sustaining stage, the stated values of bravery and honour demanded that one to stick by one's comrades and by one's superiors, irrespective of whether they enjoyed the personal affections of their subordinates, as did the broader political system on whose behalf they served. In addition to the possibility of a formal punishment, a soldier who challenged the

[58] Alexander, *Life*, vol. I, 77–8, 82–90, 144; For another soldier who did not integrate into his mess, see: Uhlmann, *Abwechslende Fortün*, 19.

[59] Laukhard, *Leben und Schicksale*, 143–4, 150.

established norms by exhibiting dishonour, personal cowardice or by abandoning his peers could incur social death. This was an unbearable price to pay at the hands of one's most immediate and, for many eighteenth-century soldiers, only available social network. Coercive means were limited and they could not be fully enforced in combat. The direct remunerative gains to be made in battle were negligible, especially when compared to the risks taken. It was the primacy of normative compliance that prompted the majority of men to fight when ordered. It also helped them to hold their posts long enough. Here lies the collective cause of old-regime combat motivation.

Concluding Remarks

Due to a strange twist of fate, Prussian Pastor Christian Täge came to observe the opening moves of the battle of Zorndorf from inside the Russian formation. The sun glittered on the weapons of the Prussian troops as they slowly advanced towards the strong defensive position occupied by the Russian army. As the enemy continued its measured and majestic approach, the senior Russian chaplain, accompanied by numerous assistants carrying religious banners, rode along the line blessing the troops. After they were thus sanctified with the sign of the cross, the soldiers drank from small flasks that they kept under their belts and concluded by loudly shouting 'URA', the Russian battle cry, thus 'demonstrating their determination to meet the approaching enemy'. Täge remembers what he calls the dreadful and beautiful moment when the Prussian army suddenly wheeled into an oblique order. First, the pounding of the Prussian drums was heard, but as they moved closer Täge recognised the music played by the oboists. It was the Lutheran hymn 'Ich bin ja, Herr, in deiner Macht', whose melody, as Täge states, he could never hear again without feeling great sadness. On their side, the Russians firmly kept to their formation in perfect silence. Then the artillery opened fire, hell broke loose and Täge retired to safer spot.[1]

Täge saw more than just the initial manoeuvres typical of an old-regime battle. He also witnessed the simple and, at the same time, powerful means intended to reinforce one's own resolve and weaken that of the enemy. Like many of the other factors considered over the preceding pages, the mental preparation for combat was both individual and collective, both formal and informal. Basic coping strategies – prayer, alcohol and fatalism – were all there. Music and shouting, intended as much to distract oneself as to intimidate the enemy; solemn rituals, be it the intake of an individual portion of vodka or the singing of an inspiring hymn to the regimental band; the empowering feeling of being part of a large collective; and the disempowering thoughts when seeing

---

[1] Täge, *Lebensgeschichte*, 179–81.

a collective just as large and unified advancing towards you from the other side: all formed part of the final all-out effort intended to defeat fear and overcome the basic instinct of self-preservation. In the case of Zorndorf, all of these proved spectacularly successful even by old-regime standards. By the day's end, one-third of the Prussians and as many as half of the Russians, an overall total of some 30,000 men, were killed or wounded, but neither side broke. However, the success of both armies in avoiding disintegration and retaining their effectiveness as military forces was not just a product of one morning. Combat was the final stage in long process which prepared soldiers physically, but also mentally. While there can be as many individual coping strategies as there are fighters, they become active only once the basic initial resolve to enter combat is firmly established. This volume concentrated on the broader social forces which helped to make this resolve possible.

Desertion offered the most obvious alternative open to those unwilling to serve and fight. This option was constantly available, from the day the recruit first took the bounty or was conscripted. Then came the campaigns with their long marches, which strained whatever means of control had been originally in place. Moreover, Zorndorf was not the first major battle fought by the Prussian and the Russian field armies during the Seven Years War. Their ranks had many veterans who have been in combat before. Nonetheless, over 70,000 men made it to Zorndorf that morning. The battle started at 9 am with a two-hour cannonade, followed by the first Prussian infantry attack. After a fire fight from a distance of as little as forty metres, Russian troops counterattacked with bayonets. Russian heavy cavalry was sent in pursuit of the fleeing enemy, only to be counterattacked in turn by the Prussian cavalry reserve, which hacked its way into the Russian right wing. A further series of desperate attacks and counterattacks followed. As ammunition ran out, men fought hand to hand with bayonets and musket butts. Some soldiers escaped into the surrounding forests and swamps. Täge himself tried to leave the battlefield in the company of a wounded Russian general.[2] However, the majority of the men fought on until the approaching darkness forced the opponents to separate, almost twelve hours after the battle had originally begun. Next morning, both armies still eyed each other across the same field. This study argues that those who fought, survived and stayed in the ranks did so willingly.

---

[2] Täge, *Lebensgeschichte*, 182–8. For another extraordinary account of Zorndorf, but from the other side of the battlefield, see: Hoppe, 'Wahrhafte Schilderung', 185–91; For good modern descriptions of the battle, see: C. Duffy, *Russia's Military Way*, 86–91; C. Duffy, *Frederick the Great: A Military Life*, 163–72; The best recent study of the battle is Adam Storring's forthcoming *Zorndorf, 1758*.

The mutual slaughter in Zorndorf is a dramatic but not unique instance, demonstrating that coercion alone cannot explain the motivation of common soldiers in the armies of old-regime Europe. Even if it is assumed that discipline in these armies was as brutal as its traditional portrayal would suggest, it is hard to believe that it could surpass the sheer ferocity of old-regime combat experience, which ran contrary to every human instinct. However, it is the virtual impunity with which reluctant soldiers could escape from military service throughout much of the period which reveals the greatest single weakness of the conventional historiography. On this point we are left with a further paradox. With the possible exception of monks and convicts, soldiers were the most closely-controlled group in early-modern society. Their time, their clothes and even their posture were all subject to orders and regulations. Moreover, their physical description, as recorded in the regimental rolls, formed what was probably the closest eighteenth-century equivalent of a modern identity database. Nevertheless, in spite of all these measures, most deserters were not recaptured at all, while others took advantage of pardons and the overall leniency of a system which was unable to stem desertion by its own means. The fact that desertion could be curtailed only with the help of civilians is revealing of the weakness of direct control mechanisms in eighteenth-century Europe. Moreover, what does it tell us about the actual power wielded by old-regime authorities, not only over their military forces, but also over the general populace?

Just like their civilian counterparts in early-modern Europe, old-regime common soldiers do not come across as passive or indifferent. There were numerous means available by which these men could challenge the system of which they were a part. However, it is actually the mutineers and the defiant soldiers who provide the best proof for the basic acceptance of the established army hierarchy. The demands put forward by the men of the line typically aimed to address a specific grievance, not to overhaul the military system. On their side, the officers responded by compromising, even if they would rarely admit this fact openly. The smooth functioning of eighteenth-century armies could not have been achieved without a substantial degree of negotiation and pragmatism. This is not to say that old-regime military discipline was lenient, or that eighteenth-century armies did not have their share of sadistic officers and NCOs. Nevertheless, military service in this period was not a straightforwardly coercive enterprise, as it has commonly been portrayed. Moreover, the soldiers were not entirely toothless, and the mere possibility that men of the line could retaliate against a brutal officer must have kept the latter in check to some extent.

The importance of seeing old-regime common soldiers as actors rather than victims of historical processes and their personal circumstances comes across most clearly when one considers their motivation to enlist. Most eighteenth-century armies were heavily dependent on voluntary recruitment, but persuading a man to take the bounty was a task only half done; the recruit also had to be convinced to stay. Thankfully for the recruiters, military service either appealed or, at least, was a likelier resort for men of a particular type. This was a known fact, and it prompted armies to present themselves to their would-be soldiers as a realm of honour, joy and plenty. Some recruits found this self-fashioning to be too rosy, and absconded, but many more remained. Whatever was promised initially, what was actually offered proved satisfactory enough for the majority. Military service could bring a degree of material stability, but the recruits had another important consideration in mind. Rather than trying to advance through their original social milieu, the army offered these men an alternative system. It was this institutional aspect that clearly appealed to many. The association with a higher class, direct service under nobles and the monarch, gentlemen's clothes and status and, at their left side, a sword. The culture of honour in old-regime armies encompassed not only the officers but also the rank and file, where it prompted a sense of corporate identity, professional pride and *esprit de corps*. It also cultivated a distinctively military form of masculinity, marked by a stated indifference to pain and hardship.

The horizontal bonds which these values helped to create in peacetime became all the more crucial when the army went on campaign. Irrespective of what soldiers might have felt as individuals, they were subject to a code of behaviour which required fighting, bravery and sticking by your comrades as long as it was possible. Admittedly, this system still contained an inherent element of compulsion, but this was very different from the model suggested by previous scholarship. The desire to retain the respect of one's peers proved stronger than the fear of battle. Nevertheless, old-regime soldiers did not fight just because they were afraid of disappointing their immediate messmates. The problem with overstressing primary group-based analysis is that it leaves out the broader fabric of values that held armies together. As a self-selecting group, soldiers often had a history of refusing to take the path laid out for them by their families and native communities, and thus tended to be defiant rather than deferential types. Yet most saw their relations with their officers in strikingly positive terms. This attachment was the product of contractual obligation and moral authority rather than force. The officers' orders were obeyed because these they were considered legitimate, but also because the soldiers were not necessarily all that indifferent to what they were fighting for. The sense that war was fought for a good or just cause was important, as were notions of military sacrifice and glory. These values appealed to men of the line well before they were said to have been democratised by Revolutionary France.[3] If previous studies have emphasised the role of the French Revolution as a universal turning point in warfare, the current volume stresses some of the similarities and continuities between old-regime, revolutionary and, subsequently, Napoleonic armies.

In addition to the alleged contrast with the enthusiastic élan of the French revolutionary troops, there is a further reason why modern historians have often taken a dim view of the experience of common soldiers in old-regime Europe. The gradual shift from contract to standing armies, which occurred during the previous century, noticeably worsened the conditions of the rank and file. Contracts outlining the mutual responsibilities of men and their captains were replaced with a one-sided obligation of long, often lifetime, service to the state. The introduction of drill, which increased the effectiveness of a military unit as a whole, lessened the value of the individual soldier. Consequently, their status as an autonomous community operating under its own jurisdiction was progressively curtailed. Soldiers became subjects both to discipline imposed from above and to a growing number of regulations and rules aiming to control not only their professional performance, but also their personal lives. Even when marriage was not outright banned, it became harder and harder to support a family after pay rates were cut all across Europe in the late seventeenth century. Greater responsibilities, demanding drill, restrained mobility, harsher punishments and lower salaries turned the ferocious mercenaries who roamed the continent up to and including the Thirty Years War into universally despised social outcasts.[4] The current volume reveals some of the limits of this interpretation, especially concerning the extent to which the disciplining of the rank and file was accomplished. Moreover, this process of proletarianisation did not stamp out soldiers' self-perception as members of a distinct social order engaged in an inherently honourable activity. On this point, there was a substantial continuity not only between the regular armies of old-regime Europe and the people's army of the French Revolution, but also with the mercenary armies of the sixteenth and seventeenth centuries. Soldiers serving in different military systems and under different forms of

---

[3] For an excellent article on the understanding of honour in the French army after the revolution, see: Lynn, 'Toward an Army of Honor'.

[4] Parrott, *Business of War*, 167–8, 286–9. See also: Redlich, *German Military Enterpriser*, vol. II, 274–7; Burschel, *Soldner im Nordwestdeutschland*; Swart, 'From "Landsknecht" to "Soldier"'.

government could still have much in common. While it is very tempting to suggest that honour is a universal military phenomenon, one cannot maintain this without undertaking wide-ranging comparative studies across numerous periods and cultures. Nevertheless, it can safely be said that the yearning for respect, if not from society at large, then at least from one's own immediate comrades, was assuredly one of the defining features of soldiering in the lower ranks for much of the previous five hundred years.

Bibliography

N.B. Symbols

* Item written by an old-regime common soldier or a biographical account by a relative or a close acquaintance.
# Printed edition of the manuscript is available.
English translations of primary sources are mentioned when available.

Manuscript Sources

Bedfordshire and Luton Archives and Record Service, Bedford

R 769, 'Duke of Bedford's Regiment of Foot'

Institut für Stadtgeschichte, Frankfurt am Main

*#S1/367 Depositum Adolf Reuber Nr. 1, 'Tagebuch Grenadiers Johannes Reuber'
*#S5/291 [Johann Georg Schreyer], 'Brieftagebuch des Fledschers der Kursächsischen Schweizergarde'

Glasgow City Library

*Ms. 72 John Burrell, 'An Account of the Allied Army's Travels & Actions in Germany, with a Just & True Account of all the General Engagements & Skirmishes they had with the French army beginning in the year 1758 to the end of the year 1761 by Trooper/Farrier John Burrell, 2nd Royal North British Dragoons, The Scots Greys'

British Library, London

Add MS
    21,643–21,651, Miscellaneous correspondence of various persons, principally with Colonel Bouquet

38,190–38,489, Liverpool Papers
44063–44084, Loudoun Papers
*45,662, Richard Humphrys, 'Journal of Richard Humphrys, 28th Foot, 1757–62'
Mss Eur
  *#B296 Samuel Hickson Papers

Grenadier Guards Regimental Archive, London

*A03/03 George Darby 'Account of the Capture of Valenciennes by the British by Serj George Darby 1st Reg. of Guards.' (13 August 1793) 'Account of the Battle of Lincelles by do.' (26 August 1793)
B09/004 'Monthly Returns'
D3/002, 'Deserter Record 1760–1820'
*E6/003, William Pell 'A Narrative of the Life of Sergeant William Pell, First Foot Guards, (Written by Himself) From his first Inlisting, Jany 18th 1779'

National Archives, Kew, London

HCA – Records of the High Court of the Admiralty
  HCA 30 Admiralty Miscellanea
WO – War Office
  WO 1 War Office and Predecessors, In Letters and Miscellaneous Papers
  WO 28 Records of Military Headquarters
  WO 71 Judge Advocate General's Office: Courts Martial Proceedings and Board of General Officers' Minutes
  WO 85 Judge Advocate General's Office: Deputation Books
  WO 284 Gibraltar Garrison: Orders

Templer Study Centre, National Army Museum, London (NAM)

1950-10-9 'Recruiting Poster for 88th Regiment of Foot'
*#1959-02-46, 'Account of the raid on St. Malo by sergeant Porter of Grenadier company, 23rd foot', 5 June 1758
1968-07-260 'Order book of Ensign Chaytor 3rd Foot Guards in Germany 1–26 May 1762'
1969-07-17 'Recruiting Poster of the 1st Battalion of Pennsylvania Loyalists'
*1972-01-36 (1), 'Account of American service and letters by James Green'
1975-11-30 'Recruiting poster for the 6th (1st Warwickshire) Regiment of Foot (1795)'
*1976-06-5 'Journal kept by an anonymous non-Commissioned officer or soldier between 29 Mar-19 May 1791'

*1976-06-16 'Manuscript letter by John Vardin of the 86th reg, of foot – service in 1802'

*1976-07-40 'Manuscript letter written by gunner James Hardcastle addressed to Hardcastle's father' (1743)

#1976-09-3 'Orderly book kept by officer in 18th Regiment of Foot, in North America, chiefly encamped outside Boston 26 Jun 1774–5 Jun 1775'

*1976-10-35 'Letter 1803; sent by a soldier in the 84th Regiment of Foot to the Father of Sergeant James Kaye'

1980-12-21 'Recruiting poster for the King's Light Dragoons' (1779)

*1986-11-1 '9 Letters of Sergeant Calder (American War) 1778–5'

*1987-10-7 'Manuscript letter written by Corporal Samuel Blomeley, Coldtstream Guards, to Thomas Ford, a clerk at the Bank of England, describing their voyage in Ireland (2 July 1798)'

1992-07-261 'Poster of the Sussex Light Dragoons' (1779–80)

*1992-12-146 'A Sort account of the Life and Transactions of James Thrupp'

*2001-01-611 'Letter from Johnston Abercromby, 3rd Battalion Grenadiers, to his wife Betsy, describing the capture of various French West Indian Islands' (27 April 1794)

2001-02-400 Major George Nicholson, 'Transactions in the Buffs from 1744 to 1776 included'

2002-07-251 'Statement re: Riot committed by soldiers in Aberdeen the night of the first of August last [1746]'

*2004-03-75 (1) 'Two manuscript letters written by Private James Morgan, Coldstream Guards to his father'

* 2008-06-4 'Soldier's entire letter written by Private W. Hopkin, 6th Company, 4th Regiment, Madras European Infantry, from Madras Hospital, Fort St, George Madras to England dated 16th February 1786'

*#2009-07-31 [John Matson], 'Journal of an unidentified private soldier, 100th regiment of foot relating to the Second Mysore War'

Centre of Kentish Studies, Maidstone

*U1350 Z9A, James Miller, 'Memoirs of an Invalid'

New York Historical Society, New York

*RV Bremner, John, 'Diary and Memorandum Book, 1756–1764'

Bodleian Library, Oxford

G.Pamph. 2850(2) Recruiting poster of the Third Regiment of Foot Guards (1795)

Archives Nationales, Paris

Mar – Fonds Marine
B4 Campagnes

Bibliothèque Nationale, Paris

NUMM-109500, [Joseph-Charles Bonin], 'Voyage au Canada, dans le nord de l'Amérique septentrionale, fait depuis l'an 1751 à 1761' [Accessible online]

Green Howards Regimental Museum, Richmond, Yorkshire

M 383 'Counter Petition on behalf of ensign Lemisden and George Clark Apprentice'

Médiathèque André Malraux, Strasbourg

*Fonds Patrimoniaux MS 15 Georg [Daniel] Flohr, *Reisen Beschreibung von America welche das Hochlöbliche Regiment von Zweybrücken hat gemacht zu Wasser und zu Land vom Jahr 1780 bis 84. Geschehen zu Strassburg den 5 . . . anno 1787*

Österreichisches Staatsarchiv, Vienna

KA – Kriegsarchiv
    ML –Musterliste

Service Historique de la Défense, Vincennes

GR – Armée de Terre
    1 J Conseils de guerre d'Ancien Régime, 1740-1792
    Fonds privés
        1 KT (témoignages)
        *#800 Fonds Amblard
        1 Kmi (microfilms)
        78 Microfilm Amblard
    1 M Catalogue général des manuscrits des archives du ministère de la Défense
    YA – Archives administratives du département de la Guerre XVIIe-XVIIIe Siècles
    YC – Contrôles de troupes

Library of Congress, Washington

*'MCC 1907 Milton S. Latham Journal'

Published Primary Sources

Adye, Stephen Payne, *A Treatise on Courts Martial, also an Essay on Military Punishments and Rewards*, 5th edn, (London: J. Murray and S. Highley, 1799)

*Aitken, James, 'The Voluntary Confession of James Aitken, Commonly Called John the Painter', *Universal Magazine of Knowledge and Pleasure*, 60 (March, 1777), 148–50

*Alexander, Alexander, *The Life of Alexander Alexander, Written by Himself*, John Howell (ed.), 2 vols., (Edinburgh: William Blackwood, 1830)

*Allfärtty, Johann Gottlieb, *Friedrich des Großen letzter Dragoner*, Gustav Rieck (ed.), (Breslau: Verlag Komptoir, 1838)

*Amblard, André, 'Histoire des campagnes de l'Armée de Rochambaud en Amérique', in Francis Barbe (ed.), 'De Lussas vers l'aventure ... dans l'Histoire de France', *Revue de la Société des Enfants et Amis de Villeneuve-de-Berg*, Nouvelle Série, 57 (2001), 183–98, 58 (2002), 239–56, 59 (2003), 183–90, 60 (2004), 229–42

*Ancell, Samuel, *A Circumstantial Journal of the Long and Tedious Blockade of Gibraltar*, (Liverpool: Charles Wosencroft, 1784)

*Andrew, James, 'The last Speech, Confession and dying words of James Andrew, who was executed in the Grassmarket of Edinburgh, upon Wednesday the 4th day of February 1784 for the horrid crime of Highway Robbery', in R.C. and J.M. Anderson, *Quicksilver: A Hundred Years of Coaching 1750–1850*, (Newton Abbot: David & Charles, 1973), 174–7

*Asteroth, Johann Valentin, *Valentin Asteroth's Tagebuch aus dem amerikanischen Unabhaengigkeitskrieg, 1776–1783*, (Zweigverein, Treysa and Ziegenhain: Verein für Hessische Geschichte und Landeskunde, 1966)

— 'The Asteroth Diary', in *Diaries of a Hessian Chaplain and Chaplain's Assistant*, Bruce E. Burgoyne (ed. and tr.), (n.p.: Johannes Schwalm Historical Association, 1990), 17–60

— *Das Tagebuch des Sockenstrickers Johann Valentin Asteroth aus Treysa (1776–1831)*, Heinz Krause (ed.), (Schwalmstadt-Treysa: Stadtgeschichtlicher Arbeitskreis, 1992)

*Astley, Philip, *Remarks on the Profession and Duty of a Soldier*, (London: P. Astley, 1794)

*Aulenbach, John Philip, 'Autobiography of Philip Aulenbach', J.A. Shaffer (tr.), in Daniel Luther Roth (ed.), *Acadie and the Acadians*, 3rd edn, (Utica, New York: LC. Childs, 1891), 361–5

*Aytoun, James, 'Private Soldiers in the Eighteenth Century', *The Cornhill Magazine*, 54 (1923), 653–64

— *Redcoats in the Caribbean*, A.S. Lewis (ed.), (Blackborn: East Lancashire Regiment Museum, 1984)

Barrington, William Wildman, *An Eighteenth-Century Secretary at War: The Papers of William Viscount Barrington*, Tony Hayter (ed.), Publications of the Army Records Society 4, (London: Bodley Head, 1988)

Bates, Ephraim Tristram, *The Life and Memoirs of Mr. Ephraim Tristram Bates, commonly called Corporal Bates, a Heart Broken Soldier*, (London: Malachi, 1756)

*'The Battle of Minden – 1 August, 1759', Charles Firth (ed.), *JSAHR*, 7 (1928), 126–8

Beccaria, Cesare, *On Crimes and Punishments and Other Writings*, Richard Bellamy (ed.), Richard Davies (tr.), Cambridge Texts in the History of Political Thought, (Cambridge University Press, 1995)

*Beeger, Friedrich Wilhelm, *Seltsame Schicksale eines alten preußischen Soldaten*, (Ueckermünde, 1850)

*Behrens, Johann Heinrich, *Lebensgeschichte des 105 Jährigen in Wolfenbüttel lebenden Invaliden-Unterofficiers Joh. Heinr. Behrens, eines Zeitgenossen und Kriegers Friedrichs des Grossen*, (Wolfenbüttel: L. Holle, 1840)

*Bense, Johann, 'A Brunswick Grenadier with Bourgoyne: The Journal of Johann Bense, 1776–1783', Mary C. Lynn (ed.), Helga Doblin (tr.), *New York History*, 66 (1985), 421–44

*Bernos, Charles-Étienne, 'Souvenirs de campagne d'un soldat de régiment Limousin (1741–1748)', *Carnet de Sabretache*, 10 (1902), 668–90, 737–62

*Berrepo, George William, 'Letter to his Mother' (2 July 1776), in Eileen A. Robertson (ed.), *The Spanish Town Papers: Some Sidelights on the American War of Independence*, (London: Cresset Press, 1959), 73–5

*Bersling, Franz, *Der böhmische Veteran: Franz Bersling's Leben, Reisen und Kriegsfahrten in allen fünf Welttheilen*, Gustav Rieck (ed.), (Schweidnitz: F.D.A. Franke, 1840)

*Beß Georg, 'Aus dem Tagebuch eines Veteranen des siebenjährigen Krieges', *Zeitschrift des Vereins für hessische Geschichte und Landeskunde*, Neue Folge, 2 (1869), 193–241

*Bishop, Matthew, *Life and Adventures of Matthew Bishop of Deddington in Oxfordshire*, (London: J. Brindley, 1744)

Bland, Humphrey, *A Treatise of Military Discipline: In Which Is Laid Down and Explained the Duty of the Officer and Soldier thro' the Several Branches of the Service*, (London: S. Buckley, 1727)

*Bleckwenn, Hans (ed.), *Preußische Soldatenbriefe*, Altpreußicher Kommiss 19, (Osnabrück: Biblio, 1982)

*[Blennie, George], *Narrative of a Private Soldier in his Majesty's 92d Regiment of Foot, Written by himself*, 2nd edn, (Glasgow University Press, 1820)

*Bonin, Charles Joseph, *Travels in New France by J.C.B.*, Sylvester K. Stevens, Donald H. Kent and Emma Edith Woods (eds.), (Harrisburg: Pennsylvania Historical Commission, 1941)

Boswell, James, *Life of Johnson*, R.W. Chapman (ed.) Oxford World's Classics, (Oxford University Press, 2008)

*Bräker, Ulrich, *The Life Story and Real Adventures of the Poor Man of Toggenburg*, Derek Bowman (tr.), (Edinburgh University Press, 1970)

— 'Lebensgeschichte und natürliche Ebentheuer des Armen Mannes im Tockenburg', Johann Heinrich Füßli (ed.) in Claudia Holliger-Wiesmann, Andreas Bürgi, Alfred Messerli et al. (eds.), *Sämtliche Schriften*, 5 vols., (Munich and Bern: Beck and P. Haupt, 1998–2010), vol. IV, 414–470

*Briefe preußischer Soldaten aus den Feldzügen 1756 und 1757 und über die Schlachten bei Lobositz und Prag, Grosser Generalstab (ed.), Beiträge und Forschungen zur Geschichte des Preußischen Heeres 2, (Berlin: Mittler 1901)

**Bristow, James, *A Narrative of the Sufferings of James Bristow, Belonging to the Bengal Artillery, during Ten Years of Captivity with Hayder Ally and Tippoo Saheb*, 2nd edn, (London: J. Murray, 1794)

**Brown, Robert, *An Impartial Journal of a Detachment from the Brigade of Foot Guards Commencing February 25th 1793, and Ending 9th May 1795*, (London: John Stockdale, 1795)

**Brown, Thomas, *A Plain Narrative of the Uncommon Sufferings and Remarkable Deliverance of Thomas Brown*, 2nd edn, (Boston: Fowle and Draper, 1760)

**Bryson, Andrew, *Andrew Bryson's Ordeal: An Epilogue to the 1798 Rebellion*, Michael Durey (ed.), Irish Narratives, (Cork University Press, 1998)

**Burke, William, *A Memoir of William Burke a Soldier of the Revolution*, (Hertford, Massachusetts: Case, Tiffany and Company, 1837)

**Butler, Robert, *Narrative of the Life and Travels of Sergeant B. Written by Himself*, (Edinburgh: David Brown, 1823)

**Büttner, Johann Carl, 'Narrative of Johann Carl Buettner in the American Revolution', in Susan E. Klepp, Farley Grubb and Anne Pfaelzer de Ortiz (eds.), *Souls for Sale: Two German Redemptioners Come to Revolutionary America*, (University Park: Pennsylvania State University Press, 2006), 201–51

**Cameron, Duncan, *The Life Adventures and Surprizing Deliverances of Duncan Cameron, Private Soldier in the Regiment of Foot, Late Sir Peter Halket's*, 3rd edn, (Philadelphia: James Chattin, 1756)

**Coates, Joseph, *The Narrative of a Soldier*, (Worcester: Thomas Hayes, 1836)

**Cobbett, William, *The Autobiography of William Cobbett: The Progress of a Plough-Boy to a Seat in Parliament*, W. Reitzel (ed.), (London: Faber, 1933)

**Cranfield, Thomas, *The Useful Christian: A Memoir of Thomas Cranfield, for about Fifty Years a Devoted Sunday-School Teacher*, (London: Religious Tract Society, 1844)

**Crawford, William, 'The Narrative of William Crawford, Private Soldier of the 29th Regiment of Foot', Don N. Hagist (ed.), *JSAHR*, 86 (2008), 315–27

— 'A Narrative of the Life and Character of William Crawford', in Don N. Hagist, *British Soldiers, American War: Voices of the American Revolution*, (Yardley, Penn.: Westholme, 2012), 60–72

**Cura, Franz Karl, 'Franz Carl Cura's Tagebuch über dessen betheiligung am österreichischen Erbfolgekriege', Joseph Würdinger (ed.) *Oberbayerisches Archiv für vaterländische Geschichte* 38 (1879), 1–41

— *Promemoria des Burghauser Hofkaminkehrermeisters an seine Kriegstaten im österreichischen Erbfolgekrieg: 1741–1745*, Max Dingler (ed.), Burghauser Geschichtsblätter, Kleine Reihe 1, (Burghausen: Stadtarchiv, 1968)

*Davis, Christian, *The Life and Adventure of Mrs. Christian Davis, Commonly Call'd Mother Ross*, (London: R. Montagu, 1740)

*Dayes, John, *Memoir of the Military Career of John Dayes, Late Paymaster Sergeant of the 5th Regiment of Foot*, Gareth Glover (ed.), (Huntington: Ken Trotman Publishing, 2004)

*Deane, John Marshall, *A Journal of Marlborough's Campaigns during the War of the Spanish Succession, 1704–1711*, David G. Chandler (ed.), Special Publication of the Society for Army Historical Research 12, (London, 1984)

*Dillon, John, *A Short Account of Mr. John Dillon*, (Bristol: P.Wine, 1772)

Ditfurth, Franz Wilhelm von, *Einhundert historische Volkslieder des Preußischen Heeres von 1675–1866*, (Berlin: Mittler, 1869)

*Döhla, Johann Conrad, 'Tagebuch eines Bayreuther Soldaten aus dem nordamerikanischen Freiheitskrieg 1777–1787', W. Von Waldenfels (ed.), *Archiv für Geschichte und Altertumskunde von Oberfranken* 25 (1912–3), Nr. 1. 81–201 and Nr. 2 107–224

— *A Hessian Diary of the American Revolution*, Bruce E. Burgoyne (tr.), (Norman: University of Oklahoma Press, 1990)

*Döhlemann, Johann Christoph, 'Diary of Johann Christoph Döhlemann, Grenadier Company, Ansbach Regiment March 1777 to September 1778', Henry J. Retzer (tr.), *Hessians*, 11 (2008), 11–7

*Dominicus, Johann Jacob, *Aus dem siebenjährigen Krieg: die Tagebuch des Musketiers Dominicus*, Dietrich Kerler (ed.), (Munich: C.H. Beck, 1891)

*[Dorman, John], 'Interesting Memoir of John Dorman (1709–1819)', *Gentleman's Magazine*, 89 (1 February 1819), 131–5

*Dresel, Johann Hermann, 'Ein brief des Wiblingwerder Bauernsohnes Johann Hermann Dresel aus dm Siebenjährigen Krieg', Rolf Dieter Kohl (ed.), *Der Märker: landeskundliche Zeitschrift für den Bereich der ehem. Grafschaft Mark und den Märkischen Kreis* 28 1979, 82–4

*Dreyer, Joseph Ferdinand, *Leben und Taten eines Preußischen Regiments-Tambours, von ihm selbst beschrieben in seinem 93ten Lebensjahre*, Altpreußicher Kommiss 22, (Osnabrück: Biblio, 1975), [1810]

*Duckett, Valentine, 'The Life, Last Words, and Dying Speech of Valentine Duckett, Who was shot for Desertion, on Boston Common, Friday Morning, Sept. 9, 1774' in Don N. Hagist, *British Soldiers, American War: Voices of the American Revolution*, (Yardley, Penn.: Westholme, 2012), 83–9

Esterhazy de Gallantha, Joseph, *Regulament und unumänderlich gebräuchliche Observations-Puncten, sowhol in Militär-ceremoniel als Öconomicis*, (Gavi: 1747)

*'Extracts from Journal of the Particular Transactions during the Siege of Quebec', in Arthur Doughty and G.W. Parmelee (eds.), *The Siege of Quebec and the Battle of Plains of Abraham*, 6 vols., (Quebec: Dessault & Proulx, 1901), vol. V, 167–89

Farquhar, George, *The Recruiting Officer*, Tiffany Stern (ed.), (London: Methuen Drama, 2010)

*Field, James, *A Devout Soldier* (Dublin: Moffat & Company, 1869)

*Flachsharr, Ludwig, 'Journal from New York to the Prisoners in the American Custody and Return to New York' in Henry J. Retzer, 'The 1783 Visit to the Hessian Yorktown Captives', *Hessians*, 20 (2007), 58–61

*Flemming, Karl Wilhelm Friedrich, 'Aus dem Tagebuche eines sächsischen Artilleristen', Paul Arras, Paul (ed.), *Wöchentliche Beilagen zu den Bautzener Nachrichten* (1891), 11–2, 15–16, 18–19, 26–27, 30–1, 34, 39, 43, 47, 58–60

*Flohr, Georg, *The American Campaigns of Georg Daniel Flohr*, Robert A. Selig (ed. and tr.), (Forthcoming)

*Fox, Ebenezer, *The Adventures of Ebenezer Fox in the Revolutionary War*, (Boston: Munroe & Francis, 1847)

*Fox, George, 'Corporal Fox's Memoir of Service, 1766–1783: Quebec, Saratoga, and the Convention Army', John A. Houlding and G. Kenneth Yates (eds.), *JSAHR*, 68 (1990), 146–68. Republished in Don N. Hagist, *British Soldiers, American War: Voices of the American Revolution*, (Yardley, Penn.: Westholme, 2012), 200–14

Frederick the Great, *Œuvres de Frédéric le Grand*, Johann D.E. Pruess (ed.), 30 vols., (Berlin: R. Decker, 1846–56)

— *Die Werke Friedrichs des Großen*, Gustav Berthold Volz (ed.), 10 vols., (Berlin: R. Hobbing, 1913–4)

— *Frederick the Great on the Art of War*, Jay Luvaas (ed. and tr.), (New York: Free Press, 1966)

*Gee, James, 'Memoirs of an Eighteenth-Century Soldier's Child', Andrew Cormack (ed.), *JSAHR*, 87 (2009), 221–4

*Glantz, Andreas Christoph, *Auszüge aus Briefen von Andreas Christoph Glantz aus Harsleben, während des französischen Krieges in den Jahren 1792–1794 an seine Frau und Verwandte in Harsleben geschrieben*, (Halberstadt: Delius Wittwe und H. Matthias, 1794)

*Grace, Henry, *The History of the Life and Sufferings of Henry Grace*, (Basingstoke: H. Grace, 1764)

*Green, William, *Where Duty Calls Me: The Experiences of William Green of Lutterworth in the Napoleonic Wars*, John and Dorothea Teague (eds.), (West Wickham: Synjon Books, 1975)

*Greenleigh, John, *The Veteran Soldier; An Interesting Narrative of the Life of the Late Serjeant Greenleigh*, (London: Religious Tract Society, 1822)

*Griffith, W. 'Memoirs and Spiritual Experience of the late Mr. W. Griffith, Senior', *The Spiritual Magazine and Zion's Casket*, (London, 1849), 118–22; 151–6; 182–6; 204–8; 242–6; 271–74; 307–10

Grose, Francis, *A Classical Dictionary of the Vulgar Tongue*, (London: S. Hooper, 1785)

*Grotehenn, Johann Heinrich Ludwig, *Briefe aus dem siebenjährigen Krieg, Lebensbeschreibung und Tagebuch*, Marian Füssel, Sven Petersen and Gerlad Scholtz (eds.), Potsdamer Schriften zur Militärgeschichte 18, (Potsdam: Militärgeschichtliches Forschungsamt, 2012)

*Haime, John, 'The Life of Mr. John Haime, Written by Himself' in *Methodists*, vol. I, 210–36

*Hale, James, *The Journal of James Hale: Late Sergeant in the Ninth Regiment of Foot*, (Cirencester and London: Philip Watkins and Longman, 1826)

*Hall, John, 'Letter to Sergeant Cabe', (September 26, 1709) in *The Tatler* 87, (October 29, 1709)

*Henly, Peter, *The Life of Peter Henly: Otherwise Peter Robinson, of Wooton Bassett of Wilts containing an account of his travels and adventures ... Written by himself*, (Calne: W. Baily, 1799)

*Hickson, Samuel, 'Diary of Samuel Hickson, 1777–1785', Basil La Bouchardiere (ed.), *Bengal Past and Present*, 49 (1935), 5–54

*Hoffman, Johann Ernst, 'Letter to his mother, (1733)' in Jürgen Kloosterhuis, *Legendäre "lange Kerls": Quellen zur Regimentskultur der Königsgrenadiere Friedrich Wilhelms I., 1713–1740*, (Berlin: Geheimes Staatsarchiv Preußischer Kulturbesitz, 2003), 171–2

*Hoppe, 'Wahrhafte Schilderung der blutigen Schlacht bei Zorndorf, von einem alten preußischen Soldaten, welcher 34 Jahr gedient und jetzt (1793) noch lebt', in Carl Daniel Küster (ed.), *Officier-Lesebuch: Historisch-militarischen Inhalts mit untermischten interessanten Anekdoten*, (Berlin: Carl Matzdorff, 1793), 178–94

Howe, William, *General Sir William Howe's Orderly Book at Charlestown, Boston and Halifax, June 17 1775 to 1776 26 May*, Benjamin Franklin Stevens (ed.), (London: B.F. Stevens, 1890)

*Hülsenberg, Kaspar, 'Letter from Grenadier Kaspar Hülsenberg to his wife', (21 January 1745), in *BBS*, 289–9

*[Hutton, Samuel], *The Life of William Hutton and the History of the Hutton Family*, Llewellynn Jewitt (ed.), Chandos Library, (London and New York: Frederick Warne and Scribner, Welford and Armstrong, 1872)

*J.R., 'Journal of the Years 1776 to 1784 Gott Save the King J.R.', Bruce E. Burgoyne (tr.), *Hessians*, 4.2 (1992), 30–39

*Jarvis, Stephen, 'An American's Experience in the British Army', Charles M. Jarvis (ed.), *Connecticut Magazine* 11 (1907), 191–215, 477–90

*Johnson, John, 'Memoirs of the Siege of Quebec and the Total Reduction of Canada', in Arthur Doughty and G.W. Parmelee, *The Siege of Quebec and the Battle of Plains of Abraham*, 6 vols., (Quebec: Dessault & Proulx, 1901), vol. V, 75–166

Johnson, Samuel, 'The Bravery of the English Common Soldier', in Donald J. Greene (ed.), *The Yale Edition of the Work of Samuel Johnson: Vol. X Political Writings*, (New Haven, 1977), 281–4

* [Jonas], *A Soldier's Journal*, (London: E. and C. Dilly, 1770)

*'A Journal of Captain's Cholmley's Batman', in Charles Hamilton (ed.), *Braddock's Defeat*, (Norman: University of Oklahoma Press, 1959), 1–35

*'A Journal of the Expedition up the River St. Lawrence', in Arthur Doughty, and G.W. Parmelee, *The Siege of Quebec and the Battle of Plains of Abraham*, 6 vols., (Quebec: Dessault & Proulx, 1901), vol. 5, 1–11

*Kappes, Jermias, 'March Route from Hessen to America: Jeremias Kappes, "Captaine d'Armes" Regiment v. Knyphausen', Henry J. Retzer (ed.), *Hessians*, 7.4 (2004), 7–14

*Kenward, William, *A Sussex Highlander: The Memoirs of Sergeant William Kenward 1767–1828*, Denis Kenward and Richard Nessbitt-Dufort (eds.), (Sedlescombe: Whydown Books, 2005)

— *A Military Life: The Life of William Kenward, 1767–1828*, Guy Mather (ed.), (Eastbourne: Whale-back Press, 2005)

*Kirkwood, Robert, *The Memoirs and Adventures of Robert Kirk, Late of the Royal Highland Regiment*, (Limerick: J. Ferrar, [1775])

— *Through so Many Dangers: The Memoirs and Adventures of Robert Kirk, Late of the Royal Highland Regiment*, Ian McCulloch and Timothy Todish (eds.), (Toronto: Robin Brass Studio, 2004)

*Kitz, Johannes, 'Report of My 1778 Attempted Visit to the Hessian Captives, by Johannes Kitz, Sergeant and Regimental Quartermaster', Henry J. Retzer (tr.), *Hessians* 9 (2006), 20–4

*Kleine, Carl Philipp, 'Letters of the Battalion Surgeon Carl Philipp Kleine', Henry J. Retzer (ed.), *Hessians* 14 (2011), 93–4

*Klöden, Karl Friedrich von, *Jugenderinnerungen*, Max Jähns (ed.), (Leipzig: F.W. Grunow, 1874)

*Koch, Berthold, *The Battle of Guilford Courthouse and the Siege and Surrender of Yorktown*, Bruce E. Burgoyne (ed. and tr.), (n.p., n.d.)

*Kozlov, Sergei A. (ed.), 'Okopnie Pisma Russkikh Soldat 1700goda' in *Istoriia Rossii do XX veka: Novye Podkhody k izucheniu* [Letters from the Trenches by Russian Soldiers from 1700] in [History of Russia until the 20th Century: New Approaches to Learning], (St Petersburg: Istoricheskaya Illustratziya, 2008), 198–213

Krafft, Johann Karl Philip von, 'Journal of Lieutenant John Charles Philip von Krafft, of the Regiment von Bose, 1776–1784', *Collections of the New York Historical Society*, 15 (1882), 1–202

Küster, Carl Daniel, *Bruchstück seines Campagnelebens im siebenjährigen Kriege*, (Berlin: Karl Matzdorff, 1791)

La Mettrie, Julien Offray de, *Machine Man and Other Writings*, Ann Thomson (ed. and tr.), Cambridge Texts in the History of Philosophy, (Cambridge University Press, 1996)

*Lahatt, Charles, 'The Autobiography of the Rev. Charles Lahatt: Hessian Surgeon's Apprentice and New York Baptist Preacher', Henry J. Retzer (ed.), *Hessians* 13 (2010), 57–63

*Lamb, Roger, *An Original and Authentic Journal of Occurrences during the Late American War from Its Commencement to the Year 1783*, (Dublin: Wilkinson and Courtney, 1809)

— *Memoir of His Own Life: Formerly a Sergeant in the Royal Welch Fusiliers*, (Dublin: J. Jones, 1811)

*Lamy, *Précis historique sur le régiment d'Auvergne, depuis sa création jusqu'à présent, précédé d'une épitre aux mânes du brave chevalier D'Assas*, (Kampen, 1783)

*Laukhard, Friedrich Christian, *Leben und Schicksale*, Wolfgang Becker (ed.), (Leipzig: Koehler & Amelang, 1955)

*Lawrence, William, *A Dorset Soldier: The Autobiography of Sergeant William Lawrence*, Eileen Hathaway (ed.), (Tunbridge Wells: Spellmount, 1993)

*Le Roy, Claude-François-Madeleine, *Souveniers de C.-F.-M. Le Roy: Major d'Infanterie, Vétéran des armées de la République et de l'Empire (1767–1851),* Gabriel Dumay (ed.), Mémoires de la Société Bourguignonne de Géographie et d'Histoire 29, (Dijon: P. Berthier, 1914)

*'A Letter from a Private Soldier in Barrel's Regiment at Edinburgh, dated Jan. 19' *Gentleman's Magazine,* 16 (January, 1746), 41–2

*'Letter from Quebec (7 October 1759)', in *Derby Mercury,* (30 November 1759)

*Liebe, Georg (ed.), 'Preußische Soldatenbriefe aus dem Gebiet der Provinz Sachsen im 18. Jahrhundert', *Jahresbericht des Thüringisch-Sächsischen Vereins für Erforschung des vaterländischen Altertums und Erhaltung seiner Denkmale,* 92–3 (1911–2), 1–37

*Linn, Edward, 'The Battle of Culloden – 16 April 1746 – as Described in a Letter from a Soldier of the Royal Army to His Wife', *JSAHR,* 1 (1921–2), 21–4

List und Lustige Begebenheiten derer Herren Officiers auf Werbungen, Altpreußicher Kommiss 1, (Osnabrück: Biblio, 1971), [1741]

*Löffler, Johann Friedrich, *Der alte Sergeant: Leben des Schlesiers J. F. L.,* Gustav Rieck (ed.), (Breslau: Graß, Bart und Comp., 1836)

*Macdonald, John, *Autobiographical Journal of John MacDonald, Schoolmaster and Soldier, 1770–1830,* Angus Mackey (ed.), (Edinburgh: Norman MacLeod, 1906)

*Mackellow, John, *Autobiography of John MacKellow,* (London: Richard Barrett, 1863)

*MacLeod, Donald, *Memoirs of the Life and Gallant Exploits of the Old Highlander Sergeant Donald MacLeod,* (London: D. and D. Stuart, 1791)

*Matson, John, *Indian Warfare or the Extraordinary Adventures of John Matson, Written by himself,* (London: Effingham Wilson, 1842)

*McBane, Donald, *The Expert Swords-Man's Companion or the True Art of Self Defence* (Glasgow: James Duncan, 1728)

— 'The Expert Swords-Man's Companion or the True Art of Self Defence' in Mark Rector (ed.), *Highland Swordsmanship: Techniques of Scottish Swordmasters,* (Union City, Calif.: Chivalry Bookshelf, 2001), 21–85

*Miller, Benjamin, 'The Adventures of Benjamin Miller, during His Services in the 4th Battalion Royal Artillery, from 1796–1815', *JSAHR,* 7 (1928), 9–51

*Miller, James, 'The Diary of James Miller. 1745–50', J.H. Leslie (ed.), *JSAHR,* 3, (1924), 208–26

*Miller, John Philip, 'The Papers of John Philip Miller, "Hessian Private"', Frederick S. Weiser (ed), *Hessians,* 5.1 (1993), 19–24

*Millner, John, *A Compendious Journal of all Marches, Famous Battles, Sieges and Other Most Note-Worthy, Heroical, and Ever Memorable Actions of the Triumphant Armies of the Ever-Glorious Confederate High Allies in their Late and Victorious War against the Powerful Armies of Proud and Lofty France … begun A.D. 1701, and ended in 1712,* (London, 1733)

*Morley, Stephen, *Memoirs of a Sergeant of the 5th Regiment of Foot, containing the Account of his Service in Hanover, South America and the Peninsula,* (London: J. Elliot, 1842)

*Nichol, Daniel, 'Diary Excerpts' in MacKenzie MacBridge (ed.), *With Napoleon at Waterloo and other unpublished Documents of the Waterloo and Peninsular Campaigns*, (London: Francis Griffiths, 1911), 9–68, 86–111, 203–44

*Nottenbaum, Hermann, 'Aus Westfälichen Feldpostbriefen des siebenjährigen Krieges', Eduard Schulte (ed.), *Westfalen* 9 (1918), 85–91

*Payne, Thomas, 'The Life of Mr. Thomas Payne, Written by Himself', in: *Methodists*, vol. I, 436–48

*Pearson, Andrew, *The Soldier who Walked Away: Autobiography of Andrew Pearson a Peninsular War Veteran*, Arthur H. Halley (ed.), (Liverpool: Bullfinch, 1987)

Peter the Great, *Instruksii i artikuli voieniie, prim tom zhe kratkie primechaniya*, [Military Articles and Instructions, with Short Annotations], (St. Petersburg, 1714)

*Pickert, Johann Christoph, *Lebens-Geschichte des Unterofficier Pickert: Invalide bey der 7.ten Compagnie*, Gotthardt Frühsorge and Christoph Schreckenberg (eds.), (Göttingen: Wallenstein, 2006)

*Plummer, Samuel, *The Journal of Samuel Plummer, A Private in the 22d Regiment of Foot: Containing an Account of His Voyage by Sea and His Journies on Land: Embracing a Period of Twenty Years, the Principal Part of Which Time Was Spent in the East Indies*, John Riles (ed.), (London: T. Cordeux, 1821)

*Popadishev, Ilya O., 'Vospominaniya Suvorovskova Soldata', [Memoirs of a Soldier of Suvorov] in S. N. Semanov (ed.), *Alexander Vasil'evich Suvorov*, Russkii Mir v Litsakh, (Moscow: Russkii Mir, 2000), 58–107

*Popp, Stephan, '*Popp's Journal*', Joseph Rosentgarten (ed.), *The Pennsylvania Magazine of History and Biography*, 26 (1902), 25–41, 245–54

*Porter, John, 'An Account by an Eye-Witness of the Expedition against St. Malo in May and June, 1758', *Royal United Services Institute Journal*, 58 (1914), 755–63

*Recknagel, Caspar, 'The Diary of Caspar Recknagel', Bruce E. Burgoyne (tr.) *Hessians*, 5.2 (1994), 42–9

Reglement für das Kaiserlich Königliche gesammte Feld-Artilleriecorps, (Vienna: Johann Thomas von Trattner, 1757)

Reglement für die sämmentlich-Kaiserlich-Königliche Infanterie, (Vienna: Johann Thomas von Trattner, 1769)

Reglement Vor die Königl. Preußische Cavallerie-Regimenter, (Berlin, 1743)

Reglement Vor die Königl. Preußische Infanterie, (Berlin, 1743)

Regulament und Ordnung nach welchem sich gesambte unmittelbare Kayserliche Infanterie in denen Hand-Griffen und Kriegs Exercitien sowohl, als in denen Kriegs Gebräuchen gleichförmig zu achten haben, (Vienna: Krauss, 1737)

*Reuber, Johannes, *Diary of a Hessian Grenadier in Colonel Rall's Regiment*, Bruce E. Burgoyne (ed. and tr.), (n.p., 2006)

*Riedel, Christian Friedrich Gottfried, *Patriotisches Schreiben eines Musketiers von Regiment Churfürst an seinen Freund über die Unwahrscheinlichkeit und Unmöglichkeit einer würcklichen Rebellion in Sachsen*, (Dresden: J.S. Gerlach, 1794)

*Robertson, David, *The Journal of Sergeant D. Robertson, Late 92d Foot: Comprising the different Campaigns between the Years 1797 and 1813*, (Perth: J. Fisher, 1842)

*Robertson, George, 'Two letters of Corporal George Robertson RA from the campaign of 1793' in Alfred F. Scott (ed.), *Everyone a Witness: The Georgian Age: An Anthology*, (London: Martins, 1970)

*Rossignol, Jean Antoine, *La vie veritable de citoyen Jean Rossignol*, Jean Barrucand (ed.), (Paris: E. Plon, 1896)

A Royal Dragoon in the Spanish Succession War, Christopher Thomas Atkinson (ed.), Special Publication Society for Army Historical Research 5, (London: Gale and Polden, 1938)

Rules and Articles for the better Government of Her Majesties Land-Forces in the Low-Countries and Parts beyond the Seas, (London: Charles Bill, 1708)

Rumyantsev, Piotr, *Dokumenty*, P. K. Fortunatov, (ed.), 3 vols., (Moscow: Voinizdat 1953–9)

*Schimmel, Johann Christian, 'Kurze Lebensbeschreibung des preußischen Veteranen Johann Christian Schimmel' *Zeitschrift für Kunst, Wissenschaft und Geschichte des Krieges*, 10 (1827), 188–200

*Schreyer, Johann Georg, *Wahl und Krönung Leopolds II. 1790: Brieftagebuch des Feldschers der kursächsischen Schweizergarde*, Erna Berger and Konrad Bund (eds.), (Frankfurt am Main: Kramer, 1980)

*Schultze, Johann, 'Soldat Johann Schultze, an seine Verwandten, Arneburg, 13. August 1723, in *BBS*, 282–4

*Scot John, 'The Remembrance: or The Progress of Lord Portmore's Regiment', in James Ferguson (ed.), *The Scots Brigade in the Service of the United Netherlands, 1572–1782*, Publications of the Scottish History Society, 3 vols., (Edinburgh University Press, 1899–1901), vol. III, 307–577

*Seume, Johann Gottfried, 'Adventures of a Hessian Recruit', *Proceedings of the Massachusetts Historical Society*, 2nd Series, 4 (1887), 2–12

— 'Memoir's of a Hessian Conscript: J. G. Seume's Reluctant Voyage to America', Margarete Wölfel (tr.), *William and Mary Quarterly*, 3rd Series, 5 (1948), 553–70

— 'A Hessian Conscript's Account of Life in Garrison at Halifax at the Time of the American Revolution', Winthrop Bell (ed.),' *Collections of the Nova Scotia Historical Society* 22 (1947), 125–46

— *Werke*, Jörg Drews (ed.), 3 vols., *Bibliothek deutscher Klassiker* 85–6, (Frankfurt am Main: Deutscher Klassiker Verlag 1993)

*Shaw, John Robert, *John Robert Shaw: An Autobiography of Thirty Years, 1777–1807*, Oressa M. Teagarden and Jeanne L. Crabtree (eds.), (Athens: Ohio University Press, 1992)

*Shipp, John, *Memoirs of the Extraordinary Military Career of John Shipp, Late a Lieutenant in His Majesty's 87th Regiment of Foot, Written by Himself*, 3 vols., (London: Hurst, Chance and Co., 1829)

*Slater, George, 'Egypt 1801: A Letter from a Sergeant of the 28th Foot, to his Mother, at Longroyd-Bridge, near Huddersfield', *JSAHR*, 7 (1928), 117–9

*Sohr, Friedrich Christian, *Meine Geschichte*, (Görlitz: J. F. Fickelscherer, 1788)

*Sonnenfels, Joseph von, *Ueber die Liebe des Vaterlandes*, (Vienna: Joseph Kurzböck, 1771)

*Stang, Georg Adam, 'March Routes of George Adam Stang, Oboist Bayreuth, the 19th of January 1784', Bruce E. Burgoyne (tr.) *Hessians* 5.2 (1994), 31–41

*Staniforth, Sampson, 'The Life of Mr. Sampson Staniforth, Written by Himself', *Methodists*, vol. II, 324–49

*[Starkov, Yakov], *Raskazi Starova Voina o Suvorove*, [Tales of an Old Soldier about Suvorov], (Moscow: Universiteskaiia Tipografiia, 1847)

*Steininger, Johann, *Leben und Abenteuer des Joh. Steininger*, Gustav Diezel, (ed.), (Württemberg: Wachendorf, 1841)

*Steller, Jung Heim, 'Letters from Private Jung Heim Steller to His Parents, 1777–1778', Donald M. Londahl-Smidt (ed.), Henry Retzer (tr.), *Hessian*, 5.2 (1994), 1–3

*Stephanie, Gottlieb, *Stephanie des jüngern sämmtliche Lustspiele*, 6 vols., (Vienna: Ghelen, 1771–81)

*Steube, Johann Casper, *Wanderschften und Schicksale von Johann Casper Steübe, Schuhmacher und italiän. Sprachmeister in Gotha*, (Gotha: Ettinger, 1791)

*Steuernagel, Carl Philip, 'A Brief Description', in Marie E. Burgoyne (ed.), Bruce E. Burgoyne (tr.), *Hessian Letters and Journals and a Memoir*, (Westminster, Md.: Heritage Books 2006), 99–199

*Stevenson, John, *A Soldier in Times of War or the Military Life of Mr. John Stevenson*, (London: W. Brittain, 1841)

*Stihell, Christopher, 'Song Brought in a Letter to His Parents', Gerda Balding (tr.) in 'Complaints of a Mercenary – 1776', *Hessians*, 7.4 (2004), 21

*Sturgeon, John, 'John Sturgeon – 39th Foot', *The Dorsetshire Regimental Journal*, 16 (May, 1947), 80–2

*Sullivan, Thomas, *From Redcoat to Rebel: The Thomas Sullivan Journal*, Thomas Lee Boyle (ed.), (Westminster, Md: Heritage, 2006)

*Surtees, William, *Twenty-Five Years in the Rifle Brigade*, (Edinburgh: William Blackwood, 1833)

Suvorov, Alexander V., *Dokumenty*, Georgii P. Merschenko (ed.), 4 vols., (Moscow: Voinizdat, 1949–1953)

Täge, Christian, *Christian Täge's ehemaligen Russischen Feldpredigers, jezigen Pfarrers in Pobethen, Lebensgeschichte*, August Samuel Gerber (ed.), (Königsberg: Heinrich Degen, 1804)

*Thompson, James, *A Bard of Wolfe's Army: James Thompson, Gentleman Volunteer, 1733–1830*, Earl John Chapman and Ian Macpherson McCulloch (eds.), (Montreal: R. Brass Studio, 2010)

*Todd, William, *The Journal of Corporal Todd, 1745–1762*, Andrew Cormack and Alan Jones (eds.), Publications of the Army Records Society 18, (London: Sutton Publishing, 2001)

*Tory, John, *A Journal of the Allied Army's Marches, from the First Arrival of the British Troops, In Germany to the Present Time*, 2nd edn, (Osnabrück: J.W. Kisling, 1762)

Tuch'kov, Sergei A., *Voienji Slovar: zakluchaiushij naimenovanija ili termini v Rossijskom sukhopuinom voijske upotreblijaemaije*, [Military Dictionary of Common Expressions and Terms Employed in the Russian Land Forces], (Moscow: Kuchkovo Pole, 2008)

*Uhlmann, Markus, *Das abwechslende Fortün oder das veränderte Schicksal eines Jünglingen: Ein Reisebericht aus der Zeit des Siebenjährigen Kriegs*, Jean-Pierre Bodmer (ed.), Mitteilungen der Antiquarischen Gesselschaft in Zürich 50.1, (Zurich: Schweizerisches Landesmuseum, 1980)

*Vernon, William, *Poems on Several Occasions by William Vernon, Private soldier in the Buffs*, (London: W. Vernon, 1758)

*Watson, Thomas, 'Some Account of the Life Convincement and Religious Experience of Thomas Watson, Written by Himself,' in Don N. Hagist, *British Soldiers, American War: Voices of the American Revolution*, (Yardley, Penn.: Westholme, 2012), 106–22

Whitehead, John Frederick, 'The Life of John Frederick Whitehead Containing his Travels and Chief Adventures', in Susan E. Klepp, Farley Grubb and Anne Pfaelzer de Ortiz (eds.), *Souls for Sale: Two German Redemptioners Come to Revolutionary America*, (University Park: Pennsylvania State University Press, 2006), 51–162

*Wiemar, Hermann Heinrich, 'Letter to Judge Kaspar Dietrich Marck in Schwerte', (7 February 1741) in *BBS*, 246–8

*Williamson, Peter, *French and Indian Cruelty Exemplified in the Life of Peter Williamson, Disbanded Soldier*, (York: N. Nickson, 1757)

*Wilson, John, 'The Journal of Sergeant John Wilson, 1694–1727', David G. Chandler (ed.), in *Military Miscellany II*, Publications of the Army Records Society 23, (Stroud: Sutton Publishing, 2005)

Witzleben, August von, *Aus alten Parolebüchern der Berliner Garnison zur Zeit Friedrichs des Großen*, (Berlin: Mittler, 1851)

*Wood, James, *Gunner at Large: The Diary of James Wood R.A. 1746–1765*, Rex Whitworth (ed.), (London: L. Cooper, 1988)

*Wray, Samuel, *The Military Adventures of Private Samuel Wray 61st Foot 1796–1815*, Gareth Glover (ed.), (Godmanchester: Ken Trotman Publishing, 2009)

*Wright, Duncan, 'The Life of Mr. Duncan Wright, Written by Himself', in *Methodists*, vol. I, 317–32

*Young, Robert, 'The Last Words, and Dying Speech of Robert Young, Who is to be Executed at Worcester this day, November 11th, 1779', in Don N. Hagist, *British Soldiers, American War: Voices of the American Revolution*, (Yardley, Penn.: Westholme, 2012), 140–7

*Zahn, Johann Gottfried, 'Ein Soldatenbrief aus der Zeit des siebenjährign Krieges, Max Könnecke, (ed.), *Mansfelder Blätter: Mitteilungen des Vereins für Geschichte und Altertümer der Grafschaft Mansfeld zu Eisleben* 8 (1894), 74–8

Published Secondary Sources

Allmayer-Beck, Johann Christoph, 'Von Hubertusburg nach Jena: Die preußische Armee am Ende des 18. Jahrhunderts von außen gesehen', in Peter Baumgart, Bernhard R. Kroener and Heinz Stübig (eds.), *Die preußische Armee: zwischen Ancien Régime und Reichsgründung*, (Paderborn: F. Schöningh, 2008), 121–32

Allmayer-Beck, Johann Christoph, and Erich Lessing, *Die kaiserlichen Kriegsvölker: von Maximilian I. bis Prinz Eugen, 1479–1718*, (Munich: C. Bertelsmann, 1978)

Amelang James S., *The Flight of Icarus: Artisan Autobiography in Early Modern Europe*, (Stanford University Press, 1998)

Anderson, Fred, *The Crucible of War: the Seven Years' War and the Fate of Empire in British North America, 1754–1766*, (New York: Alfred A. Knopf, 2000)

Anderson, Matthew Smith, *War and Society in Europe of the Old Regime, 1618–1789*, (London: Fontana, 1988)

— *The War of the Austrian Succession, 1740-1748*, (London: Longman, 1995)

Andrews, Richard M., *Law, Magistracy, and Crime in Old Regime Paris, 1735–1789*, (Cambridge University Press, 1994)

Ardant du Picq, Charles, *Études sur le combat: combat antique et combat moderne*, 8th edn, (Paris: Chapelot, 1914)

Atkinson, Christopher Thomas, 'A Soldier's Diary of the Seven Years' War: Journal of William Todd', *JSAHR*, 29 (1951), 118–27, 158–69

Atwood, Rodney, *The Hessians: Mercenaries from Hessen-Kassel in the American Revolution*, (Cambridge University Press, 1980)

Audoin-Rouzeau, Stéphane, and Annette Becker, 'Violence et consentement: la culture de guerre du premier conflit mondial', in Jean-Pierre Rioux and Jean-François Sirinelli (eds.), *Pour une histoire culturelle*, L'univers historique, (Paris: Seuil, 1997), 251–71

Babits, Lawrence E., and Joshua B. Howard, *Long Obstinate and Bloody: The Battle for Guilford Court House*, (Chapel Hill: University of North Carolina Press, 2009)

Bachman, Jerald G., David R. Segal, Peter Freedman-Doan and Patrick M. O'Malley, 'Does Enlistment Propensity Predict Accession? High School Seniors' Plans and Subsequent Behavior', *AFS* 25 (1998–9), 59–80

Bachman, Jerald G., Lee Sigelman and Greg Diamond, 'Self-Selection, Socialization, and Distinctive Military Values: Attitudes of High School Seniors', *AFS* 13 (1987–8), 169–87

Bachman, Jerald G., Peter Freedman-Doan, David R. Segal and Patrick M. O'Malley, 'Distinctive Military Attitudes among US Enlistees, 1976– 1997: Self-Selection versus Socialization', *AFS* 26 (1999–2000), 561–85

Bachman, Jerald G., David R. Segal, Peter Freedman-Doan and Patrick M. O'Malley, 'Who Chooses Military Service? Correlates of Propensity and Enlistment in the U.S. Armed Forces,' *Military Psychology* 12 (2000), 1–30

Bagensky, Bogislav von, *Regiments Buch des Grenadiers Regiments könig Friedrich Wilhelm IV. (1. Pommerschen) Nr. 2*, (Berlin, 1892)

Barnett, Correlli, *Britain and Her Army: A Military, Political and Social History of the British Army, 1509–1970*, (London: Cassell, 2000) [1970]

Bartlett, Thomas, 'Army and Society in Eighteenth-Century Ireland' in William A. Maguire (ed.), *Kings in Conflict: The Revolutionary War and its Aftermath, 1689–1750*, (Belfast: Blackstaff, 1990), 173–82

— 'Indiscipline and Disaffection in the French and Irish Armies during the Revolutionary Period', in David Dickson and Hugh Gough (eds.), *Ireland and the French Revolution*, (Dublin: Irish Academic Press, 1990), 179–201

Bartov, Omer, *The Eastern Front, 1941–45: German Troops and the Barbarisation of Warfare*, 2nd ed., (Basingstoke: Palgrave, 2001)

Battistelli, Fabrizio, 'Peacekeeping and the Postmodern Soldier', *AFS*, 23 (1996–7), 467–84

Baule, Steven, and Don N. Hagist, 'The Regimental Punishment Book of the Boston Detachments of the Royal Irish Regiment and 65th Regiment, 1774–1775', *JSAHR*, 88 (2010), 5–18

Beattie, J.M., *Crime and the Courts in England, 1660–1800*, (Oxford: Clarendon Press, 1986)

— *Policing and Punishment in London, 1660–1750: Urban Crime and the Limits of Terror*, (Oxford University Press, 2001)

Behrisch, Lars, 'Social Discipline in Early Modern Russia, Seventeenth to Nineteenth Centuries', in Heinz Schilling and Lars Behrisch (eds.), *Institutionen, Instrumente und Akteure sozialer Kontrolle und Disziplinierung im frühneuzeitlichen Europa*, (Frankfurt am Main: Klosterman, 1999), 325–57

Bell, David, *First Total War: The Age of Napoleon and the Birth of War as We Know It*, (Boston: Houghton Mifflin Company, 2007)

Bercé, Yves-Marie, *Histoire des Croquants: Étude des soulèvements populaires au XVIIe siècle dans le sud-ouest de la France*, Mémoires et documents publiés par la Société de l'École des Chartes 22, (Geneva: Droz, 1974)

Berkovich, Ilya, 'Discipline and Control in Eighteenth-Century Gibraltar', in Kevin Linch and Matthew McCormarck (eds.), *Britain's Soldiers: Rethinking War and Society, 1715–1815*, Eighteenth-Century Worlds 5, (Liverpool University Press, 2014), 114–30

Bertaud, Jean-Paul., *The Army of the French Revolution: From Citizen-Soldiers to Instrument of Power*, R.R. Palmer (tr.), (Princeton University Press, 1988)

Black, Jeremy, *European Warfare, 1660–1815*, Warfare and History, (London: UCL Press, 1994)

Blanning, T.C.W., *The French Revolutionary Wars, 1787–1802*, Modern Wars, (London: Arnold, 1996)

Bleckwenn, Hans, 'Bauernfreiheit durch Wehrpflicht: ein neues Bild der altpreußischen Armee', in Johann Christoph Allmayer-Beck et al., *Friedrich der Große und das Militärwesen seiner Zeit*, Vorträge zur Militärgeschichte 8, (Herford: Mittler, 1987), 55–72

Blickle, Peter, *Deutsche Untertanen: ein Widerspruch*, (Munich: Beck, 1981)

Bois, Jean-Pierre, *Les anciens soldats dans la Société Française au XVIIIe siècle*, (Paris: Économica, 1990)

Boscawen, Hugh, *The Capture of Louisbourg, 1758*, Campaigns and Commanders 27, (Norman: University of Oklahoma Press, 2011)

Bourgois, Philippe I., *In Search of Respect: Selling Crack at El-Barrio*, Structural Analysis in the Social Sciences, (Cambridge University Press, 1995)

Bracken, Patrick J., 'Hidden Agendas: Deconstructing Post Traumatic Stress Disorder', in Patrick J. Bracken and Celia Petty (eds.), *Rethinking the Trauma of War* (London: Free Association, 1998), 38–59

Brewis, Alfred, 'The Order of Merit: 5th Regiment of Foot, 1767–1856', *JSAHR*, 5 (1923), 118–24

Britt, Thomas W., and James M. Dickinson, 'Morale during Military Operations: A Positive Psychology Approach', in Thomas W. Britt, Carl Andrew Castro and Amy B. Adler (eds.), *Military Life: The Psychology of Serving in Peace and Combat*, 4 vols., (Westport, Conn: Praeger Security International, 2006), vol. I, 157–84

Bröckling, Ulrich, *Disziplin: Soziologie und Geschichte militärischer Gehorsamsproduktion*, (Munich: Fink, 1997)

Brooks, Jeffrey, *When Russia Learned to Read: Literacy and Popular Literature, 1861–1917*, (Princeton University Press, 1985)

Browning, Reed, *The War of the Austrian Succession*, (Stroud: Alan Sutton, 1994)

Brumwell, Stephen, *Redcoats: The British Soldier and War in the Americas, 1755–1763*, (Cambridge, 2002)

— *Paths of Glory: The Life and Death of General James Wolfe*, (London: Hambledon Continuum, 2006)

Bulloch, John Malcolm, 'Soldiering and Circuses' *JSAHR*, 8 (1929), 183–9

Burroughs, Peter, 'Crime and Punishment in the British Army, 1815–1870', *English Historical Review*, 100 (1985), 545–71

Burrows, John William, *The Essex Regiment, 1st Battalion (44th)*, 2nd edn, (Southend-on-Sea: J. H. Burrows, 1931)

— *The Essex Regiment, 2nd Battalion (56th) (Pompadours)*, 2nd edn, (Southend-on-Sea: J.H. Burrows, 1937)

Burschel, Peter, *Soldner im Nordwestdeutschland des 16. und 17. Jahrhunderts: sozialgeschichtliche Studien*, Veröffentlichungen des Max-Planck-Instituts für Geschichte 113, (Göttingen: Vandenhoeck & Ruprecht, 1994)

Büsch, Otto, *Militärsystem und Socialleben im alten Preußen, 1713–1807: die Anfänge der sozialen Militarisierung der preußisch-deutschen Gesellschaft*, Historische Kommission zu Berlin, Veröffentlichungen 7, (Berlin: De Gruyter, 1962)

Cameron, Iain A., *Crime and Repression in Auvergne and Guyenne, 1720-1790*, (Cambridge University Press, 1981)

Carter, Brian, *Matthew Bishop of Deddington in Oxfordshire: A Forgotten Voice from the 18th Century*, (Witney, Oxon: The Elmore Press, 2008) Also available online at www.deddington.org.uk/__data/assets/pdf_file/0005/2939/Bishop complete.pdf (Last accessed 7 October 2016)

Certeau, Michel de, *The Practice of Everyday Life*, Steven Rendall (tr.), (Berkley: University of California Press, 1984)

Chandler, David, G., *Marlborough as Military Commander*, (London: Batsford, 1973)

— *The Art of Warfare in the Age of Marlborough*, (London: Batsford, 1976)

— 'The Captain General 1702–14', in David G. Chandler and Ian Beckett (eds.), *The Oxford Illustrated History of the British Army*, (Oxford University Press, 1994), 67–91

Chartrand, René, 'Britannia Badge of the 9th Foot', *JSAHR*, 63 (1985), 189

— 'Punishment for Cowardice, Quebec, 1759', *JSHAR*, 66 (1988), 186

Chodoff, Elliot P., 'Ideology and Primary Groups', *AFS*, 9 (1982–3), 233–48

Childs, John, *Armies and Warfare in Europe 1648–1789*, (Manchester University Press, 1982)

Clark, Christopher, *The Iron Kingdom: A History of Prussia 1600–1947*, (London: Allen Lane, 2006)

Clausewitz, Carl von, *On War*, Michael Howard and Peter Paret (eds.), (Princeton University Press, 1976)

Cochet, François, *Survivre au front, 1914–1918: Les poilus entre contrainte et consentement*, (Saint-Cloud: 14–18 Editions, 2005)

Coffman, Edward M., *The Old Army: A Portrait of the American Army in Peacetime, 1784–1898*, (New York: Oxford University Press, 1986)

Colley, Linda, *Britons: Forging the Nation 1707–1837*, (New Haven: Yale University Press, 1992)

Conway, Stephen, '"The Great Mischief Complain'd of": Reflections on the Misconduct of British Soldiers in the Revolutionary War', *William and Mary Quarterly*, 3rd Series, 47 (1990), 370–90

— *The War of American Independence, 1775–1783*, Modern Wars, (London: Arnold, 1995)

— 'The Mobilization of Manpower for Britain's Mid-Eighteenth-Century Wars', *Historical Research*, 77 (2004), 377–404

— *War, State and Society in Mid-Eighteenth-Century Britain and Ireland*, (Oxford University Press, 2006)

— 'The Eighteenth-Century British Army as a European Institution', in Kevin Linch and Matthew McCormarck (eds.), *Britain's Soldiers: Rethinking War and Society, 1715–1815*, Eighteenth-Century Worlds 5, (Liverpool University Press, 2014), 17–38

Cooley, Charles Hurton, 'Social Organization', in *The Two Major Works of Charles H. Cooley*, (Glencoe, Illinois: Free Press, 1956) [1909]

Corvisier, André, *L'Armée française de la fin du XVIIe siècle au ministère de Choiseul: Le soldat*, 2 vols., Publications de la Faculté des lettres et sciences humaines de Paris. Série 'Recherches' 14–5, (Paris: Presses universitaires de France, 1964)

— *Les contrôles de troupes de l'Ancien Régime*, 4 vols., (Paris: État-major de l'armée de terre, Service historique, 1968–1970)

— *Armies and Societies in Europe, 1494–1789*, Abigail T. Siddall (tr.), (Bloomington: Indiana University Press, 1979)

Coss, Edward, *All for a King's Shilling: The British Soldier under Wellington, 1808–1814*, Campaigns and Commanders 24, (Norman: University of Oklahoma Press, 2010)

Costa, Dora L., and Kahn, Matthew E., *Heroes & Cowards: The Social Face of the War*, NBER Series on Long-Term Factors in Economic Development, (Princeton University Press, 2008)

Cotton, Charles A., 'Institutional and Occupational Values in Canada's Army', *AFS*, 7 (1980–1), 99–110

Cuénin, Micheline, *Le duel sous l'Ancien Régime*, Histoire des hommes, (Paris: Presses de la Renaissance, 1982)

Davis, Natalie Zemon, *Society and Culture in Early-Modern France: Eight Essays*, (Stanford University Press, 1975)

De Ortiz, Anne M. Pfaelzer, 'German Redemptioners of the Lower Sort: Apolitical Soldiers in the American Revolution', *Journal of American Studies*, 33 (1999), 267–306

Dejob, Charles, 'Le Soldat dans la litterature française au XVIIIe siècle', *Revue Politique et Littéraire*, 4ième Série, 12 (1899), 449–58

Denby, David J., *Sentimental Narrative and the Social Order in France: 1760–1820*, Cambridge Studies in French 47, (Cambridge University Press, 1994)

Depréaux, Albert, *Les Affiches de recrutement, du XVIIe siècle à nos jours*, (Paris: J. Leroy & Cie, 1911)

Dinter, Elmar, *Hero or Coward: Pressures Facing the Soldier in Battle*, (London: Frank Cass, 1985)

Donagan, Barbara, *War in England, 1642–1649*, (Oxford University Press, 2008)

Dorman, James E., 'ROTC Cadet Attitudes: A Product of Socialization or Self-Selection?' *Journal of Political and Military Sociology*, 4 (1976), 203–16

Dornfest, Walter T., 'An Unusual Case of Discipline', *JSAHR*, 68 (1990), 65

Doyle, William, *The Ancien Regime*, 2nd edn, (Basingstoke: Palgrave, 2001)

Duffy, Christopher, *The Army of Frederick the Great*, Historic Armies and Navies, (Newton Abbot: David and Charles, 1974)

— *Fire and Stone: The Science of Fortress Warfare 1660–1860*, (Newton Abbot: David and Charles, 1975)

— *The Army of Maria Theresa: The Armed Forces of Imperial Austria, 1740–1780*, Historic Armies and Navies, (New York: Hippocrene Books 1977)

— *Russia's Military Way to the West: Origins and Nature of Russian Military Power 1700–1800*, (London: Routledge & Kegan Paul, 1981)

— *Frederick the Great: A Military Life*, (London: Routledge & Kegan Paul, 1985)

— *The Fortress in the Age of Vauban and Frederick the Great, 1660–1789*, (London: Routledge & Kegan Paul, 1985)

— *The Military Experience in the Age of Reason*, (London: Routledge & Kegan Paul, 1987)

— *Eagles over the Alps: Suvorov in Italy and Switzerland, 1799*, (Chicago: Emperor's Press 1999)

— *Instrument of War*, vol. 1 of *The Austrian Army in the Seven Years War*, (Rosemont, Illinois: Emperor's Press, 2000)

— *Through German Eyes: The British & the Somme 1916*, (London: Weidenfeld & Nicolson, 2006)

— *By Force of Arms*, vol. 2 of *The Austrian Army in the Seven Years War*, (Chicago: Emperor's Press, 2008)

Duffy, Michael, 'The British Army and the Caribbean Expeditions of the War against Revolutionary France, 1793–1801', *JSAHR*, 62 (1984), 65–73

Dull, Jonathan R., *The French Navy and American Independence: A Study of Arms and Diplomacy, 1774–1787*, (Princeton University Press, 1975)

Eckert, Helmuth, 'Ulrich Bräkers Soldatenzeit und die preußische Werbung in Schaffhausen', *Schaffhausener Beitrage zur Geschichte*, 53 (1976), 122–90

Eder, Markus, *Crime and Punishment in the Royal Navy of the Seven Years War, 1756–1763*, (Aldershot: Ashgate, 2004)

— *"At the Instigation of the Devil" Capital Punishment and the Assize in the Early Modern England, 1670–1730*, (Hilgertshausen-Tandern: Markus Eder, 2009)

Eighmey, John, 'Why Do Youth Enlist?: Identification of Underlying Themes', *AFS*, 32 (2006–7), 307–28

Elias, Norbert, *The Civilizing Process*, rev. edn, Edmund Jephcott (tr.), 2 vols., (Oxford: Basil Blackwell, 1978–82)

Elton, Geoffrey, *The Practice of History*, (Sydney University Press, 1967)

Emsley, Clive, 'The Military and Popular Disorder in England 1790–1801', *JSAHR*, 61 (1983–4), 10–21, 96–112

Engelsing, Rolf, *Analphabetentum und Lektüre: zur Sozialgeschichte des Lesens in Deutschland zwischen feudaler und industrieller Gesellschaft*, (Stuttgart: Metzler, 1973)

Englund, Peter, *The Battle of Poltava: the Birth of the Russian Empire*, (London: Gollancz, 1992)

Etzioni, Amitai, *A Comparative History of Complex Organizations: On Power, Involvement and their Correlates*, rev. edn, (New York: Free Press, 1975)

Evans, Richard J., *Rituals of Retribution: Capital Punishment in Germany, 1600–1987*, (Oxford University Press, 1996)

Fann, Willerd R., 'On the Infantryman's Age in Eighteenth Century Prussia', *Military Affairs*, 41 (1977), 165–70

— 'Peacetime Attrition in the Army of Frederick William I, 1713–1740', *Central European History*, 11 (1978), 323–34

Faris, John H., 'Economic and Noneconomic Factors of Personnel Recruitment and Retention in the AVF', *AFS*, 10 (1984–5), 251–75

Field, M.D., 'Middle Class Society and the Rise of Military Professionalism', *AFS*, 1 (1975), 409–42

Forrest, Alan I., *Conscripts and Deserters: The Army and French Society during the Revolution and Empire*, (New York: Oxford University Press, 1989)

— *Napoleon's Men: The Soldiers of the Revolution and the Empire*, (London: Hambledon and London, 2002)

Fortescue, John William, *A History of the British Army*, 6 vols., (London: Macmillan, 1910–30)

Foucault, Michel, *Discipline and Punish: The Birth of the Prison*, Alan Sheridan (tr.), (London: Allen Lane, 1979)

— 'The Subject and Power', in Herbert L. Dreyfus and Paul Rabinow (eds.), *Beyond Structuralism and Hermeneutics*, 2nd edn, (University of Chicago Press, 1983), 208–26

French, David, *Military Identities: The Regimental System, the British Army, and the British People, c. 1870–2000*, (Oxford University Press, 2005)

Frevert, Ute, *Man of Honour: A Social and Cultural History of the Duel*, Anthony Williams (tr.), (Cambridge: Polity, 1995)

Frey, Sylvia R., 'Courts and Cats: British Military Justice in the Eighteenth Century', *Military Affairs*, 43 (1979), 5–11

— *The British Soldier in America: A Social History of Military Life in the Revolutionary Period*, (Austin: University of Texas Press, 1981)

Fritz, Stephen, '"We are trying . . . to change the face of the World" – Ideology and Motivation in the Wehrmacht on the Eastern Front: The View from Below', *Journal of Military History*, 60 (1996), 683–710

Furet, François, and Jacques Ozouf, *Reading and Writing: Literacy in France from Clavin to Jules Ferry*, Cambridge Studies in Oral and Literate Culture 5, (Cambridge University Press, 1982)

Füssel, Marian, 'Der Wert der Dinge: Materielle Kultur in soldatischen Selbstzeugnissen des Siebenjährigen Krieges', *Militär und Gesellschaft in der Frühen Neuzeit*, 13 (2009), 104–21

Fussell, Paul, *The Great War and Modern Memory* (Oxford University Press, 1975)

Gabriel, Richard A., and Paul L. Savage, *Crisis in Command: Mismanagement in the Army*, (New York: Hill and Wang, 1978)

Garnham, Neal, 'Military Desertion and Deserters in Eighteenth-Century Ireland', *Eighteenth Century Ireland*, 20 (2005), 91–103

Gat Azar, *A History of Military Thought from the Enlightenment to the Cold War*, (Oxford University Press, 2001)

Gates David, *The British Light Infantry Arm c. 1790–1815: Its Creation, Training and Operational Role*, (London: Batsford, 1987)

Gatrell, V.A.C., *The Hanging Tree: Execution and the English people 1770–1868*, (Oxford University Press, 1994)

Gaude, Michael R., 'Military Justice in a "Hessian" Regiment in America, 1777–1783', *Hessians*, 10 (2007), 1–12

Gawthrop, Richard and Gerald Strauss, 'Protestantism and Literacy in Early Modern Germany, *Past and Present*, 104 (1984), 43–55

George, Alexander L., 'Primary Groups: Organization and Military Performance' in Roger W. Little (ed.), *A Handbook of Military Institutions*, (Beverly Hills: Sage Publications, 1971), 293–318

Gilbert, Arthur N., 'The Regimental Courts Martial in the Eighteenth Century British Army', *Albion*, 8 (1976), 50–66

— 'An Analysis of Some Eighteenth-century Army Recruiting Records', *JSHAR*, 54 (1976), 38–47

— 'Army Impressment during the War of the Spanish Succession', *The Historian*, 38 (1976), 689–708

— 'Military and Civilian Justice in Eighteenth-Century England: An Assessment', *The Journal of British Studies*, 17 (1978), 41–65

— 'Charles Jenkinson and the Last Army Press', *Military Affairs*, 42 (1978), 7–11
— 'Military Recruitment and Career Advancement in the Eighteenth-Century', *JSAHR*, 57 (1979), 34–44
— 'British Military Justice during the American Revolution', *The Eighteenth Century: Theory and Interpretation*, 20 (1979), 24–38
— 'Why Men Deserted from the Eighteenth-Century British Army', *AFS*, 6 (1979–80), 553–67
— 'The Changing Face of British Military Justice 1757–1783', *Military Affairs*, 49 (1985), 80–4
Girard, Georges, *Le service militaire en France à la fin du règne de Louis XIV: racolage et milice (1701–1715)*, (Paris: Plon-Nourrit, 1921)
Gooch, John, *Armies in Europe*, (London: Routledge & Kegan Paul, 1980)
Gorman, Linda, and George W. Thomas, 'Enlistment Motivations of Army Reservists: Money, Self-Improvement, or Patriotism?', *AFS*, 17 (1990–1), 589–99
Goulden, R.J., 'Deserter Bounty Certificates', *JSAHR*, 50 (1972), 161–8
Griffith, Paddy, *The Art of War of Revolutionary France, 1789–1802*, (London: Greenhill Books, 1998)
Guy, Alan J., *Oeconomy and Discipline: Officership and Administration in the British Army 1714-63*, (Manchester University Press, 1985)
— 'The Army of the Georges 1714–1783', in David G. Chandler and Ian Beckett (eds.), *The Oxford Illustrated History of the British Army*, (Oxford University Press, 1994), 92–111
— 'The Irish Military Establishment, 1660–1776', in Thomas Bartlett and Keith Jeffery (eds.), *A Military History of Ireland*, (Cambridge University Press, 1996), 211–30
Hagemann, Karen, *"Mannlicher Muth und Teutsche Ehre": Nation, Militär und Geschlecht zur Zeit der Antinapoleonischen Kriege Preussens*, Krieg in der Geschichte 8, (Paderborn: F. Schöningh, 2002)
Hagist, Don N., 'Unpublished Writings of Roger Lamb, Soldier in the American War of Independence', *JSAHR*, 89 (2011), 280–90, 90 (2012), 77–89
— *British Soldiers, American War: Voices of the American Revolution*, (Yardley, Penn.: Westholme, 2012)
Harari, Yuval Noah, *Renaissance Military Memoirs: War History and Identity, 1450–1600*, Warfare in History, (Woodbridge: Boydell Press, 2004)
— 'Martial Illusions: War and Disillusionment in Twentieth-Century and Renaissance Military Memoirs', *Journal of Military History*, 69 (2005), 43–72
— 'Military Memoirs: A Historical Overview of the Genre from the Middle-Ages to the Late Modern Era', *War in History*, 14 (2007), 289–309
— *The Ultimate Experience: Battlefield Revelation and the Making of Modern War Culture, 1450–2000*, (Basingstoke: Palgrave Macmillan, 2008)
— 'Scholars, Eyewitnesses, and Flesh-Witnesses of War: A Tense Relationship', *Partial Answers: Journal of Literature and the History of Ideas*, 7 (2009), 213–28
— 'Armchairs, Coffee, and Authority: Eye-witnesses and Flesh-witnesses Speak about War, 1100–2000,' *Journal of Military History*, 74 (2010), 53–78

Härter, Karl, 'Soziale Disziplinierung durch Strafe? Intentionen frühneuzeitlicher Policeyordnungen und staatliche Sanktionspraxis', *Zeitschrift für historische Forschung* 26, (1999), 365–79

Hayter, Tony, *The Army and the Crowd in Mid-Georgian England*, (London: Macmillan, 1978)

Hedlund, Erik, 'What Motivates Swedish Soldiers to Participate in Peacekeeping Missions: Research Note', *AFS*, 37 (2011–2), 180–90

Henderson, John, 'The Irish Rebellion of 1798: Two First Hand Accounts', *JSAHR*, 52 (1973), 34–46

Herek, Gregory M., and Aaron Belkin, 'Sexual Orientation and Military Service: Prospects for Organizational and Individual Change in the United States', in Thomas W. Britt, Carl Andrew Castro and Amy B. Adler (eds.), *Military Life: The Psychology of Serving in Peace and Combat*, 4 vols., (Westport, Conn: Praeger Security International, 2006), vol. IV, 119–42

Hippler, Thomas, *Citizens, Soldiers and National Armies: Military Service in France and Germany, 1789–1830*, War, History and Politics Series, (London: Routledge, 2008)

Hitoshi, Kawano, 'Japanese Combat Morale: A Case Study of the Thirty-Seventh Division', in: Mark Peattie, Edward Drea and Hans van de Ven (eds.), *The Battle for China: Essays on the Military History of the Sino-Japanese War of 1937–1945*, (Stanford University Press, 2011), 328–53

Hobsbawm, Eric J., 'The Machine Breakers', *Past and Present*, 1 (1952), 57–70

Hochedlinger, Michael, *Austria's Wars of Emergence, 1683–1797*, Modern Wars in Perspective (Harlow: Longman, 2003)

Holmes, Richard, *Firing Line*, (London: Cape, 1985)

— *Redcoat: The British Soldier in the Age of Horse and Musket*, (London: Harper Perennial, 2001)

Hopkin, David M., 'La Remée: The Archetypal Soldier as an Indicator of Popular Attitudes in the Army in Nineteenth-Century France', *French History*, 14 (2000), 115–49

— 'Storytelling, Fairytales and Autobiography: Some Observations on Eighteenth- and Nineteenth-Century French Soldiers' and Sailors' Memoirs', *Social History*, 29 (2004), 186–98

Houlding, John A., *Fit for Service: The Training of the British Army*, (Oxford: Clarendon Press, 1981)

Houston, R.A., *Literacy in Early Modern Europe: Culture and Education, 1500–1800*, 2nd edn, (Harlow: Longman, 2002)

Howard, Michael, *War in European History*, rev. edn, (Oxford and New York: Oxford University Press, 2009)

Huck, Stephan, *Soldaten gegen Nordamerika: Lebenswelten Braunschweiger Subsidientruppen im amerikanischen Unabhängigkeitskrieg*, Beiträge zur Militärgeschichte 69, (Munich: Oldenbourg, 2011)

Hughes, Michael J., *Forging Napoleon's Grand Armée: Motivation, Military Culture, and Masculinity in the French Army, 1800–1808*, Warfare and Culture Series, (New York University Press, 2012)

Hurl-Eamon, Jennine, 'Did Soldiers Really Enlist to Desert their Wives? Revisiting the Martial Character of Marital Desertion in Eighteenth-Century London', *Journal of British Studies*, 53 (2014), 356–77

— *Marriage and the British Army in the Long Eighteenth Century: 'The Girl I Left Behind Me'*, (Oxford University Press, 2014)

— '"Youth in the Devil's Service, Manhood in the King's": Reaching Adulthood in the Eighteenth-Century British Army', *The Journal of the History of Childhood and Youth*, 8 (2015), 163–90

Hynes, Samuel, *The Soldiers' Tale: Bearing Witness to Modern War*, (London: Pimilco, 1998)

— 'Personal Narratives and Commemoration', in Jay Winter and Emmanuel Sivan (eds.), *War and Remembrance in the Twentieth Century*, Studies in the Social and Cultural History of Modern Warfare 5, (Cambridge University Press, 1999), 205–20

Hytier, Adrienne, 'The Decline of Military Values: The Theme of Deserter in Eighteenth-Century French Literature', *Studies in Eighteenth Century Culture*, 11 (1982), 147–161

Ingrams, Richard, *The Life and Adventures of William Cobbett*, (London: HarperCollins, 2005)

Ingrao, Charles W., *The Hessian Mercenary State: Ideas, Institutions, and Reform under Frederick II, 1760–1785*, (Cambridge University Press, 1987)

Jackson, Joshua J., Felix Thoemmes, Kathrin Jonkmann, Oliver Lüdtke and Ulrich Trautwein, 'Military Training and Personality Trait Development: Does the Military Make the Man, or Does the Man Make the Military?', *Psychological Science*, 23,(2012), 270–7

James, Lawrence, *Warrior Race: The British Experience of War from Roman Time to the Present*, (London: Little, Brown and Company, 2001)

Jany, Curt, *Geschichte der Preußischen Armee vom 15. Jahrhundert bis 1914*, 2nd updated edn by Eberhard Jany, 4 vols., (Osnabrück: Biblio, 1967)

Jennings, Francis, *Empire of Fortune: Crowns, Colonies, and Tribes in the Seven Years War in America*, (New York: Norton, 1988)

Jomini, Antoine-Henri de, *Précis de l'Art de la Guerre*, (Paris: Anselin, 1837)

Jurikson, Håkan, 'Russkije voijnoplennie v Visinge', [Russian Prisoners of War in Wisingsborg] in Lena Jonson and Tamara Toschendal-Salijicheva (eds.), *Poltava: Sud'ba Plijenikh i vzaimodeijstvije Kultur*, [Poltava: The Prisoners' Fate and Cultural Interaction], (Moscow: Rossiiskii gosudarstvennyi gumanitarnyi universitet, 2009), 183–206

Karsten, Peter (ed.), *Motivating Soldiers: Morale or Mutiny*, Military and Society 3, (New York: Garland, 1998)

Keegan, John., *The Face of Battle*, (London: Jonathan Cape, 1976)

— *A History of Warfare*, (London: Hutchinson, 1993)

Keep, John L.H., *Soldiers of the Tsar: Army and Society in Russia, 1462–1874*, (Oxford: Clarendon Press, 1985)

Kellett, Anthony, *Combat Motivation: The Behavior of Soldiers in Battle*, International Series in Management Science/Operations Research, (Boston: Kluwer-Nijhoff, 1982)

Kennedy, Catriona, 'John Bull into Battle: Military Masculinities and the British Army Officer during the Napoleonic War, in Karen Hagemann, Gisela Mettele, Jane Rendall (eds.), *Gender, War and Politics: Transatlantic Perspectives, 1775–1830,* War Culture and Society, 1750–1850, (Basingstoke: Palgrave Macmillan, 2010), 127–46

Kennett Lee, *The French Armies in the Seven Years' War: A Study in Military Organization and Administration,* (Durham, NC: Duke University Press 1967)

Kier, Elizabeth, 'Homosexuals in the U.S. Military: Open Integration and Combat Effectiveness,' *International Security,* 23.2, (1998–9), 5–39

Kiernan, Victor Gordon, *The Duel in European History: Honour and the Reign of Aristocracy,* (Oxford University Press, 1986)

King, Peter, *Crime, Justice, and Discretion in England 1740–1820,* (Oxford University Press, 2000)

Kleinman, Arthur, *The Illness Narratives: Suffering, Healing, and the Human Condition,* (New York: Basic Books, 1988)

Kloosterhuis, Jürgen, 'Donner, Blitz und Bräker: Der Soldatendienst des "armen Mannes von Tockenburg" aus der Sicht des preußischen Militärsystems', in Alfred Messerli and Adolf Muschg (eds.), *Schreibsucht: Autobiografische Schriften des Pietisten Ulrich Bräker (1735–1798),* Arbeiten zur Geschichte des Pietismus 44, (Göttingen: Vandenhoeck und Ruprecht, 2004), 129–187

Kopperman, Paul E., 'The Stoppages Mutiny of I763', *Western Pennsylvania Historical Magazine,* 69 (1986), 241–54

— '"The Cheapest Pay": Alcohol Abuse in Eighteenth-Century British Army', *Journal of Military History,* 60 (1996), 445–70

Krebs, Daniel, 'The Making of Prisoners of War: Rituals of Surrender in the American War of Independence 1776–1783', *Militärgeschichtliche Zeitschrift,* 64 (2005), 1–29

Kroll, Stefan, *Soldaten im 18. Jahrhundert zwischen Friedensalltag und Kriegserfahrung: Lebenswelten und Kultur in der kursächsischen Armee 1728–1796,* Krieg in der Geschichte 26, (Paderborn: F. Schöningh, 2006)

Kunisch, Johannes, *Der kleine Krieg: Studien zum Heerwesen des Absolutismus,* Frankfurter historische Abhandlungen 4, (Frankfurt am Main: F. Steiner, 1973)

— 'Das "Puppenwerk" der stehenden Heere: ein Beitrag zur Neueinschätzung von Soldatenstand und Krieg in der Spätaufklärung', *Zeitschrift für historische Forschung,* 17 (1990), 49–83

Latzel, Klaus, '"Schlachtbank" oder "Feld der Ehre"? Der Beginn des Einstellungswandels gegenüber Krieg und Tod 1756–1815', in Wolfram Wette (ed.), *Der Krieg des Kleinen Mannes: Eine Militärgeschichte von unten,* 2nd edn, (Munich: Piper, 1995), 76–92

— 'Vom Kriegserlebnis zur Kriegserfahrung: theoretische und methodische Überlegungen zur erfahrungsgeschichtlichen Untersuchung von Feldpostbriefen', *Militärgeschichtliche Mitteilungen,* 56 (1997), 1–30

Leetham, Arthur, 'Old Recruiting posters', *JSAHR,* 1 (1921–2), 119–21, 131–3

Lemmings, David, *Law and Government in England during the Long Eighteenth Century: From Consent to Command*, Studies in Modern History, (Basingstoke: Palgrave Macmillan, 2011)

Lepre, George, *Fragging: Why U.S. Soldiers Assaulted their Officers in Vietnam*, (Lubbock: Texas Tech University Press, 2011)

Little, Roger W., 'Buddy Relations and Combat Performance', in Morris Janowitz, *The New Military: Changing Patterns of Organisation*, Studies in Social Organization 1, (New York: Russell Sage Foundation, 1964), 195–224

Lonn, Ella, *Desertion during the Civil War*, (New York: The Century Co., 1929)

Lorenzen-Schmidt, Klaus-Joachim, and Bjørn Poulsen (eds.), *Writing Peasants: Studies on Peasant Literacy in Early Modern Northern Europe*, (Kerteminde: Lanbohistorisk Selskab, 2002)

Lorgnier, Jacques, *Maréchaussée: Histoire d'une revolution judicaire et administrative*, 2 vols., (Paris: L'Harmattan, 1994)

Loriga, Sabina, *Soldati: L'istituzione militare nel Piemonte del Settecento*, Storia e scienze sociali, (Venice: Marsilio, 1992)

Ludwig, Ulrike, 'Der Zauber des Tötens: Waffenmagie im frühneuzeitlichen Militär', *Militär und Gesellschaft in der Frühen Neuzeit*, 13 (2009), 33–49

Luh, Jürgen, *Ancien Régime Warfare and the Military Revolution: A Study*, Baltic Studies 6, (Groningen: INOS, 2000)

Lynn, John. A., *The Bayonets of the Republic: Motivation and Tactics in the Army of Revolutionary France, 1791–94*, (Urbana: University of Illinois Press, 1984)

— 'Toward an Army of Honor: The Moral Evolution of the French Army, 1789–1815', *French Historical Studies*, 16 (1989), 152–73

— *Giant of the Grand Siècle: The French Army, 1610–1715*, (Cambridge University Press, 1997)

— 'The Treatment of Military Subjects in Diderot's *Encyclopédie*', *Journal of Military History*, 65 (2001), 131–65

— *Battle: A History of Combat and Culture*, (Boulder, Colo.: Westview Press, 2003)

MacCoun, Robert J., 'What is Known About Unit Cohesion and Military Performance', in National Defense Research Institute (ed.), *Sexual Orientation and U.S. Military Personnel Policy: Options and Assessment*, (Santa Monica, Calif: RAND, 1993), 283–331

Mackay, I.H., 'A Recruiting Flag of the 2nd Battalion 78th Highlanders (Roos-Shire Budds), 1804', *JSAHR*, 17 (1938), 176

Mackillop, Andrew, *'More Fruitful than the Soil': Army Empire and the Scottish Highland, 1715–1815*, (East Linton: Tuckwell Press, 2000)

Maillard, Brigitte, 'Maréchaussée et répression des troubles de subsistances au XVIIIe siècle', in André Corvisier et al. (eds.), *Combattre, Gouverner, Écrire: Études réunis en l'honneur de Jean Chagniot*, Hautes Études Militaires 25, (Paris: Institut de stratégie comparée, 2003), 503–15

Malfoy-Noël, Dorothée, *L'Épreuve de la Bataille, 1700–1714*, Premières Armes 5, (Montpellier: Presses universitaires de la Méditerranée, 2007)

Mandelbaum, David G., *Soldier Groups and Negro Soldiers*, (Berkeley: University of California Press, 1952)

Manigart, Philippe, and David Prensky, 'Recruitment and Retention of Volunteers: Problems in the Belgian Armed Forces', *AFS*, 9 (1982–3), 98–114

Manning, Frederick J., 'Morale, Cohesion, and Esprit de Corps', in Reuven Gal and A. David Mangelsdorff, *Handbook of Military Psychology*, (Chichester: Wiley, 1991), 453–70

Marshall, S.L.A. *Men against Fire: The Problem of Battle Command*, (Norman: University of Oklahoma Press, 2000), [1947]

McCormack, Matthew, 'Dance and Drill: Polite Accomplishments and Military Masculinity in Georgian Britain', *Social and Cultural History*, 8 (2011), 315–30

McCorry, Helen C., 'Desertion and Discipline, North Britain, 1751–53', *JSAHR*, 69 (1991), 221–32, 70 (1992), 114–7 and 189–97, 71 (1993), 42–50, 72 (1994), 142–59

McGowen, Randall, '"Making Examples" and the Crisis of Punishment in Mid-Eighteenth Century England', in David Lemmings (ed.), *The British and their Laws in the Eighteenth Century*, (Woodbridge: Boydell Press, 2005), 182–205

McNeill, William H., *The Pursuit of Power: Technology, Armed Force, and Society since A.D. 1000*, (University of Chicago Press, 1983)

— *Keeping Together in Time: Dance and Drill in Human History*, (Cambridge, Mass.: Harvard University Press, 1995)

McPherson, James M., *For Cause and Comrades: Why Men Fought in the Civil War*, (New York: Oxford University Press, 1997)

Melton, James van Horn, *Absolutism and the Eighteenth-Century Origins of Compulsory Schooling in Prussia and Austria*, (Cambridge University Press, 1988)

Michon Georges, *Justice Militaire sous la Révolution*, Bibliothèque d'histoire révolutionnaire. Nouvelle série 6, (Paris: F. Alcan, 1922)

Middleton, Richard, 'The Recruitment of the British Army, 1755–1762', *JSAHR*, 67 (1989), 226–38

Miller, Laura L., and Williams, John Allen 'Do Military Policies on Gender and Sexuality Undermine Combat Effectiveness?, in Peter D. Feaver and Richard H. Kohn (eds.), *Soldiers and Civilians: The Civil-Military Gap and American National Security*, BCSIA Studies in International Security, (Cambridge, Mass.: MIT Press, 2001), 361–402

Möbius, Sascha, '"Bravthun", "entmannende Furcht" und "schöne Überlauferinnen": Zum Männlichkeitsbild preußischer Soldaten im siebenjährigen Krieg in Quellen aus Magdeburg, Halle und der Altmark', in Eva Labouvie (ed.), *Leben in der Stadt: Eine Kultur- und Geschlechtergeschichte Magdeburgs*, (Cologne: Böhlau, 2004), 79–96

— 'Die Kommunikation zwischen preußischen Soldaten und Offizieren im Siebenjährigen Krieg zwischen Gewalt und Konsens', *Militärgeschichtliche Zeitschrift*, 64 (2004), 325–53

— '"Haß gegen alles, was nur den Namen eines Franzosen führet"? Die Schlacht bei Rossbach und nationale Stereotype in der deutschsprachigen Militärliteratur der zweiten Hälfte des 18. Jahrhunderts', in Jens Häseler and Albert Meier (eds.), *Gallophobie im 18. Jahrhundert*, Aufklärung und Europa 15, (Berlin: Berliner Wissenschafts-Verlag, 2005), 123–58

— *Mehr Angst vor dem Offizier als vor dem Feind? Eine mentalitätsgeschichtliche Studie zur preußischen Taktik im Siebenjährigen Krieg*, (Saarbrücken: VDM Verlag Dr. Müller, 2007)

Moore, Brenda L., 'The Propensity of Junior Enlisted Personnel to Remain in Today's Military', *AFS*, 28 (2001–2), 257–78

Morrison, Ian A., 'Survival Skills: An Enterprising Highlander in the Low Countries with Marlborough', in Grant G. Simpson (ed.), *The Scottish Soldier Abroad 1247–1967*, The Mackie Monographs 2, (Edinburgh: John Donald Publishers, 1992), 81–96

Moskos, Charles, *The American Enlisted Man: The Rank and File in Today's Military*, (New York: Russell Sage Foundation, 1970)

— 'From Institution to Occupation: Trends in Military Organization', *AFS*, 4 (1977–8), 41–50

— 'Institutional/ Occupational Trends in Armed Forces: An Update', *AFS*, 12 (1986–7), 377–82

— 'Institutional and Occupational Trends in Armed Forces', in Charles Moskos and Frank R. Wood (eds.), *The Military: More than Just a Job?*, (Washington DC: Pergamon-Brassey's, 1988), 15–26

Muir, Rory, *Tactics and the Experience of Battle in the Age of Napoleon*, (New Haven: Yale University Press, 1998)

Murtagh, Harman, 'Irish Soldiers Abroad, 1600–1800', in Thomas Bartlett and Keith Jeffery (eds.), *A Military History of Ireland*, (Cambridge University Press, 1997), 296–314

Muth, Jörg, *Flucht aus dem militärischen Alltag: Ursachen und individuelle Ausprägung der Desertion in der Armee Friedrichs des Großen*, Einzelschriften zur Militärgeschichte 42, (Freiburg im Breisgau: Rombach, 2003)

Nafziger, George, *Imperial Bayonets: Tactics of the Napoleonic Battery, Battalion and Brigade as Found in Contemporary Regulations*, (London: Greenhill, 1996)

Nipperdey, Thomas, 'Probleme der Modernisierung in Deutschland', *Saeculum*, 30 (1979), 292–303

Nosworthy, Brent, *The Anatomy of Victory: Battle Tactics, 1689–1763*, (New York: Hippocrene, 1990)

Oates, Jonathan, 'The Manchester Regiment of 1745', *JSAHR*, 88 (2010), 129–51

Oestreich, Gerhard, *Neostoicism and the Early Modern State*, Brigitta Oestreich and H.G. Koenigsberger (eds.), David McLintock (tr.), Cambridge Studies in Early Modern History, (Cambridge University Press, 1982)

Oman, Charles, *Wellington's Army*, (London: E. Arnold, 1912)

Ozment, Steven, *The Bürgermeister's Daughter: Scandal in a Sixteenth-Century German Town*, (New York: St. Martin's Press, 1996)

Paret, Peter, *The Cognitive Challenge of War: Prussia 1806*, (Princeton University Press, 2009)

Parker, Geoffrey, *The Military Revolution: Military Innovation and the Rise of the West, 1500–1800*, 2nd ed., (Cambridge University Press, 1996)

Parrott, David, *The Business of War: Military Enterprise and Military Revolution in Early Modern Europe*, (Cambridge University Press, 2012)

Peace, Richard, 'The Nineteenth Century: The Natural School and its Aftermath, 1840–55', in Charles A. Moser (ed.), *The Cambridge History of Russian Literature*, (Cambridge University Press, 1992), 189–247

Peters, Jan, 'Zur Auskunftsfähigkeit von Selbstsichtzeugnissen schreibender Bauern' in Winfried Schulze (ed.), *Ego-Dokumente: Annäherung an den Menschen in der Geschichte*, Selbstzeugnisse der Neuzeit 2, (Berlin: Akademie Verlag, 1996), 175–90

Prebble, John, *Mutiny: Highland Regiments in Revolt, 1743–1804*, (London: Secker & Warburg, 1975)

Pröve, Ralf, *Stehendes Heer and städtische Gesellschaft im 18. Jahrhundert: Göttingen und seine Militärbevölkerung, 1713-1756*, Beiträge zur Militärgeschichte 47, (Munich: Oldenbourg, 1995)

— 'Dimension und Reichweite der Paradigmen "Sozialdisziplinierung" und "militarisierung" im Heiligen Römischen Reich', in Heinz Schilling and Lars Behrisch (eds.), *Institutionen, Instrumente und Akteure sozialer Kontrolle und Disziplinierung im frühneuzeitlichen Europa*, Ius Commune, Sonderhefte 127 (Frankfurt Am Main: Klosterman, 1999), 65–85

Raeff, Marc, *The Well-Ordered Police State: Social and Institutional Change through Law in the Germanies and Russia, 1600–1800*, (New Haven: Yale University Press, 1983)

Rea, Robert R., 'Military Deserters from British West Florida', *Louisiana History: The Journal of the Louisiana Historical Association*, 9 (1968), 123–37

Redlich, Fritz, *The German Military Enterpriser and His Work Force: A Study in European Economic and Social History*, 2 vols., Vierteljahrschrift für Sozial- und Wirtschaftsgeschichte, Beihefte 47–8, (Wiesbaden: F. Steiner, 1964–5)

Reese, Roger R., *Why Stalin's Soldiers Fought: The Red Army's Military Effectiveness in World War II*, Modern War Studies, (Lawrence: University Press of Kansas, 2011)

Riasanovsky, Nicholas V., *Russian Identities: A Historical Survey*, (Oxford University Press: 2005)

Rice, Howard C. and, Anne S.K. Brown, *The American Campaigns of Rochambeau's Army 1780–1783*, 2 vols., (Princeton University Press, 1972)

Richardson, Frank M., *Fighting Spirit: A Study of Psychological Factors in War*, (London: Cooper, 1978)

Roberts, Michael, 'The Military Revolution, 1560–1660', in Michael Roberts, *Essays in Swedish History*, (London: Weidenfeld & Nicolson, 1967), 195–225

Robinson, Paul, *Military Honour and the Conduct of War: From Ancient Greece to Iraq*, Cass Military Studies, (London: Routledge, 2006)

Robson, Eric, 'The Raising of a Regiment in the War of American Independence, with Special Reference to 80th and 94 Regiments', *JSAHR*, 27 (1949), 107–9

Rodger, N.A.M., *The Wooden World: An Anatomy of the Georgian Navy*, (London: Collins, 1986)

Rogers, Clifford J., 'Tactics and the Face of Battle', in Frank Tallett and D.J.B. Trim (eds.), *European Warfare, 1350–1750*, (Cambridge University Press, 2010), 203–35

Rogers, H.C.B., *The British Army of the Eighteenth Century*, (London: Alan and Unwin, 1977)

Rogg, Matthias, '"Wol auff mit mir, du schoenes weyb": Anmerkungen zur Konstruktion von Männlichkeit im Soldatenbild des 16. Jahrhunderts' in Karen Hagemann and Ralf Pröve (eds.), *Landsknechte, Soldatenfrauen und Nationalkrieger: Militär, Krieg und Gesechelchterordnung im historischen Wandel*, Geschichte und Geschlechter 26, (Frankfurt am Main: Campus, 1998), 51–73

Rogulin, N.G., *'Polkovoie Ucherezhdenie' A. V. Suvorova i Pekhotnie Instrukzii Ekaterinenskova Vremeni* [Suvorov's 'Regimental Disposition' and the Infantry Manuals from the time of Catherine the Great], (St Petersburg: D. Bulanin, 2005)

Rothenberg, Gunther E., *The Art of Warfare in the Age of Napoleon*, (London: Batsford, 1977)

Ruff, Julius R., *Crime, Justice and Public Order in Old Regime France: The Sénéchaussées of Libourne and Bazas, 1696–1789* (London: Croom Helm, 1984)

— *Violence in Early Modern Europe, 1500–1800*, New Approaches to European History 22, (Cambridge University Press, 2001)

Rush, Robert S., *Hell in Hürtgen Forest: The Ordeal and Triumph of an American Infantry Regiment*, Modern War Studies, (Lawrence: University Press of Kansas, 2001)

Sabean, David Warren, *Power in the Blood: Popular Culture and Village Discourse in Early Modern Germany*, (Cambridge University Press, 1984)

Sackett, Paul and Anne Mavor, (eds.), *Attitudes, Aptitudes, and Aspirations of American Youth: Implications for Military Recruitment*, (Washington DC: National Academies Press, 2003)

Sampson, Richard, *Escape in America: The British Convention Prisoners 1777–1783*, (Chippenham: Picton, 1995)

Sasson-Levy, Orna, *Zehuyot be-madim: gavriyut ve-nashiyut ba-tsava' ha-Yisre'eli*, [Rights in Uniform: Masculinity and Femininity in the Israeli Army], (Jerusalem: Magnes, 2006)

Schofield, Roger S., 'Dimensions of Illiteracy in England, 1750–1850', in Harvey J. Graff (ed.), *Literacy and Historical Development: A Reader*, rev. edn, (Carbondale: Southern Illinois University Press, 2007), 299–314

Scott, James C., *Domination and the Art of Resistance: Hidden Transcripts*, (New Haven: Yale University Press, 1990)

Scott, Samuel F., *The Response of the Royal Army to the French Revolution: the Role and Development of the Line Army, 1787–93*, (Oxford: Clarendon Press, 1978)

— *From Yorktown to Valmy: The Transformation of the French Army in the Age of Revolution*, (Niwot: University Press of Colorado, 1998)

Scouller, R.E., *The Armies of Queen Anne*, (Oxford: Clarendon Press, 1966)

Segal, David R., 'Measuring the Institutional/Occupational Change Thesis', *AFS*, 12 (1986–7), 351–76

Segal, David R., Peter Freedman-Doan, Jerald G. Bachman and Patrick M. O'Malley, 'Attitudes of Entry-level Enlisted Personnel: Pro-Military and Politically Mainstreamed', in Peter D. Feaver and Richard H. Kohn (eds.), *Soldiers and Civilians: The Civil-Military Gap and American National Security*, (Cambridge, Mass: MIT Press, 2001), 163–212

Selig, Robert A., 'A German Soldier in America, 1780–1783: The Journal of Georg Daniel Flohr', *William and Mary Quarterly*, 3rd Series, 50 (1993), 575–90

Seniavskaija, E.S., *Protivniki Rossij v Voinakh XX Veka: Evoliutsia Obraza Vraga v Soznanij Armij i Obshechestva*, [Russia' Adversaries in the Wars of the 20th Century: The Evolution of the Image of the Enemy as perceived by the Army and Society], (Moscow: ROSSPEN, 2006)

Seriu, Naoko, 'Déserteur et femme-soldat en marge de l'institution militaire au milieu du XVIIIe siècle', in André Corvisier et al. (eds.), *Combattre, Gouverner, Écrire: Études réunis en l'honneur de Jean Chagniot*, Hautes Études Militaires 25, (Paris: Institut de stratégie comparée, 2003), 709–22

Shils, Edward A., and Morris Janowitz, 'Cohesion and Disintegration in the Wehrmacht in World War II', *Public Opinion Quarterly*, 12 (1948), 266–315

Shoemaker, Robert B., *The London Mob: Violence and Disorder in Eighteenth-Century Britain*, (London: Hambledon and London, 2004)

Showalter, Dennis, 'Tactics and Recruitment in Eighteenth Century Prussia', *Studies in History and Politics/Etudes d'Histoire et de Poltique*, 3 (1983/4), 15–41

— 'Weapons and Ideas in the Prussian Army from Frederick the Great to Moltke the Elder' in John A. Lynn (ed.), *Tools of War: Instruments, Ideas and Institutions of Warfare, 1445–1871*, (Urbana: University of Illinois Press, 1990), 177–210

— 'Hubertusburg to Auerstädt: The Prussian Army in Decline?', *German History* 12 (1994), 308–33

— *The Wars of Frederick the Great*, Modern Wars in Perspective, (London: Longman, 1996)

Siebold, G.L., 'Military Group Cohesion', in Thomas W. Britt, Carl Andrew Castro and Amy B. Adler (eds.), *Military Life: The Psychology of Serving in Peace and Combat*, 4 vols., (Westport, Conn: Praeger Security International, 2006), vol. I, 185–201

Sikora, Michael, *Disziplin und Desertion: Strukturprobleme militärischer Organisation im 18. Jahrhundert*, Historische Forschungen 57, (Berlin: Duncker und Humblot, 1996)

Silverman, Lisa, *Tortured Subjects: Pain, Truth, and the Body in Early Modern France* (University of Chicago Press, 2001)

Skelley, Alan Ramsay, *The Victorian Army at Home: Recruitment and Terms and Conditions of the British Regular, 1859–99*, (London: Croom Helm, 1977)

Smith, Leonard V., *Between Mutiny and Obedience: The Case of the French Fifth Infantry Division during World War I*, Princeton Legacy Library, (Princeton University Press, 1994)

Snape, Michael, *The Redcoat and Religion: The Forgotten History of the British Soldier from the Age of Marlborough to the Eve of the First World War*, (London: Routledge, 2005)

Spater, George, *William Cobbett: The Poor Man's Friend*, 2 vols., (Cambridge University Press, 1982)

Spierenburg, Pieter Cornelius, *The Spectacle of Suffering: Executions and the Evolution of Repression: From a Preindustrial Metropolis to the European Experience*, (Cambridge University Press, 1984)

— 'Knife Fighting and Popular Codes of Honor in Early Modern Amsterdam' in Pieter Cornelius Spierenburg (ed.), *Men and Violence: Gender, Honor and Rituals in Modern Europe and America*, History of Crime and Criminal Justice Series, (Columbus: Ohio State University Press, 1998), 103–27

Spring, Matthew H., *With Zeal and with Bayonets Only: The British Army on Campaign in North America, 1775–1783*, Campaigns and Commanders 19, (Norman: University of Oklahoma, 2008)

Stahl, Michael J., Charles W. McNichols and T. Roger Manley, 'An Empirical Examination of the Moskos Institution-Occupation Model', *AFS*, 6 (1979–80), 257–69

Starkey, Armstrong, *War in the Age of Enlightenment, 1700–1789*, (Westport, Conn.: Praeger, 2003)

Steppler, Glenn A., 'British Military Law, Discipline, and the Conduct of Regimental Courts Martial in the Later Eighteenth Century', *English Historical Review*, 102 (1987), 859–86

— 'The British Army on the Eve of the War', in Alan J. Guy (ed.), *The Road to Waterloo: The British Army and the Struggle against Revolutionary and Napoleonic France*, (Stroud: Alan Sutton, 1990), 4–15

Stewart, Frank Henderson, *Honor*, (University of Chicago Press, 1994)

Stone, Lawrence, 'Literacy and Education in England, 1640–1900', *Past and Present*, 42 (1969), 69–139

Storring, Adam, *Zorndorf: 1758*, (Solihull: Helion & Company, forthcoming)

Stouffer, Samuel A., et al, *The American Soldier: Adjustment during Army Life*, Studies in Social Psychology in World War II, vol. 1, (Princeton University Press, 1949)

— *The American Soldier: Combat and its Aftermath*, Studies in Social Psychology in World War II, vol. 2, (Princeton University Press, 1949)

Strachan, Hew, *European Armies and the Conduct of War*, (London: Allen & Unwin, 1983)

Streets-Salter, Heather, *Martial Races: The Military, Race and Masculinity in British Imperial Culture, 1857–1914*, Studies in Imperialism, (Manchester University Press, 2004)

Stuart-Smith, James, 'Military Law: Its History, Administration and Practice', *Law Quarterly Review*, 85 (1969), 478–504

Swart, Erik, 'From "Landsknecht" to "Soldier": The Low German Foot Soldiers in the Low Countries in the Second Half of the Sixteenth Century', *International Review of Social History*, 51 (2006), 75–92

Tatum, William P., '"The Soldiers Murmured much on Account of this Usage": Military Justice and Negotiated Authority in the Eighteenth-Century British Army', in Kevin Linch and Matthew McCormarck (eds.), *Britain's Soldiers: Rethinking War and Society, 1715–1815*, Eighteenth-Century Worlds 5, (Liverpool University Press, 2014), 95–113

Taylor, Gabriele, *Pride, Shame and Guilt: Emotions of Self-Assessment*, (Oxford: Clarendon Press, 1985)

Thompson, E.P., 'The Moral Economy of the English Crowd in the Eighteenth Century', *Past and Present*, 50 (1971), 76–136

Thoral, Marie-Cécile, *From Valmy to Waterloo: France at War, 1792–1815*, Godfrey Rogers (tr.), War Culture and Society, 1750-1850, (Basingstoke: Palgrave Macmillan, 2011)

Tóth, István György, *Literacy and Written Culture in Early Modern Central Europe*, Tünde Vajda and Miklós Bodóczky (trs.), (Budapest: Central European University Press, 2000)

Uhle-Wettler, Franz, *Höhe- und Wendepunkte deutscher Militärgeschichte*, (Hamburg: Mittler, 2000)

Upton, Anthony F., *Charles XI and Swedish Absolutism*, Cambridge Studies in Early Modern History, (Cambridge University Press, 1998)

Van Creveld, Martin, *Fighting Power: German and U.S. Army Performance, 1939–45*, Contributions in Military History 32, (Westport, Conn: Greenwood Press, 1982)

— *Supplying War: Logistics from Wallenstein to Patton*, 2nd edn, (Cambridge University Press, 2004)

Voigtländer, Lutz, *Vom Leben und Überleben in Gefangenschaft: Selbstzeugnisse von Kriegsgefangenen 1757 bis 1814*, (Freiburg im Breisgau: Rombach, 2005)

Von Hirsch, Andrew, *Criminal Deterrence and Sentence Severity: An Analysis of Recent Research*, (Oxford: Hart, 1999)

Watson, Alexander, *Enduring the Great War: Combat, Morale and Collapse in the German and British Armies, 1914–1918*, Cambridge Military Histories, (Cambridge University Press, 2008)

Way, Peter, 'Rebellion of the Regulars: Working Soldiers and the Mutiny of 1763–1764', *William and Mary Quarterly*, 3rd Series, 57 (2000), 761–92

— 'Class and the Common Soldier in the Seven Years' War', *Labour History*, 44 (2003), 455–81

— 'Memoirs of an Invalid: James Miller and the Making of the British-American Empire in the Seven Years War', in Donna T. Haverty-Stacke and Daniel J. Walkowitz (eds.), *Rethinking U.S. Labor History: Essays on the Working Class Experience, 1756–2009*, (New York: Continuum, 2010), 25–53

Webb-Carter, B.W., 'Colonel Wellesley's Standing Orders to the Thirty-Third Regiment, 1798', *JSAHR*, 50 (1972), 65–77

Wehler, Hans-Ulrich, *Modernisierungstheorie und Geschichte*, Kleine Vandenhoeck-Reihe 1407, (Göttingen: Vandenhoeck und Ruprecht, 1975)

Weitz, Mark A., *More Damning than Slaughter: Desertion in the Confederate Army*, (Lincoln: University of Nebraska Press, 2005)

Wernitz, Frank, *Die Preußichen Freitruppen im Siebenjährigen Krieg 1756–1763: Entstehung, – Einsatz – Wirkung*, (Wölfersheim-Berstadt: Podzun-Pallas, 1994),

Westbrook, Stephen D., 'The Potential for Military Disintegration', in Sam C. Sarkesian (ed.), *Combat Effectiveness: Cohesion, Stress, and the Volunteer Military*, Sage Research Progress Series on War, Revolution and Peacekeeping 9, (Beverly Hills: Sage, 1980), 244–78

Wilson, Peter H., 'Violence and Rejection of Authority in Eighteenth-Century Germany: The Case of the Swabian Mutinies of 1757', *German History*, 12 (1994), 1–26

— *War, State and Society in Württemberg, 1677–1793*, (Cambridge University Press, 1995)

— *German Armies: War and German Politics, 1648–1806*, Warfare and History, (London: UCL Press, 1998)

— 'Warfare in the Old-Regime 1648–1789', in Jeremy Black, (ed.), *European Warfare, 1453–1815*, (Basingstoke: Macmillan, 1999), 69–95

— 'Social Militarization in Eighteenth-Century Germany', *German History*, 18 (2000), 1–39

— 'The Politics of Military Recruitment in Eighteenth-Century Germany', *English Historical Review*, 117 (2002), 536–68

— *From Reich to Revolution, German History: 1558–1806*, European History in Perspective, (Basingstoke: Palgrave Macmillan, 2004)

Winter, Jay, *Sites of Memory, Sites of Mourning: The Great War in European Cultural History*, Studies in the Social and Cultural History of Modern Warfare 1, (Cambridge University Press, 1995)

Wishon, Mark, *German Forces and the British Army: Interactions and Perceptions, 1742–1815*, War, Culture and Society, 1750–1850, (Basigstoke: Palgrave Macmillan, 2013)

Woloch, Isser, *The New Regime: Transformations of the French Civic Order, 1789–1820s*, (New York: Norton, 1994)

Wong, Leonard, Thomas A. Kolditz, Raymond A. Millen and Terrence M. Potter, *Why They Fight? Combat Motivation in the Iraq War*, (Carlisle, Penn.: US Army War College, 2003)

Woodruff, Todd, Ryan Kelty and David R. Segal, 'Propensity to Serve and Motivation to Enlist among American Combat Soldiers', *AFS*, 32 (2005–6), 353–66

Wyatt-Brown, Bertram, *Southern Honor: Ethics and Behavior in the Old South*, (New York: Oxford University Press, 1982)

Young, Peter, *The Fighting Man: From Alexander the Great's Army to the Present Day*, (London: Orbis, 1981)

Unpublished Dissertations

Planchais, Julien, *Les Déserteurs Français pendant la Guerre de Sept Ans ou de la Désertion*, unpublished Mémoire de Maîtrise, Université de Paris 1 Panthéon-Sorbonne, (2000)

Steppler, Glenn A., *The Common Soldier in the Reign of George III, 1760–1793*, unpublished DPhil Dissertation, University of Oxford, (1984)

Storring, Adam, *Zorndorf: Frederick the Great and the Russian Threat*, unpublished MPhil Dissertation, University of Cambridge, (2007)

Online Resources

Grant, Duncan, 'Letter to his father' (12 September 1777), http://redcoat76 .blogspot.com/2012/04/duncan-and-margaret-grant-21st-regiment.html

Hagist, Don N., *British Soldier, American Revolution* http://redcoat76.blogspot .com

Plumb, Thomas, 'Letter to his Brother' (22 February 1777), http://redcoat76 .blogspot.com/2013/01/thomas-plumb-22nd-regiment-of-foot.html

Index